3^{00}

Pursuing Innocent Pleasures

Alexander Pope in his garden. Oil painting by Jonathan Richardson, 1738. In a letter to Lord Burlington, William Kent in 1738 speaks of seeing this portrait in Richardson's lodgings and describes it as portraying "Pope in a mourning gown with a strange view of the garden to shew the obelisk as in memory to his mothers Death, the alligory seem'd odde to me . . . " (*Corr.* iv. 150).

PETER MARTIN

Pursuing Innocent Pleasures

The Gardening World of

ALEXANDER POPE

Archon Books
1984

© 1984   Peter Martin   All rights reserved
First published 1984 as an Archon Book
an imprint of The Shoe String Press, Inc.,
Hamden, Connecticut 06514

The paper in this book
meets the guidelines for permanence and durability
of the Committee on Production Guidelines for Book Longevity
of the Council on Library Resources.

Printed in the United States of America

Publication of this book
was assisted by a grant from the Publications Program
of the National Endowment for the Humanities,
an independent federal agency.

Library of Congress Cataloging in Publication Data

Martin, Peter, 1940–
    Pursuing innocent pleasures.
        Bibliography: p.
        Includes index.
    1. Pope, Alexander, 1688–1744—Aesthetics. 2. Pope,
Alexander, 1688–1744—Knowledge—Botany. 3. Pope,
Alexander, 1688–1744—Homes and haunts. 4. Gardens—
England—Design—History—18th century. 5. Landscape
gardening—England—History—18th century. 6. Gardeners—
England—Biography. 7. Poets, English—18th century—
        Biography. I. Title.
    PR3637.A35M3   1984   821'.5   84-488
            ISBN 0-208-02011-X

for
Cynthia
Andrew and Claire

Contents

Plates

Frontispiece: Alexander Pope. Oil Painting on canvas by Jonathan Richardson, 1738. Courtesy of the Yale Center for British Art, Paul Mellon Collection.

1. Joseph Spence. Engraving (1739) by George Vertue from a painting by Isaac Whood (now missing). Courtesy of the Osborn Collection, Beinecke Rare Book and Manuscript Library, Yale University.

2. Martha and Teresa Blount. Oil painting by Charles Jervas. Courtesy of the University of Newcastle.

3. Hardwick and Mapledurham. Hand-colored aquatint. Drawn by J. Farington and engraved by J. C. Stadler. 1793. Courtesy of the Colonial Williamsburg Foundation. 15⅞″ x 13½″.

4. "White Knights, the Seat of Sr. Hen. Englefield, Bart." Hand-colored drawing by F. Blyth and engraved by R. Godfrey. 1776. Courtesy of the Colonial Williamsburg Foundation. 8¾″ x 10½″.

5. Detail from "A Map of the Parish of Rowsham. . . ." Measured by Edward Grantham. 1721. Courtesy of T. Cottrell-Dormer. 34¼″ x 24⅜″.

6. *Plan of Rousham*. Pen and wash, possibly by Charles Bridgeman. Ca. 1725. Courtesy of the Bodleian Library, Oxford.

7. "A View of the Earl of Harrington's House towards the Garden at Petersham in Surry." Hand-colored line engraving. Drawn by A. Heckel and engraved by Stevens. Ca. 1750–55. Courtesy of the Colonial Williamsburg Foundation. 10½″ x 15⁹⁄₁₆″.

8. "A View from Richmond Hill up the River." Engraving of an oil painting by Antonio Joli. Engraver unknown. Mid-eighteenth-century. The painting is the property of the Borough of Twickenham and is 25″ x 47″. Courtesy of the Colonial Williamsburg Foundation.

9. "A View of the House and part of the Garden of His Grace the Duke of Argyl at Whitton." Drawn and engraved by W. Woollett. Ca. 1755. Courtesy of the Colonial Williamsburg Foundation. 14¼″ x 20½″.

10. "Taste." Anonymous engraving. Ca. 1731–32. Attributed to William Hogarth by John Nichols, *Biographical Anecdotes of William Hogarth* (2nd ed., London, 1782), but see W. K. Wimsatt, *The Portraits of Alexander Pope* (New Haven: Yale University Press, 1965), pp. 115–17. Courtesy of the Trustees of the British Library. 9⅛″ x 6⅝″.

11. "South View of Chiswick." Hand-colored line engraving. Artist unknown. Ca. 1750–60. Courtesy of the Colonial Williamsburg Foundation. 10¼" x 15½".

12. View of the southwest gardens from the terrace, Chiswick. Pen and wash by Jacques Rigaud. 1734. Reproduced by permission of the Trustees of the Chatsworth Settlement. 14" x 27½".

13. *Plan du Jardin & Vüe des Maisons de Chiswick.* Drawn and engraved by John Rocque. 1736. Plates 82–83 from J. Badeslade and J. Rocque, *Vitruvius Britannicus volume the fourth* (London, 1739). Courtesy of the Trustees of the British Library. 23¼" x 30".

14. Chiswick canal, cascade, and gardens southwest of the house. Engraved by Claude Du Bosc after P. Rysbrack. Ca. 1730. Reproduced by permission of the Trustees of the Chatsworth Settlement.

15. Chiswick gardens and house. Engraved by W. Woollett after J. Donowell. 1753. Reproduced by permission of the Trustees of the Chatsworth Settlement.

16. "A View of the Back Front of the House & Part of the Garden of the Earl of Burlington, at Chiswick, with a distant View of the Orangery, Greenhouse, Inigo Jones's Gate, &c." Drawn by J. Donowell. 1753. Courtesy of the Colonial Williamsburg Foundation. 11" x 161/2".

17. "A View taken on Twickenham Common." Black and white engraving, drawn and engraved by J. Boydell. 1753. Courtesy of the Colonial Williamsburg Foundation. 9" x 16".

18. Detail of the Twickenham area, from John Rocque. *An Exact Survey of the City's of London, Westminster . . . and the Country Near Ten Miles* (1746), plate 15. Courtesy of the Trustees of the British Library.

19. Pope's sketch of house front, interior, and portico. Add. MS. 4809, f. 86v. Courtesy of the Trustees of the British Library. 1½" x 3".

20. Pope's sketch of a Palladian building. Add. MS. 4809, f. 84v. Courtesy of the Trustees of the British Library. 2" x 2½".

21. Pope's villa. Engraving by Nathaniel Parr after Peter Rysbrack. 1735. Courtesy of J. D. Hunt.

22. View of Pope's house, taken from the *Newcastle General Magazine, or Monthly Intelligencer*, 1 (January 1748). Engraved by T. Smith. Courtesy of the Newcastle-upon-Tyne City Libraries. 8" x 19".

23. Garden plans sketched by Pope, in his Homer MSS. Add. MS. 4808, f. 186v. Courtesy of the Trustees of the British Library. 2½" x 6½" and 2½" x 6½".

24. Garden plan sketched by Pope, in his Homer Mss. Add. MS. 4809, f. 97. Courtesy of the Trustees of the British Library. 4" x 4¼".

25. "A Plan of Mr. Pope's Garden as it was left at his Death." Drawn by John Searle and published in his *Plan of Mr. Pope's Garden* (London, 1745). Courtesy of the Trustees of the British Library. 8" x 19".

26. Redrawing of Searle's plan of Pope's garden by James Sambrook. Courtesy of George Bell & Sons, publishers.

27. John Searle's "perspective View" of Pope's grotto, in his *Plan of Mr. Pope's Garden*. Courtesy of the Trustees of the British Library.

28.   Drawing of the garden entrance to Pope's grotto, 1824, by John Buckler. Add. MS. 36371, f. 29. Courtesy of the Trustees of the British Library.

29.   Shell Temple in Pope's garden. Pen and sepia drawing by William Kent. Ca. 1725–30. Courtesy of the Trustees of the British Museum. 15⅝″ x 11⅜″.

30.   Pope's sketch of what looks like a "green theater," possibly for his own garden. Ca. 1725. Add. MS. 4809, f. 227v. Courtesy of the Trustees of the British Library.

31.   Drawing of Pope's obelisk, 1826, by John Buckler. Add. MS. 36371, f. 32. Courtesy of the Trustees of the British Library.

32.   Allen Bathurst, first Earl of Bathurst. Oil painting by Sir Godfrey Kneller. Courtesy of the Courtauld Institute of Art, University of London.

33.   "A Plan of Riskins, Near Colnbrooke, Garden of Allen, Lord Bathurst," by Stephen Switzer, taken from *Ichnographia Rustica* (1742), vol 3. Courtesy of William Brogden.

34.   Detail of Riskins from John Rocque, *Topographical Map of Middlesex* (1754). Courtesy of the Trustees of the British Library.

35.   Detail of "Percy Lodge" [Riskins] from John Rocque, *Topographical Map of Berkshire* (1761). Courtesy of the Trustees of the British Library.

36.   Kip's perspective view of Cirencester (1712), published in Sir Robert Atkyns's *The Ancient and Present State of Glostershire* (2nd ed., 1768). Courtesy of the Trustees of the British Library.

37.   "A Plan of the Home Park at Cirencester" by Samuel Rudder, in *A New History of Gloucestershire* (London, 1779). Redrawn by Ian Teh.

38.   "Plan of Oakley Great Park" by Samuel Rudder, in *A New History of Gloucestershire*. Courtesy of the Avon County Library (Bath Reference Library).

39.   The Hexagonal Building, Cirencester Park. (Photo: W. Brogden.)

40.   Plan of the Sherborne gardens. Mid-eighteenth century. Courtesy of the Sherborne Castle Estates. Redrawn by Nigel Azis.

41.   Plan of Sherborne gardens superimposed on a modern ordnance survey map. Drawn by Nigel Azis.

42.   Detail from the map of the town of Sherborne. Surveyed and drawn by T. Ladd. 1733. Courtesy of the Sherborne Castle Estates.

43.   Watercolor painting of the east front of Sherborne Castle, with gardens. No date. Courtesy of the Sherborne Castle Estates.

44.   Detail from a map of Sherborne. Ca. late eighteenth century. Courtesy of the Sherborne Castle Estates.

45.   View south across the lake to Sherborne Castle. Engraving from John Hutchins, *The History and Antiquities of the County of Dorset*. Mid-eighteenth century. Courtesy of the Royal Commission on Historical Monuments (National Monuments Record).

46.   Pope's Seat and the cascade in Sherborne gardens. (Photo: P. Martin.)

47.   View south from Pope's Seat over the cascade to Sherborne Castle. (Photo: P. Martin.)

48. William Kent's design of a Gothic seat. Courtesy of the Sherborne Castle Estates.

49. Henry St. John, Viscount Bolingbroke. Oil painting. Artist unknown. Courtesy of the National Portrait Gallery.

50. *A Plan of Dawley in the County of Middlesex, The Seat of the Right Hon.ble Charles Earl of Tankerville, and Baron of Ossulstone.* By J. Knyff, engraved by J. Kip. Ca. 1710. Courtesy of the Public Record Office (W.O. 78/ 1208 MPH 246). 26″ x 39″.

51. Detail of Dawley Farm and surrounding area from J. Rocque, *Topographical Map of Middlesex* (London, 1754). Courtesy of the Middlesex Record Office.

52. Conjectural reconstruction of the Dawley Farm landscape. Drawn by Ian Teh.

53. Henrietta Howard, Countess of Suffolk. Oil portrait by Charles Jervas. Courtesy of the National Portrait Gallery.

54. "An Exact Plan of the Royal Palace Gardens and Park at Richmond with Syon House on the Opposite side the River Thames." By John Rocque. 1734. Courtesy of the Trustees of the British Library. 12½″ x 18¼″.

55. "View from the Summer House in Richmond Park Up the River Thames." Drawn by Chatelain and engraved by P. Benazech. 1755. Courtesy of the Trustees of the British Library. 12″ x 19¼″.

56. Conjectural reconstruction of the Marble Hill gardens as they may have looked during Pope's time. Drawn by Ian Teh.

57. View of Marble Hill from the river. By A. Heckell and J. Mason. 1749. Courtesy of the Trustees of the British Library.

58. View of Marble Hill. Late eighteenth-century engraving. Artist unknown. Courtesy of the Victoria and Albert Museum.

59. Plan of Marble Hill, from *Country Life* 39 (25 March 1916):399. Date unknown. Courtesy of *Country Life*.

60. Sketch of a garden plan, almost certainly by Pope and possibly intended for Marble Hill. Add. MS. 4809, f. 161v. Courtesy of the Trustees of the British Library. 1½″ x 1½″.

61. "Marble Hill, Twickenham, formerly the residence of the Countess of Suffolk." Drawn by John Buckler. 1831. Add. MS. 36371, f. 34. Courtesy of the Trustees of the British Library.

62. Charles Mordaunt, third Earl of Peterborough. Oil portrait by Michael Dahl. Courtesy of the National Portrait Gallery.

63. Detail of Lord Peterborough's gardens at Parson's Green, from J. Rocque, *An Exact Survey of the City's of London, Westminster . . . and the Country Near Ten Miles Round* (London, 1746). Courtesy of the Trustees of the British Library.

64. "A Geographical Description of the Priory of St. Diones [Denys] and of the Manor of Portswood . . . within the County of Southampton." Measured by Jonat. Godfrey, 10 December 1658. Courtesy of the City Record Office, Civic Centre, Southampton.

65. Detail of Bevis Mount landscape from a map of Southampton by I. T. Lewis. 1843. Redrawn by Ian Teh. Courtesy of the City Record Office, Civic Centre, Southampton.

66. "Netley Castle and Abbey," taken from *Beauties of England and Wales* (1808), engraved by S. Rawle from a drawing by J. Britton. Courtesy of the Trustees of the British Museum.

67. "Netley Abbey." Oil painting by William Marlow (1740–1813). Exhibited at the Royal Academy in 1771. Courtesy of Leggatt Brothers, London.

68. Detail of the Bevis Mount landscape from the twenty-five-inch ordnance survey map, 1866. Courtesy of the City Record Office, Civic Centre, Southampton.

69. "Pope's Walk, Bevis Hill." Drawn by F. Young. Ca. 1820s. Photographed from a faded sepia postcard. Courtesy of the City Record Office, Civic Centre, Southampton.

70. Bevis Mount landscape. Drawing by T. G. Hart. Mid-nineteenth century. Courtesy of the Southampton Art Gallery, Civic Centre.

71. Entrance to Bevis Mount. Drawn by John Buckler. 1824. Add. MS. 36363, f. 88v. Courtesy of the Trustees of the British Library.

72. Drawing of what is presumed to be Bevis Mount house. Photograph in the Lankester Collection, Southampton, destroyed in World War II. No later than the 1840s. Photographed from a reproduction in a pre–World War II article in the *Southern Evening Echo* by "Townshan," later reprinted in a volume.

73. Seat with inscription erected in the gardens of Bevis Mount by Lord Peterborough's nephew. Drawn by John Buckler. 1824. Add. MS. 36363, f. 89. Courtesy of the Trustees of the British Library.

74. "The Northwest Prospect of the City of Bristol." Hand-colored line engraving. Drawn by L. and N. Buck. 1734. Courtesy of the Colonial Williamsburg Foundation. 12½" x 21½".

75. "The Avon at Clifton." Watercolor by Thomas Stothard. 1813. Courtesy of the Trustees of the British Museum. 8" x 10¾".

76. Detail of Prior Park house and gardens from the *Survey of the Manors of Hampton, Claverton, and Widcombe*. Author unknown. Late eighteenth century. Courtesy of the Avon County Library (Bath Reference Library).

77. "Prior Park, the Seat of Ralph Allen Esq. near Bath." Engraved by Anthony Walker. 1752. Courtesy of the Avon County Library (Bath Reference Library). 11¼" x 17¼".

78. Auction map of Prior Park Estate. Early nineteenth century. Courtesy of the Avon County Library (Bath Reference Library).

79. Detail of Prior Park from Thomas Thorpe, *Actual Survey of the City of Bath* (Bath, 1742). Courtesy of the Avon County Library (Bath Reference Library).

80. View of Prior Park house and the Palladian bridge. Engraving. Artist unknown. Late eighteenth century. Courtesy of the Avon County Library (Bath Reference Library).

Preface

This is a book about Pope's life as a landscape gardener and the milieu of gardening in which he dwelled for most of his adult life. Its purpose is to reconstruct the landscapes in which he interested himself and to recapture as much of the spirit, detail, and biographical color of his gardening as evidence has allowed. Since landscaping was an art that came second in Pope's life only to his poetry and that often consumed more of his time and creative energy than did even the poetry, this account suggests some new contexts from which his poetry emerged and presents him as a personality who throughout his life found endless satisfaction, fulfillment, and energy in gardens.

My emphasis lies in garden history. Garden history is rapidly being recognized as a relatively neglected window into the past, capable of recapturing much that would otherwise be lost or remain nebulous in the areas of literature, history of ideas, social and economic history, horticulture, biography, politics—the list goes on. My discussions of some of Pope's favorite gardens include information that has not been published before and that broadens what we know about English landscaping in the first half of the eighteenth century. I describe in some detail the layout of these gardens, relying on the evidence as far as it takes us and sometimes venturing into the twilight of reasoned conjectures where it does not. My treatment of the gardens may be distinguished from Morris Brownell's in *Alexander Pope and the Arts of Georgian England* (1978), which appeared after I had completed most of this book, by my deliberate emphasis on the designs of the gardens and on the people who laid them out.

Brownell's study has explained the larger backgrounds and canvases against which Pope landscaped, including his ideas and feelings about open landscape, and Maynard Mack in his eloquent *The Garden and the City* (1969) and John Dixon Hunt in *The Figure in the Landscape* (1976) have analyzed the symbolic and literary importance of the poet's thinking about gardens, landscapes, and grottoes. In my work art and literary criticism (of which there is not too much in these pages), as well as biography, help illustrate what was for Pope the continuity and coherence of his life as a gardener. I hope this biographical approach succeeds here also in not only uncovering some of the excitement and personal commitment behind the poet-gardener's life, but also suggesting how his ideas about gardening evolved gradually from his reading, traveling, notions about art and morality, politics, and friendships. More explicitly than has been shown before, I believe, this book accounts for the emotional impulses behind Pope's gardening—how it affected and was affected by people, was impelled by a determination to help his friends take the lead in demonstrating new landscaping tastes and images, and became suffused with overtones of his nostalgia for old-fashioned virtues. I hope therefore I bring the reader close to Pope the man.

The original debt in the preparation of this volume is to Professor Arthur W. Hoffman, who many more years ago than I care to admit, helped me discover the importance of this subject to the civilization of the English "Augustan" period. Since then I have accumulated a long list of debts to persons, institutions, and libraries. Many of these are acknowledged in notes, but I should especially like to register my debt to the late Edward Malins, who carefully read my manuscript and on several occasions offered penetrating commentary and suggestions for revisions; Professor Maynard Mack, whose book *The Garden and the City* years ago began to influence my study and who also read my book in manuscript and offered me valuable guidance; Professor Morris Brownell, who read the manuscript and made useful observations; Peter Dixon; Peter Howe, controller of Sherborne Castle (Dorset), for his assistance in placing before me papers and maps connected with Sherborne and guiding me around that landscape; James Sambrook for some early encouragement and for showing me the site of Bevis Mount; Kenneth Woodbridge, who spared me from errors on Sherborne; Dr. Peter Willis for sending me chapter 3 of his book on Charles Bridgeman in advance of publication; Tim McCann, archivist in the West Sussex Record Office, for assitance with Ladyholt; Lord Egremont for permission to cite from the Bolingbroke Papers at Petworth House, West Sussex; the Duke of Beaufort for permission to cite from the Scudamore Papers at Badminton House; the Right Honorable Simon Wingfield Digby for permission to use papers and plans at Sherborne Castle; Lord Bathurst for assistance in understanding the Cirencester landscape; T. Cottrell-Dormer of Rousham House, Oxfordshire, for permission to cite from the Rousham poems; the poet Ted Walker, himself an ardent gardener, for reading parts of the manuscript; Norman Kitz for permission to cite from the "Amica" poems; Ian Teh for his expert drafting of several landscape plans; and Louise Osborn for her help at the Birmingham Public Library. Norman Fiering, editor of publications at the Institute of Early American History and Culture, and Terry Myers, of the College of William and Mary, also have assisted me in the later stages of this work.

I likewise am grateful for permission to use and cite from the manuscripts and other holdings, and for help from the staff, at these record offices and libraries: the Beinecke Rare Book Library at Yale University, Trustees of the British Museum and British Library, Avon County Library (Bath Reference Library), Bedfordshire County Record Office, Birmingham Public Library, Bodleian Library, Buckinghamshire Record Office, Dorset Record Office, Middlesex Record Office, Morton Arboretum (Lisle, Illinois), Public Record Office (London), Sheffield Central Library, City Record Office (Civic Center, Southampton), and Surrey Record Office. For permission to publish certain illustrations, I am indebted to the Trustees of the Chatsworth Settlement, Trustees of the British Museum and British Library, Courtauld Institute of Art (University of London), National Portrait Gallery, George Bell and Sons, William Brogden,

Colonial Williamsburg Foundation, Leggatt Brothers, Greater London Council, Newcastle-upon-Tyne City Libraries, Yale Center for British Art (Paul Mellon Collection), John Dixon Hunt, Royal Commission on Historical Monuments (National Monuments Record), *Country Life*, and Victoria and Albert Museum (Department of Prints and Drawings). Thanks must also be extended to the Garden History Society for their permission to include chapter 4 on Sherborne, which was, in a different form, previously published in *Garden History*. I am indebted to James R. Baron of the College of William and Mary for his translations of some Latin passages.

I am grateful to the American Philosophical Society for a grant that enabled me to carry on my work in England during an awkward time. A word of gratitude also to Ruth L. Watkins, who typed the manuscript with impressive accuracy and efficiency. The Colonial Williamsburg Foundation has been generous with assistance in obtaining certain illustrations and in covering typing costs. Finally, without my wife's constant help and encouragement I could not have written this book; I dedicate it to her.

Introduction

In 1713 Pope spoke out publicly for the first time on gardening. He was twenty-five and had already begun to emerge as England's new poetic genius. Joseph Addison had praised his precocious *Essay on Criticism* in 1711, and the year following Richard Steele had published his *Messiah* in *The Spectator*. *The Rape of the Lock* was a sensation in 1712, and that was soon followed by his well-regarded topographical poem, *Windsor Forest* (1713). Then toward the end of the year Pope's poetic Muse aspired to soar "with no middle flight" when he began to take subscriptions for a translation of the *Iliad*, a considerably lucrative excursion that in 1719 enabled him to move to a villa with five acres of ground alongside the Thames at Twickenham. His travels in the realms of gold continued until he finished his *Odyssey* in 1725. For about ten years he had not written much original poetry, but in the preceding seven or so he had drunk at a different fountain of creativity and inhabited (in Keats's phrase) "the bosom of a leafy world." Compelled and inspired by his need for a garden at Twickenham, he had become a gardener—in spirit and in practice.

Few of Pope's friends could have anticipated his enthusiasm for the art of gardening in the 1720s. Even the example provided by his father's gardens at their house in Windsor Forest, the brief essay on the art of gardening in 1713, an early introduction to the Earl of Burlington's gardens at Chiswick House, his friendship with Lord Bathurst, and his discovery of Homer's sketches of gardens and landscape in the *Odyssey* did not portend that he would become one of England's foremost gardening authorities in the first half of the century. Indeed, it is likely that Pope was not himself determined to have a splendid garden when he was deciding where to settle; before he decided on Twickenham he was thinking of accepting Burlington's offer of a small plot of ground for a "palozzotto" in urban London, north of Piccadilly Street.[1] He finally decided on Twickenham, but not primarily for reasons of gardening space.[2] Expense, health, privacy, personal preference for the countryside, and his (Catholic) religion all weighed heavily in his choice. And before he saw his Twickenham plot, of course, he did not know what style of garden the "situation" required.

As any dedicated gardener knows, possession and control of a garden are what generate a love of growing plants and a talent for deciding where to put them. That was Pope's experience. More than that, his use of his garden as a source of identity and personal expression further perpetuated his work with it and thereby turned it into a unique illustration of "a manner so truely Poetical"; "in a word," wrote an anonymous tourist in 1742, it was not possible that it "cou'd be design'd by any Body but Mr. Pope."[3]

Garden designing and horticultural pursuits promptly became immensely reassuring to Pope. Throughout his life he found them practically and spiritually fulfilling. They did not of course comprise an art in his life as important or brilliant as poetry, but they had the advantage over his poetry in remaining almost entirely undistracted by the diet of animosity and frustration that frequently attended his poetic activity. The reason for this pure enjoyment was partly that landscaping engaged him in the private use of his imagination and genius, as distinct from the more public use of it in his poetry. His landscaping and horticultural companions and collaborators were of his own choosing and he was not obliged to work with anyone who displeased him. For a poet who all his life was the target of one kind or another of peevish and indignant attacks, and who was regularly driven to retaliate in print, it was vital to have a major artistic focus like landscaping that was, except for the tempest caused by the publication of the *Epistle To Burlington*, relatively free from hostile criticism.

Equally, landscaping compensated Pope for the physical limitations imposed on him by ill health and a frail constitution. New ideas of landscape design, the certainties and regularity of the seasons, planting, and vegetable and fruit harvesting generated in him an enormous amount of mental energy and activity, and in consequence inspired a type of mobility he called "rambling." He rambled (or took excursions) every summer throughout accessible parts of England to visit friend after friend at estate after estate. In 1719 he boasted that there were no fewer than five houses, all in different counties, that he could visit in the summer. Although in later years he complained that his life "in thought and imagination is as much superior to my life in action and reality as the best soul can be to the vilest body" (3:156),[4] he did not do too badly. We know from his letters that he visited over fifty seats, including both smaller villas and grander houses of his aristocratic friends in the home counties, the Midlands, the west, and the southwest.[5]

Garden historians (except for Brownell) have neglected the actual gardens and landscapes Pope designed or helped design, apart from his own garden, in favor of his aesthetics or so-called theories. This is something like analyzing a poet without properly considering his poems. This book focuses more on what he achieved as a landscaper. The "Genius of the Place" was the primary text he consulted—he said as much in his gardening poem, the *Epistle to Burlington*. Since the Genius dwells in the landscape, not primarily in the mind of the landscaper (although it collaborates with him—"Paints as you plant, and, as you work, designs"), and since Pope felt that directly or indirectly it governed all his landscaping objectives,[6] we must look chiefly to the landscapes for evidence of that collaboration. If Pope was anything as a landscaper, he was practical. He based his designs on his close knowledge of individual landscapes. He was not a bookish gardener.

English garden history in the early eighteenth century—that important period during which gardens took on the essentially English character that (with varying emphases) has determined ever since much of the look of the countryside—is elucidated by the stories of the eleven or so gardens told in the book. Gardens are seldom (as far as the historian is concerned) well enough documented to afford a really good idea of what they looked like. Plans and maps, of course, are the best help concerning the outlines, shapes, and arrangement of landscapes, but their help is one-dimensional, resembling the evidence presented by aerial photography. I have found a few such maps as well as literary evidence to document further the gardens, but Pope has been the best help of all. What sometimes happens in garden history is that one individual who is especially closely connected with a garden provides the key whereby the mysteries of a garden are partially unlocked. If the person, as in the case of these gardens, happens to be the unrivaled literary genius of the age, the prospects are especially good that he will in one way or another unfold to us several dimensions of the gardens. By doing this for these gardens, Pope has illuminated a great deal about the rapidly changing garden fashions at the time.

But how did he come to be such an authority on garden design and with what special artistic perspective did he pursue these "innocent pleasures"? If his poetry was highly allusive, so was his gardening. It was based on classical ideas of landscape which with a modern poetic sensibility (and a deep knowledge of the English tradition of descriptive verse especially from Spenser to Waller and Milton) he adapted in order to emphasize the pictorial (picturelike) and the emotive. These chiefly literary sources were only part of the story, though; his landscaping was inspired mainly by his past experiences, among them his rural education as a boy in Windsor Forest and his father's "forest" landscaping on the seventeen acres around their house, Whitehill, at Binfield in Windsor Forest;[7] the three hundred or so painting lessons he took from his friend Charles Jervas in 1713–14, from which he learned the value (not applied to landscape until later) of perspective and the use of light and shade; the lectures on astronomy he heard delivered, also in 1713, by William Whiston at Button's Coffee House, which simultaneously awakened his mind to the vastness of space and sharpened his appreciation of prospects of open landscape; and his work on translating the *Iliad* (beginning in 1715) and then later the *Odyssey* through which he was surprised to discover and determined to demonstrate Homer's genius at composing prospects and landscape gardens.

Pope always placed great store by useful or practical landscaping, in the form of fruit gardening, silviculture, agriculture, livestock farming, and the responsible use of water. As far as his own designing went, at Twickenham and elsewhere, he practiced Horace's principle of "*simplex munditiis*," promoted by Stephen Switzer in *Ichnographia Rustica* (1718), whereby the classical principle of utility was complemented by parts of the garden where elegance and decency—"amiable simplicity" not "idle or mean fussiness"—could fulfill man's pleasure and needs. Pope not only raised pineapples and a variety of vegetables that he habitually shared with friends, but he also kept bantam hens and beehives, as we may conclude from one of a number of poems I have recently discovered by an anonymous female admirer of his, written in 1741:

> I've not so much as spoke to Mr. P——e,
> Tis true indeed, some time ago I spent
> Two Hours, in his little Paradise,

> While he was absent, and I in the Gardens;
> I must confess, I idoliz'd the Trees,
> And doated on each Walk, that gave him Pleasure;
> Some Bantam Chickens only did attend me,
> Walk^d when I walk'd, and when I sat stood still,
> As tho' the little Creatures wou'd inform me,
> How much they reverenc'd their Masters friend;
> Nor were the busy Bees less entertaining,
> For they all seem'd to hum their Master's praise.

This same poet later was invited by Pope to dinner at Twickenham and in a poem on the experience bore witness to the utility of the poet's garden; she seems to suggest that Pope preferred vegetables, dairy food, and meat from his own demesne such as chicken or fish from the Thames, "wholesome Eating" at "a small Expence":

> the meal was this;
> Spinage, and Eggs, Bread, Butter, *Indian-Root*,
> And some cold Fish, I think, was added to't;
> No *Epicure*, 'tis plain, but what was good,
> He introduc'd a vegetable Food.

At the bottom of the page the poet notes that the Indian Root is a "Sort of Endive, that grows in his Garden."[8]

He was also fortuitously prepared to promote other important elements of the landscape garden: the associative, the iconographic, and the emblematic. Early in his career as a poet he had shown a susceptibility to moods and reveries induced by moonlit landscapes, gothic fables, French romances, the exoticism of Eastern literature, and ruined abbeys and castles or venerable old buildings like the colleges of Oxford. He liked such moods to be evoked in landscapes and once was delighted, under moonlight, to find that he could feel contemplative even in such a courtly and formal landscape as Hampton Court. If a scene could make him feel that way with only its natural endowments, he was particularly responsive to it—it was not the landscape, incidentally, but the moonlight at Hampton Court that moved him. In the estates considered in this book, we thus see him repeatedly trying to feel, or wishing he could feel, the associative elements of landscapes to which end he would encourage the use of temples, sculpture, inscriptions, water effects, gothic garden-buildings and sundry suggestions of the antiquarian. He may have outgrown this romantic inclination (he called it the "maze of fancy") in his poetry, but never in his taste for landscape. In his book *The Figure in the Landscape*, J. D. Hunt has linked Pope's landscaping ideas to his undiminished delight in dreams and visions.

Although Pope was more accustomed to landscaping "green fields and groves, flow'ry meadows and purling streams"—the characteristic terrain from which the English landscape-gardening movement was born—he was nonetheless responsive to and eager to find English rocks, precipices, and panoramic views that could suggest romantic associations and match his readiness to be emotionally moved and transported in a garden. His surviving letters contain several excited descriptions (there must have been many more) of mountains, steep cliffs, gorges, sweeping prospects, rushing rivers, and the crumbling remains of old monuments of English history. In such moods he demanded something more romantic from a landscape garden than even the naturalized or liberated landscapes of his close friends, with their gentle hills and contrived waterworks, could provide.[9] Sherborne, Bevis Mount, and Prior Park were exceptional in his view precisely because they were well endowed with the kinds of dramatic scenes he relished in open landscape. At Sherborne, only a few hundred feet away from the house and semiformal gardens, he could enjoy the view of some ancient ruins at the top of a craggy hill. Swift was used to this kind of landscape in Ireland; Pope was not.

Separate chapters are not devoted to the better-known gardens of Stowe and Rousham, or Hagley Park (Worcestershire), either because they have been thoroughly analyzed and chronicled elsewhere or because Pope's contribution to them appears to have been minimal and is poorly documented. But he was exceedingly fond of them and spent many hours walking in them, and they enable us to place his gardening taste in a better perspective. For these reasons short sections on them are included, somewhat out of chronological order, in chapter 1. Stowe and Chiswick happen to be gardens laid out by great Whig lords, unlike all the others addressed here, with whose Tory and (sometimes) Catholic owners Pope was on much more intimate terms than he was with either Lord Cobham or Lord Burlington. The politics of these lords, however, did not diminish Pope's appreciation of their achievements in their gardens; art and taste ruled first. They were the antitheses of the Timons in the land, the imitating fools whom Pope generally associated with Whig opportunism, dullness, and insensitivity to the "Genius of the Place." *To Burlington* was a sweeping endorsement of Burlington's use of his wealth to promote the heavenly gift of good sense in art, and Stowe was the one exemplary garden Pope mentioned in it. In more private and domestic ways, though, he found, cherished, and contributed to the same confluence of personal and artistic virtues in the Tory rather than Whig gardens featured in this study.[10] These gardens also have the virtue for us of being better documented in terms of Pope's own life.

Ironically, Pope would be shocked, in spite of his frequently expressed indifference to the fate of his works of this kind, if he could see today how little of his or his close friends' landscaping survives. His own garden has completely disappeared, although the grotto, pillaged of its beautiful ornamentation, still exists underneath a convent that stands in place of his house. Even he could not have anticipated the peevishness of Baroness Howe, who purchased his house and gardens simply to destroy them and thereby get rid of the tourists. There is not a trace left of Bevis Mount, either landscape or house; the former is now buried by a densely populated housing estate. Dawley Farm lies beneath the EMI factory near Uxbridge. Riskins is a forlorn place not yet entombed by layers of concrete but deprived of its house and infested with brambles, weeds, and rubbish. None of the gardens of Marble Hill survives, although the house does in its pristine beauty, having recently been restored by the Greater London Council. The rest of the story is not so bleak. The Chiswick gardens are now being restored to match the beautiful Palladian house; and Cirencester, Sherborne, and Prior park, if not unaltered, have not been ravaged. As for Stowe and Rousham, they are two of the most complete surviving gems of early eighteenth-century landscape gardening in England.

JOSEPH SPENCE
Engraving by VERTUE, from an oil portrait, now missing,
painted in 1739 by ISAAC WHOOD

Plate 1. Joseph Spence. Engraving by George Vertue, from an oil painting in 1739 by Isaac Whood. The
painting is now missing.

1

A Master Key to Popery in Gardens

Bearing in mind Pope's fondness for putting things down on paper, one may be surprised and disappointed to discover how little he wrote on gardens. Compared with professional landscapers like Stephen Switzer, Batty Langley, and Richard Bradley, or with men of letters like William Shenstone and Horace Walpole, he contributed little to the gardening literature of his age.[1]

Pope was an amateur gardener, and a fairly private one at that, with a greater interest in designing his own garden at Twickenham and helping his close friends with the designs of theirs than in writing treatises on the subject. Furthermore, we are expecting the wrong thing from the wrong person if we expect the greatest English poet of the first half of the eighteenth century to have collected his thoughts on the aesthetics of garden design toward a theoretical exposition. The closest he ever got to explaining his principles of good design in a technical as distinct from an artful manner was in his disconnected remarks over the years to Joseph Spence, his sometime chronicler.[2] But the more probable and significant reason why Pope never wrote extensively about this (in his own mind) most important of the sister arts to poetry is that for him gardening never became an objective study to the extent it did for the writers of gardening manuals or histories. To borrow John Dixon Hunt's phrase, Pope was not so much a figure on the landscape as a figure *in* the landscape.[3]

Gardening and (metaphorically speaking) the garden were, as Maynard Mack has unfolded to us, part of the core of Pope's self-image, maintaining itself as a vital dimension in his life and writing at least from the year 1719, when he moved to his villa in Twickenham, to the end of his days.[4] He could and did use gardens to delineate his moral concerns, but he was not inclined to write extensively about them scientifically. What he did publish on the art of gardening had a strong private or personal edge to it. It grew out of his life and involvement with the natural world and was part of the mask he self-consciously presented to his society.

After Pope first wrote about contemporary gardening fashions in the 13 September 1713 issue of *The Guardian*, he waited eighteen years before writing anything else for the public on the subject. In 1731 he may have had a hand in the anonymously published *Dawley Farm*, honoring his friend Bolingbroke's landscaping. Later that year came his bombshell, *To Burlington*, the critical fallout of which compelled him to write his last public defense of the new gardening, the delightfully ironic *A Master Key to Popery or a True and Perfect Key to Pope's Epistle to the Earl of Burlington*. Today we also benefit from his more casual gardening remarks as recorded by Spence and edited in modern times by the late James Osborn, although Pope's contemporaries (except for a few friends) did not know them. In 1737 Pope actually published his own letters, and it was then that his public discovered his private and extensive opinions of particular gardens and landscapes. The letters go a long way to lighting up the world of his gardening because they bring together his concepts and his practice.

The "rules of gardening"

Pope subscribed to the common notion in his day, as he put it to Spence, that "a sketch or analysis of the first principles of each art with their first consequences might be a thing of most excellent service."[5] In this spirit, two years before he died he confided in Spence that as far as he was concerned the "rules" governing the new spirit of English gardening could be reduced to three "heads" or principles: "the contrasts, the management of surprises, and the concealment of the bounds."[6] This was nothing new in 1742. For more than twenty years Pope and a number of friends had been demonstrating variety through contrast and the pictorial interplay of light and shade, as well as through the opening up of prospects within gardens and between gardens and surrounding landscape. Even William Kent had found his way into the garden in the 1730s after concentrating for years on painting and furniture design. Horace Walpole, in fact, gave Kent most of the credit for popularizing the new aesthetics of "painting in gardening";[7] Kent was "painter enough," he judged, "to taste the charms of landscape, bold and opinionative enough to dare and to dictate, and born with a genius to strike out a great system from the twilight of imperfect essays."[8] In the second quarter of the century there were also writings like Langley's *New Principles of Gardening* (1728) and Switzer's *Ichnographia Rustica* (extended 1742 edition) to testify to the rapidly evolving art of English gardening. It was the excitement and proliferation of new gardening ideas during this period that may well have induced Pope to wish to reduce the increasingly complex subject to three major, comprehensible elements.

Pressed by Spence to clarify his choice of words, Pope explained that by contrast he meant "colouring" through "the disposition of lights and shades."[9] Variety, he added, a fundamental element in tasteful garden design, is included in the contrasts and enhances the surprise element.[10] Pope asked Spence to recall his couplet in *To Burlington*, published about a decade earlier, that succinctly put the case for the new English mode of garden design: "He gains all points, who pleasingly confounds,/Surprizes, varies, and conceals the Bounds" (55–56). The consequent pictorial effects within the garden itself were complemented by the elimination of walls, no mere afterthought in Pope's rules. Walls could impose rigid constraints upon the entire garden layout by isolating the pictorial interplay of features within the garden and not allowing them to relate freely with the landscape outside. The "capital stroke," as Horace Walpole put it, in his *History of the*

Modern Taste in Gardening (first published in 1771), was the use of a "ha-ha," a sunken fence; while permitting the boundaries of a garden to be concealed at the same time as they were preserved, the "ha-ha" let into the garden the various views of surrounding countryside.

Pictorial effects fascinated Pope in garden layouts. He was always striving for them. Almost all his gardening remarks recorded by Spence strike this theme, and in his letters he frequently judged gardens with them in mind. One can easily imagine him habitually inspecting the garden potential of landscapes with the eye of a painter, composing prospective garden scenes in his mind as a painter does on a landscape and judging their merit against the pictorial criteria that he well understood, chiefly as a result of his painting lessons with Charles Jervas.[11] "All gardening is landscape-painting," he told Spence in 1734, "just like a landscape hung up."[12] Pointing to some trees in his own garden in 1739, he observed: "Those clumps of trees are like the groups in pictures."[13]

With such remarks Pope was delineating his idea of the picturesque in a garden.[14] If we accept Spence's judgment that Pope's idea of the picturesque as versified in the earliest parts of *Windsor Forest* (1704) was "like his ideas afterwards for gardening,"[15] then long before he had his own garden or took painting lessons he discovered and articulated—unbelievably, at the age of sixteen—his ideal of landscape and garden beauty. He first discovered this ideal in the forest and in his father's garden at Whitehill House, Binfield. Moreover, these relevant early passages of *Windsor Forest* describing countryside scenes cogently summarize some of the ideas of landscape beauty he maintained for the rest of his life. This landscape of his youth is "harmoniously confus'd;/Where Order in Variety we see,/And where, tho' all things differ, all agree" (lines 14-16). At the age of about nineteen, in *Sapho to Phaon* (ca. 1707), he had hit upon the phrase "Sylvan *Genius* of the Place," part of which he later used in *To Burlington* to allude to his conception of the presiding designer of a natural scene's harmonious order through variety and contrast. As both a spiritual and an artistic influence inherent in the land, the Genius "paints" continually, so that the "Groves of *Eden*, vanish'd now so long" in a sense are revitalized endlessly. In a garden, it collaborates with the enlightened gardener. While in the following lines Pope is not, it seems, thinking of gardens, although he mentions lawns, later he will adapt to gardens his ideas about light and dark, grovework, color, contrasting shapes, variety of elevation, movement, and perspective:

> Here waving Groves a checquer'd Scene display,
> And part admit and part exclude the Day;
>
> . . . .
>
> There, interspers'd in Lawns and opening Glades,
> Thin Trees arise that shun each others Shades.
> Here in full Light the russet Plains extend;
> There wrapt in Clouds the blueish Hills ascend:
> Ev'n the wild Heath displays her Purple Dies,
> And 'midst the Desart fruitful Fields arise,

That crown'd with tufted Trees and springing Corn,
Like verdant Isles the sable Waste adorn.

(17–18, 21–28)

Whether he was looking at Lord Peterborough's two hills at Bevis Mount, the Physic Garden at Oxford, Lord Bathurst's Riskins, a swan lit up by the sparkling sun as it glided "amidst the shade of a tree over the water on the Thames" at Twickenham, or "at first blush" the "sombre" and "rich" prospects of "natural views,"[16] it was the likeness of a garden to a picture, of open landscape to a garden, that he enjoyed discovering and talking about.

The "amiable simplicity of unadorned nature"

Pope's *Guardian* essay in 1713 spoke with a bold new voice in English gardening history, but today it is rather a disappointment.[17] While it suggests that at his father's house in Binfield he was well schooled in both horticulture and garden planning, and demonstrates that he already placed a premium on "Painting at Pleasure" in gardens and the "useful Part of Horticulture," the essay is highly derivative. Its inspiration and authority are chiefly literary, which invites the speculation that Pope's first strong opinions about gardens may be traced to ancient and contemporary writing, not so much to existing gardens and living gardeners. Indeed, as both Maynard Mack and John Dixon Hunt have argued, Pope's gardening at Twickenham, as well as his grotto there, were indebted more to imagined classical, especially Roman, garden practice, drawn from literary sources and modern Italian villa examples, than to new English notions of landscape possibilities.[18] While in the essay Pope does cite Martial's "*Baiana nostri Villa*" as a clue to the garden beauty which his friend thought was rare in English "Villa's"—an architectural term, notes Hunt, that included both house and garden with strong Italian (classical and modern) overtones—he does not refer as we might have expected, to his father's Binfield garden at all, except possibly in his opening allusion to "my House in the Country," nor to any pleasing landscapes such as Lord Bathurst's Riskins Park, which he conceivably knew by 1713.[19] There is little sign in the essay that he had wrestled with the practical problems of garden design. He tells his readers that as gardeners they should be guided by the "Simplicity of unadorned Nature"—a phrase that meant much more to them than it does to us—and translates Homer's description in the *Odyssey* of the gardens of Alcinous to illustrate a classical taste for garden beauty of which he felt there was little trace left in England in 1713. He pretty well leaves it at that, however, except for a brief comment on the Homer passage and a hilariously absurd "Catalogue of Greens [bushes] to be disposed of by an eminent Town-Gardiner." The catalogue satirizes the pervasive taste for topiary and other "Fantastical Operations of Art."

Certainly the *Guardian* essay perpetuated a reaction against the Dutch and French formal styles that had overwhelmed England in the second half of the seventeenth century. Stephen Switzer, for one, cited it for support in his influential *Ichnographia Rustica* (1718) as he advocated a greater freedom and extensiveness in gardening. Pope's originality in this essay, however, was not so much in his ideas as in the way he presented them. Though he borrowed heavily from Joseph Addison and Sir William Temple as well as from the country house poem tradition of the preceding century, not to mention Homer's description of Alcinous's gardens, unlike his sources he organized their ideas into a direct and swift attack upon "the modern Practice of Gardening" in which, he said, the point appeared to be to "recede" from nature rather than study and imitate it. The vigor of the piece amounted to a call for immediate reform, whereas earlier pronouncements by Temple, the Earl of Shaftesbury, and Addison had remained conversational and analytical in tone.

At the heart of the essay is Pope's early Homeric exercise, the translation of Homer's account of Alcinous's gardens in book 7 of the *Odyssey*. It is supposed to illustrate everything the poet is advocating about garden design. Apparently he was still pleased with it over a decade later (after five years of very active gardening) when he was translating the entire epic because he included it without a single change. In his youthful enthusiasm, Pope declares that this garden was "the most beautiful Plan of this sort that can be imagined"; he adds that Sir William Temple, whose essay "Upon the Gardens of Epicurus, or, of Gardening, in the year 1685" prophetically illumined new trends in garden layouts, judges Homer's account as containing "all the justest Rules and Provisions which can go toward composing the best Gardens."[20] Pope does not say what he means by "this sort" of garden, though its four-acre size gives us a clue. He makes much of its smallness. It is his first comment on the garden and he argues, very much with the grand and formal French garden style in mind, that the English have lost sight of "simplicity" in their gardening—a word with which he equates Greek and Roman gardening.[21] We shall see as we proceed through Pope's favorite landscapes, including his own, that the smallest garden areas always pleased him most. His father's garden at Binfield in which he was living in 1713 was small;[22] very likely, as I have said, this garden was the "little Retirement" in which his expert gardening friend found "that Beauty which he always thought wanting in the most celebrated Seats, or if you will Villa's, of the Nation." To Pope the delicate mixture of pictorial effects within a small space was infinitely more interesting and worthy of gardeners "capable of Art" and "fond of Nature."

The balance of Pope's remarks on Alcinous's gardens may be traced directly to Temple, thus proving that Temple's was one of the greatest early and formative influences upon the young poet's ideas of what a tasteful garden should be. In his essay Temple cites classical sources for his gardening ideas, including Homer, Xenophon, and "other Greek Authors"—as well as the Chinese;[23] he also imparts the philosophy, shared by a number of Stuart and Jacobean poets, that a well-conceived garden is useful, respectful of nature, economical, and serviceable to the community.[24] With his love of seventeenth-century poets, Pope was already in 1713 familiar with this body of thought, but Temple's forceful application of it to gardening apparently made a dramatic impression on the young poet. Years later in *To Burlington* Pope may even have taken Temple's accusing phrase, "greater sums may be thrown away without effect," describing gardeners who try to force nature, for his own indictment of Timon's villa, where all cry out, "What sums are thrown away!'' (100). Looking back in 1752, Spence confirmed both Temple's and Addison's early influence upon the new style: "Milton's paradise is chiefly like a new natural taste. Sir William Temple guessed at it, and Addison has many strokes toward it in the *Spectators*. [The new style] began to be practised a few years after the publication of the *Spectators*.[25]

What is a bit surprising is the extent of Pope's reliance on Temple's actual wording. To begin with, he echoes Temple's remark that Homer's account was made "at the pleasure of the painter" with his own that both Homer and Virgil in their verses were capable of "Painting at Pleasure."[26] He continues by observing that the garden was fenced with a "green Enclosure" for reasons of defense (from the elements), and then repeats Temple's notion about the garden conveniently "joining to the gates of the Palace" almost in the same words: "for Conveniency join'd close to the Gates of the Palace." This concept, too, became central to the poet's idea of good sense and hospitality in gardening. Timon in *To Burlington* was mocked because to get to his house from his garden "up ten steep slopes" you "dragg'd your thighs." The several features following, which Pope thought worthy of emphasis, he mentions in almost exactly the same order Temple listed them. There were the lofty trees—"suffered" or allowed to grow to their full height, Pope says, with a slap at "People of the common Level of Understanding" who delight in stunting the growth of trees so they can indulge their false wits as tree sculptors. Intelligent fruit culture also endowed Alcinous with "a continual succession of fruits throughout the whole year." And the prominence of two fountains, elevated "remarkably" above the rest of the gardens rather in the fashion of the mounts that Pope thought crucial to garden variety, enhanced the pictorialism within the enclosure at the same time as they irrigated the gardens and supplied the nearby town with water. Here again Pope adapted and strengthened Temple's phrasing. One fountain was "for the use of the garden," wrote Temple, "and the other of palace." Pope said that the fountains were channeled by conduits or ducts, "one of them to Water all Parts of the Gardens, and the other underneath the Palace into the Town, for the Service of the Publick."

Pope makes more of the plants in the garden than Temple did. All his life he was curious about plants, experimenting with them for the benefit of his own and others' gardens. Cultivation of pineapples, grapes, vegetables, and a wide variety of trees commanded enormous amounts of his time. This illustrates his commitment to the gardening principle *in utile dulce*. His comment about letting trees grow tall, for example, may be traced to his father's forest gardening at Binfield; he once alluded in a poem to the "Forest planted by a Father's hand."[27] Lord Bathurst at Cirencester Park won his admiration as a landscaper partly because of his forest gardening—"Who plants like BATHURST," he asked in *To Burlington*. "A tree is a nobler object than a prince in his coronation robes," he told Spence.[28] In his letters he frequently pauses over the beauty and promise of many varieties of trees. As for fruit and vegetables, he is careful to remark (whereas Temple was not) that Alcinous's four acres, like his own five acres later on, were divided into three other sections besides the ornamental gardens: an orchard, a vineyard, and an herb and kitchen garden. Rather than cite Temple here, incidentally, in the notes to his complete *Odyssey* translation, he turns to Eustathius, who specified "a grove for fruits and shade, a vineyard, and an allotment for olives and herbs."[29]

To Pope, this division of a small garden was a testament to gardening genius, but disappointingly his essay offers only this brief observation on the subject:

> The *Vineyard* seems to have been a Plantation distinct from the *Garden*; as also the *Beds of Greens* mentioned afterwards at the Extremity of the Inclosure, in the Nature and usual Place of our *Kitchen Gardens*.

It is also disappointing that instead of using the note to the passage in his complete *Odyssey* to reflect on modern gardening in the 1720s, he lapses into a somewhat irrelevant exposition on whether any tree can bear fruit all year long.

Pope's debt to Addison in the essay is also striking. A few of Addison's *Spectator* papers have been credited with urging a higher regard for open and natural landscape and a freer and more practical approach to gardening (notably nos. 414 and 477),[30] but Pope's reliance upon him is somewhat slavish. Brownell has called Addison's ideas about gardens and landscape speculative and vague as compared with Pope's bolder satire on the degeneracy of modern tastes, but a close comparison of their texts reveals that Pope, young and as yet relatively inexperienced with garden design, has almost plagiarized Addison. Perhaps this was his way of flattering the famous man whose support for his intended *Iliad* translation he keenly wanted—he may, in fact, have translated the gardens of Alcinous passage to show Addison his poetic prowess as a translator.[31]

Dear to Addison's heart was the pleasure with profit concept in English landscaping, as he stated it in *Spectator* no. 414, with which he anticipated the *ferme ornée* or ornamental farm that really caught on in England toward the middle of the century. The first point Pope makes about the Alcinous passage as well as Virgil's sketch of the Corycian's gardens is just that one. "These (one may observe)," he says, "consist intirely of the useful Part of Horticulture, Fruit-Trees, Herbs, Water, &c." This comes after the passage on the superiority of "unadorned Nature" over the "nicer Scenes of Art," which looks much like a student's plagiarism of Addison's phrase in *Spectator* no. 414, "There is something more bold and masterly in the rough careless Strokes of Nature, than in the nicer Touches and Embellishments of Art." Addison speaks of the "nobler and more exalted kind of Pleasure" nature confers, while Pope speaks of the "loftier Sensation of Pleasure." Where Addison laments that English gardeners who "instead of humouring Nature, love to deviate from it as much as possible," Pope grumbles that they seem to study how they may "recede from Nature." To illustrate this point Addison takes a swipe at topiary work:

> Our Trees rise in Cones, Globes and Pyramids. We see the Marks of the Scissars upon every Plant and Bush. I do not know whether I am singular in my Opinion, but, for my own part, I would rather look upon a Tree in all its Luxuriancy and Diffusion of Boughs and Branches, than when it is thus cut and trimmed into a Mathematical Figure; and cannot but fancy that an

Orchard in Flower looks infinitely more delightful, than all the little Labyrinths of the most finished Parterre.[32]

Pope is at his best in his essay when he takes up Addison's cue and wittily embellishes the patent absurdity of citizens like the cook who "beautified his Country Seat with a Coronation Dinner in Greens, where you see the Champion flourishing on Horseback at one end of the Table, and the Queen in perpetual Youth at the other."

Except in applying his theme of good country house ownership and responsibility to gardening, Pope does not go beyond Temple or Addison in this essay. But the piece does signal more than a passing interest in garden design. Coming so soon after Addison's essay, it also renewed the growing offensive against the increasingly outmoded French and Dutch dominance. But unlike both Temple and Addison, and the third Earl of Shaftesbury, who celebrated the "genuine order" of nature over the "formal mockery of princely Gardens,"[33] Pope does not use this opportunity to promote a new aesthetic of landscape freedom and irregularity—or new ways of reading the relation of man and his environment. This he was not to do until he wrote *To Burlington* almost two decades later.

The influence of Pope the gardenist upon British gardening was scarcely at all strengthened by his writing. It was through his practical work that he exerted his powerful influence. His letters helped spread his influence, but it was what others said and wrote about his garden designs that created his reputation. Almost nothing about his garden was published within his lifetime; yet by the year of his death it was famous across the country and a favorite focus for tourists.[34]

Garden styles

The proliferation and overlapping of certain terms to describe the evolution of garden fashions in the eighteenth century have made these terms annoyingly inadequate.[35] Pope himself almost never used the terms *formal, informal, transitional, natural, wild, picturesque, rococo*, and so on, yet he was able to communicate his precise ideas of what he liked and disliked about gardens. While such terms can at times usefully refer in a general way to a body of taste, the problem with them, of course, is that they changed in meaning throughout the century. An "informal" garden design in 1725 may well have been judged "formal" in 1775, or perhaps transitional. Pope's idea of the picturesque was considerably different from William Gilpin's during the great popularity of the so-called picturesque school later in the century. Pope's carefully worked out balance between art and nature at Twickenham would have struck Launcelot ("Capability") Brown as cramped and stiff. For his part, Pope as easily might have shivered at the thought of Brown's vast and open landscapes—which could have brought to his mind his satiric lines in *To Burlington* about Villario, "Tir'd of the scene Parterres and Fountains yield,/He finds at last he better likes a Field" (87–88), or about Timon, who shivers at the breeze coming off his oceanic pond or Brobdingnagian lake.

Pope never applied the word *formal* to the dominant French and Dutch garden fashions; nor did he ever use the word to describe the deadening influence of constraint and regularity that he and his contemporaries increasingly felt emanated from those fashions. He preferred to sound the alarm with a phrase like "Fantastical Operations of Art," or a cataloguing of the sins of unimaginative gardeners as in his sketch of Timon. Moreover, to his strong and precise dislike of rigid French and Dutch gardening[36] he joined a distaste for morally weak gardeners, chiefly Whiggish, whose sterile and egocentric taste led them to follow their own self-glorifying leads instead of nature's. That, too, was part of the outmoded autocratic pattern in landscaping that he first moved against in the *Guardian* and that lay behind his portrait of Timon the demigod, lord of the relics of his pitiable efforts to show off his self-importance. It may have been Pope who without particular reference to gardening, put this sentiment forcefully in an earlier *Guardian* (no. 169), contrasting imaginative freedom with the "Impiety" of brutish rural squires who do not attend to "the Drama of Nature" and are unlikely "to be sensible to its Greatness and Beauty, to be delighted with its Harmony, and by these Reflexions to obtain just Sentiments of the Almighty Mind that framed it." Add to this his comprehensive disdain for any design that appeared to be barren of creativity, variation, and good sense, and the picture of what he rejected—what might be labeled formal—is fairly complete. Monotony is the enemy of imaginative life, whether in the form of vast regularity, flatness, stagnating water, rigidity of straight lines and geometric shapes, or impenetrable walls. There must be movement, variety, and fluidity. There must also be dynamic meaning to a garden through some form, howsoever subtle, of iconographic allusions and associations whereby the owner may provide ideas for the mind of the visitor to exercise upon and also honor historical and legendary aspects of the place or his own contributions to his country and family.[37]

With all that said, it is important to qualify Pope's position in the process of garden naturalization that we associate with the new style. He tells his contemporaries that they must follow nature but not that they should let her look unimproved:

> But treat the Goddess like a modest fair,
> Nor over-dress, nor leave her wholly bare;
> Let not each beauty ev'ry where be spy'd,
> Where half the skill is decently to hide.
>
> (*To Burlington*, 51–54)

If he is alert to nature and consults the Genius of the Place—the resident spirit or character of a situation—the gardener will be able to transcend mere taste and fashion, whether outmoded or current. The point about Pope is that he was not caught up in a comprehensive program of garden liberalization to purge the garden of most of the shackles of "nice Art." There was much more nuance and subtlety in his gardening ideas than such a view would suggest. His conception of gardening being like landscape painting, "like a landscape hung up," alone proves that. George Clarke points up the danger of seeing Bridgeman's, Pope's, Kent's, and others' contributions to the new style as installments in the "predestined development towards the kind of landscape which approximates to a painting by Claude" or toward the promised land of revolutionary landscape freedom.[38] This is the Whig interpretation of gardening, perpetuated largely

9

by Horce Walpole in his *History of the Modern Taste in Gardening* (1782), who held that what these early protagonists in the unfolding English gardening Renaissance really wanted was ultimately achieved by the so-called high phase of landscape gardening, the picturesque school.[39] This was just not true. Pope of course had no idea of himself as a transitional figure in landscaping history, though he did see himself as a pioneer. He did not garden in the present with reference to the future.

An early passage from his Preface to the *Iliad* (1715) reveals the care he was beginning to take, under the influence of Charles Jervas's painting lessons, in exploring through gardens a balance between art and nature; he never abandoned this search, though to proponents of the picturesque later in the century such a passage as this would have sounded hopelessly out of date:

> As in the most regular Gardens, Art can only reduce the beauties of Nature to more regularity, and such a Figure, which the common Eye may better take in, and is therefore more entertain'd with. . . . Our Author's [Homer's] Work is a wild Paradise, where if we cannot see all the Beauties so distinctly as in an order'd Garden, it is only because the Number of them is infinitely greater.

It is up to the observer or reader to be painter enough to perceive how nature and art "conspire" to create the *Iliad*, or a tree, or a tasteful garden. Homer understood, just as any painter-gardener must, that "'Tis one thing to be tricked up, and another not to be dress'd at all. Simplicity is the Mean between Ostentation and Rusticity."[40]

But there was more to Pope's individual delineation of variety in a garden, especially his own, than the mere creation of varied scenes in which art and nature are delicately balanced. John Dixon Hunt has incisively explained that Pope preferred symmetry mixed with surprising and varied patterns in a garden not only because the combination intensifies the experience of a garden's variety—a notion he shared with Addison—but also because the contrast enlivens the mind and gives it more to think about and respond to. "What is always in question for Pope and these early gardenists," writes Professor Hunt, "is a garden's adequate provision of a sufficient variety to occupy the mind."[41] Whether a garden's style is essentially symmetrical or artificially natural is always of less moment to Pope than that a garden be designed with an alertness to what demands it can place upon an active and demanding intelligence. Thoughts must be allowed to wander productively and satisfyingly in the garden, not be herded by rigid preconceptions or insulted by the banal frivolities of an egocentric Timon. Under the right evocative spell of moonlight, historical associations, romance, or visions and dreams, even a "formal" garden can satisfy mental needs. Hence on one occasion in the moonlight Pope is delighted with the sensation that even in St. James Park he can entertain visions and dreams. Certainly he found it easier to do that in Stowe's Elysian Fields, but the point is that the layout of a landscape was not for him the only catalyst.

Although Pope's taste ran to smaller gardens—"Pope in Miniature," James Thomson called it[42]—he could enjoy huge landscape gardens if they contained areas that felt small and private, conducive to meditation. While Lord Bathurst's vast demesnes at Cirencester made him feel uneasy, some wooded recesses and varied acres close by the house redeemed for him both the park and Bathurst the gardener. It was the same at Stowe, with which design Pope had little, if anything, to do..[43] He made a habit after 1724 of stopping at Stowe about once a year to see the gardens and buildings that Sir John Vanbrugh and Charles Bridgeman had begun to design in 1719. By 1724 Stowe was already justly famous for the landscape being laid out by its owner, Richard Temple, Viscount Cobham—to whom Pope was to address his first moral epistle (1734). In 1725 Pope certainly had a lot on his gardening plate. He was nearly finished with the first stage of his own garden, contributing to the Digbys' Sherborne, loyal to and deeply involved with Cirencester's gardens, and demonstratively proud over his garden designs at Mrs. Howard's Marble Hill. But it was to Stowe perhaps more than to any other landscape that he returned again and again "with fresh Satisfaction."

"If any thing under paradise could set me beyond all Earthly Cogitations; Stowe might do it," he spontaneously announced in August 1731 to his friend John Knight of Gosfield, Essex (3:217). Regrettably, he never described the gardens in any detail, perhaps because they were so well known to his friends and he visited regularly. We may instead pick up a clue to his fondness for the early gardens from a remark made by Sir John Perceval, first Earl of Egmont, in a letter of 1724 to Daniel Dering: "The gardens by reason of the good contrivance of the walks, seem to be three times as large as they are. . . . You think twenty times you have no more to see and of a sudden find yourself in some new garden or walk, as finish'd and adorn'd as that you left. Nothing is more irregular in the whole, nothing more regular in the parts, which totally differ the one from the other." Bridgeman's vistas stretching out from various rond-points, especially from Vanbrugh's focally placed Rotunda, and intersecting with each other to enclose many garden areas of differing size, shape, and pattern, produced what must have seemed like an unending plan of variety and surprise. That combination belied the actual dimensions of the gardens—only twenty-eight acres in 1724, Lord Perceval wrote. It was still about six times larger than Pope's garden, but the achievement of so many artistic effects within that area was analogous to Pope's technique within a "small compass" at Twickenham. The illusion of greater size was also enhanced by Bridgeman's skillful use of the ha-ha or sunken ditch, which as Perceval testified "leaves you the sight of a bewtiful woody country, and makes you ignorant how far the high planted walks extend."[44] This feature alone must have pleased Pope, whose appreciation of open landscape framed into a composition by walks, trees, windows, arched doorways, or whatever natural or artificial device was always especially keen. It was a far cry from the imprisoning walls that Timon threw up around his gardens.

While Pope's enthusiastic allusion to paradise at Stowe makes sense in terms of all we have already observed about his gardening, we should not lose sight of Lord Perceval's judgment of the balance between the "irregular in the whole" and the "regular in the parts" and what this suggests about Pope's early tastes. Parterres, an octagonal pond, geometrically shaped setting for buildings, a dominant north-south axis, and straight lines of trees enunciated Stowe's pattern of regularity. When Pope said on that occasion in 1731 that the gardens were more beautiful than when he last saw them, perhaps two summers earlier, and that they were "much enlarged, & with variety," he was undoubtedly describing (at least in part) the results of enclosing a stretch of pasture land called Home Park within the gardens. This ambitious scheme included laying out a belt or walk around the extensive perimeter together with strategically placed buildings and temples commanding sweeping vistas of one another and of the earlier gardens nearer the house. This was the stage Stowe's plan had reached when Pope perpetuated the fame of the gardens with his compliment in *To Burlington*: "Nature shall join you, Time shall make it grow/A Work to wonder at—perhaps a STOW" (69–70). Regularity, however, still was visible everywhere. Indeed, by midcentury the gardens were coming to be regarded as old-fashioned. The Marchioness de Grey wrote in 1748 that in her view the layout was "a stiff set Plan"; she added that "Nature has done very little for it, & Art so much that you cannot possibly be deceived.[45] There were too many buildings crowding each other, she thought, and not enough sense of space or freedom. One can only wonder whether Pope's garden would have struck her as similarly "stiff" and overcrowded.

"Romantic taste"

It is because Pope shared Martha Blount's "Romantic taste" for landscaping that he wrote more to her about gardening than to anyone else. He enjoyed mythologizing her into a latter-day shepherdess with a quaint preference for lambs and heifers cropping grass within view of houses and gardens because he knew intimately her judgment and sensibility regarding landscape. Like Eve, she "raves upon tying up the rose-trees," he declared to Knight in 1729, and "talks much of seeing the lawn enlarged, and the flocks feeding in sight of the parterre, and of administering grass to the lambs, and crowning them with flowers, etc." (3:68). Having both grown up amid or near the shades of Windsor Forest,[46] they recognized they were kindred spirits. Occasionally she sent him descriptions, too, of landscape and gardens. He visited Stonor Park and the surrounding landscape near Oxford in 1717 because of "the romantic description you gave me of it," he told her (1:429); and then a few days later could not resist sending her his own reflections on that romantic landscape: "I rid over hanging hills, whose tops were edgd with Groves, & whose feet water'd with winding rivers, listening to the falls of Cataracts below, & the murmuring of Winds above" (1:429–30). Martha Blount is, in fact, a key to what we may call Pope's own appreciaton for visually dramatic gardens. Without his letters to her, we would know far less than we do about his gardening.[47]

When Pope told Martha that he hoped to find the idea of her in Stowe's Elysian Fields, he was making a connection between a garden and a dream or vision. Professor Hunt writes about how the reading of romances was held to induce images of enchanting landscapes, as in Addison's linking of Leonora's garden with her extensive reading of such literature (*Spectator*, no. 37). It was the same with Pope's idea of Martha Blount. He encouraged her to read such stuff and once, according to Spence, even wished to write a romance himself. He may have understood a connection between such reading and a state of innocence where the mind inhabits enchanting realms of fancy; this view would

Plate 2. Martha and Teresa Blount. Oil painting by Charles Jervas. Courtesy The Laing Art Gallery, Tyne and Wear County Council.

be consistent with his perception of her childlike innocence and her consequent responsiveness to evocative and natural landscapes. Perhaps she did all her life read romances because for all of Pope's life she remained the perfect "Idæa" of a gardening companion.

To return to Stowe's gardens, we are able to see how Pope's always enthusiastic response to them is heightened by their evolution toward the romantic in the 1730s. If he was taken with the results of Bridgeman's and Vanbrugh's teamwork in the 1720s, he was positively overwhelmed by the poetic addition of the Elysian Fields to the west in the 1730s. Writing to Martha Blount from Stowe on 4 July 1739, he reveals an enthusiasm for landscape that not only confirms his taste for the pictorial but also shows how his taste has become more closely linked to the emotive or poetic in gardens: "I never saw this Place in half the beauty & perfection it now has. ... This Garden is beyond all description [in] the New part of it; I am every hour in it, but dinner & night, and every

Plate 3. Hardwick and Mapledurham, the home of the Blount family. Drawn by Joseph Farington and engraved by J. C. Stadler, 1793.

hour Envying myself the delight of it, because [not] partaken by You, who would *See* it better, & consequently enjoy it more. . . . Adieu. I'm going into the Elyzian Fields, where I shall meet your Idæa" (4:185–86).

It was in the Elysian Fields that, according to Sir Thomas Robinson in a 1734 letter to Lord Carlisle, designs had recently begun "after Mr. Kent's notion"; and Spence about 1752 recorded Philip Southcote's opinion that those new gardens were "the painting part" of Cobham's landscape.[48] It is certain that the area was more romantically pretty than any other area of Stowe's gardens by that date, and that the impression it left upon people as a painterly composition of great variety within a small area was eminently matched to Pope's brilliance as a landscaper. It contained a felicity of physical features that in the late 1720s and 1730s Pope was looking for more and more in an evocative garden: a grotto; a serpentine; a little "sacred" valley into which water issued from the grotto; steep grassy banks (as at Sherborne, Bevis Mount, and Prior Park) with thin screens of trees that Kenneth Woodbridge tells us were characteristic of Kent's effort to create a sequence of pictures as one walked around; two little domed temples for images of the classical-pictorial; the Temple of Ancient Virtue overlooking the pretty valley from the Great Cross Walk linking the older gardens with the new.[49]

It is commonly accepted now that Pope, together with other literary friends of Cobham's, helped articulate the governing iconography of the Elysian Fields, its "Poetick

Plate 4. "White-Knights, the Seat of Sr. Hen. Englefield, Bart.," 1776. The Blount sisters frequently stayed here; from it they could conveniently visit Pope at Binfield in Windsor Forest.

Plan," as Gilbert West prophetically wrote in his poem *Stowe*, in 1732.[50] Political, classical, and Addisonian themes were introduced into the design.[51] He may even have gone further and influenced the siting of the temples of Ancient Virtue and British Worthies in concert with allusions to sacred landscapes in the *Aeneid*. The opportunity for those allusions existed specifically because of the little valley with a small stream running along its bottom near the house. It was a naturally secluded retreat; all the gardener had to do was untangle the overgrown thickets, eliminate unwanted trees, and add the appropriate buildings and stonework. Pope was drawn to secluded spots in gardens created by hilly terrain or depressions and deep cuts in the ground. He must have noticed the overgrown and neglected valley on his first known visit to Stowe in 1724, the very year incidentally he first visited the Digbys at Sherborne Castle and was enraptured by the "Solemnity" and "prodigious Beauty" of a deep and shady valley cut out by the River Yeo, with views "more romantick than Imagination can form them" (2:238–39). He may not have known it fully then, but at Sherborne he was on the threshold of comprehending the philosophical and imaginative uses within a garden of romantically dramatic variety of elevation colored by thick woods, the sound and sight of water, rustic stonework of grottoes and old seats and bridges, and anything else that might be an aid to philosophical reflection.[52] That is not to say he was unaware of the exhilarating emotional effects upon him of hilly or romantic—a word he used several

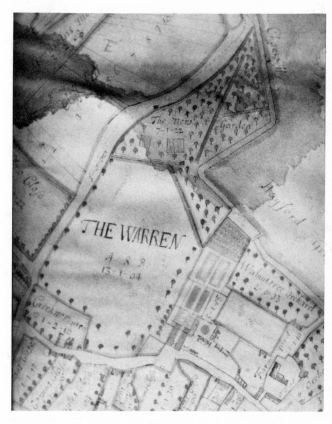

Plate 5. "A Map of the Parish of Rowsham . . . " 1721. Measured by Edward Grantham. This estate map shows the gardens before Bridgeman's alterations, with terraces north of the house and "the New Garden" with square ponds.

times—scenery; his poem *Eloisa to Abelard* (1717) and his letters (such as the one about Stonor) had already shown how very responsive he could be to the melancholy and reflective moods engendered by hills, cliffs, and valleys. But he had not yet experienced intimately, or designed, gardens with such dramatic topography. Chiswick House, Marble Hill, Cirencester, Riskins, Dawley Farm, and his own garden were all relatively flat. A major new key to Pope's garden design was about to emerge when he saw Sherborne.

Sherborne, in fact, may have influenced (via a circuitous route) the Elysian Fields. As he looked up from the bottom of the valley along the wooded banks at Sherborne, already aware of the historical iconography around him, Pope wondered if a classical temple would complete the allusive character of the spot. "I could very much wish," Pope confided in Martha Blount, "a little Temple built on a neighboring round Hill that is seen from all points of the Garden & is extremely pretty. It would finish some Walks, & particularly be a fine Termination to the River to be seen from the Entrance into that Deep Scene I have describd by the Cascade where it would appear as in the clouds, between the tops of some very lofty Trees that form an Arch before it, with a great Slope downward to the end of the said river" (2:239). That was never done at Sherborne, but with the Temple of Ancient Virtue overlooking the Elysian Fields Pope may have finally

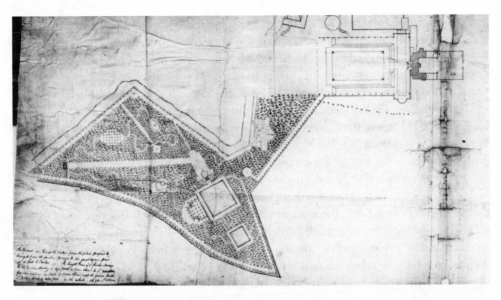

Plate 6. Plan of the gardens of Rousham, attributed to Charles Bridgeman, ca. 1725. This shows the garden as it was when Pope praised it in a letter to Martha Blount in 1728 (2:513).

used the concept. The pictorial allusiveness in that garden treatment did, in any event, determine a new course in the history of English landscape gardening.

At Rousham, in Oxfordshire, the seat of Pope's close friends the Dormer and Cottrell families, he knew another garden, much smaller than Stowe, which from the earliest of his known visits in 1728 attracted him like a magnet year after year during his rambles (see plates 5 and 6). It was the kind of garden with slopes and banks, private recesses, ponds and cascades, and thick groves cut with serpentine walks for which he developed an increasingly keen taste in the 1730s—gardens that he could "lose" himself in like Lord Peterborough's Bevis Mount, Ralph Allen's Prior Park, or Lord Lyttelton's Hagley Park. Before the late 1730s it was Bridgeman's, not Kent's, layout that roused his enthusiasm, although he himself very likely contributed some ideas.[53] It sounds as if he had never before seen the garden when he writes to Martha Blount in September 1728 with this unqualified testimony: "I lay one night at Rousham, which is the prettiest place for water-falls, jetts, ponds inclosed with beautiful scenes of green and hanging wood, that ever I saw" (2:513). The pleasures of Rousham, which still exist today, were heightened for him because the garden was small, though it stretched out some distance along the gentle river Cherwell, and commanded convenient views across the river to the farm fields and soft hills beyond. The enjoyment he took there was similar to his enjoyment of the dramatic interplay of hill, wood, water, and buildings in the Elysian Fields, at Sherborne, or at Dodington, Sir William Codrington's seat near Bath, which he praised in the same letter to Martha: "Their [Elizabethan] house is pretty enough, the situation romantic, covered with woody hills tumbling upon one another confusedly, and the garden makes a valley betwixt them, with some mounts and waterfalls."

17

Further evidence of Pope's developing eye for and enjoyment of Albano-like, hilly, idealized natural garden settings is that he applies the word *prettiest*, not *romantic*, to Rousham. Concerning landscape, he held the word *romantic* in reserve for natural scenery or gardens that were "uncommon" owing to moods of venerable solemnity, long or lofty prospects, remoteness and wildness, and age. He knew few gardens, even in the new styles popularized by Bridgeman and Kent, that possessed these qualities, although he conveyed the privacy of the hidden "Avenues" in his own garden when he told Aaron Hill in 1731 that it was both "Poetical" and "Romantic" (3:188). The Elysian Fields may have qualified as romantic, but all Pope says (not very helpfully) in 1739 is that this spot was "beyond all description." Rousham after Kent's alterations beginning in 1737 may also have deserved the word, but Pope says nothing in his surviving letters about Kent's designs there. Before Kent, the Bridgeman layout with winding walks through "wildernesses" is tied together too much with straight parapet walks, regularly shaped ponds, terraces, and a "Bridgmannick" theater to elicit the word from Pope. Nor is Rousham dramatically hilly or steep enough.[54]

With this outline of Pope's preparation and "first principles" in the art of gardening, then, we may step into the garden. If he was not totally original in his ideas, he was witty and energetic in disseminating them. The history of landscape gardening in the first half of the century is to an amazing extent the history of his encouragement and artistic support of the owners of the landscapes analyzed in the following chapters.

2

Chiswick and Twickenham

The Beginnings Along the Thames

When Pope moved into his villa at Twickenham in 1719, he naturally made that section of the Thames more famous than it had ever been before. He was thirty-one and already England's most distinguished living poet. Also, coinciding with the attention he was receiving for his recently completed *Iliad* translation, the move aroused some new public interest in Twickenham and its surroundings. The area, to be sure, had for years enjoyed a reputation for fashionable society and beautiful homes—the "Elysian Shades" of Richmond Park and gardens were just a stone's throw down the river—and it had even been a haunt of poets for over one hundred years.[1] But Pope's choice of it as a home, although not the only or even the major factor in its new popularity, freshened its reputation. Within a decade after his move his villa had become a popular landmark on the river and the area had absorbed an influx of residents who discovered it as the ideal semirural setting for country homes.[2]

Pope also quickly became known as a leading innovative gardener along the Richmond-Twickenham section of the Thames, which eventually generated still more interest in the area and contributed to its reputation as a testing ground for new landscaping ideas—the venue of avant-garde English gardening. Many writers bore witness to this bustle of landscaping. "Inchanting" or "Matchless VALE OF THAMES," James Thomson called it in *The Seasons*,

> beyond what'er the Muse
> Has of Achaia or Hesperia sung!
> A vale of bliss! O softly-swelling hills!
> On which the Power of Cultivation lies,
> And joys to see the wonders of his toil.
> ("Summer," 1432–36)

In addition to the area's natural beauties, Thomson was celebrating its visual improvement through energetic landscaping. So was Daniel Defoe, writing in the early 1720s, when he compared the area favorably with the banks of the Seine in Paris, the Danube above and below Vienna, and the Po as it passed through the classical landscape of Turin.

Plate 7. A view of Petersham House. The innovative gardening existed up and down the hill, which can be seen rising to the right. Drawn by A. Heckel and engraved by Stevens.

He was particularly impressed by the same resourcefulness of the inhabitants:

> *In a Word*, nothing can be more beautiful; here is a Plain and pleasant Country, a rich fertile Soil, cultivated and enclosed to the utmost perfection of Husbandry . . . Villages fill'd with . . . Houses, and the Houses surrounded with Gardens, Walks, Vistas, Avenues, representing all the Beauties of Building, and all the Pleasures of Planting.[3]

Another traveler, John Macky, as early as 1722 had written about the "abundance of Curious Seats" in the area,[4] one of them being Lord Rochester's Petersham Lodge, whose remarkably wild and imaginative gardens (plate 7) on the slopes of Richmond Hill had surprised and delighted Samuel Molyneux back in 1713.[5] He went up Richmond Hill to enjoy its famous view and was struck by how the scene of the vale below had dramatically taken on a classical look with all its new villas and gardens; drawing an analogy with an Italian Renaissance landscape, he called the landscape below "the Frescaty of England."

A contemporary painting by Antonio Joli showing the view of the river from Richmond Hill (plate 8) illustrates the classical pose that the area had assumed. The river winds through what looks like an idealized Italian landscape such as the English knew well from the sixteenth-century paintings by Claude Lorrain and Gaspar Poussin.[6] Twickenham, in fact, had become known for this classical look; Macky, for example, encouraged this reputation by judging Lady Ferrers's villa as passable "in Italy for a delicate Palace" and Secretary James Johnston's villa (which appears in Joli's painting) as

20

Plate 8. "A View from Richmond Hill up the River," from an oil painting by Antonio Joli, mid-eighteenth century. The village of Twickenham appears in the distance, with the house of James Johnston (who was Pope's "Scoto" in the *Epistle to Cobham*) at center-right.

"exactly after the Model of the Country-Seats in Lombardy."[7] There was also the Duke of Argyll's villa (plate 9), Whitton Park, to classicize the scene.

Besides showing the villas studding the landscape, Joli's painting also reveals that the hand of the landscaper has been at work on a large scale. Copses and rows of trees are carefully placed to separate gardens from fields where livestock graze, groves embrace villas, and villas are surrounded by extensive lawns. The semirural character of it all appears like a paradise for gardeners. As in the Renaissance Italian landscape, the villas and the soft lines of a natural style of landscaping complement each other gracefully.

This blending of the symmetry and regularity of classical architecture with the freer and more natural use of landscape was one of the guiding motifs in the early stages of the so-called gardening revolution. It was an idea of design that came over from the Renaissance garden in Italy, but its genesis was in the desire for freedom, simplicity, and naturalness. Shaftesbury had pointed the way in 1709 when he implored his countrymen to abandon "the formal mockery of princely gardens" (*The Moralists*, 1709); Addison had continued the fight in the *Spectator* (1712) when he urged the less autocratic use of landscape; and now the theme was being articulated through the fusion of classical simplicity with landscape freedom. "Classical architecture and the landscape garden," wrote Professor Rudolf Wittkower, "appear thus as two inter-related aspects of a Renaissance in the arts fostered by, and expressive of, the blessings of a free commonwealth."[8]

In this context, we may introduce, from Pope's circle of friends, our first protagonist in the story of the redesigning of England's landscape. Richard Boyle, third

Plate 9. The house and garden at the Duke of Argyll's seat, Whitton. Drawn and engraved by W. Woollett, ca. 1755.

Earl of Burlington (1695–1753), a close friend of Pope's by 1716, accelerated the Palladian revival that not only classicized English building for the rest of the century but also encouraged the partnership, which we catch sight of in the Joli painting, between classical architecture and an increasingly more natural or informal style of landscaping.[9] After his second visit to Italy, to Vicenza where he studied Palladio, Burlington enthusiastically led the Palladian movement, established his own circle of professional and amateur architects, patronized worthy disciples of Palladio like Colin Campbell, designed several villas for others, and eventually redesigned his own house at Chiswick into a Palladian gem. A satirical engraving, "Taste" (ca. 1731–32), showing the gateway at Burlington's Palladian house at Piccadilly with a statue of William Kent at the top and Pope on some scaffolding spattering paint on the innocent public below (plate 10) suggests something of the extent to which Burlington's architectural and artistic circle flourished in the ensuing years—although this particular engraving aimed its satire chiefly at Pope's so-called gardening poem, *To Burlington* (1731), and its purportedly indiscriminate attack on the taste of nobility such as the Duke of Chandos. Whereas Burlington did not begin to redesign Chiswick House until 1725, however, he imme-diately set about altering the grounds upon his return from Italy, where he had had ample time to study Roman Renaissance gardens—as had his protégé, William Kent, who joined him at Chiswick in 1719.[10] It was with Pope's visit to Burlington at Chiswick

Plate 10. "Taste," an anonymous satirical engraving of Lord Burlington's gate at Chiswick House, 1731–32.

House in 1716, three years before he moved to Twickenham, that a new and influential chapter in English landscaping history may be said to have begun.

Lord Burlington's Chiswick House

Pope's visit to Chiswick House in March 1716 was probably his first one.[11] He conveyed something of his immediate delight in the house, gardens, and Burlington's guests to Martha Blount: "I am to pass three or four days in high luxury, with some company at my Lord Burlington's; We are to walk, ride, ramble, dine, drink, & lye together. His gardens are delightfull, his musick ravishing" (1:338). This visit was part of a preliminary visit to the Chiswick area next to the Thames (plate 11) three weeks or so before Pope and his parents moved from Binfield to a house in Mawson's New Buildings by the Thames. On that occasion, Burlington took the opportunity of entertaining the young and already famous poet at his Jacobean house only a short walk from Mawson's. Pope must have been excited about the prospect of being one of Burlington's neighbors. Handel, who with John Gay had been given lodgings at Burlington house and at the time had charge of Burlington's music, was also there and "ravished" Pope with his music (1:338); and the gardens, perhaps as a theatrical setting for the music, or perhaps just the busy activity in them—for Burlington had just begun the first stage of his alteration of the landscape—Pope found "delightful." When the move finally occurred in April, Pope informed his Catholic friend John Caryll that he and his parents had "fixed at Chiswick under the wing of my Lord Burlington" (1:339), a phrase that suggests his sense of the strength of Burlington's artistic encouragement and leadership.

After Burlington returned from his first Italian tour in 1715, charged with glorious images of the Italian Renaissance, mainly of Palladian buildings and classical gardens, he began the so-called first stage of alterations to his landscape.[12] L. Knyff's early view of Chiswick (ca. 1700; published in his and J. Kip's *Britannia Illustrata* [1707]) shows that surrounding the old Jacobean house at the time was a formal and symmetrical garden, well endowed with rectangular areas. Since the gardens delighted Pope on his first visit, either Burlington in less than one year had already worked considerable changes or, as is more likely, the poet was responding more to the aura of creativity that was being generated by this wealthy patron or "Apollo" of the arts. By July, however, he was telling Charles Jervas, his friend and painting tutor, that the gardening and building were proceeding apace: Burlington's "Gardens flourish, his Structures rise, his Pictures arrive, and (what is far nobler and more valuable than all) his own good Qualities daily extend themselves to all about him" (1:347). Also at about this time, Gay, a frequent visitor at Chiswick, addressed an epistle to Burlington before departing on a journey to Exeter that alludes to the latter's architecture and landscaping, and to how Pope made himself at home in the gardens:

> While you, my Lord, bid stately Piles ascend,
> Or in your *Chiswick* Bow'rs enjoy your Friend;
> Where *Pope* unloads the Bough within his reach,
> Of purple Grape, blue Plumb, or blushing Peach;
> I journey far...[13]

While the reference to Pope is disappointing because it pictures him merely picking fruit off trees, an entirely conventional image taken from the country house poem of the

Plate 11. A south view of Chiswick from across the Thames. Hand-colored line engraving, ca. 1750–60. Artist unknown.

previous century, it is redeemed by Gay's joke about the diminutive Pope being able to reach only the low-hanging branches. It also points to the poet's lifelong fondness for fruit and orchards.

Burlington's intention to alter his landscape in 1715 offered Pope what amounted to an early apprenticeship in the application to landscape of the painter's skills he had learned from Charles Jervas in 1713. That apprenticeship taught him something about Renaissance Italian gardening and crystallized his unfocused ideas about how classical pictorial landscape could be recreated in an English garden. What complicates the question of who influenced whom, and how much, at Chiswick is that William Kent was there after 1719.[14] He came, as Burlington hoped, to fulfill his promise as a history painter. According to Kenneth Woodbridge, however, after ten years in Italy Kent knew Italian gardens exceedingly well and was in a unique position to draw inspiration as a landscape gardener from them, not so much from the painting of Claude Lorrain or Gaspar Poussin.[15] Kent did not seriously turn to garden design until the 1730s, but this does not of course mean that the "Signior," as he was nicknamed by Pope and his circle, did not apply his genius to Burlington's gardens immediately. Certainly there were many Italian garden features in the gardens, including the cascade and grotto, views of surrounding countryside from elevated terraces and mounts, and Burlington's use of classical garden-buildings. Another Italian feature at Chiswick, which Kent is known to have used elsewhere in the 1730s and 1740s, was the pictorial succession of garden scenes that presented itself to a visitor walking through the grounds.[16] Still, Pope knew Chiswick gardens at close hand for nearly three years before Kent appeared, during

25

which time he would certainly have had a say in Burlington's alterations. He himself understood the beauty of classical garden-buildings, perhaps the most famous feature of Burlington's landscape. We recall his suggestion to Martha Blount that what Sherborne needed was a temple at the top of the valley; he also confessed to Spence in 1728 his long-held desire to plant "some old Roman temple, in trees."[17] As for the succession of scenes throughout a garden, this fulfilled admirably Pope's early taste for variety and surprise. The concept was central to his entire landscaping approach, as he stated in *To Burlington*: "Parts answ'ring parts shall slide into a whole,/Spontaneous beauties all around advance" (66–67).[18]

Pope began to use these techniques soon after his move to Twickenham in 1719, the year Kent arrived, so it is likely that he had experimented with them already at Chiswick. Horace Walpole, as we have seen, thought it was possible that Pope even advised Kent at Rousham and that the area there known as Venus's Vale was "planned on the model of Mr Pope's [garden and grotto]." He added with certitude that Kent's famous designs in the Prince of Wales's gardens at Carlton House were "borrowed from the poet's at Twickenham."[19]

Although Pope never traveled to Italy, we have seen that his pictorialism owed a great debt to Italian art, as well as to a deep understanding of the ancients and how they looked at nature.[20] His Preface and Notes to the *Iliad*, for example, are extremely responsive to Homer's skill in the verbal painting of landscape: "he not only gives us the full Prospects of Things, but several unexpected Peculiarities and Side-Views, unobserv'd by any Painter but *Homer*."[21] As a brand of the pictorial, Pope's style was more like that of the ancients than baroque or of the Renaissance. Apart from portrait painting, on which Jervas concentrated with his pupil, he and Pope occupied themselves with Roman landscapes during the lessons. Possibly in the autumn of 1715, Pope wrote a poem, the *Epistle to Mr. Jervas*, which he sent to the painter with, appropriately, a new edition (1716) of Dryden's translation of Dufresnoy's poem on painting, *De Arte Graphica*. In his poem Pope alludes to the classical landscapes his "wand'ring fancy wrought" while he was Jervas's pupil:

> *Rome*'s pompous glories rising to our thought!
> Together o'er the *Alps* methinks we fly,
> Fir'd with ideas of fair *Italy*.
> With thee, on *Raphael*'s Monument I mourn,
> Or wait inspiring dreams at *Maro*'s Urn:
> With thee repose, where *Tully* once was laid,
> Or seek some ruin's formidable shade;
> While fancy brings the vanish'd piles to view,
> And builds imaginary *Rome* a-new.
>
> (24–32)

Believing that his kind of history painting was superior to the portraiture from which Jervas was then making a living, Pope told Jervas that his "first Pieces," the paintings of classical subjects, were the ones that "future Painters are to look upon as we Poets do on the *Culex* of *Virgil*, and *Batrachom.* of *Homer.*"[22] He then urged Jervas to return to history painting: "The Ancients too expect you should do them right; those Statues from which you learned your beautiful and noble Ideas, demand it as a piece of Gratitude from you" (1:376-77).

While Pope was observing and undoubtedly participating in the re-creation of an Italian landscape at Chiswick, he was of course being stimulated in the classical vein through his hard work on the *Iliad*, which, as Lady Mary Wortley Montagu said, was another way of rendering English soil "classick ground." And he received another stimulus about that time from George Berkeley, who wrote to him from Naples in November 1717 describing a "noble Landscape," sung by Homer and Virgil, "which would demand an Imagination as warm, and numbers as flowing as your own, to describe it" (1:446). Berkeley vividly described for Pope the "romantic Confusion" of the landscape on the island of Inarime precisely because he knew the poet would respond warmly to it. Pope would have caught the obvious point behind Berkeley's description regarding the pictorial effects of a classical landscape that might be explored in a translation of Homer and in gardens.

Initially, Burlington's interest in the gardens appears to have been chiefly an extension of his overriding passion for architecture. During the period between the Italian trips, he engaged most energetically in what Jacques Carré has called a type of pedantic gardening, in which nature was relegated to a backdrop role for the museumlike display of classically inspired garden structures: the "visitor was probably expected to meditate on the notion of taste rather than enjoy the proximity of plants and trees."[23] But Pope thought enough of the gardens in 1719 to want to show them to some ladies, possibly the Blount sisters, who were staying in London at the time: "I had promised to entertain 'em," he told Burlington, "the only way I could, by a sight of your Gardens this Evening" (2:2). It is tempting to speculate that he wanted to show the ladies some of his own ideas in the gardens. Before moving to Twickenham, it was mostly there that he pursued "very innocent pleasures, building, planting, and gardening" (2:3).

The only firm dates known for alterations done in the garden before Pope took the ladies there in 1719 are for the Bagnio (1717) and for the digging of the canal (before 1719).[24] The style of the Bagnio shows Burlington's entire dependence on Campbell; it was the first step in his plan to generate a Renaissance of the arts in England. This was the temple referred to by Burlington's agents on 22 October 1719 as being "covered with Lead,"[25] which Carré thought was the Pantheon that used to stand at the end of the Grand Allée. When the canal was dug, the dirt was piled up west of it and cleverly provided an embankment or terrace with views of the Thames, surrounding countryside, and other parts of the garden. A drawing by Rigaud, ca. 1734 (plate 12), showing the view from the embankment, suggests why Pope could have approved of the idea and relished showing it to his friends. The embankment provides just enough elevation in a generally flat garden, as his own mount did later at Twickenham, to open up several vistas within the garden and distant prospects outside the garden. The main canal winds pleasantly by the house and off into the hazy distance, not unlike the Thames beneath Richmond Hill in the Antonio Joli painting; and a host of different lines, shapes, and

Plate 12. Chiswick gardens, an engraving by Jacques Rigaud, ca. 1734. This shows the southwest gardens as viewed from the terrace.

patterns entertains the eye beneath an expanse of sky that is itself enlarged by the little elevation. It was, as Pope said of the views from a hill overlooking the Avon Gorge at Clifton, on the western side of Bristol, "like the broken Scenes behind one another in a Playhouse" (4:201).

Beyond these dates we have little to go on in determining when certain improvements were carried out. Burlington probably proceeded without delay in erecting the several buildings all over his landscape; in 1724 Macky described these buildings as follows:

> Every walk terminates with some little Building, one with a Heathen Temple, for instance the Pantheon, another a little villa, where my Lord often dines instead of his House, and which is capable of receiving a tolerably large Family; another walk terminates with a Portico, in imitation of Covent Garden Church.[26]

Before any of these were in place, or soon after, little formal settings for the buildings were established, with a generous use of clipped hedges. Clearly the buildings themselves had cultural connotations, but since these settings were planted principally as backgrounds to the buildings, they could not be said to have created scenes with emotionally evocative associations—such as in Venus's Vale at Rousham, the Elysian Fields at Stowe, or Oakley Wood at Cirencester. This lack of interplay between building and natural setting illustrates a barrenness of design in the early Chiswick gardens: there was much that was pictorial about them, which Pope must have liked, but the natural settings were too much like stage sets—passive and lacking dynamic interplay with the garden architecture. Daniel Defoe's *Tour thro' the Whole Island of Great Britain* (3rd edition, 1742), described the view from the terrace in distinctly pictorial terms of which Pope must have approved; Burlington, it observed, "has raised a Terrace, (with the Earth which came out of the River) from whence you have a Prospect of the adjacent Country; and when the Tide is up, you see the Water of the *Thames*, with the Boats and Barges passing, which greatly enlivens the Prospect."[27] What seems to have been happening at Chiswick in its earliest stages is that Burlington, whose main interest was architecture, was in a way ahead of developments in landscaping. He was eliminating parterres, regular flowerbeds, and straight lines of shrubs and topiary in keeping with the new mood of landscaping freedom, but he had not yet sufficiently recognized that garden buildings or furnishing of any kind could be integrated, thematically and emotionally, with the landscape. Pope had a deeper understanding of the ancients and their gardens and regarded a garden as a place to enjoy and consult nature, not to display architectural virtuosity as an end in itself. He held out to Burlington, when he moved to Twickenham, an example of what could be done. Eventually, Burlington began to introduce (in the Italian manner) scattered urns, herms, and statuary, which were organized to evoke an atmosphere in concert with, not apart from, nature.

Tall clipped hedges, one Italian feature that early on Burlington included in his alterations, remained in place at least for Pope's lifetime, although as time went on they looked increasingly old-fashioned. Defoe's *Tour* thought they were "too mean for the other Parts of the Garden; and it is much to be wondered his Lordship should suffer them to remain in the present Form." In addition to framing several of the buildings, they were used to line the long allées, so that standing at the center of the *patte d'oie* (see Rocque's *Plan*, plate 13), for example, one had an uninterrupted and dramatic view down the radiating paths culminating in various garden buildings.[28] But this means of enclosing areas of the garden and separating them from one another was too wall-like for Pope; he, Kent (later on), and other disciples of the new gardening preferred more natural-looking divisions.

The major landscaping innovation at Chiswick, the date and sources of which are undocumented, is the obscuration of visible boundaries; related to this change is the concealment of spatial limitations through the creation of surprises and illusions of distance. It was an innovation forced upon the Chiswick landscape because of its relatively small size and flatness, both characteristics that it had in common with Pope's garden, although his garden was not quite as flat. It has been said that the need to create the illusion of space at Chiswick was one of the distinguishing characteristics and practical sources of the English landscape garden. In fulfilling that need, Pope may have played a prominent role. Variety of elevation was useful, of course, in increasing a sense of space. Burlington is credited not only with the embankment idea near the canal but also with the creation of mounds (not mounts) that introduced prospects and some variety of elevation. His tall hedges also helped simulate a tunnellike visual effect down the allées, which appeared to lengthen them. Pope's contribution may have included suggestions about the placement of garden structures and ornaments for visual focus, and winding walks cut through thick groves in "wilderness" style flanking straight walks and allées, but his own words suggest how he was most helpful: "You may distance things by

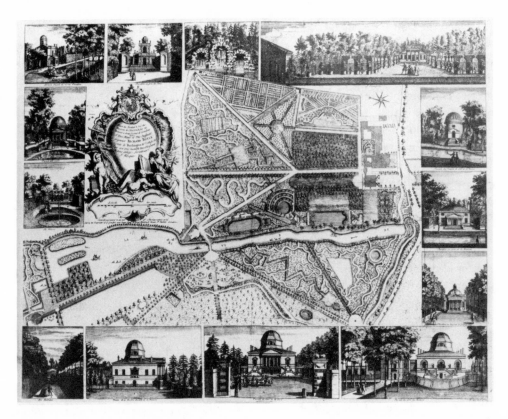

Plate 13. Plan of Chiswick gardens by John Rocque, 1736.

darkening them and by narrowing the plantation more and more toward the end, in the same manner as they do in painting"[29]—he had his eye at the moment on the cypress allée or walk leading up to the obelisk memorializing his mother at the end of his garden. With this technique in mind, Walpole judged that Pope's ideas of "retiring and assembling shades" was his most valuable contribution to landscape gardening.[30] Because there was so much going on in this garden, it felt larger than it was; the winding walks, like an irregular coastline, made for a lot of walking, as Defoe's 1742 *Tour* noted, in "the Wilderness, through which are three strait Avenues, terminated by three different Buildings; and within the Quarters are Serpentine Walks, thro' which you may walk near a Mile in constant Shade." The *Tour's* overall judgment of the uniqueness of the garden was therefore not surprising: "There is more Variety in this Garden, than can be found in any other of the same Size in *England*, or perhaps in *Europe*."[31] Chiswick definitely gave the visitor the illusion of being in a much larger garden.

By 1725, when Burlington began the extension to his old Jacobean mansion (not torn down until 1788), after the example of Palladio's Villa Rotonda, the so-called first stage of the gardens was finished.[32] About one year after the new addition was completed, Burlington published, at his own expense, Robert Castell's influential *The Villas of the Ancients* (1728).[33] In his book *The Earls of Creation*, James Lees-Milne suggested that Pliny's Tuscan villa, which Castell described and illustrated as the ideal Roman garden, inspired Burlington's irregular garden-planning at Chiswick after 1728.[34] Apart from irregularity of design, however, the uniqueness of Pliny's villa is that as a *villa rustica* its "Meadows, Vineyards, Woods, plowed Land" (to quote Castell) yielded its owner agricultural profit—some beans along with beauty. It is here that Chiswick appears to have been deficient. There is a conspicuous absence of any mention of productive gardening there. The estate, of course, had the customary kitchen gardens, but they do not seem to have been incorporated into the attitudes and designs that came to be identified with the new landscaping there; and no one else mentions the "yield" of Chiswick except for the orange trees in the Orangery. Even Defoe's *Tour* omitted any mention of productive gardening there.

This may explain the absence of that touch of enthusiasm which Pope later showed for other gardens. Between 1719 and 1732, not once is he known to have praised Burlington's gardens; compared with the other gardens that are the subject of this book, Chiswick during this time would appear to have held a minimal interest for him. Although in September 1732 he wrote to Burlington to assure him that he had always thought Chiswick's gardens and buildings to be "the finest thing this glorious Sun has shin'd upon" and that on at least three occasions he had brought "admirers" there, he also struck an ambivalent note with the curious remark, "once I brought it a Censurer, whose name I will not tell you (for his sake)" (3:313–14). The simple fact that Pope felt he had to tell Burlington he had always liked the gardens sounds suspicious, but his mention of a censurer on top of that makes the entire passage sound like faint praise. He says he is not Burlington's insincere flatterer, but he sounds like one here in light of his greater affection for places like Sherborne, Rousham, Stowe, Marble Hill, Dawley Farm, and Cirencester.

Pope's letter to Burlington may also be explained as another in the string of reassurances that he felt compelled to send Burlington after the Duke of Chandos controversy following the publication of *To Burlington* the previous December. The Chandos affair embarrassed both him and Burlington. He was contemptuous of the whispering campaign that had spread, and around February he retaliated with the amusingly ironic *A Master Key to Popery*, in which he attacked what he claimed was the absurd charge that he was mocking the Duke of Chandos's seat, Cannons Hall. Pope did this by imputing to himself mean motives in also attacking Chiswick and its Lord. "Nothing is more certain," Pope wrote anonymously, "than that the Person first & principally abus'd is the said Earl of Burlington. He [Pope] cou'd not well abuse him for *Want* of *Taste*, since the allowing it to him was the only Channel to convey his Malignity to others: But he abuses him for a *worse want*, the want of *Charity*." So much for malice; as for ill nature, stressing the word *thy*, he cites the lines,

> Another age shall see the golden Ear
> Imbrown *thy* Slope, and nod on *thy* Parterre,

in ironically asserting that in the poem the poet has told Burlington: "My Lord, your Gardens shall soon be Plow'd up, & turned into Corn-fields." He adds, "From what we have observ'd of his Prophecy of the Destruction of Chiswick Gardens, it shou'd seem as if this wretch alluded to his Lordship's want of a *Male Heir*."[35]

Plate 14. "A Prospect of the Cascade and Part of Lord Burlington's House at Chiswick." Engraving by Claude Du Bosc after P. Rysbrack, ca. 1730. Courtesy of the King's Topographical Collection, British Library.

It may not have been until Kent's first substantial garden planning at Chiswick in the late 1720s that Pope's interest in the landscape was renewed. Kent rapidly naturalized the garden by softening the banks; replacing groves and some formal planting with sloping lawns, particularly southwest and north of the new Palladian house; replacing Burlington's pyramidic cascade (see plates 14 and 15) with a beautifully rustic cascade, Italian inspired—perhaps by the one at Villa Aldobrandini in Frascati;[36] increasing the visual movement from area to area by lessening the plantations separating them; designing a wooded theater; enhancing the interpenetration of house and garden in traditional Italian fashion (plate 16); and generally heightening the "immanence of nature."[37] To Kent at Chiswick in October 1733, Spence gave credit for being the sole beginner of the natural taste, though in 1752 Stephen Wright, Kent's assistant, told Spence that the Chiswick gardens were begun five years before Wright joined Kent in 1727, thereby dating the beginning of the gardens around 1722. Wright added that the winding river was the first thing done at Chiswick.[38] Still, there is little doubt that Kent naturalized the entire landscape in the early 1730s, including the river. And it is today a restored Kent garden, beautiful with its synthesis of formal features, like rond-points from which allées radiated, terraces, hedges, and fountains, with secret recesses amid plantings flanking the allées and views of adjacent countryside.

Kent's adoption of landscape gardening as his principal vocation produced (according to the correspondence) a closer artistic rapport with Pope than he had experienced before. The three portraits of Pope that Kent painted date from the period 1725–35,

32

Plate 15. "A View of the Cascade, of Part of the Serpentine River, and of the West Front of the House of the Earl of Burlington, at Chiswick." Engraved by W. Woollett after J. Donowell, 1753. Courtesy of the King's Topographical Collection, British Library.

suggesting a closer relationship.[39] From the beginning of their friendship, Kent's eccentricities and adopted Italian manner amused Pope and his circle, making him the butt of some good-natured jokes. One can only wonder what Pope's opinion of Kent's landscaping ideas was before he proved himself as a gardener in the late 1730s at Stowe, Rousham, and elsewhere, but it appears Kent was strong-minded about his views. Pope speaks of the Signior as a garden designer for the first time not until 1733. Pope is at Lord Bruce's seat at Tottenham in Wiltshire, where the gardens considerably impressed him: "It is one of the prettiest I ever saw," he wrote to an attentive Burlington, "and one of the best Houses I ever was in, an admirable fine Library, a delicious Park, & extensive Plantations." Like most worthy gardens he saw, it started him thinking of improvements: "It wants only a few Temples & ornaments of Building, which I am contriving, in defect of better architects (who are a Rare & uncommon Generation, not born in every Family)." Another reason for his designing these improvements, he adds jokingly, is to prevent Kent, "a wild Goth" who was busy with such works, from doing them instead:

> I am told this man hath suggested an odd thing, which thro his Violence of Temper and Ungovernable Spirit of Dominion (natural to all Goths) he will infallibly erect; unless I lay a Temple in his way, which he will probably not venture to pull down. (3:417)

Kent certainly had taken Chiswick by storm. Pope made a joke of his dramatic ascendancy there, too, as a garden designer in the 1730s. No longer was any tree safe. The time had come to draw up a petition to Lord Burlington. Almost certainly by Pope,

Plate 16. The gardens behind Chiswick House. Drawn by J. Donowell, 1753.

though it was signed by nine other residents of Chiswick, one was drawn up comically protesting the threat posed to an existing tree by Kent's proposals for clearing a view from a new "Upstart Terras." There was an overripeness in the friendship of Kent and Pope in the late 1730s,[40] and the petition may reflect this; nonetheless, riotously funny in legal phrasing, it deserves to be quoted in full since it offers a glimpse of the gardening milieu in which Kent was just then emerging as professional leader:

> That whereas a Certain Tree lying, being, & standing in or on the Grounds of your Lordship, at or before or on one side or the other of a Certain Edifice of your Honour's called the Casino, hath possessed occupied and held, for the space of twenty or twenty one years or thereabouts,[41] over or under, the said Ground Place and Bank, and suffered & endured all the Changes & Vicissitudes of Wind Water & Weather in the Worst of Times. And whereas a certain Upstart Terras, hath arisen & stood opposite (tho at great distance) to your Honour's said Tree, above & before mentioned & described, which said Terras hath and can suffer no molestation, Let, or hindrance from any Shadow, Root or Branch of your said Tree, which both continued faithfully fixed to the Premises, nor ever stirred, or attempted to stir, from his said place, notwithstanding which the said Terras hath, by the Instigation of Sathan, & of William Kent, his agent & Attorney, conspiring thereunto, devised and plotted, and do at this time devise plot & conspire the Destruction, Abolition, Overthrow & Total Subversion of This Your Honour's Tree the said Tree to cut down, or saw down, or root up & grub up, & ruin for ever: We, Your Honour's humble Petitioners who have many years known,

accustomed & frequented the said Tree, sitten, reposed or disported under the Shade thereof yea and seen the said William Kent, the Agent & Attorney of the said Sathan, solace himself with Syllabubs, Damsels, and other Benefits of Nature, under the said Tree, Do, for ourselves & our Posterity, most earnestly, & jointly as well as Seperately, petition & pray, that the said Tree may remain, subsist, continue & flourish in his place, during his or her natural Life (not being absolutely certain of the Sex of the said Tree) to enjoy the Small Spot of Ground on which God & your Lordship's Ancestors of every blessed memory have placed it.[42]

This petition is a superb joke, but it is also autobiographically revealing. In addition to displaying Pope's already acknowledged love for large, majestic trees, it illustrates the high value he placed on permanency, stability, the moral value of belonging to or being rooted to a place or time, faithfulness and loyalty, steadfastness, the legacy to one's posterity, and the honoring of one's past or ancestors. Pope sees this tree as part of the history of Burlington's landscape—even as an element of the Genius of the Place, which Kent threatens to violate with one of his "Upstart," new-fangled terraces. It was there before Bridgeman began his layout, before Pope first laid eyes on Chiswick in 1716. And in his own experience it has contributed to the life of the garden by benignly encompassing the meditations, pleasures, and sportive entertainments of people (including Kent) who have lived and visited there. It has therefore merited acceptance as, let us say, an iconographic feature of the gardens. It was not invested with the historical importance of Rosamond's pond on the site of Henry II's vanished Woodstock manor, Blenheim, over which Pope in 1717 thoughtfully lingered (1:432), but such indigenous landscape features as this tree nevertheless always elicited from him thoughts about how a gardener should sensitively consult a landscape before he begins altering it. Kent, the wild Goth, charming but also the agent of Satan, threatens to upset this harmony between gardener and garden, between the tree (whatever sex it is) and the Casino.

Pope may also have seen an analogy between himself and this tree, as he often did between himself and the plants in his garden, which were always being moved about and punished by excessive cold and heat. He hoped the tree would be allowed simply to "continue & flourish in his place" and "enjoy the Small Spot of Ground" that nourished it. He had similar hopes for himself on his small spot of ground, and as we shall see he not infrequently joked with his friends about how well he did with so little. "Content with little, I can piddle here/On Broccoli and mutton, round the year," he wrote in 1734 (*The Second Satire of the Second Book of Horace*, lines 137–38). What he wished for the tree he wished for himself: simply to be allowed to exist quietly, welcome friends to his little demesne, and live out there his natural days. Just as the tree does not need to own the little spot of ground in which it has rooted itself, Pope does not need to own his villa and garden. "Well, if the Use be mine," asked Pope in the same poem,

> can it concern one
> Whether the Name belong to Pope or Vernon?

Let Lands and Houses have what Lords they will,
Let Us be fix'd, and our own Masters still.

(165–66, 179–80)

The petition contains the last known words Pope wrote about Kent and Chiswick, unless this passage he wrote in *An Imitation of the Sixth Satire of the Second Book of Horace* alludes to the fanciful technique of creating romantic landscape effects with hollow trees that Kent was not beyond using: "A most Romantic hollow Tree!/A pretty kind of savage Scene!" (176–77). Kent did not, as far as we know, contribute any designs to the gardens Pope planned in the 1730s, except for some urns that are discussed later in this chapter.[43]

"Herds, flocks, and plantations" at John Caryll's Ladyholt Park

As Pope moved confidently into Lord Burlington's circle of artists and rapidly made friends among the English nobility, and as he prepared to settle himself in his own house and garden, he began to lose interest in his Catholic intimate, John Caryll of Ladyholt Park, near Harting in West Sussex. This is a propitious moment to introduce Caryll and Ladyholt into the story of Pope's life of landscaping, even though the influence of Ladyholt on Pope's landscaping had begun to ebb by 1716–18.[44] Because Pope and Caryll had been especially close ever since they met sometime around 1703,[45] having been drawn together by their mutual friends and problems as Catholics—Caryll was Martha Blount's godfather—as well as by their love of literature, Ladyholt was the earliest large estate and landscape that Pope regularly visited and from which he may have patterned his earliest landscaping ideas. Moreover, the Caryll family, and in particular the John Caryll who was Pope's friend (there were three), gave Pope his earliest experiences of the Tudor-Stuart values of family spirit and old-fashioned country housekeeping—the "antique charities," as Pope called them (1:457)—that had been celebrated eloquently in the previous century by Jonson, Carew, and Marvell.[46] These values and the landscaping that provided the setting for them at Ladyholt were always before the young Pope's attention as he grew up at Binfield in Windsor Forest. Without them it is certain he would not have been as able as he was to focus his point of view on landscape gardening in 1713, the year he first spoke out in the *Guardian*. It is therefore unfortunate for the garden historian that after Pope moved to Twickenham and began his own landscaping, he seems rarely to have visited Ladyholt.[47]

Ladyholt Park in the Pope-Caryll friendship was a catalyst to discussions about painting, the picturesque, poetry that "painted" scenes of "woods and forest in verdure and beauty" (1:168), and landscaping that could produce some of the natural and practical (agricultural) touches of beauty that were in abundance at Caryll's estate high on the Sussex Downs. Many of them occurring before 1715, these conversations must have been among the earliest Pope would have had with anyone about such subjects.[48] The estate, with its high position, surrounded as it was by downs, fields for cultivation and grazing, and great beechen woods, and blessed with panoramic views of the sea, coastline, and Chichester, very likely displayed many of the landscape features that were to be highly prized in the landscape gardening movement. It would have been surprising if Ladyholt had not encouraged Pope, in his early twenties, to think about how less splendidly endowed landscapes could be designed by creating in them pictorial compositions such as he admired, for example, in the "poetical images and fine pieces of painting" of Thomas Tickell's poetry (1:157) in 1712 or as he "painted" in his own *Windsor Forest* (1713). It is not mere coincidence that, except for Martha Blount, it was mainly to Caryll in those early years that he revealed his responsiveness to open landscape, as in a letter in midwinter, 1712. "I am endeavouring," Pope told Caryll as he shivered at Binfield, possibly in the middle of revising *Windsor Forest*, "to raise up round about me a painted scene of woods and forests in verdure and beauty, trees springing, fields flowering, Nature laughing. I am wandering thro' Bowers and Grottos in conceit, and while my trembling body is cowering o'er a fire, my mind is expatiating in an open sunshine" (1:168). Significantly, when that early landscape sensibility bore fruit in the anonymously published *Guardian* essay, Pope was pleased but not surprised that Caryll, who knew him and his thoughts "so entirely as never to be mistaken in either," guessed that he was its author (1:176).

It was also Caryll who encouraged Pope to take painting lessons in 1713. The lessons, he thought, would train Pope's eye so that he could recreate or compose pictorial scenes like those at Ladyholt in words and oil.

As appealing as anything else to Pope about Ladyholt would have been the farming Caryll did there. It permeated the setting and was not relegated to remote parts of the estate. Caryll's useful landscaping, the combination of pleasure with agricultural profit that led eventually to the *ferme ornée*, was impressive. Farming, fishing, hunting, and forestry were all earnestly pursued to make Ladyholt serve as an economic boost to the precarious family finances that, as Catholics with double taxation and other penalties, they had to endure.[49] Pope had "long had a partiality" for Ladyholt, as he said in 1717 (1:419), perhaps because the purposefulness of the estate matched his ideas about good country housekeeping; it was not a landscape wasted in mere pleasure seeking and self-aggrandizement.

On one occasion in April 1715 when he and Pope were intending a visit to Ladyholt together, Gay wrote Caryll and amusingly alluded to the agrarian character of Ladyholt. "For my part, who do not deal in heroes or ravished ladies," he said, alluding to the work on translating Homer that Pope wanted to get on with at Ladyholt, "I may perhaps celebrate a milk-maid, describe the amours of your parson's daughter, or write an elegy upon the death of a hare." As for Pope, he pities him for his work on Homer at Ladyholt, thinking it a misplaced effort in "one of the pleasantest seats in England" (1:289). Ladyholt suited Gay's pastoral vein—his rustics were the working kind. In August 1715, when Caryll's son was about to be married, Pope complimented his friend's matchmaking ability and wondered whether he should entreat him "to seek out some shepherdess about the hills of Ladyholt for the felicity of your humble servant" (1:314). A patriarchal figure like Caryll—the paterfamilias—could do this efficiently, thought Pope; in fact, Caryll, like Bathurst later, was for Pope the essential patriarch in modern England, an image that the poet never applied to anyone who did not engage in productive landscaping of some kind. "I really long to see a true patriarch, *the lappet of whose shoe I am not worthy to loose*," he told Caryll in 1726, long after he had stopped visiting Ladyholt regularly, "and to observe once before I die, the increase of all your herds, flocks, and plantations, &c., at Lady holt" (2:393).

Throughout the Caryll papers there are references continually in private letters to domestic and agricultural economy.[50] Milk houses, cheese, butter, fish houses, the fisherman's pond, venison, fruits of many kinds, pheasant and bantam eggs, sundry crops, and coppices are mentioned over and over, as are the most detailed matters about the laborers. The most entertaining and amusing glimpses of Ladyholt's "domestic light" (Pope's phrase) come from a resident chaplain and friend of the family by the name of Thomas Hunt. While the family were abroad in France, as they frequently were, Hunt wrote to them faithfully, beginning in the 1740s, describing the goings on of all the household departments.[51] He seemed, in fact, inordinately interested in the food being produced on the estate and less concerned than might be expected with the spiritual nourishment of its employees. Nonetheless, gratifyingly, we learn from him such details about the estate as must have prevailed when Pope knew it: that it was well endowed with beeches, which in his opinion made the landscape more beautiful in the autumn than at any other time of the year;[52] that there were several fish ponds, including two called the Great Pond and Fisherman's Pond stocked with perch, trout, and carp; that the fruit and vegetables he was eating while the owners were away included melons, raspberries, strawberries, artichokes, cucumbers, figs, peaches, and pineapples; that there were several coppices, the main one of which was having a fence "finished as farr as the Gate wch gives on the Down"; that "there is never a Gate put upp att any of the Visto's of the Coppice" obstructing the views; and that the main avenue led directly to a walk on "Bushy Down," suggesting that care may have been taken to integrate the gardens with the adjacent landscape.

Pope is not known to have visited Ladyholt in the 1720s, but in 1730 he was telling Caryll nostalgically that he had "often wished to see the pleasures of that place which are external" (3:110)—that is, physical. Bathurst beat him to it in 1731, perhaps out of curiosity to see the forest-park areas, and Pope later told Caryll that Bathurst "was, and yet is, full of raptures about your park. I sincerely long to see it" (3:237). He did see it at last during one of his journeys to Bevis Mount in 1733 (3:387), but sadly, perhaps because he had Lord Peterborough's gardens on his mind, he said nothing in his letters about it. His only known remaining commitment to Ladyholt occurred in 1734, when he designed a staircase for Caryll and planned a visit "to settle the staircase plan" (3:414), which like many other proposed visits there seems to have been put off. The importance of Ladyholt as an influence on Pope's landscape gardening, then, may have been parallel to Caryll's influence on his life: it reached its zenith in those early years when Pope was at Binfield, before he had begun to move into that higher society of art and nobility that colored his gardening career. With his own garden he took a major step into that exciting milieu.

Touching his "string": building and planting at Twickenham

After about five years of translating Homer and two years of residence in Chiswick, Pope in 1719 was ready for a change. If ever in his career he felt the rival claims of art and life, it was during those years of "slavery" to Homer. Anticipating his "deliverance from poetry and slavery," in February he was already looking forward to his move to Twickenham, having decided after all to take a house and a few acres of land there instead of building in town; he would soon be found to be, he told William Broome, his collaborator on Homer, "a mere old fellow . . . pursuing very innocent pleasures, building, planting, and gardening" (2:3). He was in touch with James Gibbs about the building plans (2:4), initially perhaps regarding a house on some land of Burlington's in back of Burlington House (Piccadilly), then eventually with a view to a house on the river at Twickenham. He settled into his new home with his parents without any delay because on 26 July, Dr. Abel Evans was thanking him for his hospitality at his "pleasant House at Twickenham" (2:8).

Neither the house nor the gardens were anything to command special attention when Pope settled, but the situation certainly was, and he was beside himself with excitement about it. "The place I am in is as delightful as you can imagine any to be, in this season," he told Broome in December; "the situation so very airy, and yet so warm, that you will think yourself in a sort of heaven, where the prospect is boundless, and the sun your near neighbor" (2:19). He spoke of the "ease, the quiet, the contentment of soul, and repose of body" that refreshed and revitalized him.[53] A visitor from Newcastle in 1747–48 described the setting in these words: "*Twickenham* is a delightful Village, situated about a North Country Mile above *Richmond*, on the opposite Side of the River. Mr *Pope*'s House stands in the South-west End of the Village; the Area of the Ground is a gentle Declivity most agreeably sloping to the *Thames*" (see plate 17).[54] Pope's new Twickenham world offered him independence and must have seemed to him (at the age of thirty-two) a fulfillment of the sketch of the happy man that he had composed in his first known poem, *Ode on Solitude*, about twenty years before:

> Blest! who can unconcern'dly find
> Hours, days and years slide soft away,
> In health of body, peace of mind,
>   Quiet by day,
>
> Sound sleep by night; study and ease
> Together mix'd; sweet recreation,
> And innocence, which most does please,
>   With meditation.
>
>   (9–16)

For Pope, living next to the river was as important as any other factor in his move. From the beginning of his residence at Twickenham he responded to its pictorial beauty and its tranquil mood. He also spoke of the river in personal terms: whether he was informing Charles Jervas of his "Transplantation," "the Gods and Fate have fix'd me on

Plate 17. "A View taken on Twickenham Common." Drawn and engraved by J. Boydell, 1753.

the borders of the *Thames*, in the Districts of *Richmond* and *Twickenham*" (2:24) (see plate 18); extolling its beauties in the spring to Robert Digby, "Our River glitters beneath an unclouded Sun, at the same time that its Banks retain the Verdure of Showers" (2:44); alluding to a recent flooding, "The Prospect is prodigiously fine: It is just like an Arm of the Sea, and the Flood over my Grassplot, embraced between the two Walls, whose tops are only seen, looks like an open Bay to the Terras" (2:59); telling Martha Blount from Sherborne how much he misses Twickenham, "I . . . have seen nothing I like so well as what I left: No scenes of paradise, no happy bowers, equal to those on the banks of the Thames" (2:236); or resolving in 1742 that some present works in his garden would be "the Last Sacrifice I shall make to the Nymphs of the Thames" (4:433). After he described for Digby in 1725 the layout of his garden and grotto, his most complete description, he added, "You'll think I have been very Poetical in this Description, but it is pretty near the Truth" (2:297). In his poetry, too, especially the later ethical and satirical poems, the river for him was "my Thames," "A River at my garden's end," which he used, along with his house, garden, and grotto, to evolve a self-portrait—what Maynard Mack has called his "Muse of Satire."[55]

He did not enjoy his new demesne, however, by stretching himself out in an elbow chair, gazing at the river, sniffing the breezes, or burying himself in reading and writing. Immediately he got down to transforming his few acres. He had been gardening for a few months when he wrote to Thomas Dancastle in November that his "present Employment is Gardening" and that he had "taken 2 Acres of land last week" (2:18–19). These two acres gave him a total of five and made the garden large enough to accommodate the projects he had already planned.[56] In a December letter to Broome he wrote of

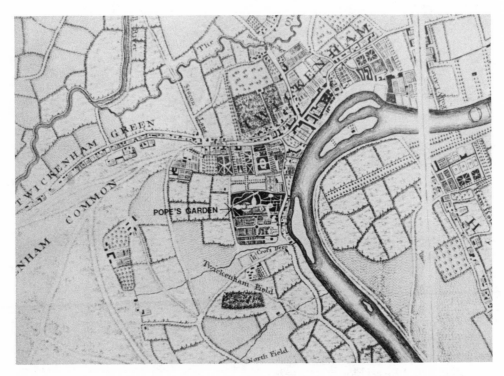

Plate 18. Detail of the Twickenham area, from John Rocque, *An Exact Survey of the City's of London, Westminster . . . and the Country Near Ten Miles Round* (1746). Pope's garden appears between the river and Twickenham Common.

"enchanted bowers, silver streams, opening avenues, rising mounts, and painted grottos (2:19)—most, of course, still only in his imagination.

After about one year in his new home, he had already executed some of these projects and was assiduously pursuing the others. He told Jervas all about it with the ethusiasm of a pupil telling his mentor about his experiments in a new medium. Not surprisingly, Pope stressed the pictorial beauties of his new homestead. He told Jervas that he had finally found a place where he could practice on a larger terrestrial canvas the principles of perspective and variety that he had learned from him a few years earlier. The following passage sounds as if Pope, out of gratitude, is dedicating the garden to him:

> I must own, when you talk of *Building* and *Planting*, you touch my String. . . .
> Alas Sir, do you know whom you talk to? One that had been a Poet, was
> degraded to a Translator, and at last thro' meer dulness is turn'd into an
> Architect. You know *Martial*'s Censure—*Præconem facito, vel Architectum.*
> However I have one way left, to plan, to *elevate* and *to surprize* (as *Bays* says.)
> The next you may expect to hear, is that I am in Debt.
>
> The History of my Transplantation and Settlement which you desire,
> would require a Volume. . . . Much more should I describe the many
> Draughts, Elevation, Profiles, Perspectives, &c. of every Palace and Garden

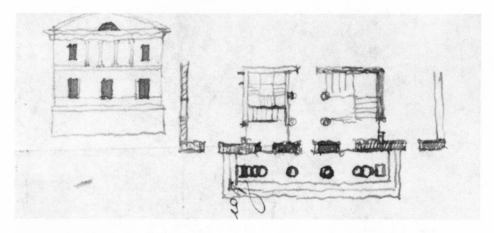

Plate 19. Pope's sketch of what might have been intended as the garden front of his house, and next to it his sketch of a portico.

propos'd, intended, and happily raised, by the strength of that Faculty wherein all great Genius's excel, Imagination. At last, the Gods and Fate have fix'd me on the borders of the *Thames*, in the Districts of *Richmond* and *Twickenham*. It is here I have passed an entire Year of my life. ... For you my Structures rise; for you my Colonades extend their Wings; for you my Groves aspire, and Roses bloom. (2:23–24)

Apart from the *Odyssey* translation and work on an edition of Shakespeare, Pope's creative energy over the next five years poured into the completion of the first stage of his garden and grotto. As Gay told Swift in February 1723, the poet "of late ... has talk'd only as a Gardiner. ... He lives mostly at Twickenham, and amuses himself in his house and garden."[57]

James Gibbs, who was impressed by the new Palladianism but remained undogmatic and maintained his independence from the Burlington circle, was helping Pope out with the drafts and elevations for the house.[58] We must, however, take seriously Pope's calling himself an architect.[59] He was, as he told Caryll in March, spending a lot of time with masons as well as gardeners (2:37), and he took pride in his knowledge of Palladianism with which he could direct what the masons were doing. At one point he complained to Caryll of the "litter" being made by the workmen, "with whom my presence," he said, "is but too necessary" (2:53). He told Robert Digby in July 1720 that he was on a diet of "Water-gruel and *Palladio*" (2:50).[60] Moreover, in the Homer manuscripts at the British Library there are two rough sketches by Pope of Palladian houses that show he tinkered with designs. One of them vaguely resembles the riverfront of his own house (plate 19), while the other could be a sketch for the side of the house fronting the London-to-Hampton road (plate 20), of which there are no known illustrations.[61] In May, by which time the reconstruction was quite advanced, he was taking a self-amused pride in the work; "My Building rises high enough to attract the eye and curiosity of the Passenger from the River," he told Digby, "where, upon beholding a

Plate 20. Pope's sketch of a Palladian building.

Mixture of Beauty and Ruin, he enquires what House is falling, or what Church is rising? So little taste have our common Tritons of *Vitruvius*; whatever delight the true, unseen, poetical Gods of the River may take, in reflecting on their Streams my *Tuscan* Porticos, or *Ionic* Pilasters" (2:44). Noting the distinctive feature of Pope's grotto entrance "below the Middle of the Front" of the house, the Newcastle visitor described briefly the appearance of the house from the river: "Over the Front Entrance into this Grotto lies a balustraded Platform, and serves the Building both as a Vestible and Portico; for a Balcony projecting from the middle Window of the second Story, and supported by Pillars resting upon the Platform, makes so much of it resemble a Portico; but the Platform extending without these Pillars, becomes more a Vestible: Add to this, the Window opening into the Balcony being crowned with a Pediment, gives the several Parts an Air of one Figure, or whole, and adds an inexpressible Grace to the Front."[62]

Pope had a little grass lawn sloping down to the river from the house, which all the riverside traffic saw and which any number of engravings of the house after 1735 clearly show (see plates 21 and 22). The view of the sloping lawn and the river from the house, and of the house from the river, was described by the visitor from Newcastle: "the lingring *Thames* glides softly by, and washes the Margin of the green Parterre; at the Head of which, as it were niched into a rising Mound, or Bank, stands the House. . . . The Sides of the Court, or Parterre, are bounded by deep Thickets of Trees, Hedges, and various Evergreens and Shrubs, ascending in a wild, but delightful Slope, beginning with these of the humblest Growth, and [,] gradually rising, end with lofty Elms and other Forest

Plate 21. Pope's villa. Engraving by Nathaniel Parr after Peter Rysbrack, 1735.

Trees."[63] None of this was lost on Pope, who saw this part of his demesne as a beautifully composed picture. In 1743, after he had completed all the gardening he was to do, as well as most of his grotto additions, he told Spence he hoped only to enhance the prospects from the house by adding "a little ornament or two at the line to the Thames"; Spence tells of his friend's plan to have stone sculptures of swans on either side of the landing place, as if flying into the river, which with the gliding Thames would satisfy his taste for landscape as it appears in motion. One day in 1728, as it happened, he had been chatting with Spence on the grassy slope by the river when a swan, illuminated by the glittering light, suddenly glided over them and the river; Pope quickly interpreted the sight as an image of the picturesque: "That idea of 'picturesque'—from the swan just gilded with the sun amidst the shade of a tree over the water on the Thames" (Spence, 613). It would be fanciful to suggest he recalled that incident fifteen years later when he mentioned to Spence the stone swans he wanted; still, in both instances he was alert to the "picturesque." In addition to the stone swans, two river gods would recline "on the bank between them and the corner seats, or temples" with inscriptions on them. Also to be provided were "two terns in the first niches in the grove-work on the sides with the busts of Homer and Virgil, and higher, two others with those of Marcus Aurelius and Cicero."[64] On the basis of the inventory of his estate, which mentions busts, it would appear that Pope carried out this plan to classicize the pictorial beauty of his riverside scene, perhaps the last garden project in his lifetime.[65]

The planting of trees, shrubs, and hedges was among the first of Pope's tasks in his garden. Considering that Edmund Curll, Pope's constant literary antagonist, was not

44

Plate 22. View of Pope's house, 1747–48, taken from the *Newcastle General Magazine* 1 (January 1748). Based upon the Rysbrack view, it shows three rows of trees within the hedge that did not appear in Rysbrack's. Pope and his dog are visible by the grotto entrance although this engraving was first published about four years after the poet's death.

likely to be generous where Pope was concerned, it is interesting that in his edition of the poet's correspondence (1735) he offered the information that John Searle, the gardener, who "has lived with Mr. *Pope* above Eleven Years . . . in the Hortulan Dialect told us, that, *there were not Ten Sticks in the Ground when his Master took the House*."[66] Searle's information was secondhand, though, since he was probably not on the scene when Pope moved in. If we accept Curll's testimony in 1735 that Searle had by then been with Pope eleven years, the gardener must have arrived to take up his duties ca. 1723–24. We know at least he was there when Lord Bathurst sent lime trees from Riskins to Twickenham in the fall of 1724.[67] These trees, if indeed they were for Pope's garden—they may have been for Mrs. Howard's Marble Hill gardens, which Pope and Bathurst at the time were planning—would have been very welcome. The growth of the trees he planted in 1719 had already begun to give him particular pleasure a year later, or so we may judge from his enthusiastic letter in May to Robert Digby: "Our Gardens are offering their first Nosegays; our Trees, like new Acquaintance brought happily together, are stretching their Arms to meet each other, and growing nearer and nearer every Hour: The Birds are paying their thanksgiving Songs for the new Habitations I have made 'em" (2:44).

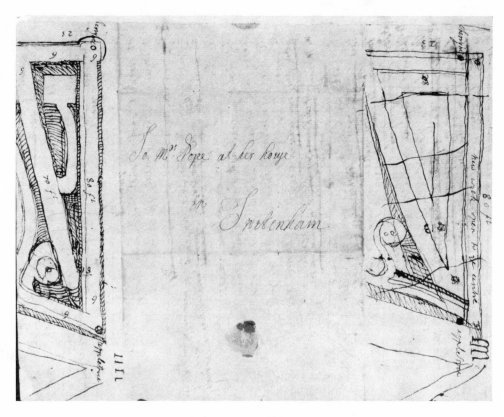

Plate 23. Garden plans, two versions for the same area, drawn by Pope.

Lady Mary Wortley Montagu particularly delighted him the following year with her praise of his trees (see his letter to her, 2:82). He received the compliment while he was staying with Bathurst at Cirencester, where he saw plantations and "opened" avenues that should have inspired any new landscaper. There were enough trees in his garden by spring 1722 to warrant his reference to the "solitary groves"—an allusion to the flanking area running almost the full length of the northern boundary and laid out in thick groves cut by winding paths.[68] This was perhaps the area for which he sketched little garden plans in his Homer manuscripts (plates 23 and 24)—ideas for arranging both curving and straight paths together with "rooms" or arbors within plantings of trees and bushes. It is well to remind ourselves at this point, incidentally, that the trees in which Pope took such pleasure in his garden were only about twenty-five years old when he died. For most of that time, and especially of course during the first decade of his residence, the trees were small and did not create the dense thickets and dark copses that we today see at Rousham, the Elysian Fields of Stowe, or any eighteenth-century garden. Having said that, we still have the account of the garden about thirty years after Pope began planting trees by the Newcastle traveler who conveys the impression that the garden was abundantly endowed with lofty elms and numbers of other trees that "unite

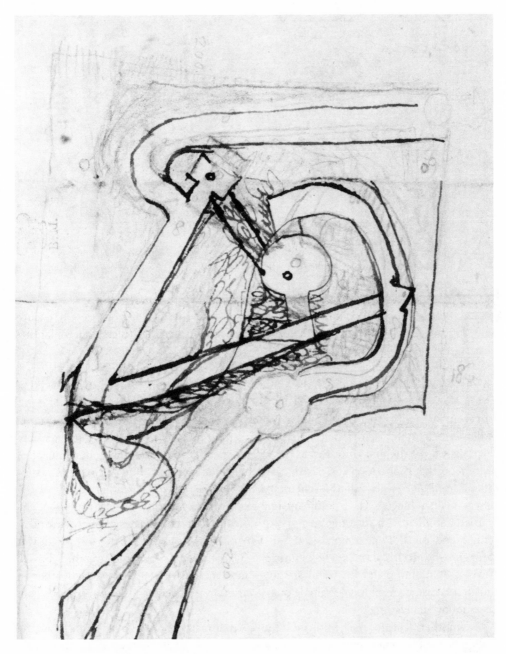

Plate 24. Garden plan drawn by Pope.

themselves more closely together, and cover the Hedges with a thick Shade," creating "Wilderness Groves" and "entangled" recesses. Pope also planted heavily with evergreens and shrubs such as laurel, bay, and holly, so that variously shaped (and naturally

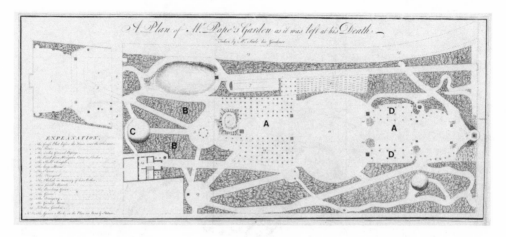

Plate 25. Pope's garden as drawn by his gardener, John Searle, in his *Plan of Mr. Pope's Garden* (London, 1745). These references have been added: A. the Great Walk; B. the Wilderness; C. grotto entrance; D. small groves.

pruned) thickets combined with the "wild and interwoven Branches of Trees" to ensure the "Privacy of the interior Parts." For a gardener who so loved trees, Pope's planting was well repaid at Twickenham.

One of the "avenues" that Pope promptly laid out was the Great Walk, shown as A in John Searle's *Plan* (plate 25). In the letter to Lady Mary just mentioned, he purred that it was a great honor "to my Great Walk, that the finest Woman in this world, cou'd not stir from it," adding that the "Walk extremely well answered the Intent of its Contriver, when it detain'd her there." The walk provided the central east-west axis in the garden, logically one of the first priorities in the layout since it established the dominating axial symmetry that such a long and narrow garden needed as a controlling element. A glance at Searle's *Plan* reveals that the scheme was therefore regular, but otherwise what the Great Walk achieved was a dominant line along which or from which sections of the garden unfolded with startling variety. With the groves on both sides of the walk, and at either end of it, Pope emphasized the irregular and pictorial. The axis itself was broken—by groups of trees, a bowling green, a large mount perhaps for watching bowls, two lesser mounts, and urns and statues—into sections that followed each other in quick succession. As Horace Walpole put it, variety was added by "the retiring and again assembling shades."[69]

Another feature that mitigated the axial impact of the Great Walk was the obliqueness of the main approach to the garden from the grotto-entrance (C), a fact that has recently been explained by James Sambrook.[70] Searle's *Plan* shows that Pope's house, which was connected to the garden by a passage or grotto running underneath the London-to-Hampton road, was not lined up with the Great Walk; it was to the south of it. The house was not only south of the main axis, but because of the angle of the road also faced northwest rather than due west (see plate 26). A visitor emerging from the grotto and proceeding along the main path from the entrance, through a wooded area that Pope

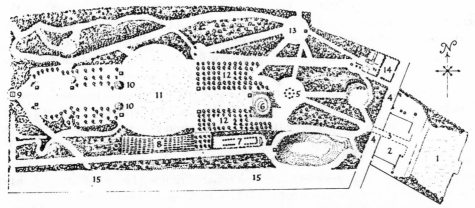

1 Grass plot between the house and the River Thames   2 The house   3 Grotto and underground passage
4 Road from Hampton Court to London   5 Shell temple   6 Large mount   7 Stoves (i.e. hothouses)
8 Vineyard   9 Obelisk in memory of Pope's mother   10 Small mounts   11 Bowling green
12 Grove   13 Orangery   14 Garden house   15 Kitchen garden
▫ Square marks indicate urns and statues

Plate 26. Redrawing of Searle's plan by James Sambrook. Courtesy of James Sambrook and Bell & Hyman, publishers.

called his "Wilderness," thus found himself entering the garden at an odd angle, not really aware of where he was with respect to the center. Before the Shell Temple was erected, at the end of this straight path the visitor found himself in a little clearing next to a mount (6), which, together with the regular groves (12) seen from that point, further obscured the main axis to the west. The visitor could also follow two other winding paths from the grotto-entrance that led to the irregularly planted northern and southern flanking sections, the latter given over mainly to kitchen gardens, a vineyard, and stoves for pineapples and other exotic plants. Even before reaching the Great Walk, then, one had already walked more than one-quarter of the length of the garden, all of it irregularly laid out.

The main garden, except for a gentle slope at the west end leading up to the obelisk to his mother's memory, was on the whole flat when he took it over, so with the trees and house cutting off prospects of the river, there really were no commanding views of surrounding countryside from the garden. When in his early letters he spoke of the prospects as "boundless," "prodigiously fine," and "rural enough" (2:19, 59, 109), he was talking chiefly about the river and the fields across it, seen from the house or the sloping lawn in front of it.[71] The mount, which he started to raise around 1720, commanded nice views, but those are not the ones of which he spoke in his early letters. The visitor in 1742 who described the garden in his journal did remark that at the upper end of the garden "a Hillock or 2 on the right side" surprised one "with an opening [prospect] to Richmond and a place or 2 more."[72] These hillocks, which John Searle in his plan of Pope's garden called "Two small Mounts," were probably built at the same time and for the same obvious reasons as the large mount.

The mount was crucial in Pope's landscaping at Twickenham. Without it the garden would have been shut off visually from the countryside. With it, not only were distant prospects let into the garden, but also views of the garden itself were possible, including the sight below of the bowls on the bowling green (11). The mount must have been completed by summer 1721[73] because by then the Blount girls were exploring it in ways that Pope might not have anticipated but that gave him pleasure and contentment; "I still see them walking on my Green at *Twickenham*," he remarked to their father, Edward, "and gratefully remember (not only their green Gowns) but the Instructions they gave me how to slide down, and trip up the steepest Slopes of my Mount" (2:86).[74] The following March he promised to "carry" Bishop Atterbury "up a Mount, in a point of view to shew you the glory of my little kingdom" (2:109). The Newcastle visitor in 1748 described the mount and what could be seen from the top of it:

> Among the Hillocks on the upper Part of the open Area, rises a Mount much higher than the rest, and is composed of more rude and indigested Materials; it is covered with Bushes and Trees of a wilder Growth, and more confused Order, rising as it were out of Clefts of Rocks, and Heaps of rugged and mossy Stones; among which a narrow intricate Path leads in an irregular Spiral to the Top; where is placed a Forest Seat or Chair, that may hold three or four Persons at once, overshaded with the Branches of a spreading Tree. From this Seat we face the [Shell] Temple, and overlook the various Distribution of the Thickets, Grass-plots, Alleys, Banks, &c.

Since Pope at the time was digging out the passage to the garden underneath his house and the road, it is likely that the displaced earth and rocks provided the fill wherewith he raised the mount. In building one, Pope was not innovative, although the mounts in a small garden like his and Mrs. Howard's at Marble Hill were not too common. Artificial mounts had been common enough in Renaissance English gardens.

The bowling green, one of the features that Atterbury would have seen from the mount, Pope mentions for the first time in his October letter to Edward Blount. Visually, it was the largest feature in the garden, eventually separating the regular groves from the smaller groves to the west and in effect dividing the garden in half. Pope was especially fond of bowling greens, admiring particularly those at Bevis Mount and Lord Oxford's Down Hall. "I'm pleasd to think your Bowling-green is one of the first of those green things I envy you the pleasure of creating," he told Oxford (2:369).[75] We can picture him at the summit of the mount, gazing contentedly at his friends playing bowls below, with the Shell Temple behind him and the house, river, and countryside beyond that.

Atterbury would also have seen the "Subterranean Passage," as Swift termed it. Without the grotto Pope would have had to cross the road in public view and risk the London-Hampton Court traffic. In 1722, when he mentioned it for the first time in a letter to Judith Cowper, it could hardly have been more than just a plain passageway, though by 1725 it had become, again in Swift's words, "a beauty which is a Piece of Ars Poetica."[76] "Wou'd you have me describe my Solitude & Grotto to you?" he asked Miss Cowper, adding some verses on the grotto and garden that he had addressed to Lady

Mary Wortley Montagu back in 1720; slightly adapted for Miss Cowper, they suggest that, even before he had turned his "blunder" or inconvenience into a famous ornament from 1722–25, he saw it as a sanctuary:

> What are the falling rills, the pendant Shades,
> The morning Bow'rs, the Evening Colonnades?
> But soft Recesses for th' uneasy mind,
> To sigh un-heard in, to the passing Wind.[77]
>
> (2:142)

The "falling rills" in the grotto, like the garden's "Solitary Groves," already in 1722 seem to be inducing "states of concentration" (Professor Mack's phrase) and providing soothing "soft Recesses." He even applied to his grotto what he (mistakenly) thought was Miss Cowper's line from a poem, *A Fit of Spleen*, "No noise but water, Ever friend to Thought." It is interesting, incidentally, that the original 1720 version of Pope's poem, as sent to John Gay, did not contain the line alluding to the grotto. Instead there was a line that spoke of the "gay parterre, the chequer'd shade"—apparently in Pope's garden. It is possible that in its first year the garden contained a small parterre with flowers as well as the delicate "chequer'd shade" of Pope's young trees. Two years later, he eliminated the poem's images of parterre and delicate tree foliage in favor of images of an evocative aquatic grotto and the fuller foliage of "pendant Shades."

Although Pope wrote romantically in the first stanza, "In vain my structures rise, my gardens grow," his little demesne was quickly taking on a natural look in its "sequestered" parts. It may also be noteworthy that he changed "The morning bower, the ev'ning colonade" to "The morning Bow'rs, the Evening Colonnades" as if to suggest that the garden's "soft Recesses" were fast multiplying.[78] We need to understand this evolution of the garden in the context of what was in the early stages, then, and to some degree always, a garden with plenty of symmetrical and regular features. As a leader of the new gardening, he did not (as we have seen) have to apologize for this. His pleasure in the garden derived partly from its combination of the symmetrical and irregular, each of which in his view enhanced the other and in the process heightened the variety of the scene.

After his visit to Twickenham in August 1723, Robert Digby put a series of queries to Pope:

> How thrive your garden-plants? how look the trees?
> how spring the Brocoli and Fenochio? hard names to spell!
> how did the poppies bloom? and how is the great room
> approved? what parties have you had of pleasure? what
> in the grotto? what upon the Thames? (2:192)

Judging by these questions, we can conclude that Pope kept rushing ahead with the design of his garden and grotto. We do not hear any more until June 1725, by which time the first stage of his planning was complete. He then told Edward Blount, in what must be reckoned the greatest misjudgment in garden history, that he had "put the last Hand" to "works of this kind, in happily finishing the subterraneous Way and Grotto" (2:296). Nothing could have been further from the truth. Breathlessly, he was telling the Earl of Strafford in October that he was "as busy in three inches of Gardening, as any man can be in threescore acres," almost losing track of the new features in the garden: "a Theatre, an Arcade, a Bowling green, a Grove, & what not?" (2:328). He never stopped toying with his grotto either.

Pope's description of the grotto for Blount in that June letter ends with the conclusion that it was all "in the natural Taste, agreeing not ill with the little dripping Murmur, and the Aquatic Idea of the whole Place" (2:297). The 1742 visitor also spoke of how the water and rustic stonework matched perfectly the "design'd irregularity of the whole" and made the grotto "look perfectly natural." Professor Mack has noticed the imaginative affiliation of the grotto with Calypso's Bower in *Odyssey* 5 and the Naiads' grotto in *Odyssey* 13, and has even wondered whether the actual plan of the grotto, and the groves and "Arcade" of trees outside the garden entrance with the winding paths leading to the entrance, may not have been inspired by Pope's current work on Homer.[79] In the absence of more specific information about what trees, apart from the elms, Pope especially desired and did plant in his garden, we may wonder whether the description of poplars and alders quivering in the "groves of living green" outside Calypso's Bower guided his choices. There were also cypresses outside Calypso's Bower, and Pope had some, we know, near the obelisk. In any case, the grotto was certainly endowed with a classical quality. During the next eighteen or so years, especially after a final spate of grotto work beginning in 1739, Pope inundated the place with minerals and ores from remote parts of England, turning it still more into a classically styled "shadowy Cave,"

> Where lingering Drops from Mineral Roofs distill,
> And Pointed Crystals break the sparkling Rill,
> Unpolish'd Gemms no Ray on Pride bestow,
> And latent Metals innocently glow.[80]

Pope's urge to indulge in "poetical" fancy or romance at Twickenham was being satisfied by the grotto. He apologized to Blount for being so very "Poetical in this Description," but insisted that "it is pretty near the Truth."[81] He explained two features of the grotto, very much the work of fancy, but deriving from his understanding of perspective and color, as analogous to a "Perspective Glass" and to the camera obscura. From the river he could look right through the grotto, through the arched entrance on the garden side, and up the "Walk of the Wilderness" (paved with "Cockle-shells, in the natural Taste") to his "open Temple," the Shell Temple (5), "wholly compos'd of Shells in the Rustic Manner." It worked in the other direction, too: "from that distance under the Temple you look down thro' a sloping Arcade of Trees, and see the Sails on the River passing suddenly and vanishing, as thro' a Perspective Glass" (2:296–97)—"a sort of continued Tube," as the anonymous observer in 1748 put it. This was one way he introduced a prospect into his garden and achieved a visual connection between the garden and the river; it also demonstrated his knowledge of the telescope, which he began to acquire at the Whiston lectures in 1713–14. As for his delight in color and

Plate 27. John Searle's "perspective View" of Pope's grotto, in his *Plan of Mr. Pope's Garden*. The view is through the opening out to the garden.

moving shapes, recent writers have shown how by means of a slit in his doorway the river scene, including hills, woods, and boats, was thrown upon the walls of a darkened room in the grotto—in the manner of a camera obscura, Pope thought.[82] Both effects increased the visual interpenetration of garden and grotto.[83]

Emerging from the grotto into the garden (see plates 27 and 28) and passing through the continuing line of the "Arcade of trees," rising slightly up a slope, a visitor came up to the Shell Temple described in 1748 by the Newcastle writer as "a Rotundo, or kind of Temple, entirely compos'd of Shells, and consisting wholly of a Cupola, or Dome, supported upon rustick Columns, so as to leave it open every Way to the surrounding Garden." This description was not of the first temple, which was built ca. 1725 and caved in about ten years later, and which Kent obviously admired for its rustic style since he drew a picture of it (plate 29), but of the second (begun in 1736), which was built on exactly the same site and in the same style. According to the 1742 visitor, it consisted that year of "a Garland of Rock Stones in the Shape of 2 Arches crossing each other," not four as the 1748 description and John Searle's *Plan* in 1745 indicate. It would appear, then, that either work proceeded slowly or Pope decided in the last months of his life to make good his promise to William Fortescue in 1736 that the second temple would "in Glory equal the First" (4:22).[84] With this remark Pope sounds as if he may be echoing (in reverse) Dryden's line on the second St. Paul's Cathedral, "The second Temple was not like the first," in *To My Dear Friend Mr. Congreve*. Modern architectural Vitruviuses like himself will ensure that his second temple is as glorious as the first, unlike the builders of the second St. Paul's, who lacked the wit and strength of a Congreve, "the best *Vitruvius*." There would be some further point in the allusion to the first gothic St. Paul's if, as

Plate 28. Garden entrance to Pope's grotto, 1824. Pencil drawing by John Buckler.

Brownell suggests, Pope was guided in building both his temples by the contemporary notion that Gothic architecture was inspired by avenues of forest trees. His temple was more Roman than Gothic in character, but we recall he had once told Spence he had an notion to plant "an old Gothic cathedral, or rather some old Roman temple, in trees."[85]

Behind that notion was not only his veneration for large old trees but also his instinct for the natural appearance such a composition would make. Both at Sherborne Castle in 1724 and Netley Abbey in 1734 Pope articulated his taste for the pictorial interaction of verdure and rustic stone. With great elder trees growing among its ruined arches and crumbling walls, Netley Abbey appeared to Pope as "ornamented" as Westminster Abbey and possessing a finer "Prospect." Surrounded by trees and shrubs, his own temple also created a fine prospect of composition. It was an important visual focus from several points in the eastern part of the garden. It looked north down an alley to the Orangery (13) and down other alleys to openings and clearings with seats or statuary; as one walked toward the center of the garden from near the boundaries, said the Newcastle writer, "the Scene opens and becomes less entangled; the Alleys widen, the Walks grow broader, and either terminate in small green Plots of the finest Turf, or lead to the Shell Temple." The seat at the top of the mount, he added, "faced the Temple."

Plate 29. William Kent's drawing of the first Shell temple in Pope's garden, ca. 1725–30. It shows the view down the "wilderness" and through the arched opening of the grotto to the river. It also shows Pope and Kent in the foreground, with Pope holding a "Perspective Glass" as he focuses on the view through the grotto.

The theater, which Pope also mentioned for the first time in 1726, is one feature either that Searle forgot to include in his *Plan* or that had disappeared by the time he drew it.[86] Pope is known to have described it only once, to Lord Oxford in March of that year: "I have just turfed a little Bridgmannick Theatre myself. It was done by a detachment of His workmen from the Prince's, all at a stroke, & it is yet unpayd for, but that's nothing with a Poetical Genius" (2:372). Presumably, he referred to the theater as "Bridgmannick" because Bridgeman's workmen created it,[87] but perhaps also because Bridgeman designed it, as he did the one at Rousham. It seems more likely, however, that Pope designed it. He had seen one at Sherborne in 1724. I have found a sketch by Pope of what is almost certainly a theater among his Homer manuscripts in the British Library (plate 30). It appears between lines 178 and 180 of *Odyssey* 24. It was sketched upon this sheet of paper before Pope used the sheet for his translation, so that he had to compose the lines awkwardly around the sketch. The sheet was the back of a letter that presumably he received shortly before he composed the lines in 1725, so that the sketch would date from that year also. The sketch shows a shape resembling Bridgeman's theater at Claremont and Sherborne's theater. He may also have got the idea of a "green

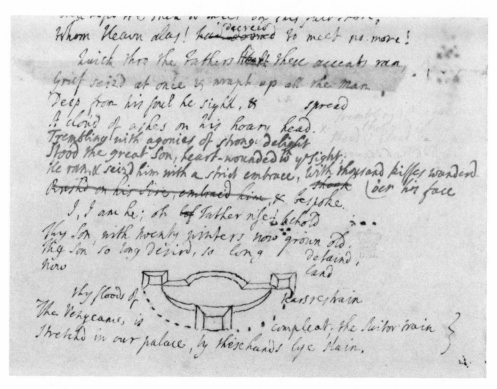

Plate 30. Pope's sketch of what may be a "green theatre" for his own garden, ca. 1725. The sketch is on a manuscript page of the poet's translation of Homer.

theatre" from Kent, who would surely have seen several in Italy. Perhaps Kent had seen the green theater at Villa Marla in Lucca, built in the second half of the seventeenth century, which Georgina Masson has called "the most charming that was ever created to fill the passing hour with amusement for the gay world of seventeenth-century Italy."[88] The theater was a beautiful and common garden feature in Renaissance Italian gardens and was usually elaborately ornamented with statuary in green niches and hedges in box and yew. It imitated, of course, the classical theater, especially in having a grass-covered promenade at the top. It also could provide some elevation for views of the countryside. Pope's theater, however, could not have been a very substantial affair, or very elevated, if it was done "all at a stroke," though we know that there must have been something toward a theater by October 1725 for him to have announced to Lord Strafford, "I have a Theatre" (2:328).

An equally important question is where the theater was located. Theaters could be used as focal points in gardens since they were large enough to be seen from some distance. If we look at Searle's *Plan*, we will notice that the other major focal point in the garden, apart from the Shell Temple at the eastern end, was at the western end of the Great Walk, where after his mother's death in 1733 Pope erected an obelisk in her memory (plate 31). According to the Newcastle visitor, the obelisk stood "upon the

Plate 31. Pope's obelisk, 1826. Pencil drawing by John Buckler.

gentle Eminence of a green Bank," so that also could have been the site of the theater. If Pope later thought the site was prominent enough for the obelisk, he may also have thought it was a suitable position for the theater. Perhaps in the long run he was not too happy with the theater in that spot, though; it was an important spot in his garden plan, but the theater, unlike the grotto, Shell Temple, and various urns and statues scattered all over the garden and especially along the Great Walk,[89] lacked (as far as we know) an iconography or spiritual interpretation. When he needed an appropriately dramatic position for the obelisk, he probably thought that the theater was the least indispensable ornament in his garden.[90]

Bridgeman's role in Pope's garden in other ways, incidentally, is unknown. The poet does not again mention him in connection with his garden; he never mentions him at all in his letters after 1726, though Bridgeman's name almost appeared in the *Epistle to Burlington* in 1731. Before the publication of the poem they appear to have had a difference of opinion, perhaps at Twickenham or at Marble Hill in 1724–26, and Pope was exasperated over the poem because Bridgeman wished to have his name removed from the line, "Lo! BRIDGMAN comes, and floats them with a Lake." Bridgeman probably read the line as an insult, either to himself or to his wealthy patrons. In any case, Pope vented some spleen when in his *Master Key to Popery* he ironically alluded to Bridgeman's excessive ambition to "please Gentlemen";

> Is it not his business to please Gentlemen? to execute Gentlemen's will and Pleasure, not his own? is he to set up his own Conceits & Inventions against Gentlemen's fine Taste & Superiour Genius?[91]

The east-west central strip of Pope's garden, including the Great Walk, groves (12), bowling green, urns, and two smaller mounts (10), surrounded by a mixture of regularity and irregularity, illustrates that it was in some respects a transitional garden. Walpole, in fact, writing at a time when picturesque gardening was the mode, singled out the groves as an exception to Pope's "exquisite judgment" in the natural taste, by which he meant of course that Pope went wrong in making the area around the mount too formal.[92]

One of the advantages to Pope's having a comfortable house and lovely gardens was that he could offer lodgings over an extended period to close friends, especially to his "exiled" friends Bolingbroke and Swift. Bolingbroke stayed with him in 1724 when he came over from France to look for an estate to purchase, and Swift stayed for two lengthy periods during the summers of 1726 and 1727. After Swift had left him in August 1726, at the end of what was a most pleasurable visit, Pope wrote to him sadly that he would never again be able to walk in his garden "without a Phantome of you, sitting or walking before me" (2:388); to which Swift replied, "I can only swear that you have taught me to dream, ... now I can every night distinctly see Twitenham, and the Grotto" (2:393). What Pope appears to have "taught" Swift was the link between dreams and gardens of which Professor Hunt has written. Pope continues to see the "Phantome" of Swift in his garden, while the latter every night sees visions of Pope in the garden. The grotto played its part, too, in Pope's comprehensive effort to unfold within his five acres a visionary scene portrayed with ideas as well as plants and stonework. But Pope's "milk" was too visionary and philosophical, thought Swift; himself a gardener, he later urged Pope, on account of his health, to sweeten his (ass's) milk with mirth by contriving "new tramgams in your Garden or in Mrs Howards, or my Lord Bolingbroke's" (3:191).[93]

Such was his garden, then, when Pope first entertained another guest, Joseph Spence, in 1726 or 1727. Since Spence later became an accomplished and influential gardener in his own right, his friendship with Pope and his knowledge of the poet's garden must be reckoned as significant facts in the history of eighteenth-century landscape gardening. We have an idea how much Spence learned from Pope from Spence's anecdotes of their conversations; and from the same source, as well as from bundles of garden maps and plans among the Spence Papers in the Osborn Collection at Yale University, we know the extent of Spence's influence on later gardeners like Philip Southcote.[94] Morris Brownell recently has even credited Spence with having written the earliest surviving detailed description of Pope's garden.[95]

Pope did not have any new garden projects underway for a few years after meeting Spence, at least not any major ones that he thought worth mentioning, except for "a triumphal arch, under which," he told Caryll in March 1733, "you shall be led into my garden" (3:358). The arch shows up in Kent's sketch of the Shell Temple.

From the beginning, Pope shared the pleasures of Twickenham life with his aged mother. Her presence naturally affected his life there; the model of a devoted and dutiful son, he was always careful to "rock the Cradle of reposing Age." When she finally died in June 1733, at the age of ninety-one, he set off on what he called a "new Æra of my life" (3:375).

As far as the garden was concerned, the effect of his mother's death was to cause him to reconsider the layout and importance of the western end, which at the time possibly featured the theater. The idea of erecting an obelisk (see plate 31) in memory of his mother must have occurred to him immediately; at least we know that he thought of it before Aaron Hill wrote to him in November offering him some shells for such an obelisk. Visiting Hill in his garden, Pope had seen him erecting a rustic obelisk with shells and apparently mentioned his own intention of building one. Hill wrote:

> The last time I had the pleasure of seeing you, at *Westminster* you were observing among some rude beginnings of rock-work, which I am designing in my garden, a *little obelisk of Jersey Shells*, over a grotesque portico for *Pallas*, against the park-wall. You, then, express'd some thoughts of improving such a use of those shells, into a nobler obelisk, among your beauties, at *Twittenham*. Allow me to *bespeak* for *myself* against next spring, the permission of presenting you the shells, materials, and workmanship; that I may have the honour to plant in your gardens a probability of being, sometimes, remember'd by the master of that growing paradise. (3:393)

Hill added that in the meantime he was sending a smaller parcel of the shells "to embellish your *marine temple* [Shell Temple], by inserting them, among the *Hollows*, between those large shells, which compose it: where being plac'd in oblique position, so as to lie open to the weather, they will enlighten the gravity, and catch a distant eye, with a kind of shining propriety." Pope would have appreciated this suggestion for some chiaroscuro effects. As it turned out, the obelisk had to wait until after he had finished with the house in 1735.

Pope's first and only mention of the obelisk was in a letter to Fortescue in March 1735 where he simply stated that he was building one. It was not just a matter of placing an obelisk at the end of the garden, however; in view of the elegiac nature of the memorial, it had to be landscaped with a proper degree of solemnity and drama. Pope hinted at solemnity and dramatic perspective in the area when in 1739 he referred to "the little cypress walk to that obelisk" to illustrate his gardening principle of perspective through light and shade.[96] The darkening and the narrowing were both achieved by the cypress walk. On Searle's *Plan*, the "nodding cypress" trees that "form'd a fragrant shade," as Pope described a dark part of Calypso's garden in *Odyssey* 5,[97] are not identified, but the small grove (D), just east of the two small mounts (10) and flanking the Great Walk, might be them, as also might the single row of trees curving toward the obelisk. In his account of the garden, Walpole was especially struck by the "solemnity of the termination at the cypresses that lead up to his mother's tomb" or obelisk.[98] The entire dramatic (visual and personal) impact of the scene was also enhanced by the gentle rise of the ground on the site. A painting by Jonathan Richardson that Pope showed Kent in November 1738 and that has recently come to light (frontispiece)[99] shows (in Kent's words) "Pope in a mourning gown with a strange view of the garden to shew the obelisk as in memory to his mothers Death—the alligory seem'd odde to me," he added (4:150). What is odd is that Kent thought the allegory was odd. On the contrary, the allegory represented an understandable climax in a garden where the poet's mental needs were continually satisfied.

The need to build another Shell Temple, the new landscaping that accompanied it, and the relandscaping around the obelisk all induced Pope, then, to embark on another phase of extensive alterations to his garden beginning in 1735. "Ever since we dined in the park, I have been planting at home," he told Fortescue in December 1735, "have catched two colds on the neck of one another, but still plant on, being resolved to finish this fine season. My alterations are what you would not conceive. Besides my shell temple is fallen down; and yet I live!" (3:511–12). In March 1736 he was trying to lure Swift into making another visit by telling him that "the gardens extend and flourish" (4:6). With "the joy of workmen" in his garden, in September he wrote to Mrs. Knight at Gosfield, "You may . . . expect to see a new garden, when you come to Twitnam" (4:30). He was rather disinclined to leave his garden at the time to go assist Lady Peterborough at Bevis Mount with her gardening, but in November he was back and busy again, declaring to Ralph Allen, "I am now as busy in Planting for myself as I was lately in planting for another" (4:40).

After this phase of gardening, Pope's garden looked very nearly like what Searle pictured in his *Plan* nine years later. Still, there were details that he had yet to see to. Kent was engaged in some work there, perhaps on the mount;[100] also, it has been mentioned that in 1743 he added some sculpture and urns to the garden by the river, sharpening the iconography of that area and bringing to an end over twenty years of landscaping on a five-acre site that by the time of his death had already become a legend.

The obelisk, the grotto, and other symbols of aids to contemplation, such as the Shell Temple, the mount, and the little secret arbors in the groves, express Pope's life and career. With its inscription,

AH EDITHA!

MATRUM OPTIMA.

MULIERUM AMANTISSIMA.

VALE.

the obelisk certainly was the most explicitly autobiographical part of the garden, but it was all in one way or another self-revealing. Pertinent inscriptions appeared on several statues, and in 1736 he contemplated a "proper Motto over my Gate" that would read, "*Mihi & Amicis*" (4:34). The one he finally decided upon in the fall of 1741 was his constant toast with Bolingbroke, "Libertati & Amicitiae," which with an "S" added after it, as he intended, meant "Sacred to Friendship and Liberty."[101]

As we look back at his gardening and correspondence during those twenty years, we should not miss Pope's close identification with his garden, not in an emblematic way but through analogies. At times he took refuge in the thought that he was more in sympathy with his plants than with the rest of mankind; or he could talk about his poetry, or lack of it, in terms of his garden. The analogies were useful to him in describing his mental state in other ways, too, not to mention the state of his health. Anyone who lived through Britain's drought in the summer of 1976 can appreciate Pope's comprehensive feelings of chaos in mind and landscape during the drought of 1723: "My body is sick, my soul is troubled, my pockets are empty, my time is lost, my trees are withered, my grass is burned! So ends my history" (2: 183). "I am stuck at Twit'nam, as fast as my own Plants, scarce removeable at this season," he declared to Mrs. Knight one July; and on a November day several years later he could say about his plants: "they will indeed out-live me (if they do not die in their Travels from place to place, for my Garden like my Life, seems to me every *Year* to want Correction & require alteration, I hope at least, for the better.)" (4:40). On another occasion, an Indian summer day in September, he alluded to his personal decay with a gesture to his garden; "the Weather is yet inviting," he said, wishing he could be visited "before I am quite decay'd (I mean all of me that is yet half flourishing, my Garden)." During a cold May in 1740, when his health was particularly poor and the coldness had him shivering, he compared his body to his garden: "I have sufferd more, in my Garden as well as in my Body, since the End of the Great Frost, than before. . . . Yet upon the Whole, my Garden would look well, & I should be well, if the Sun would but shine on us" (4:239).

It is perhaps fitting that Pope's garden did not long survive without him. He always said he was indifferent to whether it did or not. Sir William Stanhope purchased the house and garden after Pope died in 1744, and for him the poet's works in the garden were all inconsiderable. With an irony that even Pope might have found it difficult to be philosophical about, Sir William, behaving like Pope's dull Timon in *To Burlington*, altered the design of the garden beyond recognition, cut down most of the thick groves, and then, finding that this exposed the garden too much to passersby, built a wall around it. Horace Walpole's sad postscript to the garden read as follows: "there was not a Muse could walk there but that she was spied by every country fellow that went by with a pipe in his mouth."

3

The Great Patriarch

Lord Bathurst and His Parks

In his circle of gardening friends, Pope's closest friendship was with Allen Lord Bathurst. Over a period of about thirty years their friendship encompassed the earliest stages of the landscape gardening revolution. As the owner of two estates of first importance to the new movement, Riskins (or Richings) Park (near Iver, Buckinghamshire) and Cirencester Park (Gloucestershire), Bathurst enjoyed a privileged position as a practicing amateur in the vanguard of the new style; and as one of Pope's "vegetable lords," he also enjoyed the advantage of always knowing his friend's ideas and opinions on gardening.

"Primitive simplicity and good humour"

In his *Life of Pope*, Dr. Johnson remarked, "except Lord Bathurst, none of Pope's noble friends were such as that a good man would wish to have his intimacy with them known to posterity."[1] He had elaborated that notion to Boswell once, noting "how foolish was it in Pope to give all his friendship to Lords, who thought they honoured him by being with him; and to choose such Lords as Burlington, and Cobham, and Bolingbroke! Bathurst was negative, a pleasing man."[2] Johnson's entire life, agonizing as it was, and his distrust of aristocratic patrons are behind that comment, but where Bathurst was concerned he was only bearing witness to the widespread reputation of Pope's friend as a charming and pleasant landowner and member of the House of Lords. As Bathurst's only biographer has put it, Bathurst lived an extraordinarily fortunate and long life with an energy that seemed inexhaustible.[3] While it appears that many people were vexed by his occasionally erratic and unpunctual habits, most, including Pope, readily forgave this man of large tastes and lands his eccentricities on account of his humaneness and pleasantness. Pope felt easy with him and was fonder of visiting him than almost anyone else he knew. "I vow," he wrote to his friend in 1728, "I have found myself happier in sickness with you, than in health with some who are not thought bad or disagreeable Company" (2:525).

The important year for Bathurst was 1704. His father, Sir Benjamin Bathurst, died that year leaving him in possession of two large properties, Riskins and Cirencester.[4] Bathurst thereby assumed the stature of a man of considerable property on top of the favorable connections both sides of his family had enjoyed with the Court for many

Plate 32. Allen Bathurst, first Earl of Bathurst, painted by Sir Godfrey Kneller.

years.[5] In 1705 he was elected as Tory member of Parliament for Cirencester, and in 1712 Queen Anne conferred a barony upon him as one of twelve Tories she raised to the House of Lords to ensure a majority in it on the question of the Treaty of Utrecht. He had served the Tory cause courageously and attentively since 1705, and now as a peer with extensive landed interests who could call the Queen a friend and who had proved his loyalty to both Lord Oxford and Lord Bolingbroke, he emerged as a figure of some national importance. He had a promising political future to which to look forward.[6] But in just over two years the Queen died, the Tory government fell, and Bathurst's political prospects dimmed.

As it turned out, the reversal of Bathurst's political fortunes encouraged his friendship with Pope and his interest in landscaping. He had a long life yet to live—over sixty years—and his resilience and vast energy would not allow him to languish waiting for new political opportunities. With more time on his hands he could devote himself more completely to his two estates. He also sought out the leading Tory wits of the day, joining the Brothers Club with Matthew Prior, Swift, Dr. Arbuthnot (Queen Anne's personal physician), and Lords Bolingbroke and Orrery, and in 1713 fraternizing with the membership of the newly formed Martin Scriblerus Club, which included Swift, Arbuthnot, Pope, Gay, Thomas Parnell, and Robert Harley.[7] Pope, who throughout his life always seemed to take a great personal interest in "Chiefs, out of War, and Statesmen, out of Place," himself began to be attracted to Bathurst around 1713. When he

63

complained years later about not having seen Bathurst for several long months, Pope joked (as was his wont with his friend) "that there was at the latter End of Queen Anne's reign, a Poet of the name of Pope, to whom you sometimes afforded an hour of Conversation as well as reading" (3:130). Perhaps he concluded from what he saw of the Riskins landscape, which Stephen Switzer highly praised, that here was an imaginative gardener of the future. His earliest known mention of Bathurst and visit to Riskins, however, were not until August 1717, when he told Caryll that he was "obliged to pass some days between my Lord Bathurst's, and three or four [estates] more on Windsor side" (1:418).

It was sometime in the spring of 1714, during the first session of their meetings, that the Scriblerians (perhaps including Pope) took one or more excursions to Riskins to see Bathurst. Oliver Goldsmith told of such an occasion when all the members decided to walk out there and Swift fell victim to a prank engineered by Parnell. Swift apparently got a closer look at the gardens at Riskins, or at least at a summer house in it, than he planned to, having been duped into supping out there on a cold meal while the rest dined comfortably as Bathurst's guests in the main house.[8] Goldsmith's account suggests not only the ease with which Bathurst moved in the company of these wits but also that Riskins played its part in the brief history of one of the most famous Opposition literary clubs in the early eighteenth century. In June the club broke up for the summer session and, owing to the dramatic political events following the Queen's death, which scattered the members, never reassembled with the same membership.[9]

Not long after Pope moved to Chiswick in 1716, he apparently began to use Riskins as a retreat to get on with his translation of the *Iliad*, much in the way he was to use Cirencester for the same purpose by 1718. Years later Bathurst recalled that he had supplied Pope with a "tin Standish" at Riskins to hold the ink that the poet needed for his writing labors (3:133). He also recalled, with some exaggeration, that Pope "translated half Homer" at Riskins when he was "scarce awake" (3:134)—an allusion to the poet's habit of rising early and translating Homer in bed before breakfast. Bathurst, at any rate, played enough of a part in the *Iliad* translation to earn a place in Gay's celebrated poem (1720) upon Pope's completion of the project: "*Bathurst* impetuous hastens to the coast [to greet Pope upon his return from six years' imaginative journey into the Greek world]/Whom you & I strive who shall love yᵉ most."[10]

In addition to the escape Riskins offered for work on Homer—away from the "great Entertainments" in "pleasant Villas about the Thames: whose Banks are now more populous than London" (1:351), and away from the distracting and exciting new friendships Pope made with people like Burlington and John Sheffield, the Duke of Buckingham (the poet and playwright)—it offered him the chance to return to the rural setting of the forest, which he sorely missed. After only a few months of life in Chiswick, he wrote to Thomas Dancastle, one of his young friends at Binfield, about how much he missed the countryside, especially th farming life that had gone on all around them: "I ought upon this principle to rally you upon your harvest time, make pictures of my Friends tossing Wheatsheaves and raising Reeks [ricks], imagine I see you in a great Sweat and Hurry; and all that. But this I reserve till I see you; unless I should then on a sudden affect the fine Gentleman, and extoll the Innocence and Exercise of the Rural

Life." He was genuinely nostalgic for the "quiet, indolence, silence, and sauntring, that made up my whole life in Windsor Forest" (1:352). At Riskins, he could recapture a link with the agrarian impulse in general that characterized his young manhood and determined many of his landscaping ideas. The gardens possessed, as we shall see, the kind of landscape beauty to which he had referred in his *Guardian* essay with a passage from Martial about Bassus, "the true rustic, the untrimmed farm," belonging to the Roman poet's friend Faustinus at Baiae, near Naples.

Around this time Pope also got to know Robert Digby, son of William, the fifth Lord Digby, of Sherborne Castle. This friendship would turn out to be another shaping influence on Pope's conception of what a garden should be and mean. By 1720 Digby was intimately connected with Bathurst and Pope and their landscaping, spending many hours at Riskins and especially Cirencester. Pope's gardening ideas and practice always flourished in conversation with friends. He liked nothing better than to talk with them about gardening projects. Bathurst and Digby not only brought him great pleasure in these early days, but they also helped him to explore and refine new notions of landscape possibilities. Pope saw himself and his two friends as "Associates" in the "blissful Bower" of Oakley Wood, a term that suggests a feeling of magical landscaping partnership.[11] If Spence had been there to record their conversations, doubtless we would have today some vital documentation of one of the wellsprings of English landscape gardening. Sadly, there is no record of Pope and Bathurst visiting Sherborne together—indeed, Bathurst may never have gone and Pope did not make his first visit until 1724. One of Digby's numerous invitations indicates the almost visionary spirit of this triumvirate: "I have other hopes that please me too . . . these are, that you may yet make a journey westward with Lord Bathurst. . . . It grieves me to think how far I am removed from you, and from that excellent Lord, whom I love! . . . I often too consider him in other lights that make him valuable to me. With him, I know not by what connection, you never fail to come into my mind, as if you were inseparable" (2:192).[12]

One of the "lights" that made Bathurst "valuable" to Digby was a quality that Pope also appreciated in Digby himself: a rusticated lifestyle in the country, including cheerful habits of housekeeping, which they had inherited from the country house tradition. Bathurst also demonstrated a charitable concern for one's neighbors that Digby traced back to ancient Rome: "I want the publick Spirit so much admired in old Rome (2:58). Living so far from London, Digby was made much of by the other two as a rustic.[13] He played along with the idea and preened himself, half-seriously, over his own rusticity, his "primitive simplicity and good humour" (1:474). Both Riskins and Cirencester, though not as remote as Sherborne, appeared attractively old-fashioned to Pope; Cirencester especially helped turn his thoughts away from building a house in London in 1718 since these traditional values and lifestyles had always been the antitheses of city life. "Prayers and roast beef," he facetiously told John Caryll in 1717, "do actually make some folks as happy, as a whore and a bottle (1:457).[14] Bathurst urged upon him the prudence of building in the country with a thought from Horace:

> Vos sapere et solos aio bene vivere, quorum
> Conspicitur nitidis fundata pecunia villis.[15]

Such was the ancient hospitality that Pope felt "must itself soon fall to ruin" in his age. It was no small encouragement and pleasure to him to know that Bathurst's rebuilding of Oakley Grove would preserve the socioethical ideals connected with the old property. These themes were very much in his mind when in 1718 Cirencester stole over his imagination and crystallized his interest in estate management, particularly the use and design of landscape. Riskins, however, preceded Cirencester in Pope's life, so we will first take a look at its gardens and from the available evidence reconstruct it as it might have looked when, if we are to believe Goldsmith, the Scriblerians visited it as a group in 1714.

Riskins: the "extravagante bergerie"

Ironically, there exists more verbal evidence regarding the Riskins gardens after Bathurst sold the estate in 1739 to Algernon, Earl of Hertford, later the seventh Duke of Somerset, than while he owned it. In his correspondence, Pope mentions Riskins (without description) only a few times, in spite of the probability that until April 1735, when Bathurst gave over the use of the estate to his son Benjamin, he saw it regularly. The odd verbal sketch of its gardens before 1735 comes from other pens.

It is the Countess of Hertford to whom we are indebted for verbal descriptions. She was an enthusiastic gardener and amateur poet, as well as patroness of Isaac Watts, James Thomson, and William Shenstone, among others.[16] Her letters to her son[17] and the Countess of Pomfret[18] (1740–43) contain several detailed descriptions of the gardens as they were both before and after she and her husband altered them. Still, her letters give little idea of the general layout of the landscape; for a picture of the layout in its earlier stage, we are indebted mainly to Stephen Switzer.

The date of Switzer's "regulated Epitomy" or plan of the grounds (plate 33) is not known; he perhaps intended it for publication in *The Practical Kitchen Gardener* (1727), which he dedicated to Bathurst, the "best of Masters, best of Friends."[19] He had been influenced by Addison's 1712 *Spectator* essay on productive landscape gardening and quoted large sections of it in his first major work, *The Nobleman, Gentleman, and Gardener's Recreation* (1715), which presented his ideas on what he called "Rural and Extensive Gardening." He did not mention Pope's *Guardian* essay (though he did so much later in the "Proemial Essay" to his 1742 edition of *Ichnographia Rustica*). Because of the popularity of *Recreation*, he expanded it in 1718 into his three-volume first edition of *Ichnographia Rustica*, later expanded again for the second edition in 1742.[20] These books abound with advice on garden design, and they especially influenced the progress of English gardening during the fifteen years after the *Recreation* appeared. It is therefore important to the garden historian that Switzer dedicated the 1718 *Ichnographia* to Bathurst. Only six years had elapsed since Addison's plea for more practical gardening and three since Switzer himself had articulated the concept in *Recreation*, but here were Bathurst and Riskins being hailed as promoter and prototype of a distinctly new movement in gardening. It is impossible to say with certainty whether Switzer, in

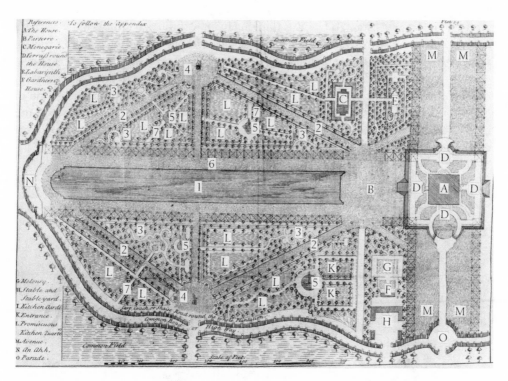

Plate 33. Stephen Switzer, "A Plan of Riskins, Near Colnbrooke, Garden of Allen, Lord Bathurst," from *Ichnographia Rustica* (1742). There references have been added: 1. the canal; 2. turfed paths; 3. "wilderness" or "labyrinth" at "every Angle"; 4. grand "rond-points" with statuary; 5. fountains; 6. grass borders to the canal; 7. "private Hedge Rows or Walks."

collaboration with Bathurst and in his capacity as nurseryman,[21] was at all responsible for the *ferme ornée* at Riskins, or whether, when he first saw it, the landscape already was a *ferme ornée*—the product of Bathurst's enthusiasm over Addison's essay.[22]

Switzer's connection with Riskins appears to have lasted well into the 1730s— conceivably until 1735, when Bathurst handed over the estate to his son, though before then Bathurst's finances had not allowed him to indulge in significant landscaping concurrently with work at Cirencester. Since Switzer says in *Ichnographia* (1742) that he and Bathurst were by 1727 "best of friends," however, why then did he not in his published writings after 1718 acclaim the remarkable landscaping that his friend, with Pope's close attendance, was achieving at Cirencester as well? There were two possible reasons why he did not. In the first place, Cirencester was not a *ferme ornée*, and it was this which Switzer, in extending Addison's argument, was promoting. Second, in terms of scale, Riskins was far more compatible with Switzer's ideas than was Cirencester.

For all its beauties, Cirencester's vastness likely proved a slight embarrassment to Switzer, as it did to Pope. When Switzer spoke out boldly in 1718 against the wasteful expense of laying out vast estates which "the Folly of this and past Ages hath run into whereby that most innocent and harmless Employ [gardening], is become a Burthen too great for the biggest Estate,"[23] he was thinking mainly of the powerful Whig lords who hoped to display their wealth through their huge landscaping projects. William Brogden argues that Switzer did not perpetuate the association of formality with autocracy, and he wished to keep politics and garden design separate.[24] In 1718 he does not mention Charles Bridgeman, who was employed to lay out many of these extravagances, and of whom Switzer was jealous, but in 1742 he does refer to him. Unfairly, Switzer fixes the blame for such grandiosity on Bridgeman's vanity rather than on the social and political conditions of the day:

> This aiming at an incomprehensible Vastness, and attempting at Things beyond the reach of Nature, is in a great measure owing to a late eminent Designer in Gardening, whose Fancy could not be bounded; and this notion has been in many Places carried so far, that no Parterre or Lawn that was not less than 50 or 60 Acres, some of them 80, 90 or 100, were by him esteemed capacious enough, though it sometimes took up the whole Area of Ground, and made the Building or Mansion-house in the middle look very small, and by no means proportionable to it. . . . The same extravagant way of thinking prevailed also to a great degree, in that otherwise ingenious Designer, in his Plan of Lakes and Pieces of Water, without any regard to the Goodness of the Land, which was to be overflowed: But which he generally designed so large, as to make a whole Country look like an Ocean.[25]

Here Switzer may be recalling Pope's sketch of Timon's gardens in *To Burlington*,

> Greatness, with Timon, dwells in such a draught
> As brings all Brobdignag before your thought.
> To compass this, his building is a Town,
> His pond an Ocean, his parterre a Down;
>
> (103–6)

or he may have remembered Pope's ambiguous compliment to Bridgeman in this couplet from the first version of the same poem, subsequently altered to include Lord Cobham's name instead,

> The vast Parterres a thousand hands shall make,
> Lo! BRIDGMAN comes, and floats them with a Lake.[26]
>
> (73–74)

"Floats" was a technical agricultural term for flooding an area in order to create a lake, but in this part of the poem it is one of three verbs, along with "make" and "cut," pejoratively used to suggest rude and impulsive landscaping. Pope certainly satirized Bridgeman with that couplet, but he (unlike Switzer) relied heavily on the gardener for landscaping ideas and their execution. It is just that he was never beyond criticizing even his best friends' gardening (including Bathurst's) when he decided bad taste was getting the upper hand. For his part, Switzer was repeating a thesis that he had first urged about twenty-seven years earlier. To him Riskins represented the antithesis of the great estates with which Bridgeman had been associated.

Switzer described for the public (in 1718) his idea of a landscape design that would afford the owner "continual Profit and Employ"; it can be taken as a fair description of Riskins:

> if his Grounds were handsomly divided by Avenues and Hedges; and if the little Walks and Paths that ought to run through and betwixt them, were made either of Gravel or Sand; and if there were Trees for Shades with little Walks and purling Streams, mix'd and incorporated one with another, what cou'd be more diverting? And why, is not a level easy Walk of Gravel or Sand shaded over with Trees, and running thro' a Corn Field or Pasture Ground, as pleasing as the largest Walk in the most magnificent Garden one can think of?[27]

Indeed, why not? Pope would have agreed.

Although it is likely that Switzer did not draw his "Epitomy" of Riskins until perhaps almost ten years later, making it unreliable as evidence of what the estate looked like in 1718, we may suppose that he would not have dedicated his work on rural and extensive gardening to Bathurst if Riskins had not then illustrated the principles of design that his book recommended.

Throughout the Riskins gardens there is a thorough integration of practical and pleasure gardening: small "wildernesses," fountains, "Promiscuous Kitchen Quarters," and areas of grass with statuary and seats are combined in all sorts of arrangements around the central axis provided by the straight canal; and intersecting the whole scheme are numbers of straight and twisting paths of various widths. Moreover, apart from the straight canal, whose only formal aspect is its straightness, and the traditional-looking menagerie and labyrinth (maze) that occupy a small western section just west of the parterre, formal features are almost nonexistent. Some symmetry is provided by wide slanting turfed paths (2 in plate 33) east and west of the canal and by the shape of the perimeter of the garden established by the "Common Road or High Way," but otherwise traditional elements either have been blurred or do not appear at all. From the grass parterre (B) several turfed paths lead off naturally, diminishing its squarish shape, and the parterre is opened up on the south side by the long grass borders (6) to the canal, which lead all the way to the edge of the landscape at the southern end of the canal. Fountains (5) are unobtrusive and in some places even hidden in "wildernesses" (3). As Switzer explains in his comments on the plan, space does not allow him to include the entire design of the estate; he does not show any of the gardens north of the house, so their design and extent are unknown.

Switzer's remarks on Riskins are quoted at length because they indicate not only his pleasure with the "*Roman* Genius" of the place but also his sense (in 1742) of his own contribution to the principles of the *ferme ornée*. Long favored by "the best Genius's of *France*," the *ferme ornée* is now likely, he says, to be perfected in Great Britain if "the Farms and Parks of *Abbs-Court*, Riskins, Dawley-Park, now a doing" are any indication.[28] Furthermore, he adds, "the *Roman* Genius" for combining practical and ornamental gardening is nowhere more evident than in this advancing taste in Britain:

> The Plan annex'd to this Appendix . . . is a regulated Epitomy of a much larger Design portraited and lay'd out, by the Right Honourable the Lord *Bathurst* at *Riskins* near *Colnbrooke*, upon the Plan of the *Ferme Ornée*, and the Villa's of the Ancients; the Lawns round about the House are for the feeding of Sheep, and the insides of the Quarters for sowing of Corn, Turnips &c. or for the feeding of Cattle. One thing I would observe in this Plan, that besides the main walks [2] which go strait diagonal ways, and round the whole plantation, there are also little private Hedge-Rows or Walks [7] round every Field about six or eight Foot wide, and in some Places they run a-cross the Field where it is large; and particularly at every Angle [of the field] there is a little piece of Wood in the form of a Labyrinth [3].

He concludes by reminding his readers that long before anyone in Britain began to lay out the *ferme ornée* he had been advocating its superiority over "any Kind of Gardening when the Farm is walled or paled in."[29] Switzer's citing of Roman authority for the *ferme ornée* was in line with the classical revival early in the century and the habit of matching up architectural and landscaping innovations with literary and actual examples from ancient times—especially after Robert Castell's *Villas of the Ancients Illustrated* was published in 1728, to which Switzer alludes in *A Farther Account of Rural and Extensive Gardening* (1728–30). The *ferme ornée* clearly fell within Castell's *villa rustica* category because while produce was important in it, complete self-sufficiency was less vital than the visual beauty resulting from the union of the useful and the irregular in nature. The *Villas of the Ancients* aside, however, Switzer could have found support for citing classical precedence from Pope alone, beginning with the *Guardian* essay and on up through the translations of Homer to the poetry of the 1730s.[30]

While Switzer was preparing the Appendix with the "Epitomy" for publication in the 1742 *Ichnographia*, the Earl and Countess of Hertford were busily at work there changing the landscape. In 1739 they moved from their "Hermitage" at St. Leonard's Hill in Windsor Forest, which they had found too small but where the Countess had become an enthusiastic gardener. She was immediatly charmed by Riskins. Herself a poet, she delighted in the literary associations of the landscape and felt she had to write to her closest friends about the romantic beauties there that inspired both her poetry and her gardening. Two of those friends were Lady Luxborough, Lord Bolingbroke's sister, who several years earlier had settled into her own small "farm-garden," Barrell's, and played the part of the "farmeress" there under the influence of her brother; and the Countess of Pomfret, on the Continent, to whom Lady Hertford wrote frequent, long, and expressive letters about her life at Riskins. From her letters to these women, in addition to those to her son Beauchamp, we learn about Riskins as it was when her husband purchased it and after they had altered it from 1740 to 1743. Except for Switzer's plan and Lady Hertford's letters, we would know nothing of the gardens as Bathurst left them, and as Pope, Swift, and Gay knew them.

From the start, Lady Hertford was attracted by the importance of Riskins in years gone by as a meeting place for some of the famous wits of the age, all friends of Bathurst's: Swift, Pope, Gay, Dr. Arbuthnot, Congreve, Prior, Bolingbroke, and Addison. Most of them were in their own way important gardeners or writers about gardening, but Lady Hertford seemed bewitched only by their literary fame. During one of her first spring walks through the arbors that were spread all over the landscape, she discovered something that with some exhilaration she related to Lady Pomfret: "We have an old covered bench with many remains of the wit of my Lord Bathurst's visitors, who inscribed verses upon it. Here is the writing of Addison, Pope, Prior, Congreve, Gay, and (what he esteemed no less) of several fine ladies."[31]

She cites one of these verses:

> Who set the trees shall he remember
> That is in haste to fell the timber?
> What then shall of thy woods remain,
> Except the box that threw the main?

With the large canal at Riskins providing the natural expanse of water that Cirencester lacked, Bathurst was fond of taking friends onto it in some "bark" constructed from timber he had felled, and the verses may allude to this. Without indulging in the speculation that Pope wrote these lines, we may note that they echo certain lines in his verse, as when Calypso tells Ulysses in book 5 of the *Odyssey*,

> Go, fell the timber of yon' lofty grove,
> And form a Raft . . .
>
> (210–11)

or when in his verses on *Gulliver's Travels* (1727) he has Glumdalclitch mourn over the vanished tiny Grildrig,

> Hast thou for these now ventur'd from the Shore
> Thy Bark a Bean-shell, and a Straw thy Oar?
> Or in thy Box, now bounding on the main?[32]

Be that as it may, Lady Hertford added one of her own verses to the old bench in memory of the glory with which these wits had endowed Riskins:

> By Bathurst planted, first these shades arose;
> Prior and Pope have sung beneath these boughs:
> Here Addison his moral theme pursu'd,
> And social Gay has cheer'd the solitude.

Lady Hertford's first reference to Riskins in a letter to Lady Pomfret in November 1739 also connects Pope with her new home:

We have now taken a house just by Colnbrook.[33] It belongs to my Lord Bathurst; and is what Mr. Pope, in his letters, calls his *extravagante bergerie*. The environs perfectly answer that title; and come nearer to my idea of a

71

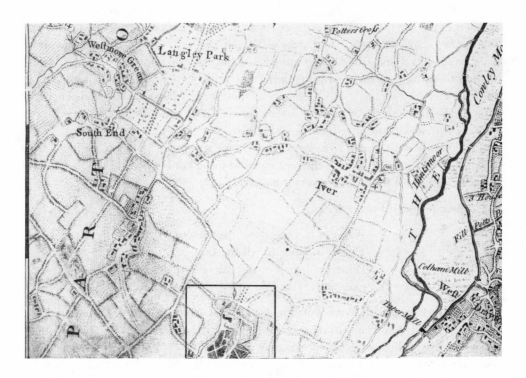

Plate 34. Detail of Riskins from J. Rocque, *Topographical Map of Middlesex* (1754), showing the gardens roughly as they were during Lady Hertford's ownership.

scene in Arcadia, than any place I ever saw. The house is old, but convenient;[34] and when you are got within the little paddock it stands in, you would believe yourself an hundred miles from London, which I think a great addition to its beauty.[35]

Fortunately, her letter apparently never reached Lady Pomfret so she had to write her another, more detailed description of Riskins the following April:

It stands in a little paddock of about a mile and a half round; which is laid out in the manner of a French park, interspersed with wood and lawns. There is a canal in it about twelve hundred yards long, and proportionably broad;[36] which has a stream continually running through it, and is deep enough to carry a pleasure-boat. It is well stocked with carp and tench; and at its upper [northern] end there is a green-house [orangery?] containing a good collection of orange, myrtle, geranium, and oleander trees. This is a very agreeable room; either to drink tea, play at cards, or sit in with a book, in a summer's evening.[37]

It is not clear what she meant by "in the manner of a French park," though the woods and lawns laid out along the central axis of the canal may have reminded her of the dominant canal treatment at Versailles and other less imperial French gardens (see plates 34 and 35).

Plate 35. Detail of "Percy Lodge," formerly called Riskins, from J. Rocque, *Topographical Map of Berkshire* (1761).

The navigable part of the water at Riskins was limited to the straight canal, but Lady Hertford speaks elsewhere of other waters in the grounds that were more naturalized and like serpentine brooks. Switzer's plan does not show it, but there was in Bathurst's time such a brook entering the estate from some meadows (not owned by Bathurst) to the northwest and winding its way to the head of the canal near which, according to Lady Hertford, sat the greenhouse or orangery. Before Switzer drew his "Epitomy," its course might have been underground, passing by the menagerie to the head of the canal. Sometime after this Bathurst turned it into a visual asset by widening it and bringing it to the surface—if, that is, we are to believe a writer over fifty years later who claimed that Bathurst "was the first person who ventured to deviate from straight lines, in a brook which he had widened at Riskins near Colnbrook. . . . Lord Strafford who paid him a visit remarked how little more it would have cost, to have made the course of the brook in a straight direction."[38]

It was in the area of the menagerie and labyrinth that Bathurst must have altered his landscape most after Switzer drew his "Epitomy." Further on in her letter to Lady Pomfret, Lady Hertford speaks of a romantic corner of the garden complete with a cave or grotto out of which issued a spring, "little more than a rude heap of stones . . . not without charms for me": "A spring gushes out at the back of it; which, falling into a basin (whose brim it overflows), passes along a channel in the pavement, where it loses itself." It could have been this grotto to which Robert Digby had referred on 2 July 1725, when he recalled the pleasures of Pope's and Gay's company in "the Temple, in the Greenhouse

& the Grotto" (2:305). By exposing what was until then probably a subterranean stream, in a single stroke Bathurst created a picturesque scene anticipating the cascades and springs in, for example, the Venus's Vale at Rousham and the Elysian Fields at Stowe. He then had the gardener's priceless and enviable commodity, a serpentine brook; all he needed was more space in which to scatter additional trees, position benches and statuary, and wind some paths.

Lady Hertford hints at how and where he realized the additional space in a letter to Lady Luxborough in 1742, where she mentions "a channel cut of 22 feet wide which falls into a [basin?] where the menagerie was, and from thence runs in a serpentine stream to the head of the canal, at the entrance of which it forms a cascade and falls about 18 inches."[39] The menagerie and, next to it, the traditional labyrinth or maze were among the few formal features of the garden that appear in Switzer's "Epitomy"; by replacing them with irregularly placed arbors, "through all which there are winding paths," Bathurst or his successors efficiently naturalized the garden. This is the sort of naturalization of which Pope was so fond in his own garden, and at Sherborne, Stowe, Marble Hill, and Bevis Mount. It especially consisted of the treatment of labyrinthine walks leading to secret arbors in groves bordering straight walks.

We do not know whether or not Bathurst had this little cascade of eighteen inches where the serpentine stream fell into the canal, which had an island in it,[40] but Lady Hertford says definitely that her husband was responsible for the (straight) channel, twenty-two feet wide, which emptied into a basin on the site of the old menagerie and flowed in a north-south direction. It was connected to the main canal by means of a basin and Bathurst's widened serpentine stream.[41] The Hertfords also purchased "a little pasture farm which is just without the pale because there is a very pretty brook of clear water which runs through the meadows to supply our canal, and whose course winds in such a manner that it is almost naturally a serpentine river." They clearly were fond of the water effects in the grounds. "I have a favourite elm," she told Lady Luxborough, "which is in the middle of one of the lawns and faces the canal just where the serpentine rivulet falls into it."[42] All in all, it appears that Lady Hertford's poetic tastes and temperament found congenial expression at Riskins in the romantic combination of woods, twisting paths, cascades, waterfalls, streams, meadows, and farmland. The Riskins gardens also illustrate that in the late 1730s and early 1740s the type of designs traditionally associated with Kent, what Spence called "painting in gardening" in the "national taste," was gaining wider acceptance. The fact also that it was connected with Pope and Bathurst makes it one of the important landscape gardens in the first half of the century.

The water at Riskins was always a source of pride for Bathurst and enjoyment for him and his friends, especially because until 1736 (the year after he relinquished Riskins to his son), Cirencester did not have any water. He was too sanguine when he told Pope in August of that year that the new lake at Cirencester would be "at least as big as the canal at Riskins" (4:25). Years earlier, about 1725, Pope wrote to Robert Digby (who was staying at Riskins) referring to Bathurst's projected "Improvements" in Lady Scudamore's landscape at Holm Lacy, from which he expected something like the "waters of *Riskins*, and the Woods of *Oakley* together, which (without Flattery) would be at least as good as any thing in our World." He hoped that Digby's sister, Mary, who was also staying with Bathurst, was making use of the *"Extravagante Bergerie,"* the lovely banks along the water to recover from her host's social "Ferment"—his "unwearied Request and Instigation" (2:314–15). If she were, however, she apparently ran the risk of being attacked by the ducks. Pope and Gay, too, had been set upon by these ducks earlier in the summer,[43] but this was only one of the aquatic surprises Riskins held in store for its guests. There was also the spectacle of Bathurst fishing for salmon in his canal[44] and an occasional boating on the waters—for which he was on the lookout for a gondola.[45]

Lady Hertford knew of the festivities that had flourished at Riskins when Bathurst played host to his friends, and she lyricized them in her poem on the "vacant hours (if such he knew)" he spent in Riskins' arbors:

> These arbours he for other guests had plann'd:
> Where wits might muse, or politics be scann'd.
> He stretch'd the lawn: and cut the smooth canal,
> Where Cleopatra's gilded bark might sail;
> Or nymphs more modern might admire the scene,
> Float on the wave, or dance upon the green![46]

She could not resist a critical reflection, however, upon Bathurst's instinct for vast landscaping:

> What strange delusions sway'd his tow'ring mind,
> To think himself for such a spot design'd . . .
> Within a pale of scarce two miles confin'd!

On the contrary, she pleaded forbearance for the "whimsically infectious" air of Riskins that urged her, like Bathurst, on to ambitious projects. In 1742 she mentioned some of these to Lady Luxborough, which "you would approve of."[47] That comment was more diplomatic than sincere, however, as we may gather from an incident that occurred in 1743. Bathurst came to call upon Lady Hertford bright and early one morning in May, even before her husband was up, to see the gardens. She graciously showed him her improvements but was amused that while he "seemed to approve" of them he managed to suggest about fifteen hundred pounds worth of what she deprecatingly described as "new decorations." "His eloquence strives in vain," she remarked after he had left, "to make me believe that this place wants any new ornaments to make it perfectly agreeable to my taste."[48]

If we follow her account of her alterations, we get a clearer idea still of what the garden looked like when Pope knew it. To begin with, her location of certain features, such as the stables and the kitchen garden, differs from their position in Switzer's "Epitomy." Since her letter dates from 1742, it is doubtful that she and her husband would have had time by then to make such major adjustments, especially since the relocation of the stables in the area of the old labyrinth probably meant that the main entrance to the estate was then from the west rather than from the east as Switzer pictured it. It therefore seems likely that Bathurst had changed the landscape extensively after Switzer drew his "Epitomy," though financial pressures, aggravated by his landscaping costs at Cirencester, probably compelled him to put a stop to the changes sometime before his son went to live there in 1735.

In the April 1740 letter to Lady Pomfret, Lady Hertford had mentioned the greenhouse (which doubled as an orangery) at the north end of the canal. Although in Switzer's "Epitomy" no greenhouse appears anywhere on the landscape, with only a grass parterre separating the north end of the canal from the main house, we know that a greenhouse, presumably the same one that Lady Hertford mentioned, existed at Riskins as early as July 1725.[49] We recall that Robert Dibgy had written to Pope that month envying him new "pleasures in the Temple, in the Greenhouse" (2:305). Lady Hertford also mentioned "a gravel-pit on the left hand as you went [west] from the greenhouse up to the arbour." This arbor was probably the new one that Bathurst created with the grotto in the area of the old menagerie and labyrinth because later she describes the spot as where the old menagerie was. If the gravel pit was in that area, it would have been well hidden by trees and reached by one of the several winding paths in the area. In describing the raised oval grass plot that Lord Hertford substituted for the gravel pit, she also says that the terraces around it bordered on the kitchen garden and a lane (I in plate 33). Switzer included the kitchen garden in the references to his plan, but forgot to identify it in the "Epitomy" itself; its location is therefore unknown before 1727. At least we know that in 1742—and most likely earlier—it was in that now crowded and irregular area of the old menagerie. The "channel cut of 22 feet wide" that ran along the western edge of this area was crossed by a bridge that led directly into the stables. It must have been a beautifully irregular litle area, full of surprises and variety, reminiscent of Pope's touch in his own garden. Also like Pope's garden, it contained formal features such as the oval grass plot, terraces, and the menagerie.

In a style possibly similar to the hexagon and octagon at Cirencester, Bathurst apparently began to build (according to Lady Hertford in her April 1740 letter) "in one of the woods on the farther side of the canal . . . a wooden building in a hexagon shape, which he never finished, and his succession [son] let run to ruin"; it was placed "as to see the water in two points of view." The "farther" side of the canal must have been the southwest portion of the landscape severed from the grounds around the house by the water, but it is not possible to be more precise except that it was near the water and commanded views of it in two directions. Lady Hertford also speaks of an ice house (which kept no ice) that they replaced with "a circle of horse chestnut trees." Ice houses were popular among Pope's friends. Henrietta Howard at Marble Hill, Bolingbroke at Dawley Farm, and Lord Peterborough at Bevis Mount, among others, had them.

Finally, one last feature the Countess mentions, one to which she was very partial from the start, is the Abbey Walk: "it is composed of prodigiously high beech-trees, that form an arch through the whole length, exactly resembling a cloister. At the end is a statue; and about the middle a tolerably large circle, with Windsor chairs round it: and I think, for a person of contemplative disposition, one would scarcely find a more venerable shade in any poetical description."[50] The name "Abbey Walk" and Lady Hertford's description show that the walk was deliberately conceived and ornamented to look like a Gothic cathedral. As we have seen, Pope was attracted by such use of "venerable" trees. He must have liked this treatment.

In addition to the more decorative aspects of the Riskins landscape that Lady Hertford inherited from Bathurst, its *ferme ornée* style caught her fancy, and she immediately got into the spirit of viewing herself a farmeress. Her explanation of the "convenience" of the landscape reveals this: "this is," she told Lady Pomfret in April 1740, "the cheap manner in which we keep it, since it only requires a flock of sheep who graze the lawns fine; and, whilst these are feeding, their shepherd cleans away any weeds that spring up in the gravel, and removes dry leaves or broken branches that would litter the walks."[51] In the same year she wrote a poem praising the life of "poultry, farms, and hay" that she led there.[52]

Riskins appears to have influenced the landscaping of Mrs. Howard's Marble Hill in Twickenham, where Bathurst, Pope and Peterborough teamed up as fellow gardeners beginning in 1724, though it is possible that any (unknown) alterations of the gardens at Riskins in the 1720s—the gardens Switzer knew—could, in turn, have been affected by the trio's designs at Marble Hill. Marble Hill was easily accessible to Bathurst from Riskins, and he could have conveniently sent over any materials and men needed in Mrs. Howard's gardens. The provision for livestock in the Marble Hill landscape was also indebted to Riskins, as Pope hints in some typical banter with Bathurst; if Bathurst will not "vouchsafe" to visit him at Twickenham, "let him (as the Patriarchs anciently did) send flocks of Sheep & Presents in his stead: For the grass of Marble hill springeth, yea it springeth exceedingly & waits for the Lambs of the *Mountains*, (meaning Riskins) to crop the same" (2:292). One of the few references by Bathurst himself to Riskins occurs, in fact, in a letter to Mrs. Howard about ten years later, when he alludes to her admiration of Riskins: "there is but one lady in the world that I desire to see there [in Alfred's Castle at Cirencester] and I fear I never shall have that satisfaction, though it is only to satisfy my curiosity whether she has any true taste or not, having given some marks of it by her appreciation of my works at Richkings, but no proofs of it by her own at Twickenham."[53]

Riskins must have begun to take on a deserted, though not neglected, look after Bathurst left it in 1735, though a number of Pope's friends continued to rely upon it as a convenient meeting place until then.[54] Understandably, from time to time Pope, especially, felt this. Cirencester claimed more and more of his friend's time, and he missed him; "I wish I had you at Riskins," he told Bathurst in December 1728, "So do many more here" (2:532). In 1732, while having William Cleland as a guest for seven days, Pope promised to take his guest and Dr. Arbuthnot to Riskins on an excursion: "I intend to carry them one day to Riskins with a cold dinner, purely to propagate the Fame of your gardens here, while you desert them" (3:295). By 1735, Pope's gardening world had changed drastically: not only had Riskins disappeared from his life, but so had Dawley Farm when Bolingbroke returned to France. To make things worse, Lord Peterborough died that year and Bevis Mount no longer held its remarkable attraction for him. In the wake of these events, Pope wrote Bathurst a touching, even pathetic, letter that summed up his feelings at the time. He says that at Stowe and Oxford, indeed everywhere he goes, he longs for his friend; "Your Lordship is almost my only Prop," he says, now that "two of those [Bolingbroke and Peterborough] with whom my soul rested & lean'd upon, are gone out of the Kingdom this Summer." He is feeling old and "dare hardly hope to enliven any Country Retreat so late in the year, & so late in my life," though he wishes he had gone on from Oxford to Cirencester—a "Place of Rest, where my Heart was at ease." Dull as he feels, he concludes that the "sacred silence & deep Contemplation of those groves, where 'Cum uxore & cum natis,/Dulcè ambulas in pratis, &c,'" would bear him up till the end of his life—"You animated my Youth, my Lord, Comfort my age!" (3:499–500). Largely because of the permanence of Cirencester and its lord, Pope's friendship with Bathurst, unlike that with any other of his gardening friends, did continue undiminished for the last nine years of his life.

The "joys of Nebuchadonozor"

Since in his moral poems of the 1730s Pope frequently exploited the satirical advantage deriving from the relatively diminutive size of his house and gardens—relative, that is, to the gardens of the aristocratic and landed friends he liked to visit—it is not surprising to witness in his correspondence with Bathurst his satisfaction with his littleness. He applied to Bathurst images of the "Beast" and the Patriarch to emphasize his friend's inexhaustible spirit and energy in gardening and in life generally.[55] At the same time, with these images and his reflections upon them Pope could underscore his littleness as the lord of the "Land ot Twitnam" in the face of the "absolute Monarch" of Cirencester's countless acres (see plate 36)[56]. Cirencester was important in his life partly because its vastness compelled him (not against his will) to play the Lilliputian to Bathurst's spirit of Brobdingnag. Psychologically, he needed to play on his own littleness as part of his strategy of control, as Maynard Mack has described it,[57] in order to deflate its impact on others, including his friends, and get them to laugh with him, not at him. He continually took refuge in his own projection of his friend's all-embracing capacities. He could thereby feel, especially when he was staying at Cirencester, cared for, protected, and sustained.

Lady Hertford had observed in her poem on Riskins that Bathurst's "tow'ring mind" could scarcely be accommodated by an estate whose perimeter measured less than two miles. At Cirencester it was another matter. One of the "rides" there alone was five miles long. The estate was perfectly suited to his expansive personality. He landscaped, planted (mainly trees), and built on a large scale in the park; and it amused both him and Pope that even so the achievements did not manage to keep pace with their plans and projects. Indeed, Cirencester Park epitomized him in many important ways. Pope liked to portray not only, as we have seen, this parallel between the man and his demesne but also the figure he himself cut next to Bathurst by comparing his own small demesne to Cirencester's immensity. He seems to have been particularly struck by this contrast in late summer 1725. The famous ancient royal gardens of the East came into his mind in August as fitting analogies to Cirencester. Adopting a garden-historical perspective, he confesses to Robert Digby in August 1725: "as to the hanging Gardens of *Babylon*, the Paradise of *Cyrus*, and the Sharawaggi's of *China*, I have little or no Ideas of 'em, but I dare say Lord B——t has, because they were certainly both very *Great*, and very *Wild*"

Plate 36. Kip's perspective view of Cirencester (1712), published in Sir Robert Atkyns's *The Ancient and Present State of Glostershire* (2nd ed., 1768).

(2:314–15). Compared with Bathurst's landscaping, he contentedly tells the Earl of Strafford a month later, his gardening reminded him of "the fellow that spent his life in cutting the twelve apostles in one cherry-stone" (2:328).

A very amusing exchange between the two men in September 1730 illustrates this point. Their gardens were at the center of the joke. Taking to heart the notion that Pope encouraged, that he was the poet's "master," Bathurst threatens to employ a heavy hand: "I'll cutt you off some little corner of my Park (500 or 1000 acres) which you shall do what you will with, & I'll immediately assign over to you 3 or 4 millions of plants out of my Nursery to amuse your self with." If that does not bring Pope, he threatens, in the style of one of the Eastern "Tyrants," to "send one of my wood-Carts & bring away your whole house & Gardens, & stick it in the midst of the Oakly-wood where it will never be heard off any more, unless some of the Children find it out in Nutting-season & take possession of it thinking I have made it for them" (3:134). Pope takes hold of Bathurst's fun and his reply shows the great pleasure he finds in playing the Lilliputian:

> I am sorry to find one I took for a Just Patriot, so tyrannical & oppressive in his disposition, as to think of taking from another his house & Lands, only

because they are less than his own. At this rate your Lordships poor Neighbours will fare ill, & all be swallowd in Oakley Wood. I hoped at least my Distance from you might have secur'd me from those terrible Designs of the Greater upon the Less. But if your Cart does come, & carry away my Buildings & Gardens it shall carry me too a-top of 'em; that I may be sure of a tight & safe Roof at least to lye under. . . . In good earnest, my Lord, I wish I were your Tenant in the Wood on any terms. (3:136)

He brings Martha Blount in on the joke, too, who he says offers herself to baby-sit for the children to whom Bathurst gives his house and gardens. Here one finds many of the ingredients that characterized their relationship: Bathurst's admiration of Pope's gardens and house and his understanding of the poet's relish over being esteemed a connoisseur of littleness; and Pope's respect for Bathurst's patriotism, fondness of his imperial disposition, and unending partiality for the area in the park known as Oakley Wood.

Pope benignly invokes the ghost of Nebuchadnezzar on a few occasions to suggest Bathurst's style of living and landscaping at Cirencester. It may have been Lord Bolingbroke, but it was probably Pope, who thought of wishing Bathurst in July 1732 "all the Joys of Nebuchadonozor, all the pensile Gardens, the proud Pyramids, the Ninevehs and Babels, to aggrandise and ornament your Territories; & that at length, you may be turn'd into a Happy Beast, loose among a thousand Females, to grass" (3:295). But he could turn the image upon himself ironically, as when he describes his own garden as no more than "a plate of Sallet to Nebuchadnezzar, the first day he was turn'd to graze" (2:328); or when he risks boasting about his "little kingdom" to Bishop Atterbury "like Nebuchadnezzar of the things I have made" (2:109).[58] Not without some earnestness, however, he complained to Lady Mary Wortley Montagu in September 1721 that a prolonged stay at Cirencester was liable to make him forget his own "little *Colifichies* [at Twickenham] in the daily Views of the noble Scenes, Openings, & Avenues of this immense Design at Cicester" (2:82). Lady Mary, gratifyingly, had just praised his Great Walk and put him in mind again of the example of precocity in miniature at his own doorstep.

Pope also complained occasionally of having to walk too much at Cirencester. The walk from the "bower" in Oakley Wood to the main house alone came close to finishing him off. By 1737 he was obliged to travel around Cirencester Park in a "chaise or chariot" (4:85). Remembering his last visit to England in 1727, Swift complained similarly to Bathurst of being compelled to "walk two miles to dinner with your 2500 acres of garden and not a codling to eat."[59] All of this walking suited Bathurst's regimen perfectly, and his commitment to exercise,[60] but to Pope these uses of the gardens may at times have seemed borrowed from a chapter out of Timon's book of horrors. Timon's vast gardens compelled visitors on the way into the house to sweat "thro' the length of yon hot Terrace" and drag their thighs "up ten steep slopes."[61]

Nonetheless, although the immensity of Cirencester disturbed Pope (as we shall see) on several counts, both aesthetic and moral, the stability inherent in an estate of that scale owned by a Tory sympathizer and landscaped with a freshness and a spirit of modernity enabled Pope to relax with the owner and revel in his eccentricities—something he could never do with the contemporary Timons. In addition to the psychic reassurance that Bathurst's stature and his landscape's huge scale gave Pope, the extensive planting of trees there was to him another example of morally superior Tory ideas about the uses of land. When Bathurst had joked with Swift about his fears that Walpole might take a fancy to Cirencester's acres and desire to appropriate them as an appendage to Houghton Hall (one of the most probable models for Pope's sketch of Timon's villa)[62]—"to place them as an Iland in one of his new-made fish-ponds" or to hang out under a "great Bow-window"—he let fall that he would not like it because Houghton was, in effect, a depressing example of the Whig effort to demonstrate supremacy through rapidly purchased and ill-conceived landscapes exploiting land purely for show. "In the first place," he told Swift, "I am not sure his new-made ground may hold good, in the latter case I have some reason to doubt the foundations of his House are not so solid as he may imagine."[63]

Cirencester: From "*Cotswold* Hills to *Saperton*'s fair dale"

From the start, Bathurst distinguished himself for his afforestation at Cirencester; "Who plants like BATHURST . . . ?" Pope asks in *To Burlington*, thinking of the "willing woods" (line 62) that his friend joined and planted through a comprehensive scheme of forest gardening that eventually covered thousands of acres from Sapperton to the west, acquired from the estate of the historian Sir Robert Atkyns in 1716, all the way east through Oakley Park to Home Park adjacent to the main house (see Samuel Rudder's plans of Oakley Great Park and Home Park, plates 37 and 38).[64]

The extension of the estate through the acquisition of Sapperton gave Bathurst five miles of generally level, though not flat, land in the northern parts of which springs give birth to the Thames and flow westward to the Severn.[65] He therefore had scope for extensive gardening, but his plantations were not exclusively comprised of vast wildernesses of forestry through which straight avenues ran uninterrupted for miles on end.[66] They were instead linked or, as Pope put it, joined by avenues radiating from "rond-points" and lined up with vistas of distant points in the surrounding countryside or with focal points within the park itself. With these avenues Bathurst was able to establish sections in the landscape having individual character. These were decorated with temples, buildings, seats, and the like about which more will be said later. Thus he satisfied, first Addison's, then Switzer's, relish for whole plantations thrown into a kind of scenic park.

Extensive gardening at Cirencester also included farming, from which Bathurst derived most of his estate income.[67] In his capacity as landlord, he was proud of his benevolence, as he confided to Swift in 1737: "my chief business is to take care that my Agents don't impose upon my tenants. I am for letting them all good bargains that my Rents may be pay'd as long as any rents can be pay'd, & when the time comes that there is no money, they are honest fellows & will bring me in corn & cattle I shall want."[68] It is Bathurst's farming, as well as his forestry, that Pope records and celebrates in his *Imitation*

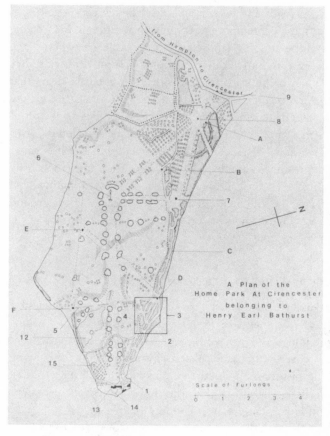

A Plan of the
Home Park At Cirencester
belonging to
Henry Earl Bathurst

Scale of Furlongs

Plate 37. Samuel Rudder's Plan of Home Park, Cirencester, from *A New History of Gloucestershire* (London, 1779). See plate 38 also for references given here. References: A. Pope's Seat; B. the Octagon; C. the Venetian Building; D. the Hexagon; E. Hartley's Temple; F. Horse Temple; G. Alfred's Hall and Garden; 1. entrance; 2. "strip" of wilderness; 3. widened area in the wilderness; 4. terracing; 5. ha-ha?; 6. obelisk; 7. convergence point of two vistas; 8. "rond-point"; 9. the Round Tower; 10. "rond-point"; 11. Sapperton Park and Plantation; 12. lake; 13. house; 14. tall yew hedge; 15. mount. Redrawn by Ian Teh, with references to garden features added.

of the Second Epistle of the Second Book of Horace; at the same time he bears witness to the large canvas on which the Earl traces his creations:

> Join *Cotswold* Hills to *Saperton*'s fair Dale,
> Let rising Granaries and Temples here,
> There mingled Farms and Pyramids appear,
> Link Towns to Towns with Avenues of Oak,
> Enclose whole Downs in Walls . . .

(257–61)

The passage hints at the integration of farming, forestation, and landscaping at Cirencester—the use of the landscape that justified its existence regardless of its ownership or longevity.

Given Cirencester's vastness, however, it would have been surprising if Cirencester Park and its lord, in spite of Pope's intimate connection with both, had escaped entirely some satiric reflections from his pen. We have just noted the irony of his reflections on Bathurst's "vast Possessions . . . Whether you call them Villa, Park, or Chace," and certainly there was a little implied criticism in those jokes about Bathurst's patriarchal

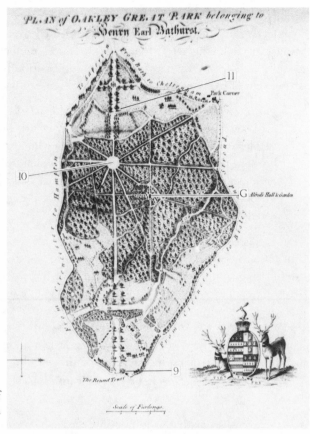

Plate 38. Samuel Rudder's plan of Oakley Great Park, Cirencester, from *A New History of Gloucestershire*.

lifestyle and tastes, the need for a cart to get around the estate, Swift's complaint about having to walk two miles to dinner, and so on. In a note to the "Argument" of *To Burlington*, Pope would castigate Timon for imagining that "Greatness *consists in the* Size *and* Dimension, *instead of the* Proportion *and* Harmony *of the* whole."[69] Quickly it should be noted that when in the poem he indicts Brobdingnagian landscapes such as Timon's, Pope is thinking chiefly of Blenheim Palace and Walpole's Houghton Hall; moreover, the poem specifically compliments Bathurst for the "encrease" (line 182) of his lands that enables him to be a good landlord. Still, two satiric passages in the poem probably also allude to what Pope thought was a landscaping blunder by Bathurst at Cirencester in 1728. An incident that occurred in the summer of 1728, not very long before Pope started to write *To Burlington*, might well have accounted for the small amount of fallout that settled on Bathurst from the general attack.

 On a visit to Cirencester in August 1728, Pope was surprised to find that Bathurst was not at home when he arrived. His lordship frequently was late for appointments, but Pope was surprised when days later he still had not turned up. While he waited he naturally had a good look at the landscape, particularly his favorite spot, Oakley Wood. He was distressed to find that Bathurst, in what he construed as a barbaric spirit, had denuded a section of "the great Vista in Oakley wood"—the Broad Avenue—almost completely of its mature and freshly transplanted trees. Pope must have been outraged because in a follow-up letter to Bathurst of 15 September he snapped that he was obliged to wait "four & twenty days" as a cooling-off period before writing. He wrote, with a strong vein of irony, as follows:

> However my Visit to your House was not wholly void of all Comfort to me: for I saw the Steeple of Ciceter stand on one side over it, and the great Vista in Oakley wood to the said Steeple by being widened beyond its former Hedges, borderd now only with some low thing which I took to be a Box-Edging on either side: Moreover I beheld with singular consolation the Back of the high Wood piercd thro, & every Tree that bore the least pretence to be Timber, totally cut down & done away. (2:517)

It was Bathurst's apparent impulsiveness that disturbed Pope. Perhaps he made a connection between this behavior and Villario's in his poem. After "ten-years toil" of careful landscaping, Villario suddenly tires of the whole business and "finds at last he better likes a Field" (87–88). Villario's recourse to a field brings to mind Pope's several jokes about Bathurst's compulsion to behave like a "Beast" in the field. It also hints at the poet's suspicion that large landowners are led into temptation in ways a gardener like himself, of a small demesne, can only guess at. For all his good sense, Bathurst may have had difficulty controlling his impulse for the grand or sweeping.

Continuing his letter, Pope rubs salt into what he sees as Bathurst's self-inflicted wounds:

> Wherby I see with delight not only the bare Prospect you have made, but also another, of the Necessity you are now reduced to, of raising some Building there: And I form to myself yet a third prospect, that you will so unwillingly & grudgingly undertake the said building [probably because of the cost], that it will be so small & inconsiderable as to oblige you to pull it down again another year, to erect a bigger & more adequate. Nevertheless my Lord (to prove I am not angry, but with a mixture of charity inclind to rectify, what I disapprove) I would not advise you to an obelisque which can bear no Diameter to fill so vast a Gap unless it literally touch'd the Skies; but rather to a solid Pyramid of 100 ft square, to the end there may be Something solid and Lasting of your works. (2:517)

A pyramid of that size, even for a patriarchal figure like Bathurst, would have been a bit ambitious, but Pope's anger and disappointment are understandable. It was the lovely trees of Oakley Wood that he first admired at Cirencester. He was especially fond of its "silvan Bower" or seat and soon began to refer to it as "the silvan seat" (1:488) or "my Bower" (1:515). His first recorded visit to Bathurst's "wood," as Oakley Wood and the bower affectionately came to be known to Pope and his friends, was in July 1718; during the rest of that year alone he visited it at least three times, commuting, as it were, between there and Stanton Harcourt while he worked on his translation of the *Odyssey*. "The minute I find there's no hopes of you," he announced to Teresa and Martha Blount in August, "I fly to the Wood. It is as fit for me to leave the World, as for you to stay in it" (1:490). Two months later with obvious relish he told them again about his life in the bower: "I am with my Lord Bathurst, at my Bower, in whose Groves we had yesterday a dry walk of three hours. It is the place that of all others I fancy, & I am not yet out of humour with it, tho I have had it some months." With his taste for the pictorial, he told the girls, he even reveled in the beauty of autumn there—"the very dying of the leaves adds a variety of colours that is not unpleasant" (1:515). In May 1722 he wanted to guide Robert Digby's sister, Mary, "thro' that enchanted Forest" of which he saw himself "as the Magician appropriated to the place, without whom no mortal can penetrate into the Recesses of those sacred Shades. I could pass whole Days, in only describing to her the future, and as yet visionary Beauties, that are to rise in those Scenes (2:115–16). And yet, here was Bathurst in 1728 hacking away at Oakley Wood just like those "leading Critics" of gardening Pope had blasted in a letter to his friend nine years earlier, critics who "are for rooting up more than they plant" and manage to banish half the trees from gardens (2:14).

Pope's reaction to his friend's deforestation may also be understood in psychological terms that point up a link between that reaction and his gardening ideas. As Professor Hunt observed, Pope's allusion to himself as a magician in Bathurst's "enchanted Forest" underlines his provision for the role of dreams and visions in a garden. He measured Oakley Wood's value as a garden, as he did his own garden, Stowe's Elysian Fields, and all the major landscapes featured in this book, partly by how readily he could imagine a world of romance and fantasy within its recesses. As if to find solace, he told the Blount sisters, he could "fly to the Wood" and thus "leave the World"; or he could inhabit a world of fancy in "My Bower"—note the possessiveness. He saw himself there as something of a Spenserian protagonist amid blissful shades. "Mr Gay is as zealously carry'd to the Bower by the force of Imagination," he had told Bathurst back in 1718, "as ever Don Quixote was to an Enchanted Castle" (1:477). A prerequisite for entering this sanctuary was the ability to see "visionary Beauties." When Bathurst cut down the trees, the spell was broken. Pope's psychic disturbance is understandable.

It has been suggested that Bathurst may have done this to clear an area for what became known as the Seven Rides, shown by Samuel Rudder in his *History of Gloucestershire* as a large opening in the woods with seven rides leading off concentrically in all directions.[70] In any case, Pope did not think it was justified. Could Bathurst have passed through his mind when he decided to slip these lines into *To Burlington* describing landscaping that is done without "Sense":

> Or cut wide views thro' Mountains to the Plain,
> You'll wish your hill or shelter'd seat again.
> Ev'n in an ornament its place remark . . .
>
> (75–77)

Although in a note to these lines Pope, anticipating the Man of Ross syndrome that he would generate in the *Epistle to Bathurst*, remarks that a "wealthy citizen" in Hertfordshire did this by removing some beautiful woods at a cost of 5,000 pounds,[71] that specific dramatic example is, like Timon, one instance of a general malaise in English landscaping to which Pope is alluding. The word "ornament" in its satiric application could be read to include the pyramid Pope facetiously suggested to fill up the space and all such structures set up by landscapers who had insufficient regard for the "Genius of the Place." He did mention a pyramid in his description of Cirencester quoted above— "there mingled Farms and Pyramids appear"—and in 1732 he and Bolingbroke continued the joke, wishing Bathurst all "the proud Pyramids, the Ninevehs and Babels, to aggrandise and ornament your Territories" (3:295).

There could also be a partial allusion to Bathurst's blunder in the passage describing Sabinus and his son, if we think of Sabinus as an oblique allusion to Bathurst's father, Sir Benjamin, and his son as Bathurst himself:

> Thro' his young Woods how pleas'd Sabinus stray'd,
> Or sat delighted in the thick'ning shade,
> With annual joy the red'ning shoots to greet,
> Or see the stretching branches long to meet!
> His Son's fine Taste an op'ner Vista loves,
> Foe to the Dryads of his Father's groves,
> One boundless Green, or flourish'd Carpet views,
> With all the mournful family of Yews;
> The thriving plants ignoble broomsticks made,
> Now sweep those Alleys they were born to shade.
>
> (89–98)

Sabinus's son has replaced his father's nobler forest trees with evergreens, particularly yews, so as "to make way for such little ornaments as Pyramids of dark-green, continually repeated, not unlike a Funeral procession."[72] Pope belittles his entire impulsive landscape scheme by imagining the yews as no more than rows of suspended broomsticks perpetually engaged in the mockery of sweeping a boundless or endless capet of lawn that has been unrolled between them. To Pope this scene is the antithesis of a noble alley of venerable trees simulating a Gothic cathedral. It is superificial and merely clever.

These images, particularly the one of the brooms, may perhaps be ironically glimpsed in Pope's anonymous *Master Key to Popery*.[73] Pretending to be another outraged critic of *To Burlington*, he ridicules this inimical reading-between-the-lines of his poem by finding another victim that no one else has found—Bathurst. He achieves his parody of the critics, but in the guise of "defending" Bathurst against the writer of the epistle, he mentions enough accurate details about him and his landscaping perhaps to imply that Bathurst, after all, may fit into the satiric picture. In that event, the burlesque would be double-edged and carefully disguised—disguised if in his comments on the above passage about Sabinus and his son, he vaguely identifies Bathurst with Sabinus and his son Benjamin with Sabinus's son: "If he [Lord Burlington] had one [a male heir], he had been probably treated like another of his *Friends*, the Lord Bathurst: whose noble Plantations at Cirencester he prophecy's with like Malignity shall be destroy'd & lay'd levell by his Lordships *Son*; for which no doubt, that ingenious and sober young Gentleman is much oblig'd to him."

After quoting the lines, he remarks, "I wonder this piece of Malice has escap'd all the Criticks; and I suspect it was to screen this Author, that his gentle Friend Lord Fanny [Lord Hervey] apply'd to this Nobleman the Character of Villario." There then follows the description of Villario from the Epistle, the last two lines of which are:

> Tir'd with the Scene Parterre & Fountains yield,
> He finds at last he better likes a Field.
>
> (87–88)

Lord Hervey, or Sporus—the "mere white Curd of Ass's milk" in Pope's *Epistle to Dr. Arbuthnot* (line 306)—was probably the last man in England who would defend Pope from anything. In addition to parodying Hervey and perhaps alluding somewhat to Bathurst in the Sabinus passage, the Villario imputation enables Pope to add the humorous reflection that Bathurst, like the "Beast" Pope often good-naturedly likened him to, finds "he better likes a Field." Ironically defending Bathurst even from this Villario charge, Pope pokes fun at his taste for wide open spaces and asserts some facts about his landscaping: "For first, my Lord Bathurst is known to be of the most constant temper in the world in all his Pleasures: Secondly, he never was a *Florist*, is so much an Enemy to *nice Parterres*, that he never mows, but grazes them, & thirdly, has no water at Cirencester to squander away in Mænders."

Turning now to Pope's contribution to the landscaping at Cirencester,[74] we discover that it began almost immediately after he saw it for the first time in July 1718. On that occasion he went with Gay; the planting was then still in its very early stages, but that did not prevent either of them from being thoroughly delighted. Like Don Quixote in an enchanted castle, Gay saw the wood as a cave of Montesinos, "planted" it with myrtles, and peopled it with nymphs. Besides trees, the only thing lacking was water—"a Christal Rivulet to purl thro the Shades." But unlike Bathurst's friend and "prose-man," Erasmus Lewis,[75] neither Gay nor Pope owned that he was disturbed by this. Gay wrote a little pastoral poem about Cirencester, which has been lost, in which he resolved to include an abundance of woods and water.[76] Pope, too, was resolved to hear "no reasons" against the wood, but he could not resist offering a jaunty little verse about Lewis's objections in his "Lines to Bathurst":

> A Wood? quoth Lewis; and with that,
> He laughd, and shook his Sides so fat:
> His tongue (with Eye that markd his cunning)
> Thus fell a reas'ning, not a running.
>   Woods are (not to be too prolix)

Collective Bodies of strait Sticks.
It is, my Lord, a meer Conundrum
To call things Woods, for what grows und'r 'em.
For Shrubs, when nothing else at top is,
Can only constitute a Coppice.

. . . .

If this a Wood you will maintain
Meerly because it is no Plain;
Holland (for all that I can see)
Might e'en as well be termd the Sea.[77]

The lack of water at Cirencester, however, remained a serious flaw in the middle of a gardening movement that set a high premium on water effects. Six of the Timon sketch's fourteen lines attacked the aridity of Timon's gardens, though he (unlike Bathurst) aggravated the problem with ludicrous garden ornaments embracing water that was not there. It is not clear whether Bathurst was thinking of the absence of water or the planting to date when, inviting Pope for another visit on 14 August, he referred to his garden as "oddly bad"; but he urged the poet to be "as free with it as if it were entirely your own" in giving his opinion of how it came to be that way: "You know there is nothing in it can be spoilt" (1:488).

By October 1718 they were both deep in projects and plans. Pope reported faithfully to the Blount sisters, "I write an hour or two every morning, then ride out a hunting upon the Downes, eat heartily, talk tender sentiments with Lord B. or draw Plans for Houses and Gardens, open Avenues, cut Glades, plant Firrs, contrive water-works, all very fine and beautiful in our own imagination" (1:515). Bathurst's search for prospects and new avenues remained theoretical until he decided he would lay aside theory and go "directly to Practice" in September 1719. "Alas, what a Fall will that be?" Pope mused; "A new Building is like a new Church, when once it is set up, you must maintain it in all the forms, and with all the inconveniences; then cease the pleasant luminous days of inspiration, and there's an end of miracles at once!" (2:14). We do not know for certain what this building was, but the avenues and glades they were planning must have been in Oakley Wood, perhaps in a long strip of probably recently planted "wilderness" along the northern boundary of the estate extending from the house to the wood (2 in plate 33). This strip, eventually threaded with winding paths, was needed as a picturesque and "secret" access to the wood, so it must have had early priority in any new designs. Rudder described a serpentine walk through this strip turning off to the west directly from the main entrance to the house:

> Turning to the right . . . the walk divides; one branch leading to the terrace [4]
> the other running by the side of it, in a serpentine direction above a mile in
> length finely arched over and shaded by a thick plantation of firs, beech, and
> other woods, through which it passes. At suitable distances it communicates
> with the terrace, where are several buildings and benches, for the con-
> venience of shelter and rest.[78]

This terrace, as Rudder described it, is reminiscent of the northern terraces at Sherborne as Pope was to describe them in 1724. Rudder said:

> The terrace is sheltered on the north by flowering shrubs and ever-greens, completely covered for their height the thick plantation, thro' whose shady arcades and bowers the serpentine walk meanders. It is separated from the Deer-park, to the southward, by a low cut hedge and fosse, over which it commands a distant prospect of the north of Wiltshire; and it terminates at a handsome building called the Octagon [B] about a mile from the mansion-house.[79]

The benches and buildings on the terrace, which in Rudder's plan include the Octagon (B) and the Venetian Building (C), were never specified by either Bathurst or Pope in their correspondence, though from time to time they did mention, as Pope did above, that certain buildings and monuments were being planned and put up. It is therefore difficult to pin down the evolution of the landscape in terms of these structures.

Such structures, which in 1722 were yet only "visionary Beauties," were part of a comprehensive landscaping scheme. Pope spoke of the "Palace that is to be built, the Pavillions that are to glitter, the Colonnades that are to adorn them: Nay more, the meeting of the *Thames* and the *Severn*, which (when the noble Owner has finer Dreams than ordinary) are to be led into each other's Embraces thro' secret Caverns of not above twelve or fifteen Miles, till they rise and openly celebrate their Marriage in the midst of an immense Amphitheatre, which is to be the Admiration of Posterity a hundred Years hence" (2:116). Here was extensive gardening indeed. Through this Thames-Severn canal, an engineering feat whose "destin'd time" Pope did not think would come for a century,[80] Bathurst showed himself every bit as ambitious as everyone thought. As for the "Palace," Pope might have been referring facetiously to the alteration of the "Sylvan Bower" or wood house.

Work on the wood house was about to begin in September 1721, since in that month Bishop Atterbury wished them speedy success with it (2:85), but apparently it was delayed because two years later Bathurst is tempting Pope to visit him with a scheme "to begin the alteration of my wood house, and some little baubling works about it, which you shall direct as you will" (2:207).[81] Thinking of expensive long-term projects like the tunnel and glittering pavilions and colonnades, Bathurst ruefully adds that he has tired himself "with computations and designs of things which cannot be completed in my own time" (2:207); he wants to get on with what can be finished. In time he became financially pressed with his landscaping at two estates and gradually became a little more conservative over the projects that he and Pope were proposing but for which he alone would have to pay. He complained to Mrs. Howard in 1734 that "instead of admiring (as he ought to do) what is already executed," Pope is "every day drawing me a plan for some new building or other, and then is violently angry that it is not set up the next morning."[82] That was just the nature of Lady Hertford's complaint about Bathurst's visit to Riskins several year later; like Pope, Bathurst was not averse to ambitious landscaping schemes if someone else was paying for them.

By the time the wood house was complete in July 1732, it had become a castellated folly known as Alfred's Hall or King Arthur's Castle—the first, says Hussey, in a long line of such follies.[83] Eagerly inviting Pope to see it, Bathurst enjoyed the sensation of another achievement in the spirit of Brobdingnag: "I long to see you excessively, for I have now almost finished my hermitage in the wood, and it is better than you can imagine, and many other things are done that you have no idea of. . . . I will venture to assert that all Europe cannot show such a pretty little plain work in the Brobdingnag style as what I have executed here" (3:299–300).

Bathurst must have turned the wood house into a castellated "hermitage" between 1727 and 1733. Mrs. Pendarves wrote to Swift in October 1733 that Bathurst did not begin until after 1727, the year Swift saw Cirencester for the last time, because when he saw it the wood house still looked like a cottage, "not a bit better than an Irish cabin." "It is now a venerable castle," she added, "and has been taken by an Antiquarian for one of King Arthur's 'with thicket overgrown, grotesque and wild.'"[84]

During the 1720s Bathurst was occupied with a good many other landscaping projects besides the wood house, some which Pope had "no idea of." Pope was aware of some sort of scheme Bathurst dreamed up for Leighs, the Essex estate of Katherine Sheffield, the Duchess of Buckingham. Pope himself may have been doing some garden planning for the Duchess as early as his first recorded visit to Leighs in 1724 (2:259). He was a regular guest there of the dowager Duchess. Probably Bathurst himself decided to come to the aid of the Duchess, and he and Pope planned some comprehensive (and expensive) scheme at Leighs. Pope undoubtedly disappointed Bathurst when he wrote to him in November 1728 with the news that while the Duchess was "wishing (she tells me) to execute your Lordships Schemes," she believed that "they must be left to the Duke's & your own Riper Judgment, seven years hence" (2:525). The Duchess probably hesitated to commit the young Duke, who would not reach his majority for seven years, to such expenses. But conceivably Pope's mention of Bathurst's "Riper Judgment" implied the Duchess's conservatism in the face of Bathurst's ambitious designs. Her caution recalls Lady Hertford's at Riskins. At the same time, Pope told Bathurst he would be happy to use an annuity he had purchased from the Duchess, should he die in a year, to pay for a new pond in her garden. This raises the possibility that Bathurst was planning a large pond, perhaps even an "ocean," for Leighs. Pope also said he would not mind using the money to add an obelisk to the Cirencester garden should he die.

Another garden plan at Cirencester around 1728 was perhaps conceived entirely by Pope. On the back of a sheet on which he translated the *Odyssey* 10, lines 293–318, Pope sketched a plan for a labyrinthine walk in a garden.[85] The sketch dates from spring 1724, a time when Bathurst probably was still busy cutting his paths all over Oakley Wood and through the strip of wilderness already mentioned. Though some modifications may have been made over the intervening fifty years, Rudder's plan nonetheless shows a section (3) of this strip that resembles the shape and treatment of Pope's labyrinthine section. It must remain conjecture, but Pope's sketch of a serpentine path aligned to create surprises could have been intended for that section of Bathurst's garden. Rudder's plan shows that the strip of wilderness widens at this point, indicating perhaps that some special effects were designated for the area. Only just over half a mile from the house, the spot would have been in a prominent position, and from the terrace bordering it on the south the place would have commanded some fine views across Home Park. It would have been worthy of the poet's special attention.

Another major modification was carried out in 1728. It was the one that denuded an area by the Broad Avenue and angered Pope. Bathurst widened the Broad Avenue or Great Walk and extended it at the same time; thereby he managed to align it with the Cirencester church so that from any point on the avenue one could see the church steeple. According to Mrs. Pendarves, who saw it in 1733, the "grand avenue that goes from his [Bathurst's] house through his Park and wood" was by then five miles long, though not continuous. Mr. Lees-Milne noted that Home Park and Oakley Park were still separated in 1775 by a road and that about one mile of the eastern end of the Broad Walk was planted after that year. Mrs. Pendarves remarked that "when the whole design is executed it will be one of the finest places in England," but doubtless neither she nor anyone could have guessed that Bathurst's financial constraints would delay the completion of this master plan until after 1775.[86]

In the patriotic spirit of the "Great and Noble Works" that at the conclusion of *To Burlington* Pope urged Lord Burlington to pursue, Bathurst planned the following sensational projects for Cirencester in 1730: "Enclosing a Province with Walls of Stone, planting a whole Country with Clumps of Firs, digging Wells (which were extremely wanted in those parts for the very necessities of Life) as deep as to the Center, erecting Palaces, raising Mounts, undermining High ways, & making Communications by Bridges" (3:130). Available evidence, however, suggests that the large projects that Bathurst had in mind involved only the raising of buildings and monuments. Pope received from him in August 1736 two plans for a building that they had discussed previously and for which "a great quantity of very good hewn stone from the old house at Saperton" had been brought "to the great centre in Oakley wood" (4:25). The building was to be "backed with wood" so that only three of its sides were to be seen; it had to be this shape, said Bathurst, because "it is to answer three walks." The building was probably the Hexagon (D), since Rudder's plan shows three principal walks (probably dating from the 1730s) leading to the Hexagon (plate 39), located at the northwest corner of the widened area discussed above. Bathurst also remarks that the materials had to be the same as those of the "seat" because they had already been brought to the spot and he thought the "rough stone exceedingly pretty, and am ready to stand all the jokes of *Rusticus expectat*" (4:25).[87]

This seat, the same one later known as Pope's Seat, was already in place, then, by 1736. As an afterthought, Bathurst considered adding a cupola to the Hexagon, "to try the effect of the Cornish slate," the ribs of which would be done in lead and gilded or painted with gold color set off by blue slate. He was uncertain how to design the fascias and cornice, however, and thus left it to Pope to decide. He also mentions another building that was to be erected later "to answer the other diagonal which will also

Plate 39. The Hexagonal Building, Cirencester Park. Photo courtesy of William Brogden.

overlook the lake, no contemptible body of water I can assure you." This second building is almost certainly the Horse Temple (F) located across Home Park from the Hexagon and very close to the lake (12). The lake, incidentally, was painstakingly man-made without any assistance from accessible natural sources of water and was, according to Hussey, one of the first made to follow natural contours. There must have been a fine view of it from the house and from the terrace on the other side of the park. One last project that Bathurst mentions is an obelisk (6) "to terminate the view" from the house. He has already begun "to level the hill before the house" to accommodate it, so that when eventually the Doric column was raised in 1741, it sat on a truncated plateau.[88] This project, as well as the others, awaited Pope, who was giving "orders" again in August 1737 when he told Ralph Allen that before he could "be of any Service" at Prior Park he had to stay at least one week at Cirencester "to set some Works of my Lords, and some Buildings forward, setling Plans, &c" (4:84).[89]

We may conclude this survey of Cirencester Park by looking at its landscape from Rudder's point of view. About halfway along the serpentine walk, he says, you arrive at the Hexagon,

> which you ascend by a flight of half a dozen steps. It faces a vista, which
> crosses the park at right angles with the terrace, and terminates with another

little structure called the *Horse-temple*. At the end of the serpentine walk is a small building called *Pope's* Seat . . . where eight vistas concentre, and direct to prospects of neighboring churches, and other agreeable objects. One of those objects is a fine lofty column in the midst of the deer-park, supporting a colossal statue of queen Anne.

From near the Venetian Building (C), continues Rudder, the lake is clearly visible; it

looks like part of a considerable river; but 'tis only a pleasing deception, for nature, as to that element, hath dealt her favours to this place with so sparing a hand, that there is not perhaps a perennial spring to be found within it. This agreeable deception is produced by planting clumps of trees to conceal the extremities of the lake . . . [90]

One thing Bathurst was not was a version of Horace's country bumpkin waiting for miracles of nature to transform his landscape. He fully intended to make his estate one of the finest in England. If he did not, his impediment was a lack not of talent or will, but of money. His forest planting cost him enormous amounts, and these buildings and monuments he was raising were further drains upon his relatively limited resources. One could not say that he was guided by Pope's moral reflections about how estates, like fortunes, "have wings, and hang in Fortune's pow'r." When Pope made a special point of getting this message across in his *Second Epistle of the Second Book of Horace*, he had Bathurst in mind as he asked,

> All vast Possessions (just the same the case
> Whether you call them Villa, Park, or Chace)
> Alas, my BATHURST! what will they avail?
>
> (254–56)

"'Tis all a joke!" he exclaimed,

> Inexorable Death shall level all,
> And Trees, and Stones, and Farms, and Farmer fall.
>
> (261–63)

And yet Pope appears to have encouraged this disposition in *his* Bathurst to create great things. If Swift had been as close a friend of Bathurst's as he was of Bolingbroke's, he probably would have warned him, as he did Bolingbroke, of the dangers of landscaping prodigality. But Pope lived with emotional attachments to Cirencester that prevented him from doing that.

Soon after Bathurst's death in 1775 his son, the second Earl, wrote to his agent, Mr. Porter, about intended improvements to the house and garden at Cirencester: "All these things are expensive but the Desire I have of making my Father's Works as beautiful as can be will make me readily submit to the Expence for two or three years." Elsewhere he spoke of an invasion of rabbits between the Hexagon and Horse Temple and mentioned that "there were walks markd out from the Horse Temple to the Seat round the trees [?], and from thence to the new building and from that building to the Hexagon." He added that he wished to have these walks made "particularly fine . . . indeed, it will be my Desire to have the whole Park made as fine and rich as possible."[91] Thanks to this kind of eager desire for continuity at Cirencester on the part of the second and later Earls of Bathurst, much of Bathurst's and Pope's original landscaping has been preserved down to the present day.

4

Sherborne Castle

A "Situation of so uncommon a kind"

Pope took only one ramble in 1724.[1] He went to the Digby estate at Sherborne in Dorset and hoped to include a stopover at Wilton.[2] On 15 June he was on his way, but by then either had not yet arrived at Sherborne or had so recently arrived that he had not yet walked in the gardens. His letter to Martha Blount on that day, her birthday, was sent to Twickenham, where in his absence she was staying with his mother. He wrote:

> I know you wou'd both be pleas'd to hear some certain news of a friend departed; to have the adventures of his passage, and the new regions thro' which he travell'd, describ'd; and upon the whole, to know, that he is as happy where he now is, as while he liv'd among you. But indeed I (like many a poor unprepar'd soul) have seen nothing I like so well as what I left: No scenes of paradise, no happy bowers, equal to those on the banks of the Thames. (2:236)

His intended allegory here, incidentally, is psychologically revealing. He sees his rambles to and through gardens as a magical journey to celestial paradises, but none of the scenes he discovers can respond to his emotional needs as well as the garden-paradise he left behind. His follow-up letter to Martha on 22 June mentions that while he had, before he left home, perfunctorily promised to describe for her the gardens there, he now is alive with excitement over what he has seen:

> I promisd you an account of Sherborne, before I had seen it, or knew what I undertook. I imagind it to be one of those fine old Seats of which there are Numbers scatterd over England. But this is so peculiar and its Situation of so uncommon a kind, that it merits a more particular description. (2:236)

He then probably wondered why he had delayed his trip so long. In a letter to Pope the preceding summer (14 August 1723), Robert Digby says that Pope has a great part of his "philosophical reveries" in the gardens. As Professor Sherburn noted, this remark might imply that Pope had already visited Sherborne; but earlier in the letter Digby hopes Pope may yet come (2:192).[3] We know he had been promising Digby a visit since 1720 (2:48, 115, 192); and for as long a time Digby had been urging the beauties of Sherborne on Pope and inviting him to come, in one instance, we recall, with Lord

Bathurst. In spite of Sherborne's beauties, however, Digby's humility apparently restrained him from advertising the gardens as forcefully as Pope did both his own garden and Oakley Wood. By way of enticing Pope into a visit, he could praise the variety of colors, the fragrant hedges, and the immanence of nature throughout the gardens, but owing to his absorption with his own garden and Digby's readiness to meet him at Cirencester, Pope did not get around to going west until 1724, only two years before young Digby's death.

The description of the Sherborne gardens is the most detailed Pope ever wrote. Nowhere else except in his satiric verse account of Timon's gardens, which is probably not modeled on any one garden, does Pope so closely describe the physical layout of a garden. It is at least for this reason an important description. It is also important because it contains a deliberate passage on how the landscape could be enhanced pictorially. But its importance is chiefly due to Sherborne itself. Except for Ladyholt and Rochester's Petersham in Richmond, by 1724 Pope did not know another garden like it. It was dramatic and romantic. It seems likely, in fact, that Sherborne inspired Pope with new ideas for Marble Hill, especially for the rustic grottoes by the river. While Rousham, Stowe, Bevis Mount near Southampton, and Prior Park were, as Pope said of Bevis Mount, "beautiful beyond imagination," we may infer that Sherborne almost certainly, directly and indirectly, helped determine their distinctive blend of hilly naturalness, meditative allusiveness, and (in the case of Bevis Mount and Prior Park) dramatic landscape effects. But their relandscaping in the new fashion was not to begin for three or four years. Here at Sherborne Pope got a glimpse of a landscape that merited "a more particular description" and intimated some directions the landscape movement might take.

"Good without noise, without pretension great"

In view of Pope's enthusiasm for the Sherborne gardens, it is surprising that so little has been written about them.[4] In an old essay on the "dream" landscape in the eighteenth century, H. F. Clark had more to say about the gardens than anyone until Morris Brownell devoted a few pages to them in his analysis of Pope's picturesque gardening. Professor Clark devoted half a page to them, in which he correctly made two claims. Pope's description, he said, is of a garden in a state of transition "from the traditional to the new landscape style and some of Pope's own ideas of improvement." He also asserted that the garden "either suggested or actually constructed most of the elements of those landscapes which were to be the greatest achievements of the movement."[5] It is evident that to Pope the gardens "suggested" as much as they actually showed. More will be said later about Professor Clark's claims, but even with them and Professor Brownell's analysis it remains that Sherborne has not received the attention it deserves as an important early eighteenth-century landscape garden. This may well be the result of the circumstances of the creation of the gardens.

By 1724 the Digby family had mildly naturalized the seventeenth-century water and ornamental gardens in the river valley between the two castles, consisting of a T-shaped canal system, regular groves of horse chestnuts, terraces, a bowling green, a semicircular *berceau* and amphitheater, and a "triangular wilderness" just north of the "new" castle or lodge, built by Sir Walter Raleigh in 1592.[6] As we shall see, these mostly Italian and formal features pleased Pope owing to their proximity to more natural features and prospects, but the uniqueness of the garden that overwhelmed him was its romantic character north of the river valley. Here there was, and still is (the castle and gardens are open to the public), a northwest area through which the river rushed between steep banks thickly clad with huge trees; and above these banks were the "venerable broken Walls" of the ancient ruins. The Digbys either did not have to or want to "tame" or improve these northern areas. In the northwest area, as will be shown, they placed the occasional seat or bower and laid winding paths up and down the banks, but quietly they merely enhanced the natural spirit or "Genius" of the setting.

Before he describes his walk through the grounds, Pope generalizes:

> The Gardens are so Irregular, that tis very hard to give an exact idea of 'em but by a Plan. Their beauty rises from this Irregularity, for not only the Several parts of the Garden itself make the better Contraste by these sudden Rises, Falls, and Turns of ground; but the Views about it are lett in, & hang over the Walls, in very different figures and aspects. (2:237)

The wording, "sudden Rises, Falls, and Turns of ground," proves that it is the northern area he has in mind when he calls the place irregular since the Italian gardens in the river valley did not contain that element of surprise except in that the views were let into them, too. The northern area was an example of the romantic type of landscape, one of the five types classified by William Gilpin in *Practical Hints on Landscape Gardening*.[7] Since there is, then, little record of stylization in these areas of the Sherborne landscape, it is not surprising that garden historians have neglected it. Even Launcelot ("Capability") Brown left that area alone when he worked on the landscape at midcentury.

As for the ruins, their history brought to the gardens an allusive and allegorical element. Unlike William Kent at Stowe, the early eighteenth-century gardener at Sherborne did not have to rely on art to introduce such emblematic history. The ruins are of a Norman castle built for the Bishop of Sarum in the twelfth century.[8] Acquired by Sir Walter Raleigh in the late sixteenth century and passing into the Digby family in 1617, the castle had a stormy history in the seventeenth century. Unsuccessful at converting the castle into a modern home, Raleigh instead built himself the new castle across the river. Raleigh's skillful garden designing at the turn of the seventeenth century also established a distinguished gardening tradition at Sherborne well over a century before Pope first saw the gardens. According to John Coker in his *Survey of Dorsetshire*,

> Queen Elizabeth granted [Sherborne] to Sir Walter Rawleigh, who beganne verie fairelie to builde the Castell, but altering his Purpose hee built, in a Parke adjoineing to it, out of the Grounde a most fine House, which hee beautified with Orchardes, Gardens and Groves of much Varietie and great

Delight: Soe that, whether that you consider the Pleasantnesse of the Seate, the Goodness of the Soyle, or the other Delicacies belongeing unto it, it rests unparalleled by anie in these Partes.[9]

If Coker's enthusiasm is any indication, the "situation" or "Pleasantnesse of the Seate" was uncommon even then; and Coker speaks particularly of the variety of the groves and gardens, which appears to point to both the topography and Raleigh's landscape treatment. If Pope had been aware of this legacy that the Digbys inherited, it would have heightened his pleasure in 1724 immeasurably. Here was a landscape that had always remained faithful to its inception, preserved for the most part from the encroaching taste of seventeenth-century France and Holland and a continuing witness to its historic past.

Because Sherborne had important national associations before the Digbys acquired it, the family did not have to turn to someone like Kent to design an emblematic landscape, and hence neither did this dimension of the gardens gain fame for Sherborne through such professional help. The same applies to the northwest section, just south of the ruins, where there was (and still is) Raleigh's Seat. Robert Digby himself was responsive to the national associations of the place and to its importance as a place of meditation with Pope as its "Genius," much as Pope a year earlier imagined himself as the "Magician" of Oakley Wood. He wrote to Pope in August 1723:

> I have as you guess, many philosophical reveries in the shades of Sir Walter Raleigh, of which you are a great part. You generally enter there with me, and like a good Genius applaud and strengthen all my sentiments that have honour in them. This good office which you have often done me unknowingly, I must acknowledge now, that my own breast may not reproach me with ingratitude, and disquiet me when I would muse again in that solemn scene. (2:192)

What he meant was that the gardens and groves, especially in the northwest section where Raleigh's Seat was, comprised a landscape of meditation. The past was partly responsible for this by permeating the present amid the dark and romantic groves. I find it significant, too, that Digby also associated Pope with the past there, as if the poet were identified in his mind with the old-fashioned values celebrated by the house and gardens. This is especially suggestive since Pope had not then yet set foot in the gardens. Pope not infrequently had this kind of effect upon his friends, however, often deliberately. He tended to prefer Tudor-Stuart country seats like Sherborne, Stanton Harcourt, Rousham, and Dodington Hall, precisely because they evoked the "old" world and had been spared the influences of moneyed men with their large landscapes in the grand formal manner.

Another factor that might account for the relative obscurity of Sherborne as an early eighteenth-century garden is Robert Digby's stature as a landscape gardener. We have already discussed in the last chapter the gardening triumvirate of which, with Bathurst and Pope, he was a member at the beginning of the landscape movement.

Although our sources document Pope's gardening projects with Bathurst more closely, he discussed with Digby, too, the changing tastes in gardening and projects that were underway or anticipated at Twickenham, Cirencester, and Sherborne. Digby was unnecessarily mystified when in his August letter he remarked to Pope fondly about Bathurst: "With him, I know not by what connection, you never fail to come into my mind, as if you were inseparable." We have observed Bathurst's strength of personality, public and domestic, so not surprisingly he and his park at Cirencester dominated the trio's conversations and projects. At least Pope's correspondence corroborates this (see 2:44, 47, 50, 58, 115, 192). In addition to his reticence about praising Sherborne's landscape beauties, he was only the son of the owner of Sherborne while Bathurst was the lord of Cirencester. We do not know how William, Lord Digby, looked upon the new gardening ideas,[10] but the surviving correspondence suggests that it was on Cirencester and to a lesser extent Twickenham, not Sherborne, that the trio's attention was focused.

There may have been resistance at Sherborne to their grand and (in the case of Bathurst) impulsive ideas; perhaps Robert Digby was too deferential to Bathurst and too accommodating in coming to Cirencester and Twickenham, or it was just that neither Pope nor Bathurst had seen Sherborne and that therefore both were relatively uninterested in it. Still, it is interesting that Digby was fascinated by the goings-on in Oakley Wood and that Pope several times wrote to him about them, describing the visits of other members of the Digby family and once calling himself and Digby "Associates" there (2:50).

Pope enjoyed Digby and Bathurst as gardening companions partly because they, like himself, were private gardeners. As Pope once told Thomas Wentworth, the Earl of Strafford, another private gardener at his villa by the Thames and at his country estate, Wentworth Castle in Yorkshire, "I have long been convinced that neither Acres, nor Wise; nor any publick Professors of Gardening, (any more than any publick Professors of Virtue) are equal to the Private Practisers of it" (2:309).[11] But more than this, landscape gardening in the early 1720s was experimental and an adventure for amateurs like them. By the mid or late 1730s Bridgeman and Kent had fairly removed the so-called revolution in gardening from the realm of theory and exciting amateurism. In the earlier years, Pope's garden was one of the few well known in the new fashion; as for Sherborne, it was virtually unknown as a garden of any special character—and Digby, as far as we can tell, was equally unknown as a gardener.

It was not landscaping, however, that first brought Robert Digby and Pope together. When they first met, possibly in 1716—Pope's first known letter to Digby in June 1717 (1:408–09) shows that they were already well acquainted[12]—Pope was living in Chiswick and had little idea of how "rural" he would eventually become at Twickenham. In his recent portrait of the Digby family, Howard Erskine-Hill suggests that they may have met through Charles Jervas.[13] From the start they shared literary and cultural tastes, perhaps also a taste for antiquarianism, and an interest in Homer. In early letters to Robert, Pope's remarks on *Gorboduc* (1:467) and Colley Cibber's play, *The Non-Juror* (1:473), are colored by political sentiments that he also shares with his friend (and his friend's family), but otherwise he had a high regard for Robert's appreciation of wit and good sense. "If I knew how to entertain you thro' the rest of this Paper," he wrote in March 1718, "it should be spotted and diversified with Conceits all over; you should be put out of Breath with Laughter at each Sentence, and pause at each Period, to look back over how much Wit you had pass'd" (1:473).

In addition to the exemplary religiousness, honor, and dignity of the entire Digby family, their "Spirit of Goodness" (as Pope put it), which had been embodied for decades of political and religious controversy by Robert's father, William, the fifth Baron Digby,[14] it was the rural "virtue" of the family that appealed to the poet. With an allusion to the Digbys' respect for worthy clergymen, he tells Robert in the March letter that "Decency and Patience" are to be found mostly in the country, whereas "in Town we hum over a Piece of fine Writing, and we whistle at a Sermon." This was a common sentiment on behalf of the life of the country house owner, but Pope was particularly aware of it when writing to Digby. Digby's cousin, Lady Frances Scudamore, was in London at the time, and Pope could report with irony and humor that "My Lady *Scudamore*, from having rusticated in your Company too long, really behaves herself scandalously among us: She pretends to open her eyes for the sake of seeing the Sun, and to sleep because it is Night; drinks Tea at nine in the Morning, and is thought to have said her Prayers before; talks without any manner of shame of good Books, and has not seen *Cibber's* Play of the *Non-Juror*" (1:473). From Coleshill in Warwickshire, which Lord Digby and his family regarded as their principal country seat even after they acquired the Sherborne estate on the death of the third Earl of Bristol at the turn of the century,[15] Robert could only smile contentedly and agree that in the country they were surrounded with genuine "blessings and pleasures."

Among the manuscripts at Badminton House in Gloucestershire, where Lady Scudamore's daughter reigned as the third Duchess of Beaufort, there is an elegy written upon the former's death in 1733 that further illustrates the "Decency" of country life that Pope associated with the Digbys. Lady Scudamore's seat at Holm Lacy, Hertfordshire—"Where Vaga murmuring glides"—which Pope much admired, is praised through association with the owner's moral attributes. Pastoralized as Panthea, Lady Scudamore is represented in the poem as the type of ideal rural lady that Pope sketches in several of his poems. If he knew this poem, which does mention him, he would have agreed entirely with the rhetoric of praise. It was another testimony on behalf of the Digbys and blameless country life:

> From the succeeding Ages well may paint
> The Friend, the Wife, the Mother, & the Saint.

From then until Robert's death in 1726, their letters abound increasingly with comentary on landscape and gardens, deepening all the time with a mutual fondness and understanding (see 2:191–92). It would appear, in fact, that a common interest in landscaping, along with other factors already mentioned, served to sustain their relationship and increase its intimacy. Having just returned from a visit to Twickenham in late summer 1723, Digby writes combining praise of Pope's country pleasures with genuine regard for him as a dear friend:

> I thank you heartily for the new agreeable idea of life you there gave me . . . .
> As you are possessed of all the pleasures of the country, and as I think of a right mind, what can I wish you but health to enjoy them? This I so heartily do, that I should be even glad to hear your good old mother might lose all her present pleasures in her unwearied care of you, by your better health convincing them it is unnecessary. . . . If I any ways deserve that friendly warmth and affection with which you write, it is, that I have a heart full of love and esteem for you. (2:191)

The year before his death, he said again, with a touching earnestness and almost with a premonitory sense that his life was about to end and that he might never again see his friend: "I shall ever remember *your good Mother Mrs Pope* & have you in my heart, whose health I wish & prosperity in all things" (2:305).[16] The epitaph for Robert and his sister Mary—Pope's "guide" through the "enchanted Forest" of Oakley Wood—who died three years later, which Pope wrote on Lord Digby's request and which was engraved on their tomb in Sherborne Abbey, summed up Pope's feelings:

> Go! fair Example of untainted youth,
> Of modest wisdom, and pacifick truth:
> Compos'd in suff'rings, and in joy sedate,
> Good without noise, without pretension great.
> Just of thy word, in ev'ry thought sincere,
> Who knew no wish but what the world might hear:
> Of softest manners, unaffected mind,
> Lover of peace, and friend of human kind:
> Go live! for heav'ns Eternal year is thine,
> Go, and exalt thy Moral to Divine.[17]

The house and formal water gardens

Today the existing Sherborne gardens are thought to be of major interest as an example of the landscaping of "Capability" Brown. According to Dorothy Stroud, Lord Ilchester advised in 1756 that Brown ought to be consulted for some landscaping connected with a cascade, but it is not known for certain that he did any work there until 1775, when he began some general landscaping, including the floating of the present lake, which buried the formal water gardens in the river valley. He also landscaped the shores of the lake into pleasure grounds.[18] Though much of the pleasure grounds beside the lake is now overgrown, the outlines of Brown's landscaping are still visible.[19] There is no record of his having altered the northern areas except immediately alongside the lake. These areas were of course not affected by the flooding of the river valley since they begin to rise precipitously a few feet from the lake and, in the case of the northern area where

101

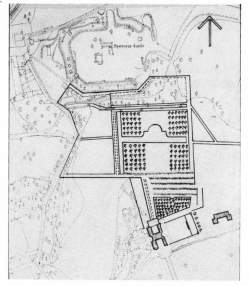

Plate 40. Plan of the Sherborne gardens as Pope saw them and as they were until "Capability" Brown's modifications in the 1770s. Found in the library at Sherborne Castle. References: 1. east front; 2. "Green walk of Standard Lymes"; 3. triangular wilderness; 4. southern terraces; 5. bowling green; 6. formal groves of horse chestnuts; 7. T-canal; 8. basin; 9. "semi-circular Berceau"; 10. river Yeo; 11. eastern long walk; 12. area of northern terraces; 13 and 14. (possible) bridges over the water; 15. circular grove; 16. old Dinney bridge in "ruinous taste"; 17. Raleigh's Seat; 18. Pope's Seat (not shown); 19. cascade; 20. old doorway leading to the main gateway of the ruins (not shown);21. highest terrace; 22. "Little, old, low wall, beside a Trench"; 23. "Natural" rising ground; 24. (possible) entrance to the ruins used by Pope (not shown); 25. main gateway to the ruins. Redrawn by Nigel Azis.

Plate 41. Garden plan superimposed on a modern ordnance survey map to show the exact position of the water gardens, terraces, and triangular wilderness in relation to the present landscape.

Pope saw four terraces crowned high up by a little wilderness, continue to rise to the level of the old castle ruins. Romantic in character, these early eighteenth-century areas represent historically a middle position between the formal seventeenth-century lake and the pleasure grounds laid out in their place later in the century. From the seats, arbors, winding walks, and ruins above, one can imagine the resident Genius of the Place watching with interest through the years the changing landscape below. And today these upper parts of the gardens appear to a visitor much as they did to Pope in 1724.

In addition to Pope's description, we have two early eighteenth-century documents that show the water gardens. The plan of the gardens (plates 40 and 41) is the earlier. It shows clearly everything Pope describes in his letter. The map (plate 42) is an

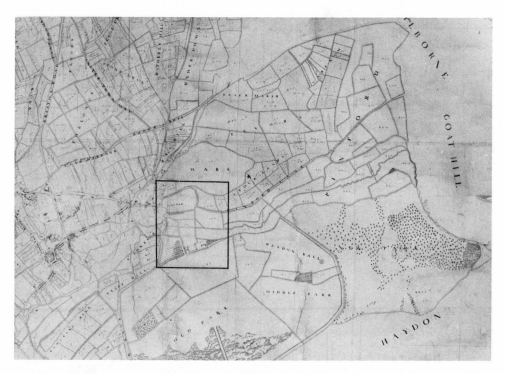

Plate 42. Map: detail from the plan of the Town of Sherborne, 1733, showing the castle and water gardens (boxed), with the outlying parks to the south and east described by Pope as "finely crownd with . . . sloping down to the house." Surveyed and drawn by T. Ladd.

undetailed enlargement of a 1733 map of Sherborne town by T. Ladd, showing its environs and also the water gardens. There is a watercolor painting of the walled formal garden on the east front of the castle (plate 43) that also predates Brown. It is painted from position B in the garden plan. It shows the raised terrace and balustrade with columns and urns at the east end and also the four small lawns with a broad gravel path intersected and bounded by narrower paths. Another map probably drawn in the late eighteenth century (plate 44) shows Brown's alterations and provides a valuable record of the Sherborne landscape altered in a major way for the first time in almost two hundred years. It shows Brown's lake and shoreline pleasure grounds, and the open grass lawn at the east front of the castle rather than the walled formal garden with the raised terrace. (A comparison with the modern outlines of plate 41 reveals that this map has some of the angles and areas wrongly drawn and shaped.)

From these records and Pope's description we can reconstruct the garden as Pope saw it and compare it with Brown's garden some fifty years later. The period for which there is little information (except for the undetailed 1733 map) is from Pope's visit in 1724 until Brown's appearance. This is especially unfortunate because while landscaping amateurism at Sherborne doubtless lost much of its color with Robert Digby's death in 1726, these were the years when the new gardening in England came to maturity with

103

Plate 43. Undated watercolor painting of the east front of Sherborne Castle with a view of the formal garden from the raised and balustraded terrace. Pope admired the "Wings of a newer Architecture with beautiful Italian Window-frames done by the first Earl of Bristol" around 1625 (2:236–37). This garden is possibly much as it was when Pope saw it, before "Capability" Brown leveled the terrace and turned the area into an expanse of lawn. The arrow marks the doorway from which Pope emerged to start his walk.

the work of Bridgeman and Kent. Some of the new ideas may have found their way there during this period.

Pope acknowledges that the Sherborne gardens were so complex and irregular that "tis very hard to give an exact idea of 'em but by a Plan." He may indeed have sketched a plan of the gardens from which to write his description: his description, checked against the garden plan, is so accurate that we may wonder if he used a sketch to remind himself about details.[20] The plan is of additional interest because it contains all the features Pope mentions in his letter and a striking correspondence in shapes, angles, and style. Only three features that he mentions do not appear on this early plan: a "circular Grove" (15 in plate 40) in the northwest section, the hermit's seat (18), and the bridge Pope crossed to reach the ruins. The location of the bridge is open to conjecture, but the southeast corner of the ruins area (24) seems the best choice (see below). The "circular Grove" is shown as somewhat triangular on the plan, and the arbor Pope mentions is omitted. As for the hermit's seat, which stood where Pope's Seat now stands, it must have been contemporary with Raleigh's Seat and the old rustic bridge (16), both shown in the plan and mentioned by Pope; its omission from the plan was most likely an oversight. If the plan was drawn decades after Pope's visit, its details conceivably were gleaned from his letter.

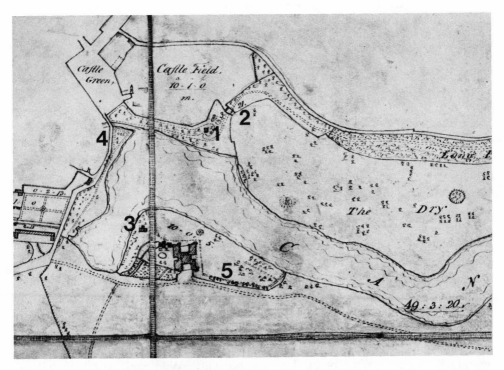

Plate 44. Detail of a map drawn after Brown flooded the river valley to create the lake and shoreline pleasure gardens. Probably late eighteenth century since it shows Brown's Bastion (1) and subterranean passageway (2), 1776–79; and Robert Adam's Orangery (3), ca. 1780. Not shown are Raleigh's and Pope's seats, and the circular grove looks more like a triangle (4). There is also a ha-ha (5). Several incorrect angles and shapes suggest it is an amateurish sketch.

The castle stands in a large and beautiful park surrounded by gentle hills "with very high Woods, on all the tops of the Hills, which form a great Amfitheatre sloping down to the house" (see plate 40). There is a beautiful southeast prospect from the castle across the old deer park toward Jerusalem Hill. On all sides, except to the north where the ruins stand, the hills are far off from the house, and the woods upon them comprise a distant background. In Pope's day there were woods close to the house on the north side, where just beyond the river Yeo there was a dark stretch of trees from west to east: "On the Garden Sides the Woods approach close, so that it appears there with a thick Line & Depth of Groves on each hand, & so it shows from most parts of the Park" (2:237).

The trees at Sherborne, incidentally, were impressive in 1724 and still are today. In addition to the large, towering, dark trees to the north (which Pope does not identify) and the distant groves of forest trees surrounding the estate, scattered all over the gardens themselves were lime trees, sundry species of fruit trees (including cherry), honeysuckles, horse chestnuts, elders, and thickets of "mixd trees." Disappointingly, Pope frequently refers to trees at Sherborne and many other gardens (including his own) without specifying many varieties. But given his profound appreciation of trees of all kinds, young and old, the fascination Sherborne held for him must have derived substantially from the abundance of wood. This was especially true in the northwest area, where they towered romantically—and still do—over the steep slopes and rushing water below. If ever Pope found trees among which to "lose" himself and sense nature's drama, it was here in 1724.

Pope starts his walk from the house through a door leading from the northeast turret into "a green Walk of Standard Lymes with a hedge behind them that makes a Colonnade" (2:237). The garden plan and the watercolor painting agree on where he found himself as he stepped through this door (A in plate 40). The painting reveals that he was outside (north) of the northern wall of the formal garden and that to his left (our right as we look at the painting) was the colonnadelike walk or row of limes (2). Neither in the painting nor in the plan does the hedge behind the limes appear, but in the painting it is barely visible by the garden wall. The painting also shows the east front of the castle with the Italian window frames that Pope admired and, with an unexplainable lapse of taste, would have "joined in the middle by a Portico covering the old Building [which] would be a noble Front."

Immediately, Pope steps into the southwest corner of "a little triangular wilderness [3], from whose Centre you see the town of Sherborne in a valley, interspersd with trees." He savors these lovely prospects and particularly enjoys gazing upon them from within the well-defined limits of the triangular "wilderness." The plan suggests that this artificial "wilderness" is irregularly planted, and as Pope later adds, "You'l be pleasd when I tell you the Quarters of the above mentiond little Wilderness are filld with these ['Honisuckles . . . the largest & finest I ever saw'] & with Cherry trees of the best kinds all within reach of the hand." One of the reasons Pope is agreeably surprised by this area is that though its perimeter is geometrically established, its plantings are profuse and varied. He relishes the consequent feeling of nature's abundance created artificially. The wilderness creates an illusion of wildness that contrasts with the lined-up horse chestnuts in the groves amidst the water gardens.

In order to interpret the special pleasure Pope took in this part of the garden, the concept of a wilderness in early eighteenth-century gardening needs to be clearly understood. *Wilderness* was a broad term denoting relatively small and totally artificial garden areas full of irregularly planted woods and winding paths, though just how irregular varied considerably. Some wildernesses were well endowed with statuary, temples, and other stonework, and were placed close to the house, as was the one at Sherborne. Others were even full of quincunxes. In "Of Gardens" (1625), Sir Francis Bacon provided for a relatively formal wilderness in his ideal "princely" garden. At Castle Howard in Yorkshire the gardens until as late as 1750 contained walled mazes flanking the southern lawn that comprised the wilderness or "wood within the walls." Such an old-fashioned "set wilderness or grove," Stephen Switzer urged in *Ichnographia Rustica* (1718), was outmoded and should be replaced by coppice woods grown from seeds or by cutting walks and groves through existing woods. While the old-fashioned wilderness shut in a visitor entirely with high walls or hedges, Sherborne's actually opened up the surrounding countryside. Pope especially enjoyed the resulting sensation of being a spectator in the *theatrum mundi*—the world as a theater. The prospect of the town of Sherborne below him "interspersd with trees" became to him in a way a controlled aesthetic experience by virtue of his viewing it from the triangular wilderness. The trees framing the prospect seemed like props on a stage. Pope delighted in perceiving this sort of analogy to human artifice within the expanse of open landscape, although this is an early and abbreviated example in his descriptive prose. We shall see later how at Netley Abbey near Southampton in the mid-1730s he sustained this delight and carefully described it for Martha Blount.

From this wilderness Pope emerged either at the northwest or northeast corner and issued "at once upon a high green Terras the whole breadth of the Garden, which has five more green Terras's hanging under each other, without hedges, only a few pyramid yews & large round Honisuckles between them." The plan shows the high green or turfed terrace with five more terraces below (4), but it does not look as if the highest extends the whole breadth of the garden, at least not the breadth of the water gardens. Probably Pope was referring to the breadth of the wilderness and the formal garden. He does not say much about these southern terraces with their views north over the water gardens and toward the ruins and Sherborne town in the distance, except to suggest that they were both formally and naturally planted—formally with pyramid yews and naturally with large honeysuckles. Sir William Temple, in his essay "Upon the Gardens of Epicurus" (1685), regarded terraces as perfectly in keeping with the "regular figures" he thought were so beautiful and reliable in a garden and especially apt on a descent where "the beauty, the air, the view makes amends for the expense, which is very great in finishing and supporting the terras-walks."[21] This undoubtedly was the case when Pope saw them. Viewed today from a boat, what is now a sloping grass bank still shows thin lines where the terraces used to be.

Pope then adds, "At the ends of these Terras's run two long Walks under the Side walls of the Garden which communicate with the other Terras's that front these opposite." He is slightly imprecise here because along the entire western side of these terraces it would have been geometrically impossible for a straight walk to have continued, without bending, into the long walk under the western wall of the water garden. The plan reveals why. An extension southward of the long walk on the west side of the water gardens would have run straight into the coppice perhaps two hundred feet west of the terraces. On the other hand, we can see from the plan that the angles on the east side of the terraces were correct for a long walk (11) extending from the highest terrace down to the water gardens and up to the northern terraces (12). At the east end of the southern terraces, however, the plan shows no walk; rather it is at the west end where a walk is shown by which to ascend and descend the terraces. The long walks apparently began only at the level of the lowest terrace. Reaching that level, Pope would have seen at both ends the garden walls and the beginning of the long walks under them.

From the lowest of the five terraces he may have gone in any direction to reach the "left corner of the Canal and the Chestnut groves in the bottome" (position C). He does not describe his path through the water garden nor even in the northern terraces but simply says of what they consisted and how they were arranged. Such a fundamentally rectangular garden on a confined and level site with no views let in may not have been

107

evocative enough for him. His description is subdued and precise—it matches exactly the layout of the area as shown in the plan:

> Between [the southern and northern terraces], the Vally is layd level and divided into two regular Groves of Horse chestnuts, and a Bowling-green in the middle of about 180 foot. This is bounded behind with a Canall, that runs quite across the Groves & also along one Side, in the form of a T. Behind this, is a Semicircular Berceau, and a Thicket of mixd trees that compleats the Crown of the Amfitheatre which is of equal extent with the Bowling-green. (2:237)

A few features in this area, as well as in Pope's description, are historically important. The T-canal (7) is French in design, with a basin (8) also formal in the French style, such as Dézallier D'Argenville illustrates frequently in his *Théorie et la Pratique du Jardinage* (1709).[22] The rectangular regularity of this area would have contrasted strikingly and pleasingly with the spreading fields, hills, and woods around. To the east of the small arm of the T-canal were four symmetrically placed horse chestnut groves (6) flanking the main arm of the T-canal and, south of it, separated by the 180-foot bowling green (5). The dimension of the bowling green is valuable because it tells us the scale for the entire garden; hence the distance between the northern and southern terraces must have been about four hundred feet. The plan also supports Pope's description of these groves as "regular," for one clearly can see that the trees are planted in straight lines.[23]

So far, everything in the water gardens is traditional. In addition, the walks (11) just inside the eastern and western walls are absolutely straight and accentuate the oblong shape of the area. No effort has been made to conceal the walls or minimize their Tudor-like formidableness. And as for the river Yeo (10), it looks as if it has been canalized as it runs next to the water gardens. Pope says that north of the groves "runs a natural River thro green banks of turf," and this is correct since this section is the river itself, not a diversion; but later he speaks of a "Wall that bounds the channel of the river," certainly a formal feature.

One feature in the water gardens that, though not irregular, can be regarded as transitional is the amphitheater; unfortunately neither it nor the thicket of mixed trees is shown in the plan. Green theaters in landscape gardens, as we have seen, had been used in Italy; they were also fashionable in France, had already been used in England, and were rapidly becoming more popular. Some member of the Digby family may have visited Chantilly, just outside Paris, some years earlier because, as the late Edward Malins showed me, the design for the Sherborne theater and its position in relation to the canal were probably taken from the design of the theater there.

These theaters usually were placed in the more remote parts of gardens and against hills or slopes. Bridgeman built an amphitheater at Claremont and at Stowe in the late 1720s and Vanbrugh one in Wray Wood at Castle Howard probably also in the late 1720s; there was also one at Rousham at least by 1725.[24] Pope told Robert Digby, as we have seen, about Lord Bathurst's intention to build "an immense amphitheatre" in the midst of which the Thames and Severn rivers would "rise and openly celebrate their Marriage."

And even in his own garden Pope, perhaps after his own design, had Bridgeman execute the "Bridgmannick Theatre" at an early stage in that garden's history, even before he had seen the French one at Sherborne.

As Pope suggests, the amphitheater and *berceau* were of the same "extent" or width as the bowling green. Providing some elevation, it too would have afforded views south over the water, bowling green, and groves of horse chestnuts, and toward the southern terraces and the castle. And from other parts of the garden it would have provided a focal point in the valley.

Though the plan shows a rectangular area (12) just north of the river where Pope says there were four terraces, it does not indicate terracing there. Nonetheless, this area is of exactly the same width as the T-canal system and in other ways conforms perfectly to Pope's description of the northern terraces. He states that just south of the old ruins was "an uppermost Terras" with three terraces below down to the river:

> Beyond that [amphitheater] runs a natural River thro green banks of turf, over which rises another Row of Terras's, the first supported by a slope Wall planted with Vines (So is also the Wall that bounds the channel of the river.) A second & third appeard above this, but they are to be turnd into a Line of Wilderness with wild winding walks for the convenience of passing from one side to the other in Shade, the heads of whose trees will lye below the uppermost Terras of all, which compleats the Garden and overlooks both that & the Country. (2:237)

The proximity of these terraces to the wildest parts of the garden and to the steepest cliffs must have encouraged Pope and Robert Digby to regard them somewhat as a transitional area between the regularity and conventionality of the water gardens and the irregularity of the north and northwest areas. The vines growing over the wall supporting the lowest terrace, as well as over the wall channeling the river (10), must have given them a natural look, but beyond that there does not seem as yet to have been any planting. After the planting that Pope says was intended, with winding paths laid out through the trees and views of the garden and countryside remaining uninterrupted, these terraces in effect were to become "wildernesses" in the same sense that the triangular wilderness near the house was one. A terrace would become a "Line" of wilderness simply because its geometric shape was long and narrow. Pope uses the word "but" to introduce this information about the proposed naturalization of the terraces, which raises the possibility that he and Digby were apologetic or embarrassed about these awkwardly formal (and misplaced) terraces and quick to say that they would not be that way long. Together with Pope's recommendations later in the letter, these projected alterations also demonstrate that the Digbys were in the process of and mood for naturalizing the gardens. Indeed, Pope's visit may have been planned just then so that he could have his say.

Possibly under the direction of Robert Digby, this naturalization of the second and third terraces was carried out sometime in the next two years before he died in 1726, though the 1733 map does not show any trees in this area.[25] It is the single plan for improvement that Pope says will definitely become a reality. H. F. Clark cited it as "the first step towards naturalising the garden" though by garden he apparently meant the areas that have already been discussed—those visibly shaped by the reach of art.[26] Pope also speaks of the uppermost terrace as completing "the garden." He was using the word deliberately in its traditional sense of being enclosed and decorated, and in the knowledge that for over a decade—ever since the writings of Addison, Switzer, and others—the idea of a garden had been extended to include landscape.

Awful, solemn, and venerable landscape

As Pope turns (at position C) from the left corner of the canal into the "very old trees" and "deepest Shade," he is just next to the river, on its south bank, and is heading west. The tone and vocabulary of his description from this point on are markedly different. He throws himself into another gear. He sounds more enthusiastic, more evocative, relishing the picturesque combination of trees, water, prospects, precipices, bower, and rustic stonework that in the next decade were to become an accepted character of the new landscape gardening. While he describes all of the preceding formal and semiformal areas in one long paragraph, he starts a new paragraph for this wild northwest area—as if to stress a new approach or attitude. From the sound of his description one might suppose him to be walking in the Lake District instead of in a Dorset country seat:

> When you are at the left corner of the Canal and the Chestnut groves in the bottome, you turn of a sudden under very old trees into the deepest Shade. One walk winds you up a Hill of venerable Wood over-archd by nature, & of a vast height, into a circular Grove, on one side of which is a close high Arbour, on the other a sudden open Seat that overlooks the Meadows & river with a large distant prospect. Another walk under this hill winds by the River side quite coverd with high Trees on both banks, over hung with Ivy, where falls a natural Cascade with never-ceasing murmurs. On the opposite hanging of the Bank (which is a Steep of 50 ft) is plac'd, with a very fine fancy, a Rustick Seat of Stone, flaggd and rough, with two Urns in the same rude taste upon pedestals, on each side: from whence you lose your eyes upon the glimmering of the Waters under the wood, & your ears in the constant dashing of the waves. In view of this, is a Bridge that crosses this Stream, built in the same ruinous taste: the Wall of the Garden hanging over it, is humourd so as to appear the Ruin of another Arch or two above the bridge. Hence you mount the Hill over the Hermits Seat (as they call it) describd before, & so to the highest Terras, again.

This is the "uncommon" situation to which Pope referred at the start of his letter, but in determining what was uncommon to him about it we need to remember that this, in fact, was not a wild landscape. It was part of a garden and for that reason seemed all the more remarkable to him. It was a microcosm of open landscape, a Netley Abbey "methodiz'd,"

Plate 45. View south across the lake to Sherborne Castle, from John Hutchins, *The History and Antiquities of the County of Dorset*. Mid-eighteenth century.

where the Genius of the Place was revealed in its native perfection by the unobtrusive use of art. As in his own garden, though more romantically, there was a preciosity in the variety of effect owing to the small scale (the steep bank was only fifty feet high) and "the fine fancy" achieved with winding walks, a grove, the use of water, and the placing of two seats. Here he is again admiring genius expressed "in a very little."

One year or two before "Capability" Brown altered the landscape by flooding the water gardens and creating his lake (plate 45), John Hutchins saw Sherborne; his description of the gardens is, significantly, almost entirely limited to the northwest area and the ruins:

> The ruins of the castle, Sir Walter Raleigh's grove, the seat of Lord Digby, a grove planted by Mr. Pope, and a noble serpentine body of water, with a fine stone bridge of several arches over it, made by the last Lord Digby, conspire to make this Seat one of the most venerable and beautiful in England.[27]

That Pope planted a grove, incidentally, is probably legendary more than factual, undoubtedly deriving from the increasingly legendary nature of his visit. The grove Hutchins had in mind could have been the area surrounding Pope's Seat (18).

Pope describes two walks in this part of the garden, the second (lower) of which remains today. The first walk wound to the left up a "Hill of venerable Wood" into the "circular Grove" (15). It could not have wound off to the right (north) since then it would have had to cross the river. He does not cross the river until he reaches the old bridge (16), which is on the second walk. This second walk remains at the bottom by the

Plate 46. Pope's Seat and cascade in the Sherborne gardens.

river until it reaches the bridge. The circular grove, which is neither shown as such in the plan (but appears as a triangle in plate 42) nor remains today, must then have been high up on the south bank of the river, its curve partially outlined by the bending river at that point. On one side of the grove was the open seat that today is known as Raleigh's Seat (17). As Pope said, it overlooks the river and cascade (19) and commands a view over them out to the meadows and distant scenes. The scene today commands the finest prospect in the entire garden and must have thrilled him. As for the arbor on the other side of the grove, it has disappeared. Today there is a small cemetery for the Keeshond dogs that the Digby family bred for several years in what must have been the center of the grove.

From this elevated position and on "the opposite hanging of the Bank" Pope saw a "Rustick Seat." Raleigh's Seat is the only one in the present garden that is "flaggd and rough"; the other seat in this area, known as Pope's Seat (18) (plate 46) and sitting by the river and cascade just where I would place the one Pope sees, is plastered and Georgian in appearance. But the "Rustick Seat" and Raleigh's Seat could not be one and the same since it was from the latter or near to it that Pope caught sight of the former. Furthermore, he specifically states that the hermit's seat, as he later calls it, was on "the opposite hanging of the Bank"—on the other (north) side of the river—and near

Plate 47. View south from Pope's Seat over the cascade to Sherborne Castle. On his visit in 1724, of course, Pope would have seen the formal water gardens instead of Brown's lake. Traces of the terraces remain on the sloping bank.

enough to the cascade and river whereby "you lose your eyes upon the glimmering of the Waters under the wood, & your ears in the constant dashing of the waves." I sat in the existing Pope's Seat (plate 47) and, because of its semicircular shape and the consequent amplification of sound, similarly "lost" myself in the moving of the water over the cascade or weir directly in front of the seat. Moreover, from Pope's Seat one enjoys just the view of the rustic Dinney Bridge crossing the stream that he saw from the hermit's seat. Perhaps there was a hermit's seat when Pope visited in 1724 that was, in commemoration of his visit, subsequently plastered over and renamed in his honor. The two pedestals are still in place. Or perhaps the "Rustick Seat" was the Gothic seat that Kent drew possibly for the Sherborne gardens (plate 48); if Kent's seat was built, the only evidence we have of his contribution to this landscape was unaccountably destroyed.

Pope's last recommendation is that a small temple be built on one of the hills surrounding Sherborne Castle, probably Jerusalem Hill, to be seen from any part of the garden:

It would finish some Walks, & particularly be a fine Termination to the River to been seen from the Entrance into that deep Scene I have describd by the Cascade where it would appear as in the clouds, between the tops of some

Plate 48. Kent's design of a Gothic seat, probably intended for Sherborne.

> very lofty Trees that form an Arch before it, with a great Slope downward to
> the end of the said river. (2:239)

More than just an eye-catcher, this classical temple would have been a distant focus especially in the prospect directly over the cascade seen along the stream from the Dinney Bridge. Pope's description of how the temple in this position would be framed by an arch of trees and the river sloping downward shows an understanding of how landscape elements in the foreground could achieve a beautifully pictorial perspective for the temple. The temple would appear to be embraced by the clouds, as were so many such temples by Italian Renaissance landscape painters like Claude Lorrain. This is a mild effort on Pope's part to classicize a part of the landscape. It would delineate a transition from the Gothic gloom of the woods near the ruins to a Grecian glory upon a distant summit. Such an iconographic journey would have anticipated by more than a decade a similar transition at Stowe. No such temple, as far as we know, was every built.

Both walks mentioned by Pope would have met at the old Dinney Bridge crossing the river—the first after having descended from Raleigh's Seat. This bridge exists today as it did when Pope saw it, with its west wall as part of the tall wall separating the garden from the old coach road from Dorchester to the north just outside. Crossing the river over the bridge, and then climbing up the north bank heading east, Pope's route mounts "the Hill over the Hermits Seat (as they call it) describd before, & so to the highest Terras, again." The word "again" indicates that Pope has completed his walk through the Sherborne gardens when at position D he meets up again with the highest terrace.

Eventually he reached the ruins. Whatever route he took to them, he was impressed (again) more by the landscape prospects there than by the perspective, variety of elevation, and solemn romanticism:

> You first see an old Tower penetrated by a large Arch, and others above it thro which the whole Country appears in prospect, even when you are at the top of the other ruins, for they stand very high, & the Ground slopes down on all sides. These venerable broken Walls, some Arches almost entire of 30 or 40 ft deep, some open like Portico's with fragments of pillars, some circular or inclosed on three sides, but exposd at top, with Steps which Time has made of disjointed Stones to climb to the highest points of the Ruin . . . (2:238)

"Awful," "solemn," and "venerable," these are qualities Pope feels in this naturally associative Gothic atmosphere of shade and antiquity. He feels awe and reverence. As stated earlier, in his mind one of the aspects of the "uncommon" situation of Sherborne was the expressive nature of the northwest area and the ruins. These emblems of centuries of national history in the ruins made it unnecessary for artificial emblems of history and tradition to be introduced there. To him the ruins seemed a natural part of the landscape, animating and dignifying it. Thomas Whately implied the type of ideal association that existed at Sherborne when he urged that emblems of history, mythology, poetry, and tradition should be introduced into landscape gardens so as to appear to be naturally present:

> as the subject does not naturally belong to a garden, the allusion should not be principle; it should seem to have been suggested by the scene; a transitory image, which irresistibly occurred; not sought for, not laboured; and have the force of a metaphor, free from the detail of an allegory.[28]

At Sherborne, this natural association was enhanced by the unstudied character of the adjacent landscape: it was a genuine example of what might be called the unlearned type of landscape. It generated poetic and philosophic moods entirely without the aid of a landscape gardener. Also without the mediation of a gardener, the scenes unfolded again as so many props upon a stage, so that the historical theme was strengthened by an inherent element of drama.

"I could very much wish this were done . . . "

Yet in the passages that follow Pope does propose that Lord Digby should set up an obelisk as a memorial to his family's defense of the castle during the Civil War; and he thinks that the ruins and adjacent landscape require artistic embellishment:

> These [ruins] I say might have a prodigious Beauty, mixd with Greens & Parterres from part to part, and the whole Heap standing as it does on a round hill, kept smooth in green turf, which makes a bold Basement to show it. The open Courts from building to building might be thrown into Circles or Octagons of Grass or flowers, and even in the gaming Rooms you have fine

trees grown, that might be made a natural Tapistry to the walls, & arch you over-head where time has uncoverd them to the Sky. Little paths of earth, or sand, might be made, up the half-tumbled walls; to guide from one View to another on the higher parts; & Seats placd here and there, to enjoy those views, which are more romantick than Imagination can form them. I could very much wish this were done . . . (2:238–39)

It is important to recognize that the several "pretty" effects Pope envisions here do not interfere with the predominant romanticism and "prodigious Beauty" of the half-tumbled walls piling up into a dramatic Gothic heap on the steep hill overlooking the gardens, nor do they belie Pope's own "principles of naturalistic design," as has elsewhere been suggested.[29] On a spiritual level, he is projecting a scene in which nature is "raised" or idealized, brought to a type of perfection, by the human mind, and by which the human mind is also raised as it exhibits the residue of nature's pure, prelapsarian genius. On an aesthetic level the green turf, greens and parterres, circles and octagons of grass or flowers, trees planted within the old walls to provide "a natural Tapistry to the Walls" (a theatrical image that is the only specific reference in Pope's account to the concealment of bounds), and paths of earth or sand connecting the several parts of the ruins with commanding views would highlight this romantic scene by framing and pictorializing it with additional perspectives, angles, curves, and shades and gatherings of green.[30] It is a type of picturesque synthesis that he achieved within his own Twickenham garden through the somewhat self-conscious blend of the central axis of the garden with the more informal perimeter areas full of meandering paths. Also as at Twickenham, the contrast of these proposed formal features with natural effects—the irregular ruins, the natural aspect of the whole area, and the panoramic prospects of surrounding countryside—had the effect of multiplying the picturesque effects in a prismatic fashion.[31] For Pope, it seems to me, this may not have amounted to a violation of nature: since the ruins and their "readable" iconography were practically as indigenous to the scene as was the Genius of the Place itself, they could be formalized in a degree to bring together their disjointed parts into a pictorial whole—a coherent visual and historical composition. It would be a pleasing composition for the walker who, like Pope, had just emerged from a scene in the northwest section almost totally lacking human ingenuity. Pope's recommendations for the historic ruins recall Vanbrugh's unsuccessful and picturesque proposal for preserving the old manor of Woodstock at Blenheim. In Vanbrugh's hands the manor would have taken on the character of a beautiful stage set; so would have the Sherborne ruins in Pope's hands.

Returning to the obelisk for a moment, we notice that Pope wants to commemorate the Digby family:

What should induce my Lord D. the rather to cultivate these ruins and do honour to them, is that they do no small honour to his Family. . . . I would sett up at the Entrance of 'em an Obelisk, with an inscription of the Fact [the defense of the castle during the Civil War]: which would be a Monument erected to the very Ruins; as the adorning & beautifying them in the manner I have been imagining, would not be unlike the Ægyptian Finery of bestowing Ornament and curiosity on dead bodies. (2:239)

The obelisk would supply, according to Maynard Mack, "a point of visual and emotional climax" to the Sherborne gardens,[32] though less distinctly than did Pope's obelisk in memory of his mother a few years later at Twickenham. It would tower over the ruins and therefore over the river valley and house. More picturesque and discreetly placed than the huge obelisk in honor of the Duke of Marlborough at Blenheim, of which Pope may have been reminded, it would stress the national and family honor connected with the ruins and the family seat.

Pope stresses two themes in his portrayal of the Digbys' relation to their seat and to the neighboring town of Sherborne. The first, filial piety, is one that he felt strongly in his own life; his feeling about this ancient virtue, as Professor Mack has explained, may have intensified through his immersion in the world of Homer from 1715 to 1725.[33] His devotion to his mother is well known and his regard for others who demonstrated the virtue was high. Addressing himself to Robert Digby's father in 1729, Pope declared: "It is you My Lord, that perpetuate your Family the best way, by transmitting thro' yourself all the Virtues of it into your Posterity" (3:52).[34] Pope tells Martha Blount that "not one of his [Lord Digby's] Children wishes to see this Seat his owne" (2:239).

Pope's second theme about the family concerns the Tudor-Stuart ideal of country house ownership. Unlike many other great landowners, says Pope, Lord Digby behaved responsibly toward his nation and neighborhood. He was, in Pope's experience, an early example of the benevolent man who appears in various forms throughout the poet's work. In spite of there being more dissimilarities than resemblances between the social status of Digby and, for example, one of Pope's benevolent heroes, the Man of Ross in *To Bathurst*, the resemblance in moral attributes was striking and useful to the poet. "I dare say," Pope says with confidence, Digby's "Goodness and Benevolence extend as far as his territories; that his Tenants live almost as happy & contented as himself" (2:239).[35] At the center of the poet's feeling is the ideal relation, already discussed in these pages, that he thought ought to exist between a country house and an enlightened civilization. He is really thinking of a rural society, largely classically inspired, that would help ward off the destructive pressures of the new age.[36]

Lord Digby's social and civic responsiveness is even sublimated by his religious consciousness, for Pope tells Martha Blount he has discovered secondhand that his Lordship at his own expense erected "a noble Monument and a beautiful Altar-piece of Architecture" in Sherborne Abbey and that he also designed "a neat Chappel for the use of the Towns-people, (who are too numerous for the Cathedral)" (2:239).[37] This is the little St. Mary Magdalen's Church in Castleton, just northwest of the ruins, built in 1714.

The fact that the Digbys had much else besides Sherborne whereby "to be lik'd" heightened Pope's pleasure over the scenes there. Art and morality were in harmony. But his pleasure was due mainly to the sensations of newness or the landscape possibilities of which he was aware at Sherborne. There were at Sherborne and in Pope's description several anticipations of later landscaping and literary techniques: associations of the

Gothic and romantic; the letting-in of prospects; the picture-conscious approach to gardening; the iconographic gardening; a model of the country house ideal that Pope later developed poetically in *To Burlington*; the portrait of the benevolent man; and the image of the tasteless and extravagant landowner whose creations in earth and stone prefigure the obscenities of the Timons and Cottas in the poems of the 1730s. As for the gardens alone, it is idle but tempting to conjecture whether, if Robert Digby had not died in 1726, Kent may have been eventually called upon in the 1730s to enhance, more than just a Gothic temple, the natural and historical features of the entire landscape, including the formal or transitional water gardens, with their French and Italian features, and the unimproved areas to the east and west of them. Robert Digby doubtless would have remained Pope's intimate friend and might have become a competent landscaper in the new fashion. In that case, it is not difficult to imagine Kent also being interested in a "Situation of so uncommon a kind."[38]

While it is regrettable that Robert Digby's early death spelled the premature end of a potentially influential partnership with Pope in the landscape movement, we can be grateful that in spite of some recent water engineering that has spoiled the area near the cascade, the north and northwest areas remain today essentially as they were when Pope saw them.

5

Bolingbroke

The Tory Farmer at Dawley Farm

Henry St. John, first Viscount Bolingbroke, was a close intellectual and philosophical friend of Pope's.[1] This Tory statesman, who briefly reached the summit of political power during the reign of Queen Anne in 1714 and fell precipitously from it with the accession of George I in the same year, for about twenty years intimately shared his ideas, schemes, and ambitions with the poet. At Pope's death, Spence recorded Bolingbroke's touching comment: "I have known him this thirty years, and value myself more for that man's love and friendship than—(sinking his head and losing his voice in tears.)."[2] For his part, Pope virtually idolized his friend, telling Spence in 1735 that he was "something superior to anything I have seen in human nature. You know I don't deal much in hyperboles: I quite think him what I say."[3] William Shenstone once added his testimony: "People of real genius have strong passions; people of strong passions have great partialities; such as Mr. Pope for Lord Bolingbroke."[4] Although the beginning of their friendship dated back to some time before Bolingbroke's political disgrace and exile to France in 1715,[5] the intimacy that eventually influenced a good deal of Pope's poetry and occasioned a garden setting for their mutual horticultural and philosophical amusement did not really develop until the statesman's first return from exile in 1723.

Pardoned and restored to his rights and possessions, though not allowed by the astute Sir Robert Walpole to take his seat in the House of Lords, Bolingbroke in 1725 purchased Dawley Manor in Harlington, Middlesex, near Uxbridge, just a few miles away from Pope's villa. This seat, which he immediately renamed Dawley Farm, quickly became the center of his political efforts to organize the opposition party, and it became well known as the venue for gatherings of political, literary, and other personalities. With his villa so near, Pope must have been one of Bolingbroke's most frequent visitors, but the road between Dawley and Twickenham was well traveled by both men because during the next ten years Bolingbroke regularly supped with the poet at his villa and conversed with him in his garden and grotto—" Where, nobly-pensive, ST. JOHN sate and thought."[6]

When Pope wrote to Lord Harcourt on 21 June 1723—two days before Bolingbroke's arrival in England—in great anticipation of his friend's return and the consequent end of his "Afflictions" (2:175), he had no idea that eventually Bolingbroke would settle quite so close to Twickenham. The area, with its proximity to London, must

Plate 49. Henry St. John, Viscount Bolingbroke. Artist unknown.

have appealed to Bolingbroke as a prime choice. When he was trying to sell Dawley in 1735, he told Sir William Wyndham: "I considered it rather as the purchase of a Seat, than of an Estate, and of a Seat near London, where such a parcel of Land together is not commonly found."[7]

His first few months were spent in London, where he made new friends and discarded some old ones—"those Insects of various Hues, which used to hum and buz about me while I stood in the Sunshine" (2:187). He also tried without complete success to shake off the habits of "retirement" that he had formed at his "Hermitage," La Source, near Orleans in France, during the preceding years. Nostalgic, however, for the philosophical "Glut of Study and Retirement" at La Source and, as he told Swift, in no hurry to reenter the political fray with its "hoarse Voice of Party" (2:187), he left England in August for his "Hermitage" to resume temporarily the life of the stoic philosopher, which he had so assiduously cultivated.

Before picking up the story of Dawley Farm, we may take a look at his romantic Château de la Source, for in its grounds he first explored the art of landscape gardening. His gardening experience there, with its heavy iconographic emphasis, prepared him admirably to be, upon his return to England, one of Pope's gardening companions and, along with Bathurst, one of the leaders in the increasingly popular *ferme ornée*.

Apprenticeship at La Source

He settled at La Source early in 1720 with his charming new wife, Marie-Claire Deschamps de Marcilly, the widow of the Marquis de Villette, from whom she had inherited a large fortune. Bolingbroke's neglected first wife, Frances Winchcombe, a favorite of Swift's, had died in 1718. Because of his marriage, he told Swift in 1723, "I have been then infinitely more uniform and less dissipated, than when you knew me and cared for me; that Love which I used to scatter with some Profusion, among the whole Female Kind, has been these many Years devoted to One Object."[8] Immediately after his marriage and settlement at La Source, he began to landscape the romantic features of its grounds, making the best of his retirement until such time as he would be able to return to England. He fancied himself a type of rural philosopher—an image he was determined to display to the world and his friends. Relative to Pope's and England's first important steps in the new landscaping, his own gardening at La Source was therefore early; it was also isolated from those early efforts by Pope, Bathurst, and others, and was all the more remarkable for being carried out in a country whose gardening tended in the direction of grand and formal proportions calculated to display wealth and power. His choice for a landscape of retreat, and his own description of his improvements there suggest that he did not lag behind his friends in England.

Bolingbroke had a lot to work with at La Source in terms of natural features. When he first saw the landscape, he must have recognized immediately its particular "Genius" and possibilities. In July 1721, a little over a year after settling at his retreat, he wrote to Swift (from whose gardening in Dublin he was later at Dawley to learn some ideas of taste), praising the setting of his landscape. It is striking how advanced his thinking was at the time concerning the potential of the scene, especially of the spring of the Loiret, a branch of the Loire: "You must know that I am as busy about my hermitage, which is between the château & the maison bourgeoise, as if I was to pass my life in it; and if I could see you now & then, I should be willing enough to do so. I have in my wood the biggest & clearest spring perhaps in Europe, which forms before it leaves the park a more beautiful River than any which flows in greek or latin verse. I have a thousand projects about this spring, and, among others one wch will employ some marble. . . . "[9] What his projects were is, for the most part, unknown. In addition to leasing the château for twenty-five hundred francs annually, however, we do know he spent some ten thousand francs on improving the house and grounds.[10]

Rapin de Thoyras visited Bolingbroke at La Source and later wrote a description of it in his *Histoire de l'Angleterre*. Describing the landscape along the Loiret, just south of Orleans, with its terraced banks frequently adorned by vineyards, he notes that La Source was "a comfortable house,"

> in the gardens of which was the spring of the curious river of which I have spoken. The spring is a kind of pond twenty or twenty-five feet square, and as wide and deep as it is when it flows into the Loire. As this noble lord does not lack money, he has made his house into a kind of château, and greatly embellished the gardens.[11]

In his letter to Swift, Bolingbroke mentions his intention of erecting marble monuments and tablets at the fountainhead of the stream and elsewhere in the garden, and asks for Swift's help to "correct" and provide inscriptions and mottoes for such tablets and monuments as would articulate the *beatus vir* theme throughout the landscape; he also mentions other features, including fine prospects, a greenhouse, and an "ally" leading to his "apartment"—for both the greenhouse and the "ally" he had already decided upon mottoes.[12]

Among the inducements to Bolingbroke's retirement at La Source were his "contempt of grandeur," as he put it, and his desire to create a setting for himself and his friends in which he could think and write about the values and virtues that he believed England rejected when it rejected him. He wanted the house and gardens to express him, or his view of himself, much as we have seen Pope's house and garden expressed him psychologically, morally, and aesthetically. His coloration of La Source reflected the mental state of a deeply disillusioned politician-philosopher. Thus it is not surprising that the principal known emphasis in his gardening at La Source was iconography. With innumerable Latin inscriptions on tablets and monuments, taken from Latin authors as well as composed by himself, he set out to commemorate his service to England and the Queen and his efforts to establish peace in Europe. Several of these tablets also bore witness to his unjust exile at the hands of what he regarded a factious and immoral government.

In his letter to Swift he included a few of these inscriptions, two of which he himself composed. One of them, which he intended to inscribe on a marble monument at the fountainhead of the Loiret (and which he hoped Swift would be able to "correct") suggests the tone and substance of the iconography at La Source:

> Propter fidem adversus Reginam, et Partes,
> Intemeratè servatam,
> Propter operam, in pace generali concilianda
> Strenuè saltem navatam,
> Impotentiâ vesanae Factionis
> Solum vertere coactus,
> Hîc ad aquae lene caput sacrae,
> Injustè exulat,
> Dulcè vivit,
> H. De B. An. &c.[13]

He proposed to place another in "a proper place, before the front of the house, which I have new built."[14] For his greenhouse he chose from Virgil, "hic ver assiduum, atque alienis mensibus aestas [Eternal spring and summer out of season],"[15] and for the "ally" he chose Horace, "fallentis semita vitae [The untrodden paths of life]."[16] The latter represents his attitude to the whole of his retreat.

In accumulating these inscriptions, Bolingbroke was guided by the same instinct for self-projection that later compelled him to fashion Dawley as a farm and himself a moral philosopher-farmer. The difference, however, was that at La Source in his early forties he was justifying his past in the manner of a sexagenarian like, for example, Lord Peterborough, who with his own accumulation of inscriptions, insignia, and emblems enshrined at Bevis Mount his great military career. La Source was a "Hermitage" for him, his friends, and his literary acquaintances; its "untrodden paths" perpetuated this mood.[17]

Whether Bolingbroke described La Source in letters (now missing) to Pope or in conversations the two would have had about gardening when the former visited England in 1723, Pope knew enough about La Source in April 1724 to compose a short poem about it and its pair of owners. In a letter that month he raised the image of Bolingbroke's wife as the "Lady of Lasource." Not entirely facetiously, Bolingbroke had been encouraging Pope to think of her as the "Revelator" at the "Hermitage," from whom the poet could derive spiritual benefits (see 2:221, 249). Pope's beatific image of her anticipated his more earnest appreciation of the devoutly Catholic Lady Peterborough at Bevis Mount, whom Lord Peterborough enjoyed describing as Pope's "female Mediatrix." As it happened, Lady Bolingbroke never ministered in the fashion of "Oracles of our Lady" (Pope's phrase) at Dawley as she had at La Source, probably because she was frequently ill and seldom at home, but in 1724 she elicited Pope's only words about Bolingbroke's landscape. "I see Visions of her and of Lasource," he said, then lapsed into poetry:

> —An me ludit amabilis
> Insania, Audire et videor pios
> Errare per lucos, amœnæ
> Quos et aquæ subeunt et auræ.
> What pleasing Phrensy steals away my Soul?
> Thro' thy blest Shades (La Source) I seem to rove
> I see thy fountains full, thy waters roll
> And breath the Zephyrs that refresh thy Grove
> I hear what ever can delight inspire
> Villete's soft Voice and St John's silver Lyre.
> —Seu voce nunc mavis acuta
> Seu fidibus, cytharave Phœbi.

> I cannot subscribe my self better than as Horace did.
> Vestris Amicum Fontibus et choris.[18]

(2:229)

Bolingbroke's withdrawal to La Source was analogous to Pope's to Twickenham five years earlier in that to some extent it was forced upon him. "Methinks quiet serves instead of happiness to Philosophers," is Pope's comment to his friend upon both their "retirements" (2:226). This poem praises the exile and his wife because they turned an inconvenience into an inspiring model of retirement. Pope portrays their landscape at La Source as an emblem of redemption and productivity, much as he proudly portrayed his own grotto years later as a retreat graced by the visits of what Maynard Mack has called alienated men, people like Bolingbroke and Peterborough.[19] Even though he had not seen, and would never see, La Source, Pope shows a sensitivity in this poem to what the

La Source meditative landscape of retreat meant to Bolingbroke. His contemplation of La Source—and Bolingbroke obviously told him much more about the place than has come down to us—induces imaginative excitement in the poet and seduces him or, as he writes, "steals away my Soul." One is reminded of Pope's allusion to Bolingbroke's lyrical and enticing "Flow of Soul" in his imitation of the *First Satire of the Second Book of Horace*— the lines on La Source are also, in fact, an imitation of lines from Horace's *Carmina* (3.4). Bolingbroke's eloquence and patriotism, and his wife Villette's religiosity, so distinctly bless and inspire their "blest Shades" that far away on the banks of the Thames another "Hermit," as Pope calls himself, draws inspiration. What he sees with his mind's eye is a landscape that reflects its owners' wisdom. He intends his brief articulation of the garden features to be taken as a clue to Bolingbroke's virtue and credentials as an enlightened philosopher-statesman; this is Pope's intention any time he connects landscape with this patriot hero. His remarks on Voltaire before he cites the poem in his letter lend credence to this, so that the poem becomes in the letter not only an echo but also a refrain of what he has just written about the patriotic responsibilities of writers and philosophers. Unlike Timon's, Bolingbroke's gardens are blessed with groves that give protective shade, fountains that are filled with water, and rivulets that "roll" dynamically and (presumably) water and refresh the landscape. The reciprocity between man and landscape even extends to nature's inspiring sounds being complemented by the "soft Voice" and "silver Lyre," images of renewal and revitalization.

Apart from the busy gardening in which he engaged at his French retreat in the early 1720s, Bolingbroke was far from idle there. As he wrote to Pope in 1724, he considered it incumbent "on every Man, that he should be able to give an Account even of his leisure, and in the midst of Solitude be of some use to Society" (2:252). And still preoccupied with mottoes, he added: "Hic sitrus est vatius was a Motto in the Stile of an Epitaph which Seneca had a mind to write over the door of a Slothful Wretch, who liv'd in his Villa like a Drone in some remote Cell of an Hive."[20] He claimed he was never so busy in all his life as he was then, but Pope "must not imagine from hence that I am writing Memoires of my Self" in the style of someone who has outlived his usefulness to his country. On the contrary, he read omnivorously and proposed writing a general history of Europe, which, among other things, would set the record straight on his achievements in the reign of Queen Anne. This he did not get around to doing until the end of the decade,[21] but he channeled his astonishing energy into an extensive reading program from which he emerged in 1725, when he returned to England, as a man of considerable learning with a wide range of intellectual interests. Pope noticed the change after his friend had settled at Dawley and he had seen their friendship grow more intimate. "Lord Bol. had not the least harm by his fall," he told Swift; "I wish he had no more by his other Fall—Our Lord Oxford had none by his[22]—but Lord B. is the most *Improv'd Mind* since you saw him, that ever was without shifting into a new body or being Paullo minus ab angelis [a little lower than the angels]" (2:332).

In the final months of his exile in France, Bolingbroke and Pope were drawing especially close to each other. He had spent much time with the poet during his few exploratory months in England in 1723, and what he hoped would be a permanent return was imminent. Furthermore, one result of his reading program was a keener interest in poetry.[23] As he told Pope with a touch of vanity, Voltaire had visited him, the "Hermit," at La Source (2:221–22).[24] He even took it upon himself to advise his friend not to look upon his Homer translations as his magnum opus, but to pursue new directions with honor "to your self, to your Country, to the present Age, and to Posterity" (2:219). They both wanted to strengthen and continue this friendship, and landscaping was a leaven that they both sensed would help achieve that end in the years to come.

The return of Bolingbroke—Odysseus

Pope told Spence in 1744 that Bolingbroke, before his return to England in 1725, had remarked: "He was not ill where he was [in France], that he had made several friendships and did not dislike the country, but if he might be *fully* restored, he should be obliged."[25] Even productive "retirement" such as he enjoyed at La Source, with considerable opportunities for original landscaping, could not come close to contenting a restless man who, like Odysseus, longed to return to his homeland, old friends, and native arena of political activity. When he was invited back in spring 1725 to claim his titles and possessions, but not his political rights, he was not slow to take up the offer. With his arrival at Dawley early that year, there begins a new stage in his and Pope's relationship, as well as a new chapter in English landscaping. Before dealing with the Dawley landscape, we may pause briefly to consider the tenor of Pope's response to Bolingbroke's return to England because it both influenced and derived from his then evolving ideas about landscaping.

It has been observed that Pope's ideal figure of the statesman in a good society, as he presented it in his imitation of Horace's *First Satire of the Second Book* and in other poems of the 1730s, may have owed less to Horace than to his work on translating the *Odyssey* in the early 1720s.[26] Bolingbroke's return and Pope's concurrent notions about the utilitarian aspect of landscape gardening are two other factors that ought to be seen as related to his work on the *Odyssey* and his concept of the patriot-statesman. These factors all converged in 1724–25 to emphasize a new dimension in English landscaping and a new theme in Pope's poetry.

It is likely that as Pope looked to Bolingbroke's return, he saw him through the classical perspective offered by Odysseus, so that his friend became a kind of Bolingbroke-Odysseus, to use Maynard Mack's phrase—the much-enduring and much-experienced exile. There were resemblances between his friend and Odysseus that encouraged this identification, such as the former's widely recognized eloquence. Pope paid his friend a considerable poetic compliment by speaking of the "Feast of Reason and the Flow of Soul" to be discovered in his company;[27] and Lord Chesterfield once remarked that "he possessed such a flowing happiness of expression that even his most familiar conversations, if taken down in writing, would have borne the press without the least correction."[28] Also like Odysseus, he was "inly pining for his native shore" (*Odyssey* 5.195). Not only that, but his country, Pope believed, sorely needed him; as with Ithaca, it was a race against time: would Bolingbroke be able to return in time to rescue

England from its accelerating pace of chaos and corruption? It was natural for Pope imaginatively to connect these two exiled heroes as he translated the *Odyssey* and, in the middle of it, welcomed the statesman home after so many years.

Maynard Mack has shown how sensitive Pope was to analogy. It partly accounted for his achievement in his *Odyssey* of magnifying two major qualities, sententiousness and pictorial and useful landscaping.[29] Just as he did this in his translation, he imagined it when he saw Bolingbroke come home and begin to landscape his "farm" at Dawley; and the two imaginative acts, the one literary and the other biographical, perpetuated each other.

The two men had seen much of each other during Bolingbroke's visit between June and August 1723, when Pope was still in the early stages of the translation and there were high hopes of Bolingbroke's return for good. The nostalgia and melancholy of some of Pope's descriptions of Odysseus's homeland and homestead before the hero's return may owe something to Bolingbroke's presence. As for the descriptions of landscape in the later books, when Odysseus is home, they may have assumed a special urgency and precision by Bolingbroke's own return early in 1725.[30] This interrelation is important to us because Pope's carefully composed topographical passages during these periods can suggest what special sense of landscape he entertained in relation to Bolingbroke.

The main theme that emerges from many such passages is *in utile dulce*—the use of terrain whereby pleasure is combined with cultivation. As we know, from Switzer onwards this had been an important theme in English landscaping, one especially promoted by Pope; but what Pope magnifies in this verse—and it is the only verse he wrote during these years—is the sententiousness that the theme is given by association with the figure of a Bolingbroke—Odysseus, the patriot and future farmer of his homeland. Describing his homeland to King Alcinous of Phaecia in book 9, Odysseus focuses on its "fruitful stores" (line 27); when he goes on to summarize the beauties of some of the islands he saw, he describes the pictorial beauties of agriculture and repeats the word "products," although it is not only man but also nature whose genius does the work. Of the home of the Cyclops, he observes that while they are "Untaught to plant, to turn the glebe and sow,"

> They all their products to free nature owe.
> The soil untill'd a ready harvest yields,
> With wheat and barley wave the golden fields.
>
> (121–24)

As for Lachæ, "here all products and all plants abound,/Sprung from the fruitful genius of the ground;/Fields waving high with heavy crops are seen" (151–53). When Odysseus at last arrives home in book 13, Athene's speech celebrating Ithaca's cultivation and the industry of its inhabitants can be read as Pope's and Bolingbroke's vision of an England with "swelling grain," "loaded trees [which] their various fruits produce," "clust'ring grapes" affording "a gen'rous juice," "Woods [that] crown our mountains, and [that] in ev'ry grove/The bounding goats and frisking heifers rove" (289–96).

We will recall that Pope's description of the gardens of Alcinous almost a decade earlier (1713), which he included in book 7, contained these same images of the pictorial and useful in gardens; yet he composed this passage presumably without any thought of Bolingbroke, or of a Bolingbroke-Odysseus persona heightened by the moral and political overtones of sagacious gardening. This is not, however, a contradiction. The fact alone that in 1713 Pope singled out the passage on the gardens of Alcinous from the entire *Odyssey* for translation and inclusion in his *Guardian* essay demonstrates that he was pleased with his early translation and the understanding of gardens that lay behind it. Although it is a pity he chose to translate Homer for his authority in the essay rather than articulate his own gardening ideas, his translation proves how important he already felt it was not to waste the landscape with sterile garden design that gratified the pride of the gardener and ignored both the "situation" of a plot of ground and the people who lived on or near it. The piece contains images of landscape use that may be read as politically allusive even that early in Pope's career. Moreover, he had come under the influence of William Whiston's astronomy lectures, which awakened his relish for the variety and beauty of "the boundless spaces of the extended Creation," and he had grown ungenerous about the "Impiety" of men who ignore a beautiful and open "Prospect of Nature."[31] It was as he impatiently waited for Bolingbroke's return in 1724 that he translated Homer's account of the gardens of Alcinous. When the time came to translate the *Odyssey*, Bolingbroke's situation and his own sharpened gardening ideas impelled him to emphasize more and more the "Patriot's" and moral being's responsibility to be the good gardener. This emphasis continued to increase in his thinking throughout the 1720s and 1730s. It found its way into print in the *Odyssey* and, if he wrote it, in *Dawley Farm* (1731); and then it squarely challenged his contemporaries in *To Burlington*.

In the final book of the *Odyssey*, the emotional climax of the hero's reunion with his father, Laertes, is heightened by the portrayal of Laertes' "cultivated land" (24. 235). By the time Pope translated this section, Bolingbroke had either been farming at Dawley or thinking of doing so for about one year. In his account of Laertes' settlement, we can imagine a glimpse of Dawley: "labour made the rugged soil a plain," on which there stood a "mansion of the rural sort,/With useful buildings round the lowly court"; and the most authentic touch is the observation that the master "seeks the field" (24. 236–56). Laertes is also presented as an ideal of "kingly Gard'ner" whose "careful hand is stamp'd on all the soil" (24. 267, 288) and who taught his famous son as a child to plant and care for trees.[32] Together with some divine help (the "Genius"), their cultivation and designs guarantee a "future vintage"—a phrase that may be taken as a symbolic portent of what is in store for England now that Bolingbroke-Odysseus is back.

To the leading Opposition gardeners, Bolingbroke's return to his homeland and his subsequent landscaping illustrated the redemptive power that enlightened landscape gardening could have on the country. The corruption in Ithaca to which Odysseus returned was in the Opposition mind so neatly analogous to the English political and social chaos to which Bolingbroke returned that Pope deliberately stressed the moral attributes of the deserving landscaper. He thus dramatized the ugly image of those usurping and landless lords who in Odysseus's absence were controlling the country and wasting its resources in useless luxury. When Eumaeus, whose rural virtues in the epic are never in doubt, denounces this background of urban sin, we may hear Pope indignantly telling Bolingbroke about the England to which the latter was returning:

> The best our Lords consume; those thoughtless Peers,
> Rich without bounty, guilty without fears!
> Yet sure the Gods their impious acts detest,
> And honour justice and the righteous breast.[33]
>
> (14.99–102)

Unlike Odysseus, Bolingbroke could not use force to regain his political rights; nevertheless, to the Opposition in 1725, he represented their main hope. With him back, they might witness "one man's honesty redeem the land."[34]

"I have caught hold of the earth..."

From the twilight of conjecture we come into certain light when we take up Bolingbroke's actual move to Dawley Farm. The first we hear of him at Dawley is in a letter from himself to Lord Harcourt on 22 March 1725: "Whilst I am here," he wrote, "troubling myself very little about any thing beyond the extent of my farm, I am the subject of some conversations in town which one would not have expected" (2:290).[35] Very likely helped by Bathurst to find Dawley, Bolingbroke seems to have paid £10,000 in deposit for the property the previous September while he was still in France, when the original purchase agreement was made. Apparently, he took up residence before he paid the balance of the £22,200 purchase price since that final transaction was not realized until 14 September 1725.[36] The property had come into the market in 1722 with the death of Charles Bennett, second Lord Ossulstone, created Earl of Tankerville in 1714, so it is possible that during his 1723 visit Bolingbroke and Bathurst had come over from nearby Riskins (four miles away) and gone over the property. It is unlikely that Bolingbroke would have decided on the property one year later had he not seen it on this visit.

As he revealed in his letter to Lord Harcourt, Bolingbroke was not slow to retitle his estate Dawley Farm from the Dawley Manor he had purchased. With its more than 400 acres of park, in addition to a 15-acre "menagerie" and 21 acres of grounds immediately surrounding the house and outbuildings, the estate certainly was large enough to be a farm, but John Knyff's Plan (ca. 1710) shows extensive formal plantations in the grand French manner (plate 50). The Dawley landscape of Knyff's Plan would have appeared to most potential purchasers at the time as a plan conducive to the extension, not obliteration, of the dramatically formal conception. It was typical of the type of huge exploitation of land carried on especially by the newly powerful and rich Whig lords who, like Pope's Timon, wished to demonstrate their financial superiority over the landed gentry or squirearchy, even if they could not claim roots in the landscape going back generations. Such exploitation meant turning hundreds of acres of otherwise arable

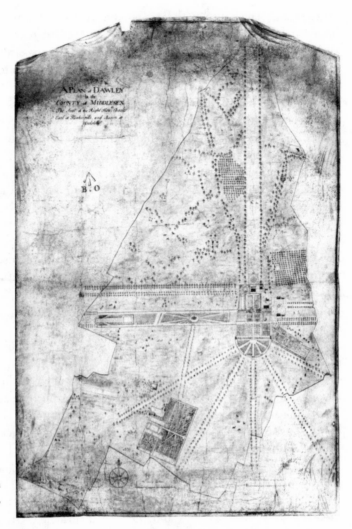

Plate 50. *A Plan of Dawley in the County of Middlesex*, by John Knyff, engraved by Kip, ca. 1710.

land into parkland crisscrossed by interminable avenues from which the owner could feast on views of his possessions. Maintenance costs were enormous, as was the loss of agricultural production.

Bolingbroke had other ideas. He resolved to play the farmer-landscaper. He had tasted the role years before at Bucklebury, his wife's seat next to the Downs in Berkshire, where Swift, whom he had entertained there in 1711, found that he had "enquired after the wheat in such a field."[37] At Dawley, however, it must have satisfied him particularly to reclaim the landscape and, as he saw it, turn it from a useless Whig-type extravagance into an apotheosis of good sense, usefulness, and sententiousness—an Opposition oasis amidst Whig deserts.

Dawley House was built by Sir John Bennett, first Lord Ossulstone, in the late seventeenth century.[38] In 1690 he enclosed about three hundred acres of farmland and laid it out in the French grand manner. Knyff's *Plan* shows exactly what he did with the enclosed land. The house, with farm buildings close by to the northeast and a stable yard immediately to the north of the house, was flanked to the south by formal walled gardens. Running north-south, and not more than twenty yards east of the walled garden and the house, was the main road from Hillingdon Common to Harlington Village, later known as Dawley Road. With the eastern boundary of the estate therefore passing just next to the house, there was little opportunity for gardens to the east; instead, long avenues lined with trees extended south from the walled garden and west in the form of a double avenue from a little court immediately west of the house. Slightly smaller, though not shorter, avenues radiated southwest from the house; and the outlying park to the north was dominated by two long avenues, neither of which was on a central axis with the house. Later these two were replaced by the Long Walk extending from the house northward to the outermost point of the estate, thereby with the southern and western avenues completing the axial design of the park.

In 1707 Charles, second Lord Ossulstone, enlarged the park to 373 acres by moving Dawley Road some distance to the east, away from the house and walled garden, and incorporating the extra land into some formal gardens fronting the eastern side of the house.[39] Certainly Dawley Road followed its later line, as shown in J. Rocque's *Topographical Map of Middlesex* of 1754 (plate 51), by the time another plan was drawn sometime from 1714 to 1722.[40]

According to this latter plan, at the time of Lord Ossulstone's death in 1722 and shortly before Bolingbroke first saw Dawley Manor, the estate consisted of extensive formal gardens and plantations, with avenues radiating in all directions over the park and encompassing the whole of the parish north of the approximate line of Bourne Avenue. The dominant impression was large-scale and comprehensive unity. In his *Spectator* no. 414, we recall, Addison had said he preferred this coherent beauty along French principles to the compartmentalized fussiness of the Dutch garden, but he had also urged—and this was the main thrust of his argument—that in England, where land was more scarce than in France, these expanses of landscape be farmed. As with politics immediately after 1714, however, the era of landscaping up to about 1720 belonged predominantly to the Whigs and the French principles. It is noteworthy that John James's influential translation into English of Dézallier d'Argenville's work, *Theory and Practice of Gardening* (1712), prompted the French style in England and that James's name appears on the reverse side of the 1714–22 plan of Dawley in the Public Record Office, possibly suggesting his connection in some way with the landscape that Bolingbroke purchased. It is also indicative of the popularity of the French style through which English gardening passed in the second decade of the century that the names of both Burlington and Bathurst appear in the list of subscribers to James's translation.

There is almost no evidence of what, if any, landscaping Bolingbroke did at Dawley during his first two years there. The earliest hint of landscaping there is provided by Pope, who on a visit to Dawley in September or October 1725 replied to a letter Bridgeman had sent Bolingbroke, sending the gardener some directions: "I hope you will fix that matter with Mrs. Howard. My Lord Bolingbroke received yours, and shall be glad to see you at your conveniency" (2:327). By this time, as we know, Bridgeman had

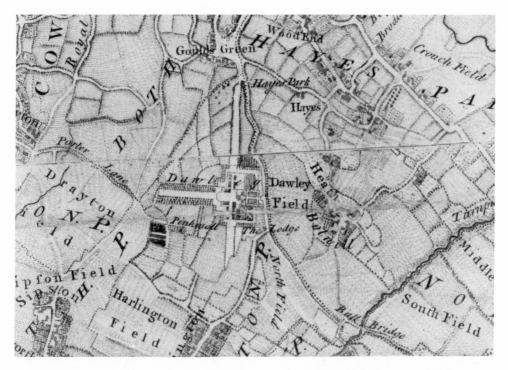

Plate 51. Detail of Dawley Farm and surrounding area from Rocque's *Topographical Map of Middlesex* (1754).

come under Pope's influence; he was currently busy implementing Pope's and Bathurst's landscape ideas at Marble Hill, and in March of the next year he was to "turf" the little "Bridgmannick Theatre" in Pope's garden. And then, apparently at Pope's suggestion, about half a year after Bolingbroke moved in, Bridgeman was to apply his modified landscaping principles toward the conversion of Dawley into a "farm."[41]

Nothing is known of the work Bridgeman may have done at Dawley. An entire year passed, Swift came for a visit and returned to Dublin—of which more will be said later—and there is no sign that any conversion of the landscape, however slight, was underway. In his only reference to Dawley after his first visit in 1726, Swift simply told Pope nostalgically that he could "every night distinctly see Twitenham, and the Grotto, and Dawley" (2:393).[42] Finally in September 1726, Bolingbroke intimated to Swift that some work was underway when he wrote of burying himself from the world in "an agreeable Sepulchre" that he hoped to bring about by "next Spring." Whether the "trifles, disagreeable in themselves" with which, as he told Swift, he was "eternally busy" were details of his financial and political affairs or preparations for the landscaping, it is not possible to say, but it is clear that he hoped to be comfortably "retired" on his converted landscape by spring 1727 (2:403).

During the months between Swift's first and second visits, Dawley house was undergoing some alterations and repairs. In September 1726, James, the third Earl of Berkeley, leased his estate at Cranford to Bolingbroke while such improvements were

131

going on.[43] We know that Pope paid a visit to Dawley just after Bolingbroke had moved out in September because Pope had a serious road accident on his way home from the estate (see 2:399–400, 401).[44] Visiting alone or rendezvousing with Bolingbroke, he might well have been there to consider and survey the projected building improvements. Landscaping must have gone on simultaneously, and it would have been surprising if, living so close to Dawley, Pope had not frequently taken the four-mile carriage ride to observe the progress of the work. Still, what is certainly strange is the complete absence of any allusions to such landscaping by Pope or anyone else. As this study shows, in every other case where his close friends embark, with or without his help, on landscaping and building, Pope mentions or describes the improvements in his letters. This silence may possibly be explained by the politically and personally sensitive position in which Bolingbroke found himself at the time and his consequent desire to avoid gossip abroad by his enemies. In any case, by February he still had not returned to Dawley. Writing to Swift in eager anticipation of his friend's second visit, Bolingbroke refers to the imminent completion of the work:

> you suffer much where you are, as you tell me in an old letter of yours which I have before me, but you suffer with the hopes of passing next summer between Dawley and Twickenham, & these hopes, you flatter us enough to intimate, support y^r spirits. . . . I am hurrying myself here [London] that I may get a day or two for Dawley, where I hope that you will find me establish'd att y^r Return. there I propose to finish my Days in ease with out sloth, & believe I shall seldom visit London, unless it be to divert myself now [and] then with annoying fools and knaves for a month or two.[45]

Bolingbroke's building is only slightly better documented than his planting in these early months. His renovation of the house was carried out according to designs by James Gibbs.[46] The intention was to convert the house from an imposingly formal edifice into a villa whose simplicity would answer to the image of a classical "farm." According to a later writer in the *Gentleman's Magazine*, the result was a two-storied house of brick with round-headed windows below a rather flat roof.[47] But possibly Pope himself best conveyed the beauty, simplicity, and harmonious proportion of the new Dawley, revised according to classical principles; these lines are from the poem *Dawley Farm* (1731), which he may have written and of which more will be said later:

> See! Emblem of himself, his *Villa* stand!
> Politely finish'd, regularly Grand!
> Frugal of Ornament, but that the best,
> And all with curious Negligence express'd.
> No gaudy Colours stain the Rural Hall,
> Blank Light and Shade discriminate the Wall:
> Where thro' the Whole we see his lov'd Design,
> To please with Mildness, without Glaring shine;

Himself neglects what must all others charm,
And what he built a Palace calls a *Farm*.[48]

(19–28)

The alterations to the house must have been extensive to have prompted the poet to say that Bolingbroke had "built" his "Palace." Bolingbroke's sister, Lady Luxborough, some years later also referred to her brother as having "built" the house.[49]

It could be that during the winter 1726–27 Bolingbroke was so occupied with these renovations and eager to return to his house that he paid little attention to the landscape, though he relished the possibilities of a farm at Dawley from the moment he settled there early in 1725. Most of his letters were headed "Dawley Farm" and he began immediately to refer to himself as the "good man" and his wife as "the good woman of Dawley" at "the farm." His renovations in early 1727 included an inscription above his threshold that read, "Beatus satis ruris honoribus." As Pope put it to Swift, alluding to Bolingbroke's resolve to be a "farmer" in the face of tempting opportunities on behalf of the Tory Opposition, "Another of our friends labours to be unambitious, but he labours in an unwilling soil" (2:395). The extent of his commitment to the idea of a farm may be gauged from his effort during the winter of 1726–27 to find a farm also for his sister, who was then living in France. Soon after he returned to his own converted farm, he told her: "I wish I could find such a farm for you as would please me in every respect. No doubt we shall do so att last, and in the meanwhile there is a poor farm in the County of Middlesex where you and yours will be always welcome."[50]

It should be stressed, then, that Bolingbroke's self-image as a farmer was not just a dilettantish pose. As early as 1717, in the first stages of his exile in France and before he had settled into his hermitage at La Source, he had given serious thought to its classical ancestry and its philosophical importance:

> Thucydides in Thracia or Xenophon in his little farm at Scillus. Far from the hurry of the world, and almost an unconcerned spectator of what passes in it, having paid in a public life what you owed to the present age, pay in a private life what you owe to posterity.... Rural amusements and philosophical meditations will make your hours glide smoothly on, and if the indulgence of Heaven has given you a friend like Laelius, nothing is wanting to make you completely happy.[51]

Bolingbroke's ideas for making a farm out of Dawley had appealed to Swift during his visit to England in 1726, but it was on the latter's second visit the following year that he was completely converted; he returned to Ireland determined to promote the *ferme ornée* in his own garden at Naboth's Vineyard, Mrs. Delany's Delville, and elsewhere.[52] Bolingbroke knew that Swift was interested in the concept of a landscaped farm, and he did all he could to engage his friend's curiosity. He talked to him about "mowers & Haymakers" and "my poor farm, which I would willingly make a rich one,"[53] and he made such an impression with the kind of landscaping he showed him that for months after his return to Ireland Swift complained about seeing "no Paulteneys nor Dawleys nor Arbuthnots." It was an exciting time for Swift, Bolingbroke, and Pope, and the landscaping gave a sense of permanence to them all. Bolingbroke summed it up with these reassuring words for Swift in the middle of the following winter: "I am in my farm, and here I shoot strong and tenacious roots: I have caught hold of the earth, (to use a Gardener's phrase) and neither my enemies nor my friends will find it an easy matter to transplant me again."[54]

By February, then, the farming was proceeding apace. "Is My Lord Bol——— at the moment I am writing," Swift asked of Gay, "a planter, a Philosopher or a writer . . . ?"[55] Pope replied with some mirth in June: he was writing his letter from Dawley, he said, somewhere out among the haystacks in the farm. His bemused description of Bolingbroke's enthusiasm for his farming, the longest and most precise we have, deserves to be quoted at length:

> I now hold the pen for my Lord Bolingbroke, who is reading your letter between two Haycocks, but his attention is sometimes diverted by casting his eyes on the clouds, not in admiration of what you say, but for fear of a shower. . . . he has fitted up his farm, and you will agree, that this scheme of retreat at least is not founded upon weak appearances. . . . As to the return of his health and vigour, were you here, you might enquire of his Hay-makers; but as to his temperance, I can answer that (for one whole day) we have had nothing for dinner but mutton-broth, beans and bacon, and a Barn-door fowl. (2:503)

Pope's mention of Bolingbroke's temperance, although done in fun, was calculated to relieve Swift's anxiety that their mutual friend was spending too much money.[56] Bolingbroke had been spending money freely on his landscaping and hospitality—there were feasts of the senses as well as of reason. It was a habit he continued until a few years later when, with his father still alive and his fortune still denied him, he came under considerable financial pressure. It may have been financial constraint in August 1729, in fact, although it could also have been political frustration, that made him tell Swift that he rued the day he decided to build at Dawley and that he little cared for his part of the country in any case.[57] That was spoken in a moment of weakness, however; in spite of the huge sums he was spending, he shared Swift's and Pope's belief (embodied in the Man of Ross) that the "Figure of living" is not a prerequisite for "the pleasure of giving." The rural values he perpetuated at Dawley demonstrated that, but to make certain that everyone realized as much he laid out some more money on a rather bizarre sort of ornament.

Pope was the first to mention this large expenditure: "Now his Lordship is run after his Cart, I have a moment left to my self to tell you, that I overheard him yesterday agree with a Painter for 200 *l.* to paint his country-hall with Trophies of Rakes, spades, prongs, &c. and other ornaments merely to countenance his calling this place a Farm" (2:503). These paintings were completed promptly and achieved a certain fame. Pope saw them in November and described them for Bathurst: "Lord Bolingbroke & I commemorated you in our Cups one day at Dawley—(Farm I should say, & accordingly there are all the Insignia and Instruments of Husbandry painted now in the Hall, that one could wish to see in the fields of the most industrious Farmer in Christendome.)" (2:525).

In spite of Pope's ironic contention that the paintings countenanced Bolingbroke's calling Dawley a farm, Pope of course knew better. Agriculture, haystacks, and carts all over the estate were authentic emblems of a commitment to the *ferme ornée*.[58] The paintings instead were modes of iconography communicating associations of the estate with virtuous, patriotic landscaping; even if considerable money was being spent, it was being used wisely and responsibly for the good of many "Hay-makers" and other laborers. There is a (verse) description of these paintings, which considers their iconographic value, in the poem *Dawley Farm*, following immediately on the lines describing the house that were quoted earlier:

> Here the proud Trophies, and the Spoils of War
> Yield to the Scythe, the Harrow and the Car;
> To whate'er Implement the Rustick wields,
> Whate'er manures the Garden, or the Fields.
>
> (29–32)

There is no false pride in this iconography—ironically, if he wrote those lines, Pope could not have anticipated Peterborough's later penchant for military emblems at Bevis Mount. "Manures" instead implies a kind of reverse snobbery; displayed in the house, the farming implements suggest the superior judgment of an owner who searches out "the Fields." This ideal figure of Bolingbroke projects a *"Contraste* of Scenes," the poet writes to the Whig landowner, "a worthless Tool" lolled "in State,/'Midst dazling Gems, and Piles of massy Plate" (lines 33, 35–36).[59] Whereas this worthless lifestyle climaxes in an "Ideot Laugh," Bolingbroke through his farming and iconography "Adds Grace to Cotts, and Dignity to Swains":

> Whilst Noble *St. J*—in his sweet Recess,
> (*By those made greater who would make him less*)
> Sees, on the figur'd Wall, the Stacks of Corn
> With Beauty more than theirs the Room adorn,
> Young winged *Cupids* smiling guide the Plough,
> And Peasants elegantly reap and sow,
> The *Mantuan* Genius, thus, in rural Strains,
> Adds Grace to Cotts, and Dignity to Swains,
> Makes *Phœbus'* self partake the Farmer's Toil,
> And all the Muses cultivate the Soil.
>
> (39–48)

Dawley Farm, which begins by comparing Bolingbroke to Apollo, glorifies him by stating that in guiding the plough and partaking of the farmer's toil and soil, he is joining some

135

select classical company—Virgil, Phoebus, and the Muses among them. The poet sees him as perfectly tuned to classical landscaping tradition.

"The dictator from the plough"

From written descriptions we learn very little about how Bolingbroke changed the Dawley landscape he acquired in 1725. There is a letter to him from Swift in 1730, continuing the analogy between Bolingbroke and the classical world, that does mention some landscape features. Especially peeved at the time by Robert Walpole, the "Dunce [that] might govern for a dozen years together," Swift discovers the image of Cincinnatus, a man of old-fashioned frugality and integrity who was literally called from his plough on his own land to save the Roman army from peril, and who then returned to his plough. He then threatens to call for Bolingbroke, "the Dictator from the plough." Taking the analogy further, he asks Bolingbroke, who cultivated this pose as a Cincinnatus, about his gardens and farm: "Pray my Lord how are the gardens? have you taken down the mount, and removed the yew hedges? Have you not bad weather for the spring-corn? Hath Mr. Pope gone farther in his Ethic Poems? and is the headland sown with wheat? and what says Polybius?"[60] The amusing allusions to Bolingbroke's spring corn and wheat aside, Swift's casual references, which I think may be taken seriously given his own involvement in gardening, do at least tell us that Dawley had a mount somewhere— the east end of the bowling green seems a likely place (see below)—and some yew hedges, but was Bolingbroke seriously considering removing them both—and if so, why? Was it his idea to put up the mount in the first place? If, as Lady Luxborough observed, Dawley's "environs were not ornamented, nor its prospects good,"[61] is it likely that Pope suggested it? As for the yew hedges, it is feasible that Bolingbroke wanted them removed simply because they bounded the gardens next to the house too much and isolated them from the surrounding farmland.

Most of the evidence about Bolingbroke's landscaping at Dawley is found in maps, however, not in written descriptions. Guided by the 1714–22 Harlington Enclosure Award map, Rocque's 1754 map, and Knyff's *Plan*, we can reconstruct the landscape approximately as it looked after Bolingbroke had turned it into a *ferme ornée* (see plate 52). One of the first things he did was to enclose his demesne with hedgerow lines (A in plate 52) that predated Lord Ossulstone's emparkment in 1690. Along this perimeter he may have provided a narrow path along which to walk and look out upon the fields on both sides. He also turned the southwest of the estate into farmland (C), removing the old menagerie. Lady Luxborough said he eventually had an annual income of £700 from this land. Then he addressed himself to consolidating two western axes, one a long avenue and the other an elaborately landscaped oblong section with square pond (see plate 50) into what looks to have been a bowling green (B) bordered on either side more naturally with several rows of trees. Rocque shows a semicircular line of trees at the east end of this bowling green that may well have been the outline of a green theater resembling the one at Sherborne or the image Pope sketched in his Homer manuscripts for what may have been a garden theater. If that is the case, Bridgeman, who was

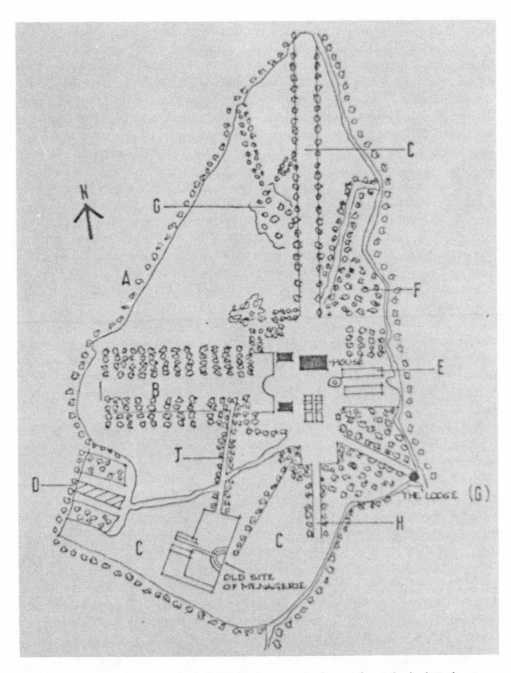

Plate 52. Conjectural reconstruction of the Dawley Farm landscape after Bolingbroke's alterations. References: A. hedgerow; B. bowling green; C. farmland; D. small canal; E. grass plots; F. orchard; G. orchard; H. southern avenue; I. long avenue; J. lime walk; K. lodge. Drawn by Ian Teh.

responsible for Pope's theater and was on the scene, could have laid it out. The features he kept were the long avenue (I), the main axis extending north from the house; a small canal (D) far to the southwest, which he naturalized by planting groves on either side; the southern avenue (H), which he widened and terminated within the park; the lime walk (J); and some of the formal pleasure gardens just south of the house. To the east, between the house and the new road on the parish boundary (ca. 1707), was a smaller avenue approaching the house, on either side of which were two small rectangular grass plots (E). The pleasure gardens adjacent to the house were themselves simplified and rendered less Dutch in style without all those geometrically shaped compartments that Knyff shows. Bolingbroke also preserved and naturalized two orchards, cherry and apple (F and G).

In place of the severe radiating avenues to the southeast that Knyff shows, Bolingbroke substituted thick groves through which one straight path led to the Lodge (K); off this path there must have been, in Pope's favorite style, meandering paths throughout the groves connecting the perimeter of the a farm to the pleasure gardens next to the house. Through the fields between the house (and the groves) and the canal there probably were small paths allowing closer views of the farm and livestock. A similar idea of paths through groves and fields was likely used to the north, on either side of the long avenue.

By 1731 Bolingbroke's conversion of Dawley into a farm conceivably was close to completion, although there is no certain evidence of this. In April Swift suggested a recipe for relaxation by recommending that Pope "Descend . . . to some other amusements [than poetry] as common Mortals do," adding: "contrive new tramgams in your Garden or in Mrs Howards, or my Lord Bolingbroke's" (3:191). This comment, while intimating that Pope had a hand in the landscaping at Dawley and that he had finished with it, does not of course tell us that Bolingbroke had finished all his landscaping; but it is probably true that the excitement had abated by 1731. The mount and yew question mentioned earlier has the ring of an afterthought about it; moreover, in a letter to his wife of 5 June 1730 Bolingbroke sounds as if he is content with what he has done: "I wish you my Dear much amusement and pleasure att Paris. Those which my farm affords are sufficient for me, and I should think myself perfectly happy if they were not passed by other circumstances."[62] That he had finished the greater part of the landscaping is borne out by the poem *Dawley Farm*, which is unlikely to have been written before both the landscaping and the building had satisfied its owner. The poem was first published in *Fog's Weekly Journal* on 26 June 1731 and written not long before then. We may infer from the poet's anonymous covering letter to the poem, which incidentally sounds much like Pope's introductory sentences to his *Guardian* essay, that the estate was ready to be brought to the attention of the public:

> I will . . . inform you, that, in my Return to this Place, I pass'd within a Mile of a fine Seat, which I was prevailed upon, by a Fellow Student, who accompanied me, to go to see; I was so charm'd with the beautiful Simplicity that appear'd in the House and Gardens, and so captivated with the good Sense, and easy Politeness of its Owner, to whom I was introduced by my Companion (who had the Honour of his Acquaintance) that it produced the following Lines, which are at your Service, if you think fit to publish them.[63]

The vacant throne: frustration and failure

Bolingbroke, it seems to me, was the ideal person to whom Pope should have addressed his important garden poem, *To Burlington*, in 1731. That he addressed it to Lord Burlington instead could stand out as an early instance or clue to Bolingbroke's dimming personal and political prospects during his ten-year residence in England. There would have been an appropriateness to Bolingbroke's assumption of the throne of the garden poem: the gardening passages in *To Burlington* would have been even more meaningful in a poem addressed to or about him, and so would have been the Tory-styled patriotism inherent in Pope's appeals for national salvation. For his part, Pope dearly wished he could give this triumphant and as yet empty throne to his philosophic friend.

The public's reception of the poem *Dawley Farm*, however, had confirmed Pope's suspicion that his friend was too politically partisan to be enthroned in a poem that purported to be a bipartisan celebration of national ideals and values. Pope also suspected that Bolingbroke, unlike Burlington and Bathurst, would never become a widely and impartially regarded man of taste. Even *Dawley Farm* turned out to be politically explosive, in its combination of allusions to Bolingbroke's politics, the ethics of enlightened estate management, and ideas of taste in landscaping and architecture—all elements that for five years Pope had seen embodied at Dawley and that he wanted to record for posterity. The poem's prefatory letter, written ironically in the persona of a disinterested university student, inflamed the inevitable party-political reaction: "two or three Gentlemen [Bolingbroke being one]," the poet wrote, "who are continually loaded with Abuse by certain Writers, who stile themselves the well-affected, are the Persons who have the warm Hearts of the People." The poem then begins by comparing Bolingbroke to Apollo, who, exiled by "Tyrannick Jove" (George I and/or Walpole), retired to "Silvan Shades, to Grots and Streams." On earth, as in heaven, he was found to be a "simple Majesty" whom swains and nymphs—that is, the common people or the "chearful Tenants" again—immediately recognized and appreciated for his "Learning, Arts, and Wisdom." Bolingbroke "has made the Fiction true" because he "Taught Patriots Policy; taught Poets Sense;/And bade all live, or die, in LIBERTY's Defence."

A crescendo of patriotism and lamentation concludes the poem; at the least, it reads like an indignant (even sour grapes) attack on an ungrateful Britain. Unlike Burlington, who in the conclusion of *To Burlington* is invoked to make "falling Arts" his care and to bring new honors to a grateful and peaceful Britain, Bolingbroke lives at Dawley "splendidly obscure" and "only for his wretched Country grieves."

Immediately, there was an angry attack on both the author and subject of the poem in the *Weekly Register*, which must have neither surprised nor disturbed Pope.[64] Upon reading it, though, he must have been glad, if he wrote the poem, that he had not presented in it the Burlington poem's carefully worked out ideas on the uses of riches with respect to landscaping, architecture, and estate management. They would not have received a fair reading there.

If it was a personal disappointment to Pope not to be able to honor and articulate Bolingbroke's and, if any, Dawley Farm's influence upon his ethical ideas by addressing a poetical epistle to him, he did at least honor his friend's philosophy somewhat in *An Essay on Man* (1733), albeit anonymously, by dedicating that poem to him.[65] According to Spence, the two men had been thinking of the gardening poem together for a long time; in May 1730 Bolingbroke had sent Pope "a long letter" that Spence said contained the "very large prose collections on the happiness of contentment." "Prodigality (in his piece)," adds Spence, "flings away all in wrong tastes. 'Tis thus in particular that some of the gardening poem will be of service."[66]

As it turned out, even addressed to Burlington the gardening poem drew upon Pope a wave of hostile criticism, largely because the enemies he had made with his *Dunciad* (1728) and *Dunciad Variorum* (1729) were quick to see openings through which they could attack him. The opening they saw and spread about town was the suggestion that in the satiric portrait of Timon's villa and gardens Pope was censoring the seat of the highly regarded Duke of Chandos, Cannons, for its dull and formal grandiosity in an age when greater freedom of landscaping was becoming a sign of good taste.[67] As we know, Pope was embarrassed, apologized to Chandos with assurances that he was not being satirized, and wrote to several of his friends to the same effect. For the public he wrote his anonymous ironic piece, *A Master Key to Popery*.[68]

This essay is mentioned now because one short paragraph in it mentions Bolingbroke and Dawley, though it points the reader ironically to Walpole's buffet at Houghton Hall. "Be it as it will," Pope wrote ironically about himself,

> this Poet is equally happy when he can abuse either [political] side. To shew his wicked Impartiality, at the same time he is squinting at Sir R. [Walpole] he has not spared his old Friend the Lord Bolingbroke.
> A gaping Triton spews to wash yr face [*To Burlington*, line 154],
> is the exact Description of the bufet at Dawley. Nothing sure can equal the Impudence of such a Guest, except the Indifference of that stupid Lord, who they say is not provok'd at it. I doubt not the Honourable Mr Pulteney wou'd have had his share, but that he, poor Gentleman! has no Villa to abuse.[69]

The "gaping Tritons" keep company with the "well-colour'd Serpents" in presiding over Timon's obscenely wasteful and ornamented buffet, so the absurdity of that buffet being compared to the buffet at Bolingbroke's farm was obvious. It is possible, in fact, that Pope intended Timon's "solemn Sacrifice" or buffet to be read as the complete inversion of the "flowing Bowl" and "Feast of Reason" at Dawley. Dawley Farm by this reading becomes an antitype of Timon's villa. Pope liked those images as applied to Bolingbroke so much that he used them again two years later in his *Epistle to Fortescue*, but by then the hostility toward Bolingbroke had, if anything, increased, and what Pope got for his trouble was a vitriolic attack in verse that contained, among others, these lines:

> To Virtue and her Friends you're not a Friend.
>
> . . . .
>
> Nor would a Jew prepare the Friendly Bowl,
> To mingle with the Flow of such a Soul.[70]

Through a period of frustration and an increasing sense of failure, Bolingbroke was encouraged by both Swift and Pope to divert his energies somewhat from politics to

"Philosophy," for which they thought his lifestyle and prospects at Dawley were becoming better suited. "I pass almost all my time at Dawley and at home," Pope told Swift in 1732; "my Lord (of which I partly take the merit to my self) is as must estrang'd from politicks as I am. . . . it is the greatest vanity of my life that I've contributed to turn my Lord Bolingbroke to subjects moral, useful, and more worthy his pen" (3:276). They also urged him to use his time to write a moral history of the age of Queen Anne (3:372-73).[71] This does not mean that Bolingbroke, in spite of his resolution in 1731 to enjoy "an uninterrupted tenor of philosophical Quiet," was in any way resigned to a life of retirement; from October 1732 to April 1733, in fact, he devoted almost every issue of his journal, the *Craftsman*, to attacking Walpole's proposed Excise Bill.[72] As for Pope, his political sympathies were more overtly expressed than ever in his poetry of the 1730s.[73] Under Bolingbroke's influence, the poetry became more Juvenalian and less Horatian as the decade progressed.[74] But the political situation was nevertheless discouraging and all of Bolingbroke's, and the "old" patriots', lingering hopes finally disappeared with the defeat in March 1734 of the Opposition's motion to repeal the Septennial Act. The general election that immediately followed returned Walpole's government with a greater majority. It was then only a matter of time before Bolingbroke left the country in July 1735 and before Dawley, the expression of many of Pope's artistic-moral values, became deserted.

At odd times during his poetry of this period Pope returned, in an autobiographical vein, to the landscape garden or farm as a supporting metaphor for his values, but when we consider how important to him landscaping continued to be, such passages are remarkably infrequent.[75] He had concluded that the landscape metaphor was not an effective poetic device in reforming his country; his new method was to chastize. Instead of "fighting with Shadows" and general propositions, he would now do all he could to raise the anger of bad men. He wrote lengthily to Dr. Arbuthnot about his new strategies while he was on his way, significantly, to Bevis Mount to get really away from the warfare. He had been tempted by Bolingbroke to bring his private gardening world into public service in his poetry, and he had been rebuked for it; he would try to avoid it in the future.

Getting rid of this "incumbrance": the sale of Dawley

Bolingbroke's sale of Dawley provides a melancholy postscript to the farm's brief history in Pope's life and in English landscape gardening. Among the archives at Petworth House, Sussex, there is a collection of letters from Bolingbroke to Sir William Wyndham, written in the years 1735-40, when Bolingbroke once more was living in France;[76] these letters document the trouble he had in selling his farm. Most important, these letters, in retrospect, throw light on his attitudes toward his farm, retirement, and politics.

For a few months after the Opposition's defeat in the general election in 1734, Bolingbroke saw much of Pope, as the latter told Swift: "I now pass my days between Dawley, London, and this place, not studious, nor idle, rather polishing old works than hewing out new" (3:444). By July of the next year, however, Bolingbroke had left Dawley and the Opposition gloom. He returned to France and settled at Chantelou, where he was determined to lead the life of a scholar. He returned to England once to stay from July 1738 to April 1739, during which time he lived mostly with Pope at Twickenham. There were political reasons for this visit, but another reason was his inability over the preceding three years to sell Dawley and his decision to take matters into his own hands.

In his first letter to Wyndham of 29 November 1735, Bolingbroke explains the reasons why he returned to France and has decided to settle there. Then, as to Dawley, he adds:

> In this light you see that the Establishment I had almost completed before the late King's death att Dawley, becomes useless to me. Tho' none of the favourable contingencys that might have happened, did happen whilst I was in England, but on the contrary even such cross events as I had no reason to apprehend, yet I might be tempted perhaps to keep a place where I have layed out so much to improve the habitation and the Estate if I remained fixed in England.

But having decided to remain in France, he asks the help of Sir William and Lord Bathurst—"who has a good tallent, & good luck too, in the management of such affairs"—in ridding him of "this incumbrance." Above all, he insists, it is crucial that the business be kept secret and that the idea of the sale be circulated as Sir William's, not his own, so that his enemies might be encouraged to find a purchaser simply to get him out of the country. Concerning a price, he admits that he bought it dearly at £23,000. He regarded it "rather as the purchase of a Seat than of an Estate." Not wishing "to make a noise, by a hagling Treaty," he would let it go, with all its improvements, for the same amount provided the purchaser would give him one or two thousand pounds per year annuity "for my Lord St. John's life," a commitment, he observed, not liable to run over three years.[77] With the money he would secure his wife's future, but he would also leave some in England in case he decided to provide himself with "some little habitation such as may suit an old, retired, attainted Philosopher, & Hermit to vegetate, languish, & dye in, if the fancy of dying att home should take me." In fact, although he wrote to Wyndham on 5 January 1736 that he thought himself "att liberty to live where I amuse myself the most, and enjoy the greatest ease"—by which he meant France—he would have much preferred to remain in England had his wife's health and tastes, and his own financial state, permitted it. This much he intimated to his sister on 3 March 1738: "As I was a farmer in England, I am a huntsman in France; and am less diverted from the latter than I was from the former Employment."[78]

With Dawley still unsold on 18 March 1736, Bolingbroke sounds more anxious and determined; if it is not sold by the end of the summer, he tells Sir William, he will feel an uneasiness that will "distress all the philosophical quiet of my life, for tho I do not wish to live like Aristippus, I cannot live like Diogenes."[79] Dawley did not sell by summer's end, and on 27 February 1737 he lowered the price impulsively and dramatically, offering it to Dr. Richard Mead,[80] who attended Pope in 1743, for the ridiculously low sum of £6,000, including the furniture. If nothing comes of these negotiations, he threatens to come to

England in May to take new measures, which might include living on his capital "att Dawley in a very retired manner as well as at Argenville."

May passed and Dr. Mead backed off, provoking this sneer from Bolingbroke: "This person it seems who wanted a Seat, & who affected to be so frank a purchaser, thinks the land too dear. He should have found a better reason, or have given none." His 5 May letter is laden with melancholy thoughts "without any reserve" about retirement and friendship. He was so fed up he even allowed himself to say that the main reason he returned to England in 1725 was out of resentment over the ill-usage he had received from his enemies. New Year's Day 1738 arrived and still Dawley was not sold. Bolingbroke was genuinely puzzled:

> I have made wrong judgments & wrong calculations many times in my life, but I never misreckoned more than about Dawley. . . . I always expected to lose vastly by it; but I hoped, and found that persons of better judgment than myself in matters of that kind believed, it would sell for some little advance above what it had cost me in the wild and naked condition in which I found it.

His phrase "wild and naked," incidentally, is puzzling since the estate pictured by Knyff in his *Plan* can hardly be called "wild." "Naked" may refer to the lack of a suitable house and garden furnishings when he bought Dawley. In his mind the wildness of the gardens when he took possession could have derived from its unproductive character—in the same sense, that is, as Timon's gardens were like a desert barren of those improvements that could have turned them into a useful and tasteful landscape.

Finally, in July he journeyed to England, staying with Pope for almost one year. In the middle of his stay, Pope thought that his friend Lord Orrery might wish to purchase Dawley. His letter to Orrery in October summarizes the confused state of affairs at the time:

> The Loss of my Lord Bolingbroke from this Neighbourhood could be recompenc'd by nothing so well [as Orrery's taking up residence at Dawley], & it has vext me at heart to think, no Man of *this Sort* was likely to succeed to the very best & most commodious House in England, as well as the cheapest. It cost him not twelve years ago near 25 thousand pound & will be sold for 5000; The Furniture, (perhaps the compleatest any where in a private house) for which an Upholsterer in my hearing offerd 3000, to take down & make money of, he will part with at the price where it is ready put up; And the Land by measurement, at the Rent it is now let at & Tenanted. There is an Advowson of 300 a year & a Royalty, which last is not to be valued nor the Timber (4:136).

Orrery as a purchaser was an attractive possibility since, as a good friend of both Swift and Pope, an English nobleman of his worth would honor Bolingbroke's memory and achievements there. He would also prevent the vulgarization of the seat by some "Child of Dirt, or Corruption" (4:136) like Joshua Vanneck—whom Pope referred to as "vile Van-muck" in *The Second Epistle of the Second Book of Horace* (line 229)—or "some Money-headed & Mony-hearted Citizen" (4:136). This Vanneck had, at Bolingbroke's expense, stayed at Dawley with his wife for two weeks under the pretense of wanting "to Examine the Wholsomness & Dryness of the House, take opinions of the Soil, & converse with the Farmers" (4:137).[81] As it turned out, Orrery was not interested. More time elapsed, and in December Pope's remark on the unresolved fate of Dawley was that "a Great House in this Nation is like a Great Genius, too good for the Folks about it" (4:153).

Almost four more months elapsed before Dawley finally was sold, and sold well, to Edward Stephenson for £26,000. Almost immediately Bolingbroke departed for France, where, according to Pope, he embarked on an entirely satisfying style of life: "his Plan of Life is now a very agreable one in the finest Country of France, divided between Study & Exercise, for he still reads or writes 5 or 6 hours a day, & hunts generally twice a week: he has the whole Forest of Fontainbleau at his command" (4:177).[82] His father eventually died in 1742, whereupon he inherited the family estate at Battersea and intermittently lived there for the rest of his life, gradually acquiring a reputation as "the Hermit of Battersea." Bolingbroke would not be pleased to know that today on the site of Dawley stands a modern factory.

6

Pope, Mrs. Howard, and Friends
at Marble Hill

Pope's involvement with Marble Hill, Henrietta Howard's country house in Twickenham, began in 1723. By July of that year it appears that Mrs. Howard already had some designs for the house, perhaps drawn up by Roger Morris, and it is likely that about one month earlier she had decided to build the house along the Thames at Twickenham in a "shot" called Marble Hill, from which the house eventually took its name. In July she wrote to John Gay, who with Pope and Swift had been her intimate friend for about three years, about some plans that Gay had stumbled upon by chance in her apartments at the Prince of Wales's house at Richmond Park. The secrecy of the project was paramount, largely because of the threat posed to her security by her long-estranged and improvident husband, Charles Howard, so Mrs. Howard appealed to Gay to keep his knowledge of the plans to himself: "There's a Necessity, yet, to keep that whole affair secret, tho' (I think I may tell you) it's almost entirely finish'd to my satisfaction."[1] Gay replied quickly that he would "not say a word more of the house."[2]

Gay was probably one of the few of Mrs. Howard's close friends, however, who had not known of the project. In spite of her need for secrecy, Pope and Lord Peterborough already knew about it, even where the house was to be. In a letter to Pope written sometime between 23 June and 14 July,[3] Lord Peterborough specifically mentioned the location: "pray doe me the favour to send me the breadth, & depth of the marble Field, you may have itt measured by moon light by a Ten foot Rod, or any body used to grounds will make a neer guesse by pushing itt over" (2:183).[4]

Mrs. Howard's means whereby to purchase land and build a house on it were due entirely to a settlement on her early in 1723 by the Prince of Wales, whose mistress she had been since 1717. Wanting her to be independent of her erratic husband, the Prince settled on her some stock worth £11,500, sundry pieces of jewelry and plate, and all of the furniture and furnishings presently in her apartments at the Prince's houses at Leicester Square and Richmond Park. Until then her adult life had been independent neither socially nor financially. Her youth was spent happily with her mother and her father, Sir Henry Hobart, the fourth Baronet, and seven other children at Blickling Hall in Norfolk, but when she was about seventeen (1698) her father died and shortly thereafter she unwisely married Charles Howard, the youngest son of the fifth Earl of Suffolk.

Plate 53. Henrietta, Countess of Suffolk. Oil painting by Charles Jervas.

The young couple went from bad to worse owing to Howard's profligacy.[5] Finally, they left England in 1713 or early 1714 for Hanover, where they pinned their hopes on the favors of the future King of England. When George I acceded to the throne in 1714 they returned and were given places in the royal household, probably because of the impression that Mrs. Howard made on the monarch and Princess Sophia, the Electress of Hanover (who died in June 1714).[6] While her husband was favored with the position of groom of the bedchamber of the King, her place was woman of the bedchamber to the Princess of Wales, where she established loyalties that, together with her personal attractiveness, subsequently won her the attentions of the Prince of Wales. She also came to the attention of the Opposition circle, including Swift, Pope, Gay, and Arbuthnot, who gathered round the Prince at Leicester House and the Lodge in Richmond Old Park.[7]

Pope first mentioned seeing her in September 1717 at Hampton Court, to which he could have been invited by Mary Bellenden, Molly Lepel, and Anne Griffin, maids of honor to Princess Caroline, who like many others in the summer months immediately following the publication of his *Works* (in June) were eager to see the young poet. He had stopped at Hampton Court on a ramble to see his "great" friends "at almost every house along the Thames" who upon the breaking up of Parliament, he said, instantly become his neighbors (1:417). From the start he was impressed by Mrs. Howard's graciousness and wit, but he was also distressed by the rigors of her life at Court, which she had apparently confessed to him, and by her state of dependency there.[8] She was in her third year of service to Princess Caroline, with many more to come. Pope addressed a poem, *The Court Ballad*, to the maids of honor in which he coyly mentioned "Mistress H——d" as one who was not "chaste"—an allusion to her sexual services rendered to the Prince.[9]

Unfortunately, no letters between Pope and Mrs. Howard during these early years have survived; nor did Pope refer to her in his letters again until 1724.[10] Gay did mention her, though, in his poem *Mr. Pope's Welcome from Greece* (1720), as one of Pope's friends who will be ready to welcome him back to the living from his "Six Years toil" of translation: "Now to my heart ye glance of *Howard* flies."[11] In fact, Gay mentions her before any of the other ladies, suggesting that by 1720 she was already one of Pope's close friends.

When Pope moved out to Twickenham in March 1719 he naturally had more opportunity to cultivate his friendship with Mrs. Howard, who spent much of her time at nearby Richmond Lodge in the old deer park of Henry VII's palace at Shene, where after his quarrel with the King in 1717 the Prince of Wales was forced to reside. He divided his time between there and Leicester House. We have seen how Pope's move launched him into a hectic period of landscaping and that Twickenham and its environs offered the ideal setting for new landscaping ideas in the following years. Since his move brought him closer to the rival Court at Richmond, perhaps inevitably he soon found himself involved in the gardening going on there under the encouragement of the intellectually alert Princess Caroline. In the months following his settlement at Twickenham, while his friendship with Mrs. Howard developed, his reputation as a gardener also grew. Eventually that reputation reached Richmond. As a prelude to our discussion of Pope at Marble Hill, we may pause therefore to look at the gardening at Richmond and consider whether his experience there may have influenced what happened three to four years later at Marble Hill: why Mrs. Howard proceeded as she did at Marble Hill in 1723, who helped her, and how its landscape was conceived.

A princely garden: Richmond Lodge

Possibly through Lords Burlington and Bathurst, and perhaps because of the landscaping that Pope set about immediately in his own garden, he soon became known to Princess Caroline as someone worth consulting about the royal gardens at Richmond, which Bridgeman was then redesigning. Whether or not Walpole was correct in citing Pope's garden as an influence upon Bridgeman and the gardens of Richmond Lodge,[12] it is likely that Pope first worked with Bridgeman in connection with them. He may in fact have seen him at Richmond Lodge in September 1719 at a meeting of gardeners, convened presumably by Princess Caroline herself.

Two years had elapsed since the Prince had been banished from Court, and it had become clear that without Hampton Court they would have to regard Richmond Lodge as their permanent country residence until the Prince acceded to the throne. Accordingly, they bought the house and grounds in 1719 and Princess Caroline immediately determined to overhaul the landscape. Gardeners were brought in to consider the design of the landscape, and apparently the Princess included Pope, presumably thinking that if any new ideas were to find their way into these royal acres, Pope just might be the man to suggest them. Pope was not pleased by the gardening symposium that resulted. He sent an account of this meeting to Lord Bathurst, which with its burlesque of the mania for topiary work contains several satirical echoes of his *Guardian* essay six years earlier:

> That this Letter may be all of a piece, I'll fill the rest with an account of a consultation lately held in my neighbourhood, about designing a princely garden. Several Criticks were of several opinions: One declar'd he would not have too much Art in it; for my notion (said he) of gardening is, that it is only sweeping Nature:[13] Another told them that Gravel walks were not of a good taste, for all of the finest abroad were of loose sand: A third advis'd peremptorily there should not be one Lyme-tree in the whole plantation; a fourth made the same exclusive clause extend to Horse-chestnuts, which he affirm'd not to be Trees, but Weeds; Dutch Elms were condemn'd by a fifth; and thus about half the Trees were proscrib'd, contrary to the Paradise of God's own planting, which is expressly said to be planted with *all trees*. There were some who cou'd not bear Ever-greens, and call'd them Never-greens; some, who were angry at them only when cut into shapes, and gave the modern Gard'ners the name of Ever-green Taylors; some who had no dislike to Cones and Cubes, but wou'd have 'em cut in Forest-trees; and some who were in a passion against any thing in shape, even against clipt hedges, which they call'd green walls. These (my Lord) are our Men of Taste, who pretend to prove it by tasting little or nothing. (2:14)

Notwithstanding Pope's mockery of this "consultation," that such a meeting was held at all and that Pope was invited testify to Caroline's passion for gardening, which Peter Willis has stated was at the center of Bridgeman's landscaping for the Crown until her death in 1737.[14] Moreover, she seems to have had the good sense to keep Pope interested and involved in the landscaping during at least the following six or seven years. Although his direct influence at Richmond is difficult to document owing to the work of professional designers like Bridgeman and, later, Kent (who in 1735 designed the rustic Hermitage there, discussed below), it appears he felt easy enough in his relationship to that landscape to borrow a detachment of Bridgeman's laborers working there in 1726 in order to turf his own "Bridgmannick" theater (2:372). Queen Caroline, of course, presumably granted this gardening favor, and others, in return for landscaping favors (ideas) that Pope had given her in the past.

Unlike the King, Caroline had a wide and generous interest in the arts and patronized artists as diverse as Charles Jervas, Sir Godfrey Kneller, John Wootton, William Kent, Henry Flitcroft, the sculptors Battista Guelfi and John Rysbrack, and many others. She acquired her enthusiasm for gardening from the royal landscape at Herrenhausen that Electress Sophia had laid out, but since her arrival in England and move into St. James's with the King and Queen in 1714 she had been unable to satisfy her enthusiasm. As for Hampton Court, she was scarcely in a position as the daughter-in-law of the unsympathetic King to take a lead in altering that royal landscape or, more to her taste, the recently completed Kensington Gardens by Henry Wise, the royal gardener first under Queen Anne and then George I.[15] Doubtless she sought out Wise, however, and talked to him about one of her two favorite subjects (the other was theology), but until the Prince of Wales acquired Richmond Lodge, talk about gardening with Wise or anyone else was pretty much all she could do to satisfy her interest.[16] Richmond therefore became a spiritual oasis for her amid the artistic wasteland of a Court where not only landscaping—George II called her landscaping "childish silly stuff"—but also books, philosophy, and theology were ignored or shunned. With Richmond as her showpiece, she could encourage the new landscaping in the 1720s.[17] Landscaping at Richmond was also another means by which, on behalf of the Prince's circle, she exerted some leadership and independence in the country, perhaps to the chagrin of the King,[18] although indifference to the arts ran in the family and the Prince himself had little use for them, including gardening, except for music and the opera.

By early 1728, when Queen Caroline appointed Bridgeman to succeed Wise in the post of royal gardener, Bridgeman had already demonstrated his expertise in private landscapes such as Stowe, Rousham, and Marble Hill, but about five years earlier, when she called for his services at Richmond, he had not yet established some reputation in the less formal style. He had not yet worked on Marble Hill, which particularly enhanced his credentials as far as the royal couple were concerned because the grounds there were the Prince's gift to Mrs. Howard; nor had his gardening yet been influenced by Pope. His career had begun back in 1709, and he had worked with Vanbrugh at Blenheim and at Eastbury (in Dorset), but in 1719–20 he was thrown into situations, employment, and friendships that changed the course of his professional work and brought him in touch with new ideas.[19]

The date when Bridgeman began laying out the grounds at Richmond Lodge is unknown, but it must have been well before October 1723, when Lady Mary Wortley Montagu, who had moved to Twickenham with Pope's help in 1719,[20] saw and loved them.[21] He must have been present at that early meeting in 1719 which Pope mocked. We know he did some work for Pope at Twickenham within a year or two of Pope's move there, so the poet may have passed on a word about him to Richmond. If Caroline had not called upon Bridgeman by early summer 1721, there was by that time another garden, in which Pope took an interest, that benefited from Bridgeman's labors. It was Down Hall in Essex, where from the summer of 1720 until his death in 1721 Matthew Prior, with Bridgeman's help, had devoted himself to improving the grounds, whose "Gardens so stately, and Arbors so thick" had great possibilities.[22] It was through his work at Down Hall that Bridgeman came under Lord Harley's patronage and became a member of his artistic coterie, the "Tory Virtuosi." Harley then asked him to landscape his estate, Wimpole Hall, Cambridgeshire, from 1720 to 1724.[23] With the architect Gibbs putting up three classical temples around the bowling green at Down Hall and Bridgeman designing two layouts—one more "adventurous" than the other but both with kitchen gardens—a spring, an encircling terrace walk, and a great walk leading down to a great basin fed by a stream, by the spring of 1721 Prior could write to Harley: "I am glad Bridgeman has begun so well. He says he will make it the finest and noblest thing

149

in England."[24] Willis compared existing plans of Down Hall and judged that Bridgeman was making the Down Hall landscape freer and more suggestive.[25] In September 1720 Prior thought well enough of Bridgeman to be calling him his "operator hortorum et sylvarum."[26] Prior died suddenly, incidentally, a few days after making this remark; had he lived, one suspects he would have become a major figure in the new landscaping.

Lady Mary Wortley Montagu, who was on good terms with Princess Caroline and fairly good terms, until 1722, with Pope, must also have put in a good word for Bridgeman. As she had been a resident and close neighbor of Pope's in Twickenham since 1719, and since she took more than a casual interest in gardens, she undoubtedly knew Bridgeman's recent work. She seemed to prefer a more irregular and natural style in gardening; even as early as 1717 out in Turkey she had noted with pleasure the rusticity and simplicity of Eastern gardens. Passing through France on her return to England in October 1718, she had little use for the excessive ornamentation of French gardens as against, even then, the simpler and less artificial English royal gardens:

> There is here an excessive prodigality of ornaments and decorations, that is just the opposite extreme to what appears in our royal gardens; this prodigality is owing to the levity and inconstancy of the French taste, which always pants after something new, and thus heaps ornament upon ornament without end or measure. (1:521)

When she returned home she found it was her friends Pope and Bathurst who seemed to be leading the way in naturalizing gardens much beyond what she remembered as the character of the royal gardens. She also discovered that far from being satisfied with the royal gardens, Princess Caroline was herself panting after something new, but not mere ornamentation. Lady Mary may have felt behind the times; nonetheless, there is no evidence that she requested Pope's help in the design of her own garden before they were estranged in 1722. Had he been asked, Bathurst might also have helped, and perhaps Bridgeman.[27] Mrs. Howard did ask, and the collaboration of those three gardeners occurred and bore fruit further up the river at Marble Hill.

By 1723, then, with much expert and original help Caroline had created at Richmond a unique royal landscape, consisting of a villa, a park, and a garden. Lady Mary saw it in 1723: "except in the Elysian Shades of Richmond," she told her sister, Lady Mar, "There is no such thing as Love or Pleasure."[28] She was not the only one who was reminded of an Eden or earthly paradise by Richmond; this became a popular analogy, with Milton's description of Eden in *Paradise Lost*, book 4, frequently being cited in accounts of the "Varieties of Nature" in the landscape.[29] John Macky approved of Richmond in 1722 because it appeared "neat and pretty" instead of with the "Grandeur of a Royal Palace"; best of all, he thought, was "the Wood cut out into Walks" with the natural feeling of "plenty of Birds singing in it, [that] makes it a most delicious Habitation."[30]

The variety of the gardens is evident from John Rocque's 1734 plan of the Richmond gardens (plate 54). The woods cut by winding paths and dotted with seats and arbors extended in a northeast direction from the Palace along the river. Across the

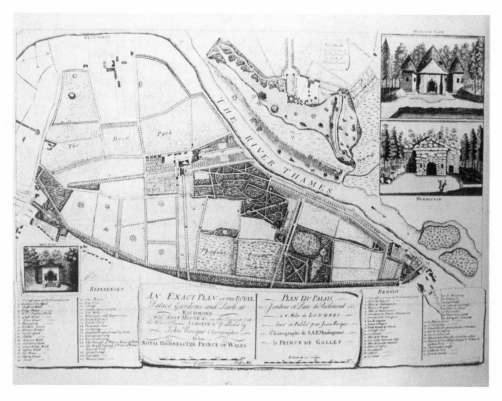

Plate 54. Plan of Richmond gardens by J. Rocque, 1734. This shows Syon House across the river and details of both the Hermitage and Merlin's Cave.

river to the north and west was pleasant countryside endowed with villas and dominated by the Duke of Northumberland's Syon House (plate 55). To the east were the deer park and fields for grazing and cultivation, so that wherever these winding paths emerged from the woods one could enjoy an open view of farmlike scenery. On the south side of the main house were the formal parterres, and to the north was a straight canal flanked by regular groves. But the regularity of even this canal area was diminished by a thin line of woods cut by winding walks with a theater—Popean/"Bridgmannick"?—at the furthermost northwest corner. As for the cultivated fields embracing and surrounding this area, Bridgeman, under whatever influence, deliberately sought to accommodate them visually within the design. Walpole mentioned this element of design, noting that when Bridgeman's "reformation gained footing, he ventured farther, and in the royal garden at Richmond dared to introduce cultivated fields, and even morsels of a forest appearance."[31]

The forest appearance may indirectly, through Pope, have owed a debt to Cirencester; woods were used to "loosen the outline of the fields and replace clumps by wavy belts of trees"; winding paths were cut through them and decorated with garden buildings, and meadows and fields of corn were "interspersed" with them.[32] In 1723 these woods cut out into walks were the "Elysian Shades" in which Lady Mary found

151

Plate 55. "View from the Summer House in Richmond Park Up the River Thames." Drawn by Chatelain and engraved by P. Benazech, 1755.

such pleasure. They contained some of the effects Pope had already achieved in his own garden, the rooms and allées arranged irregularly, resembling the northern strip of his garden that ran east-west. With its canal, groves, and grass plats, the first section, just east of the house, also brings to mind the arrangement of the water gardens at Sherborne, which Pope admired in 1724. Although William Kent later designed some garden buildings for the Richmond gardens, notably the Gothic and politically inspired extravagance known as Merlin's Cave (see detail in plate 54), at which expense Pope, Gay, and others enjoyed some satirical fun,[33] he did not alter the landscape; so Rocque's plan illustrates some of Bridgeman's early essays, in a more "naturalized" manner.

"That you might Leave that Life of hurry"

When Henrietta Howard received her settlement from the Prince in 1723 and decided to build her country retreat, she looked around her in the immediate area and saw gardens she wanted to imitate: she knew, too, whom she might call upon to help her. Pope and Bathurst immediately offered to help; and for advice with the more technical aspects of design over the extended period required to landscape a garden out of bare fields, they knew they could all rely on Bridgeman. Three other persons played vital parts in the earliest stages of Marble Hill's history: the brothers John Campbell, second Duke of Argyll, and Archibald Campbell, Earl of Ilay, of Whitton Park (see plate 9); and Henrietta's admirer, Lord Peterborough—all Pope's friends. Gay mentioned the Duke of Argyll, whom Pope knew from at least 1716 until Argyll's death in 1743, and his brother, Lord Ilay, as two of the poet's friends awaiting to give him a "Welcome from Greece" in 1720:

> See there two Brothers greet thee wth applause
> Both for prevailing Eloquence renown'd
> Argyll the brave and Islay learn'd in Laws
> Than whom no truer friends were ever found.[34]

Argyll shared Pope's dismay over Mrs. Howard's sexual drudgery and may have recommended that she be given the means whereby to achieve some independence and peace in the form of a country house. His wife, the former Mary Bellenden, maid of honor, hinted that some relief was in the offing in a letter to Mrs. Howard in 1722: "I was told before I left London that somebody that shall be nameless [Caroline?] was grown sour & crosse and not so good to you as usual, if it is so, it betrays the want of that good understanding that both you & I so often have flatter'd ourselves about, but these times I fear is over. It wou'd make one half mad, to think of miss spent time, in us both, but I am happy, & I wou'd to god you were so & ... that your circumstances were such that you might Leave that Life of hurry."[35]

When the decision to go ahead with a country house was made public early in 1723, Lord Ilay was appointed as a trustee charged with the task of finding a site and purchasing the land. He was well cast in that role; Pope's friendship with him was encouraged by Lord Ilay's enthusiasm for horticulture and landscaping—in that order. Horace Walpole recorded his intellectual interests: "He had a great thirst for books; a head admirably turned to mechanics; was a patron of ingenious men, a promoter of discoveries, and one of the first great encouragers of planting in England."[36] In 1722 he acquired an estate at nearby Whitton, where he built a house and began to landscape, stocking it with rare trees and plant specimens.[37] Since Mrs. Howard's duties at Richmond had by no means ended (she did not retire from Court until 1734), she needed a house nearby. Twickenham was a logical choice, but where in Twickenham? Pope had some suggestions; probably everyone agreed that a site with some frontage along the river was desirable or even requisite. By late June or early July 1723, as we have seen, Lord Peterborough knew that Marble Hill "shot" was to be the center of the site,[38] and in March of the next year Lord Ilay began purchasing the land.

The "gallant gardiner"

This brings us to Lord Peterborough's relationship with Mrs. Howard. Without his appearance we would know less than we do about Pope's friendship with her. He had been secretly married to Anastasia Robinson, the famous opera singer, in 1722, but his marriage did not prevent him from embarking at about the same time or shortly after on a courtship, perhaps somewhat political, of Mrs. Howard. Pope, who may have been in on the secret of Peterborough's marriage and who quickly developed—most things in Peterborough's life happened quickly—a great affection for the sexagenarian general, was aware of his friend's fondness for Mrs. Howard. Others soon began to regard him as her "gallant." Pope's first surviving letters to Peterborough not only mention Mrs. Howard but also turn their wit on the affection both men felt for her. Knowing Peterborough's delight in compliments paid to her, in his letter of July 1723 Pope pictures her "door" as an entrance to paradise.

> I will...hope to find at Mrs Howards door [at Richmond Lodge], next Sunday morning about 12 The Appearance of that Benevolent Being, without whom I had never been blest with such a Celestial Conference. A Lady of her acquaintance inform'd me, She was to be Approachd at that canonical hour; & as tis the piece of Devotion & Adoration which I shall pay with the most Zeal & Spirit. (2:178)

He then offers Peterborough a commission before Sunday to be his "sole-acting-Plenipotentiary" at her door. The lady appears in another letter that summer; sitting beside her, Pope advises Peterborough, "you yourself will own it a peculiar mark of Esteem and Gratitude, when I tell you I lose an hour of Mrs Howard's Conversation, to converse in this manner with You. She sits by my side, I look not on her, but on these lines; I give no attention to her, but indulge the remembrance of you" (2:189).

That hour of conversation might well have touched on her future gardens. We know from Peterborough's midsummer request for the dimensions of "Marble Field" that the landscape was very much on his mind. Eventually he came to be known as her "gallant gardiner" and, fired by love as much as or more than by landscape, he even wanted to claim the initiative in her gardening. With the Duke of Argyll and Lord Ilay acting as her trustees, and Lord Herbert, later the ninth Earl of Pembroke, the "Architect" Earl, supervising the building of the house,[39] this was the least he could do, he probably thought. "Fair Lady," he declared to her, "I dislike my Rivalls amongst the living, more than those amongst the dead [the Duke of Marlborough had just died in 1722], must I yield to Lord Herbert and Lord Ily...."[40] The story of his disappointment as her gardener is told in the next chapter, so we will leave Peterborough's role in the project by citing a passage from his second surviving letter to Pope that shows his eagerness to get on with preparing the ground and equipping it with outbuildings. It appears from this letter that contractual arrangements for the purchase of the land were nearly complete by Autumn 1723: "I intended to waite on Mrs Howard to day att Richmond.... I was impatient to know the issue of the affaire, and what she intended for this autumn for no time is to be Lost either if she intends to build out houses or prepare for planting, I will send to morrow to know if you can give me any account, & will call upon you as soon as I am able that we may goe together to Mrs Howards" (2:196–97).

The landscape

Lord Ilay first purchased land for Mrs. Howard in March 1724, when he acquired from Robert Parsons and Thomas Vernon four pieces of land totaling eleven and one-half acres in "Marble Hill Shot" (see plate 56).[41] Mr. Vernon, of nearby Twickenham Park, was secretary to the Duke of Monmouth, a wealthy Turkey merchant, and with

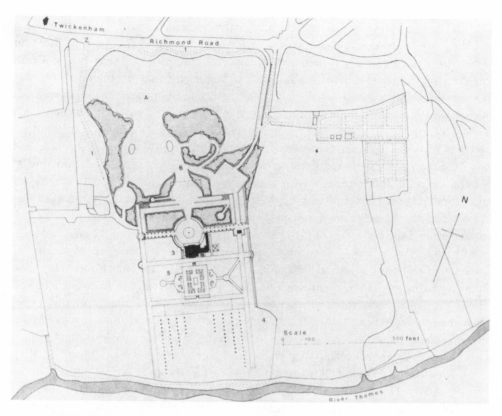

Plate 56. Marble Hill landscape reconstructed as it might have looked when Pope knew it. This drawing incorporates the sketches in plates 59 and 60 and M. Draper's drawing of Marble Hill (*Marble Hill*, p. 13) derived from a deed of 23 August 1901. References: A. the Meadow; 1. drive or path; 2. entrance; 3. the house; 4. widening possibly used for gardens; 5. area of formal gardens; 6. Pope's sketch, as shown in plate 60, drawn into the area north of the house. Drawn by Ian Teh.

Sir Godfrey Kneller was a churchwarden in the Twickenham parish church of St. Mary's; he was also Pope's landlord, so the poet conceivably acted as liaison between him and Lord Ilay. A second purchase was made in September from Robert Parsons and John Gray, whom Pope mentions five years later (3:35) in a letter to Mrs. Howard regarding the nuisance that Mrs. Vernon, widowed since 1726, had been making of herself over a road-access question in Mrs. Howard's property. In this purchase Ilay acquired for Mrs. Howard two more parcels of land: ten acres north of the "Marble Hill Shot" acreage extending up to what is now Richmond Road; and four acres south of the "Shot" reaching right down to the Thames. At that point, then, Mrs. Howard owned over twenty-five acres from Richmond Road south all the way to the river: from Richmond Road to the river about sixteen hundred feet; riverside frontage about five hundred feet; and Richmond Road frontage about a thousand feet narrowing to about eight hundred feet just north of the house. The house was sited in the middle of the initial "Marble Hill Shot" acreage where the land narrows to a width of about four hundred fifty feet, except for a small protrusion to the east (4 in plate 56).[42]

155

If Henrietta Howard had landscaped all of this acreage, her garden would have been sizable—five times as large as Pope's. Her limited means and the shape of this land induced her to confine her gardening to the narrower strip of land stretching down to the river on the south side of the house. The larger enclosure to the north (A) was perhaps circled by a drive (1) giving access to the house from the main entrance (2) off Richmond Road. It may have been landscaped in some modest manner, but there is no known record of that. The jocular references by Pope to Mrs. Howard as a shepherdess, and to her cows, suggest she may have rented some of the land as pasturage for sheep and cows and thereby created a minifarm on her estate; she thought of it as her "Meadow."[43] Or else she could have done this with some of the adjacent land. It would have made a nice rural prospect for livestock to have been feeding in the foreground as one approached the house from the main Twickenham–Richmond Ferry road or as one walked around the perimeter of the field along the railing. If some of the land had been used in this way, it would have made more credible Pope's frequent claim that at fashionable Twickenham he and his friends felt quite "rural," although Robert Digby, we know, was amused by the claim when he compared the settings of Lady Scudamore's Holm Lacy and Twickenham. "Pray when you next see Mrs Howard," he told Pope, "give my humble Service to her, & ask her whether she knows that a Scene like this is properly the Country; when she wishes to live in it. Or whether she loves the Country only as you do & would exclaim with you—How Rural we are! at Twittenham" (2:305).

The siting of Marble Hill house (3) was, as it turned out, a crucial decision in the history of Mrs. Howard's gardens. The house severed the recently acquired land into two areas. It was placed at the crest of a gentle slope gradually descending to the river, so that to the north of the house was the wider and more circular open field on flat ground, while to the south she could look down her garden to the Thames and across over the fields beyond. A verse by Horace Walpole on his Strawberry Hill suggests that the grounds of Marble Hill may have been generally regarded as flat:

> Some like to rowl down Greenwich Hill,
>   For this thing or for that,
> And some preferr sweet Marble Hill,
> Yet tho' sure 'tis somewhat flatt
> Yet Marble Hill, nor Greenwich Hill
>
>   .   .   .   .
>
> From Strawberry Hill, from Strawberry Hill
> Could ever bear the bell.[44]

The house and its immediate area of kitchen gardens, garden houses, and so on occupied an area of about two acres, leaving a garden area about the size (five acres), though not the shape, of Pope's. This was the area that commanded the attention of Pope and Bridgeman, and Bathurst and Peterborough, in 1724–25.

Despite Lord Peterborough's eagerness, the designing of the landscape did not begin until after the land was purchased outright in 1724. Pope may have had Marble Hill on his mind when he complained to Bolingbroke back in April that his Homer translation was blotting out too much of his life: "'Tis such a Task as scarce leaves a Man time to be a good Neighbour, an useful friend, nay to plant a Tree, much less to save his Soul" (2:227). Mrs. Howard's acquisition of Marble Hill was timely because it gave him, in addition to his own garden, another alternative to Homer for creative activity. His thought was on Marble Hill a good deal through the spring and summer of 1724.

Pope's first letter to Martha Blount while he was staying at Sherborne in June shows more interest in her and Mrs. Howard back home at Twickenham than in Sherborne (2:235–36). Between those two ladies a friendship had developed that Pope was encouraging. If there is a present he could wish for Martha, it is Mrs. Howard: "I am therefore very sollicitous that you may pass much agreeable time together: I am sorry to say I envy you no other companion." He says he misses the "scenes of paradise" and "happy bowers" on "the banks of the Thames" and, in his next letter, he reassures Mrs. Howard, "don't let any Lady from hence imagine that my head is so full of any Gardens as to forget hers. The greatest proof I could give her to the contrary is, that I have spent many hours here in studying for hers, & in drawing new plans for her" (2:240). He was in a mood for sketching at Sherborne, but any plans he may have drawn for Marble Hill are not known to have survived; the logical question is how much that he saw at Sherborne influenced his designs for Marble Hill.

If Pope "studied" Sherborne to get ideas for Marble Hill, he must have done so chiefly with Mrs. Howard's five acres fronting the river in mind. Unlike Pope's garden, where the five acres were on the other side of the house from the river and therefore not visible to river traffic, Marble Hill's largest garden area consisted of those five acres facing the river and containing about five hundred feet of river frontage. By June, this and the area on which the house stood were all that had yet been purchased. Thinking of that regularly shaped area, Pope may have recognized in the seventeenth-century Italianate water gardens at Sherborne just what the area required since the flat valley there between the two sets of terraces was "layd level and divided into two regular Groves of Horse chestnuts, and a Bowling-green in the middle of about 180 foot" (2:237). Still, there was little in that area of Sherborne's gardens to inspire new landscaping ideas. The area was formally bounded on one side, and split into two areas, by a canal "in the form of a T." While no canals or other artificial waterworks were needed at Marble Hill, where the Thames drifted by at the foot of the garden, the flat lawn or grass plat and, especially, the horse chestnut groves of the Sherborne valley were introduced, very likely by Pope. As it was described by a guidebook to Twickenham in 1760, this south garden contained "a fine green Lawn, open to the River, and adorned on each Side, by a beautiful Grove of Chestnut Trees."[45] In the conjectural reconstruction of the probable original layout of the gardens, these features are included. Such an expanse of grass flanked on both sides by trees was both an economical and a natural feature. Also, within the belts of trees, provided they were irregularly planted, winding paths could be laid out and interesting groves fashioned. An engraving in 1749 by Augustin Heckell and James Mason (plate 57) suggests that the groves of horse chestnuts were planted in straight rows, and I have

Plate 57. View of Marble Hill from the river, by A. Heckell and J. Mason, 1749.

drawn the trees in rows in the reconstruction, but the guidebook's depiction of a "beautiful Grove" in 1760 hints that the trees may have been less regularly planted than that. Trees in straight lines are easier to draw and, in a frontal perspective such as Heckell and Mason show, create a more stately setting for a house. A more romantic late-century engraving of Marble Hill (plate 58), showing a much more leafy river frontage after these trees had grown for half a century, gives no sign of trees in rows. The whole treatment of the grounds, however, is suspect because it does show cows drinking in the Thames, as if the gardens were so forlorn by then that the front lawn had become a pasture. The character of Marble Hill has here an ironic flavor: Mrs. Howard deliberately cultivated a rustic pose at Marble Hill, but surely never to the genuinely "rural" extent of having cows cooling themselves off on her front lawn.

The Heckell and Mason engraving also shows that at least by 1749 an open area between the trees laid out in what looks like turfed terraces (without trees) extended all the way from the house to the river. The late-century engraving also shows what look like terraces that have collapsed and been allowed to grow into softly contoured dips and rises. Neither illustration reveals any sign of what was claimed to be an original layout of the gardens, of unknown origin, reproduced in *Country Life* over sixty years ago (plate 59),[46] which I have incorporated into the reconstruction of the garden. According to this plan, a narrow strip 250 feet wide extending across the breadth of the garden immediately on the south side of the house was given over to a formal garden consisting of a central parterre with pathways leading off east and west and then dividing into two more paths on each side running into the corners of the area. This is what the 1760 guidebook referred to with the remark "the Garden is very pleasant." A pathway then

Plate 58. Late eighteenth-century engraving of Marble Hill. Artist unknown. The treatment is more romantic than in the Heckell and Mason engraving, with mature trees and unrestrained cows framing the still pristine-looking beauty of the villa.

separates this formal area from what is just barely hinted as the start of the green lawn flanked on either side by the horse chestnuts. Under the influence of Kent, "Capability" Brown, and others after them, such formal areas were quickly replaced by a sweep of lawn, so it is not surprising that by 1749 this formal area at Marble Hill had disappeared. The authenticity of this purportedly original layout, in this detail at least, is borne out by M. Draper's adapted deed-plan showing the approximate sites of original fields. In that plan the remains of the formal area are clearly shown, with even one of the paths to a corner still intact. Though it is not shown on the original plan, the area was most likely terraced with steps leading down to the lawn that covered the rest of the distance, some 450 feet, down to the river.

It is disappointing that the *Country Life* plan of the original layout is limited to the areas immediately north and south of the house, but the reason for that seems clear: the area shown is precisely the area of the garden having straight parallel sides and constituting a square with the house located just north of its center. In addition to showing the formal garden on the south side, it shows on the north side a circular drive directly in front of the house, which also appears in Draper's deed-plan and which has a regularity in character with the formal garden. In other words, this square segment of the garden had an individual style and integrity that leant itself to a separate drawing. It

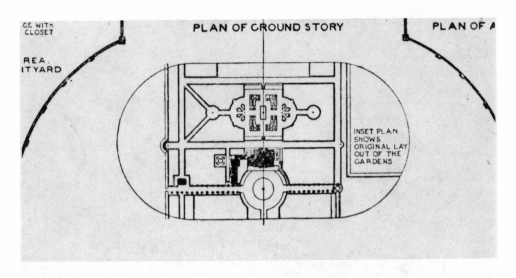

INSET PLAN SHOWS ORIGINAL LAY OUT OF THE GARDENS

Plate 59. Plan of Marble Hill, from *Country Life* 39 (25 March 1916):399. Date unknown.

was more geometrical than either the north or south areas of the estate and effectively separated the two areas.

The 1760 guidebook particularly mentioned "an Ally of flowering Shrubs, which leads with an easy Descent down to a very fine Grotto; there is also a smaller Grotto, from whence there is a fine view of *Richmond-Hill*." We can only speculate about the location of this alley—the Heckell and Mason engraving does not show anything like it—but it was probably straight and ran north-south along the eastern boundary down to the river.[47] Under the influence of Pope, who had been creating his own grotto under his house, we would expect Mrs. Howard to have created some grottoes in her own garden. It was becoming fashionable for a lady to have and decorate a grotto. Both gardens were near or next to the river, which would have provided the appropriate water effects and sounds. In Swift's poem *A Pastoral Dialogue between Richmond-Lodge and Marble-Hill*, Marble Hill speaks of its "Echoes."[48] The Thames, of course, was the most important focus in the landscape at Marble Hill: the house fronted it squarely, the southern gardens reaching their climax in the river frontage. These grottoes would have served as cool seats where one could enjoy aquatic sounds, prospects of the river with river traffic gliding by, and the romantic view of Richmond Hill as the major feature in the distant landscape. Visitors would have gravitated toward the river and would have been encouraged to do so by a landscape design that unfolded in that direction—unlike Pope's garden.

It is possible that one or two grottoes were built at Marble Hill in 1724–25 as part of the original design, but it is more likely that the creation of the main grotto coincided with the start of the second phase of Pope's grotto in 1739–40. The earliest reference to any grotto at Marble Hill may be by Mrs. Howard herself in her remark to Pembroke, "I am at this time over head and ears in Shells."[49] Pope could be expected to have

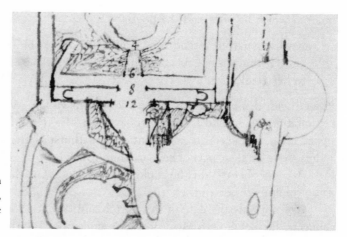

Plate 60. Sketch of a garden plan, almost certainly by Pope, perhaps intended for Marble Hill.

transferred his new enthusiasm for making grottoes to Marble Hill; he even supplied Mrs. Howard with some of the shells and Cornish minerals he was lucky enough to be receiving from William Borlase. He had helped Mrs. Mary Caesar with her grotto at Bennington Hall in the 1720s and was going to assist Mrs. Ralph Allen, too, with hers at Prior Park, but grottoes were a feature of her garden in which Mrs. Howard herself took special interest over the years, taking her cue perhaps from Kent's Hermitage at Richmond. In 1742 she was still embellishing it; George Grenville wrote to her in September sending his greetings "to the inhabitants of the Grotto (which . . . I hope goes on prosperously)."[50] If Mrs. Howard had liked to visit beaches, she could have supplied herself with shells, though her indulgence in this hobby, fashionable as it was, probably was not that deliberate—certainly not as methodical as Mrs. Delany's (Mary Pendarves), friend to Swift and Bathurst and inventor of the "flower mosaic," who by seven every morning was at work sticking shells on the walls of her grotto at Delville in Ireland and who did the same for a number of her friends.[51] The smallest of Mrs. Howard's grottoes probably served as an icehouse, to which Swift, who styled himself as the "Keeper of the Ice-House," referred in his *Pastoral Dialogue between Richmond-Lodge and Marble-Hill*.[52]

In the absence of evidence suggesting otherwise, and since the large piece of land north of the house, the "Meadow" between the house and what is now Richmond Road, was undoubtedly used for pasturage and was enclosed by a ha-ha—"ye great Ditch," as Roger Morris's account book noted[53]—it would not appear that much careful landscaping was done north of the house by Pope or anyone else. One piece of evidence, however, over which we can speculate, may provide some additional details about Pope's involvement at Marble Hill in the northern area. Preserved among Pope's Homer manuscripts in the British Library is a sketch of a garden plan by Pope that has never before been published (plate 60).[54] It is more detailed than the others in the Homer manuscripts and appears on the back of Pope's translation of a passage from *Odyssey* 17, which probably dates it as no later than June or July 1725.[55] The sketch appears on the address side of a letter Lord Bathurst had written to him (at approximately the same time) in which he informed the poet:

> I will not fail to attend Mrs Howard upon Marble Hill next tuesday, but
> Lady Bathurst is not able to come at this time, which is no small mortification
> to her. (2:298–99)

Pleased with this news of his friend's imminent visit to Marble Hill and eager for the consultation they would be likely to have over Mrs. Howard's gardens, Pope may have ripped off and retained the page containing Bathurst's letter, sketched out a plan on the address page for some part of her garden to which he had been giving some thought, and then saved the sheet so that he could translate Homer on the overleaf. The plan is in the nature of an impromptu sketch.

It is not only the date of this sketch and Bathurst's mention of Marble Hill that connects the sketch with Mrs. Howard's landscape. The landscape design it delineates also appears to connect it with the landscape north of the house. If the sketch is examined alongside Draper's adapted 1901 deed-plan and the *Country Life* drawing of the formal garden area adjacent to the house, it will be seen that the rectangular (formal) area shown at the top matches perfectly the rectangular area adjacent to the north front of the house shown on both the other plans. We are not able to check the sketch in much detail against the *Country Life* drawing because the latter leaves off just at the point where the sketch may begin and extends north, but if the sketch is presumed to be a plan for this area of Marble Hill, it offers additional detail about how the formal grounds immediately north of the house may have been laid out.

To begin with, Pope has written the numbers 4, 6, 8, and 12 along the central path extending from what might be a circular drive to the edge of the rectangle. These figures could represent the number of feet the ground rises and therefore terraces extending the width of the rectangle and leading up to the next area of the garden. The figures may otherwise simply indicate the width of the path as it proceeds north. Pope also sketched in a diagonal path from the northeast corner of the rectangle toward the center that terminates in what looks like a little arbor amidst probably some low-lying greenery. On the highest terrace or northern edge of the rectangle he also sketched in two rounded niches for seats, statuary, or other types of ornament; the niches and the adjacent long corridor or terrace could have been turfed. Thus far Pope's sketched plan is essentially formal.

Perhaps this small formal area ended abruptly, however, at a ha-ha that separated it from the "Meadow," but Pope's sketch may suggest that it did not. It is unlikely that he would have approved of such close proximity of formal gardens and the "Meadow." Even at Rousham, where open pastureland was unobtrusively separated from house and gardens by the river Cherwell and appeared very close to them, there was a long bowling green between the river and the house; and all along the perimeter of the garden the trees mediated between pastureland and the garden, preventing the occupant from feeling naked or exposed in the presence of open landscape. Pope's sketch includes groves with winding paths and straight walks cut through them leading to secret arbors and larger "rooms" or bosquets that, if Marble Hill were the subject of the sketch, would have been placed between the house and fields.

Such groves resemble his style of gardening along the northern boundary of his own garden and also that shown on two other sketches amidst the Homer manuscripts (plates 23 and 24). This sketch is more detailed than the other two, though—more detailed, in fact, than any other Pope is known to have drawn of a garden design he himself conceived. It shows how subtly he could connect naturalized groves and walks to formal areas. Rather than introduce one garden area after another rigidly without transitions, he draws into the plan a fluid relationship of features reflecting emblematically his aesthetic-philosophical principle that a person must be able to experience visual and emotional freedom as he walks through a garden. In a garden much of this is an illusory freedom, but after all it was in gardens that Pope learned to think this way about landscape. As John Dixon Hunt has written, he and his contemporaries in the early-century landscape gardening movement bequeathed just this discovery about movement of mind and body through landscape to the late-century and Romantic writers about open landscape.[56] That little sketch of Pope's is an early and superb example of his deliberate effort to represent in a small garden scene this, as yet undeveloped, style of thinking about nature and man's harmonious accommodation within it.

In Pope's sketch, a pathway from a circular area northwest of the house leads north into a large turfed clearing where four other paths converge. Two of these paths lead from arbors and wind through the trees. Another wide path cuts through the trees from the entrance to the formal area near the house. If he intended the sketch for Marble Hill, Pope shows his originality in the way he used this latter path as a transitional feature between the formal gardens and the irregular area in which he doubtless was chiefly interested. Rather than continue the symmetrical aspect of the main walk in the formal garden leading north to the wilderness, he immediately widens the path on the east side while he keeps the west side straight. As the path approaches the smaller opening to the large clearing, it has to narrow and so ends up with an oblique and curving side.

It is unlikely that Pope did this sketch for his own garden, which was already laid out and established by 1725. But John Searle's plan does reveal how closely the effects achieved at the western end of Pope's garden resemble the poet's treatment of the large clearing and its perimeter in the sketch. It is obviously the same eye that designed both. First, the shape of the clearing and its prominence and relation to other features in the sketch bring to mind Pope's bowling green, which was the single largest feature in his garden. Also like his bowling green, the clearing at its northern end contains what appear to be two small mounts situated in a manner resembling the two small mounts in Pope's garden framing the entrance to the more private western end of the garden, sacred with associations of his mother. Both the clearing and bowling green are bordered on one side by the groves with arbors and labyrinthine walks. Pope enjoyed the effects of contrast and surprise—the "retiring and assembling shades"—that resulted from placing an expanse of fine turf close to such groves so that one could emerge from the darkness and irregularity of the groves into the evenness and relative formality of the turf. Finally, there is a more precise similarity of design between the small and most westerly section of Pope's garden, containing the obelisk in memory of his mother together with two urns or statues, and the southern end of the clearing in the sketch, where he has arranged hedges or trees to create a little setting with concave wings.

As soon as the weather improved in the spring of 1725 Pope was eager to see Mrs. Howard's landscape grow, and he knew Bathurst would be, too. But getting his friend to visit Twickenham, instead of the other way around, was getting to be like asking a patriarch to visit one of his distant "children," so Pope enticed him with an image of the springing grass: "If he will not vouchsafe to visit either his Servant, or his handmaids, let him (as the Patriarchs anciently did) send flocks of Sheep & Presents in his stead: For the grass of Marble hill springeth, yea it springeth exceedingly & waits for the Lambs of the *Mountains*, (meaning Riskins)[57] to crop the same

> Till then, all Mrs Howard's Swains
> Must feed—*no* flocks, upon—*no* plains."[58]
>
> (2:292)

After Bathurst's visit, probably in June,[59] Pope went to Stowe where, off and on, he stayed for about a month, using it as a base for a busy period of rambling and gardening "from Garden to Garden" (2:314–15). As he rambled in and between gardens in July, he was thinking of refinements on what he had already designed at Marble Hill; he was also thinking of new ideas. At Stowe particularly, where Bridgeman had begun to work, he found new gardening effects to admire and study for Marble Hill, as he had the year before at Sherborne. "I've seen Mr. Pope," Martha Blount wrote to Mrs. Howard on 23 August, "as I believe you have or will very soon. He is come back very full of plans for buildings and gardens which I find is not owing so much to the beautys of Lord Cobhams as the desire he has of being serviceable to you at Marble Hill."[60]

Even by then, however, the gardens were impressive and winning some recognition. Miss Blount, whose frequent visits to Twickenham enabled her to see Marble Hill in its succeeding stages of landscaping, went on to say in her letter: "I have already often seen your House & Gardens in that place and I have carryd my way of building so far that I have passed whole days with you so very agreeably that I hope the prospect of it is not at too great a distance as you imagine." Lady Hervey also spoke of the landscaping in a letter to Mrs. Howard on 30 July: "I shall certainly visitt both you & marble-hill for I long extreamly to see, what I'm told is the prettiest thing of the Shire that can be seen."[61]

In order for the garden to have been so beautiful within one year after its landscaping had begun, the work in the grounds must have been well organized. This was Bridgeman's doing. He hired workers, arranged for tools and equipment, and saw to it that work continued through the winter—though an account for landscaping work in January 1725 records payment "For a Garden Roll[er] . . . by the order of Mr. Pope"; it was probably for the bowling green, for which also there was ordered "120 ft. of Deale Railling Cross ye Bolling Green."[62] Simple garden tools like rollers and brooms were vital in maintaining the turf of the new landscape garden, not only on the bowling green but also in large clearings such as those described above, and in arbors and pathways.[63]

Trees also were easier and more economical to care for than hedges and topiary, so that, for example, in his sketch Pope provides for a "natural wilderness" of trees. The horse chestnut groves also required little maintenance.

Other features in the gardens that were in place by June 1725 are mentioned in the account book kept by the builder, Roger Morris: "ye Mount," "Deal Railing for ye Yew Hedge," "Railing in ye Meadow," "a Style & Steps at ye Thames side," and "ye great Gate Ditch."[64] It is difficult to locate the yew hedge and the mount. The hedge would have been appropriate as a means of enclosing the circular drive; Bathurst had planted a yew hedge around an enclosure in front of Cirencester house. The mount, which according to Morris had a brick wall, could have been placed in the southern gardens and incorporated into any designs Pope had planned for that area. As for buildings in the garden, Roger Morris's accounts also mention that in 1728, following on more than one year of apparent inactivity in the building of the house, Mrs. Howard paid Morris four hundred pounds to complete some work in the house and to build "4 Buildings in the Garden." A later document describes them as being "in the Manazery [sic]," and as having "tiled roofs and pediments over the doors."[65]

In the eighteenth century, incidentally, a menagerie was an aviary. It was particularly fashionable for ladies to have them in their gardens. Swift's friend Mrs. Delany had one at Delville Park near Dublin, and Bolingbroke's sister, Lady Luxborough, wanted one in her garden at Barrells. Switzer identifies a menagerie as a major feature of Riskins in his epitome of its gardens, where it appears as a rectangular area surrounded with trees cut through by curving paths—a naturalized scheme for an exhibit of both exotic and domestic birds. But probably not many ladies were as serious about exhibiting birds in their gardens as was Mrs. Delany, who stored her menagerie with Indian pheasants and a "great variety" of other birds. Lady Luxborough's idea of one was chiefly as a chicken coop, which was consistent with her commitment to the garden as a farm; she wrote to William Shenstone in 1749: "If I had such a command of corn and water as you have [at the Leasowes], I should be apt to fall into the expense of a *ménagerie*."[66] We know Pope liked hummingbirds from the North American colonies especially and kept them in his grotto, doubtless to enhance its exotic character, although their mortality rate must have been preposterously high in that cold and clammy habitat. He received some hummingbirds from Anthony Browne's menagerie at Apscourt. Menageries or their equivalents seem appropriate adjuncts to landscape gardens in that they would have engendered an increased feeling of naturalness. Mrs. Howard's menagerie must have been a substantial affair to accommodate four buildings, but I have found no other reference to it except in Swift's *Pastoral Dialogue between Richmond-Lodge and Marble-Hill*, in which Marble Hill house speaks of "my Birds."

With all the help that Mrs. Howard enjoyed, we may wonder how much influence she herself had on her own landscape. This is impossible to determine, but Bathurst, half-seriously in a letter to her in 1727, may have provided the hint of an answer: "there is but one Lady in the World," he wrote, "I desire to see there [Riskins], and I fear I never shall have that satisfaction, tho' it is only to satisfie my curiosity whether she has any taste, or not, having giv'n some marks of it by her approbation of my works at Richkings, but no proofs of it by her own at Twitnam."[67] Her interest, however, was of course unquestionable. In particular, she seemed to be impressed by Bridgeman's workmanship and on one occasion even recommended him to the Duchess of Queensberry, who wanted to alter the layout of some of her grounds at Amesbury in Wiltshire. Writing to Gay from Windsor in 1730 about Amesbury, Mrs. Howard sounds experienced: "Mr. Bridgeman is here, and I have spoke to him about the Gardens; he says they are kept as they ought to be, and at a very reasonable expence, but he will very soon bring me the account and a positive agreement; if it be such as the Duchess approves."[68] She may have regretted recommending him, as it turned out, because he failed to keep an appointment or two at Amesbury and seems to have been difficult to locate for a few days. "We wonder we have heard nothing from Mr Bridgeman, if you chance to see him pray tell him so," Gay wrote to Mrs. Howard;[69] to which she replied exasperatingly, "I was never more peevish in my life than I have been about this Journey of Bridgeman's."[70]

Enter Dean Swift

There is no sign that after 1725 Pope did any more designing at Marble Hill, though his interest in it continued. He, and Gay too, of whom Mrs. Howard was particularly fond, continued to be frequent visitors there in the following years, even in her absence. She frequently was away because after the Prince of Wales's accession to the throne in June 1727, the Court and Mrs. Howard with it removed from Richmond to St. James's. After that she had far less time to enjoy her Twickenham retreat.

In 1726 Swift, who wrote the only poem about Marble Hill in its early history, joined Gay and Pope as an admirer of the landscape. He did not meet Mrs. Howard until his visit to England in 1726—a meeting to which Pope eagerly looked forward. It must have occurred to him that if they hit it off she might be able to promote Swift's personal interests at Court, but he was simply convinced that Swift would admire Marble Hill. Swift was one of the chief promoters of what has been described as the romantic-poetic landscape garden in Ireland.[71] He had been designing (and "ditching") his and others' landscapes in Ireland during the preceding seven years—simultaneously with Pope's landscaping at Twickenham. It was in the same breath as he mentioned Mrs. Howard for the first time in September 1725, incidentally, that Swift first acknowledged Pope's "great Atchievments in building and planting and especially of your Subterranean Passage to your Garden whereby you turned a blunder into a beauty which is a Piece of Ars Poetica" (2:325–26). It is strange that these two profoundly close friends had never before written to each other about their gardening activities.

Swift eventually arrived in England in the middle of March 1726. It was a propitious time for his visit because Pope's and Mrs. Howard's gardens were maturing and increasing in beauty. Dawley, four miles away at Uxbridge, was also taking shape, and Swift spent much time there, as well as at Cirencester. Knowing Swift's interest in landscaping and that he would wish to return to Ireland familiar with the latest English ideas, Pope had him on the move almost immediately, as he told Fortescue in April: "I have . . . been engaged in country houses and gardens, with one friend or other, and know nothing of the town. . . . Dr. Swift is come into England, who is now with me, and with whom I am to ramble again to lord Oxford's [Wimpole] and lord Bathurst's, and other places" (2:373). He also mentions that he proposes to carry Swift to Mrs. Howard's.

These landscapes must have surprised and pleased Swift since they were so different from what he had known when he left England in 1715, although he and Patrick Delany, in particular, had been in touch with the landscaping of Pope and others. They were guiding Irish gardening in the same direction, on a smaller scale since they lacked the financial resources enjoyed by their English counterparts, but with greater access to and use of romantic scenery of mountains and lakes. Swift's gardening world in Dublin during these years made contact with Pope's, so that it will be useful to pause briefly here and take a look at it.

Swift began to be consulted about gardening by his Irish friends, and actually to garden for them, at least by 1721. In his poem *The Journal* (1721), he described his gardening activities with Patrick Delany and the Reverend Thomas Sheridan at Gaulston, County Westmeath, the estate of the Rochforts.[72] In the spring and summer of 1725, he was enjoying himself at Sheridan's house at Quilca, improving the grounds there with considerable freedom and with his own two hands. By doing much of the work himself, incidentally, he probably went beyond Pope since it is unlikely that the poet's health allowed him physically to assist his friends much in their gardens. Swift wrote to Chetwode: "I live in a cabin and in a very wild country; yet there are some agreeablenesses in it, or at least I fancy so, and am levelling mountains and raising stones, and fencing against inconveniencies of a scanty lodging, want of victuals, and a thievish race of people."[73] He was still at Quilca a couple of months later, "employing and inspecting labourers digging up and breaking stones, building dry walls, and cutting through bogs, and when I cannot stir out, reading some easy trash merely to divert me."[74] He also gardened extensively on long visits to Market-Hill, the estate of Sir Arthur and Lady Atcheson, near Armagh, where Pope wrote to him in October 1728, noting that Swift was still there "planting and building; two things that I envy you for. . . ."[75]

Apart from his own garden, the garden in which Swift was most interested was Delville, the eleven-acre estate at Glasnevin, two miles north of Dublin, belonging to his good friend the Reverend Patrick Delany, fellow and tutor at Trinity College. Delany was also a friend of Pope's, and with Swift was the guest of the poet at Twickenham in 1726 and 1727. From Swift and Pope, and from landscapes like Cirencester and Marble Hill that he saw on these visits, Delany imbibed the spirit and character of the new landscaping, afterward laying out his eleven acres with wild planting and a beautiful combination of restrained formality and irregular freedom.[76] Its design resembled Pope's garden and, according to Cooper Walker, eighteenth-century Irish gardening historian, introduced Pope's style into Ireland. It was a style, Walker wrote, "by which Pope, with whom he [Delany] lived in habits of intimacy, taught him to soften into a curve the obdurate and straight line of the Dutch; to melt the terrace into a swelling bank, and to open his walks to catch the vicinal country."[77]

Sheridan's wilder and more rural and spacious gardens at Quilca provided a contrast to Delany's smaller or Popean garden near Dublin that was analogous to the contrast Robert Digby saw between Lady Scudamore's Holm Lacy and Pope's garden. While he admired Delville, Sheridan could not resist a good poetic joke, and it is he, not Swift, who may have written some good-natured verses, *A Description of Doctor Delany's Villa*, reflecting on Delville's cramped garden. This relatively unknown poem describes some of the gardening effects inspired by Pope's garden and opens by complimenting its variety and productiveness:

> ... in this narrow compass we
> Observe a vast Variety?
> Both walks, Walls, Meadows & Parterres
> Windows and Doors, and Rooms and Stairs
> And Hills, and Dales, and Woods and Feilds
> And Hay and Grass and Corn it yeilds ...

But then perhaps with a glance at Pope's style and with a Bathurst-like patriarchal manner, Sheridan concentrates on Delville's Lilliputian touches:

> A little Rivulet seems to Head
> Down thro a thing you call your Vale
> Like tears along a wrinkled Cheese,
> Like Rain along a blade of Leek.
> And this you call your sweet Meander
> Which might be suckd up by a Gander
> Could he but force his Nestling bill
> To scoop the Channel of the Rill
> Ime sure you'd make a mighty Clutter
> Were it as big as City gutter.
>   Next come I to your Kitchen-Garden
> Where one poor Mouse woud fare but hard in
> And round this Garden is a Walk
> No longer than a Taylors chalk.
> Thus I compute what space is in it
> A snail creeps round it in a miniut,
> One Lettice makes a shift to squeeze
> Up thro a Tuft you call your Trees
> And once a year a single Rose
> Peeps from the bud, but never blows
> In vain then you expect its bloom
> It cannot blow for want of room.
>   In short in all your boasted Seat
> Theres nothing but yourself, that's Great.[78]

This is the kind of poem Bathurst could easily have been moved to write about Pope's garden. While Sheridan enjoys the joke, there is also of course the undercurrent of implied praise for the Popean design. This poem is a sign of Pope's influence in

168

encouraging pictorial variety in "a small compass" among his friends and acquaintances. Delany, incidentally, made one of the more interesting comments in 1731 on Pope's recently published *Epistle to Burlington*; writing to Sir Thomas Hanmer about the outcry in London against Pope's poem, he complimented Hanmer's garden, Mildenhall in Suffolk: "One thing I regret with all my heart, that Mr. Pope was not acquainted with Mildenhall, because I am persuaded the united elegance and simplicity of your gardens had supplied him with a better standard of true taste than any yet he had met with; & methinks a just and proper praise of taste where it is, had been the best satire on the want of it...."[79]

Since Pope had his own garden, Marble Hill, Cirencester, Stowe, and others to document his landscaping tastes in 1731, Dr. Delany's comment appears a trifle beside the point; nonetheless, Sir Thomas's garden contained landscaping of which Pope would have approved, such as the placing of the bowling green so that it was surrounded by bosquets intersected by allées leading to buildings and other structures. This blend of "elegance and simplicity" illustrated for Delany the gardening principles proclaimed by Pope's poem. Although there is no evidence that Pope had seen Sir Thomas's garden, in his letter to Bathurst in September 1719, quoted above, he alluded derisively to an expression used excessively by Sir Thomas in his volume *The Garden Book*: "One declar'd he would not have too much Art in it; for my notion (said he) of gardening is, that it is only sweeping Nature."[80]

The setting of Delville also resembled Pope's. Swift thought of it, too, as a villa, and compared its position, near Dublin and along a stream called the Tolka, to Twickenham: "He [Delany] hath a Country House very agreeable within a Mile of this Town," he told Pope in one of his recurring attempts to interest the poet in coming to Dublin, "fit to lodge you, in a fine college [probably a scribal error for "country" although "college" suggests the ideal of philosophical retirement] much more retired than Twickenham."[81] In the same unpretentious fashion as Pope entertained his intellectual friends at his villa, Delany regularly gathered around him members of the intellectual community residing in nearby villas and country houses. Swift banked on this appealing to Pope; he dangled the double temptation of good gardens and good companionship in front of his friend. "I have the command of one or two villa's near this town," he wrote to Pope in May 1728 after deciding he would be unable to make the trip to England the third year in succession; "You have a warm apartment in this house, and two Gardens for amusement"[82]—Swift's own gardens around the deanery and, further off, at Naboth's Vineyard. Several years later, after his health had made him give up entirely the idea of another trip to England, he tempted Pope with a more detailed description of his garden and a sketch of the social and intellectual milieu that centered on Delany: "Dr. Delany is the only Gentleman I know who keeps one certain day in the week to entertain seven or eight friends at Dinner." After describing his garden, he added, "There are at least six or eight gentlemen of sence, Learning good humour & tast, able & desirous to please you, and orderly females, some of the better sort, to take care of you.[83]

Mary Pendarves, one of those females, later Delany's wife, in letters to Swift from England in 1733 nostalgically referred to "Dr. *Delany's* sett" and "the sociable *Thursdays*, that used to bring together so many agreeable friends at Dr. Delany's."[84] Unfortunately, during this period in England before she returned to Ireland and married Delany, Mary Pendarves did not develop a friendship with Pope, and therefore her letters, which are very descriptive of the places she saw, do not, as they might have done, describe Pope's garden or the gardens of Pope's close friends at Twickenham and close by. She stayed further down the river with her future uncle, Sir John Stanley, who was connected with Ireland, at his seat called "Paradise" in Fulham.[85] If we recall that Lord Peterborough lived exclusively at Fulham before he moved to Bevis Mount, Mary Pendarves's descriptions of this residential area next to the river as "the *Delville* of this part of the world" and as having "all the advantages of the country; as quietness, cheapness, and wholesome air,"[86] are particularly interesting.

One of the estates belonging to a friend of Pope's that she did visit for a day and a half, however, was Cirencester, which Swift had last seen in 1727. "My Lord *Bathurst* talked with great delight of the pleasure you once gave him by surprising him in his wood [Oakley Wood], and shewed me the house where you lodged," she wrote to him in October 1733, adding with some amusement: "it has been rebuilt; for the day you left it, it fell to the ground; conscious of the honour it had received by entertaining so illustrious a guest, it burst with pride."[87] As an accomplished artist who frequently painted scenes at Delville,[88] she added, "I endeavoured to sketch it out for you; but I have not skill enough to do it justice"—a considerable compliment to the landscape beauties at Cirencester. But its beauties did not make her and Bathurst "forget to talk of Naboth's vineyard and Delville." Bathurst particularly enjoyed hearing about Naboth's Vineyard from her.[89]

Edward Malins has discussed Naboth's Vineyard in some detail,[90] so it is not necessary to describe it here except to say that in his garden Swift was less poetic or symbolic (less committed to the *simplex munditiis* of Horace) and more practical than Pope in his. This is not to say that Pope, whose landscaping was simultaneous with Swift's, did not practice the princple of *in utile dulce* at Twickenham, but that Swift did it more exclusively. He raised (in his own words) "the finest paradise stocks of their age in Ireland" of apple, peach, pear, and nectarine, and he maintained a paddock in his small walled demesne complete with a horse that he fed with hay that he himself cut from another part of the garden.[91] Among the estates of Pope's friends that Swift saw on his 1726 and 1727 visits, Dawley Farm would have appealed to him as much as or more than any others (Pope's excepted) because of this practical approach to landscape. As far as we can tell, he visited Dawley more than any other garden.

When Pope carried him to Mrs. Howard's, Swift suspended his mistrust of a Court lady and joined in the fun Pope and Gay were having at Marble Hill, mainly in Mrs. Howard's absence. He would have appreciated the signs of farming he saw there with the livestock grazing in the meadow near the house, and he would have been amused by Pope's and Gay's insistence on Mrs. Howard's metamorphosis into a shepherdess, and by their jokes about her expertise on such matters as "boiling Chickens in a Wooden Bowle" (2:409). "She has as much Good nature," Pope wrote to Gay, "as if she had never seen any Ill nature, and had been bred among Lambs and Turtle-doves, instead of Princes and Court-Ladies" (2:182). Pope had earlier spoken about the "Lambs of the

Mountains" of Riskins being brought down to graze upon "the grass of Marble hill" where "Mrs Howard's Swains" might care for them (2:292).

Mrs. Howard's infrequent residence at Marble Hill, even before the organization of the new Court at St. James in June 1727, was one of the perils of her service to the Princess, but her literary triumvirate (including Swift) were able to see the lighter side of the problem. On one occasion, when one of her calves was born while she was away, the three of them happened to be staying at Marble Hill. Pope showed their Scriblerian-like playfulness in this letter to the shepherdess:

> We cannot omit taking this occasion to congratulate you upon the encrease of your family, for your Cow is this morning very happily deliver'd of the better sort, I mean a female calf; she is as like her mother as she can stare. All Knights Errants Palfreys were distinguish'd by lofty names: we see no reason why a Pastoral Lady's sheep and calves should want names of the softer sound; we have therefore given her the name of Caesar's wife, Calf-urnia; imagining, that as Romulus and Remus were suckled by a wolf, this Roman lady was suckled by a cow, from whence she took that name. In order to celebrate this birth-day, we had a cold dinner at Marble-hill, Mrs. Susan offer'd us wine upon the occasion, and upon such an occasion we could not refuse it. Our entertainment consisted of flesh and fish, and the lettice of a greek Island, called Cos. We have some thoughts of dining there to morrow, to celebrate the day after the birth-day, and on friday to celebrate the day after that, where we intend to entertain Dean Swift; because we think your hall the most delightful room in the world except that where you are. (2:435–36)

Recalling such moments from the past summer and looking forward to his 1727 visit, Swift wrote good-naturedly to Mrs. Howard from a cold Dublin in February: "I hope you will get your House and wine ready, to which Mr Gay and I are to have free access when you are safe at Court; for as to Mr Pope, he is not worth mentioning on such Occasions."[92]

Still, Swift had his doubts about Mrs. Howard's sincerity and this tended to interfere with his total enjoyment of Marble Hill. During the 1726–27 winter, in between his two visits to England, he kept in touch with her, and his friends kept mentioning her in their letters; but one feels that it was more because of her connections at Court than because of the qualities of her landscape.[93] In his correspondence he mentioned other gardens, but never hers; he could "every night distinctly see Twitenham, and the Grotto, and Dawley, and Mrs. B. [Martha Blount] and many other et cetera's" (2:393). Pope appeared to sense this reluctance, also never mentioning Marble Hill; "I shall never more think of Lord Cobham's," he wrote his friend, "the woods of Ciceter, or the pleasing prospect of Byberry, but your Idea must be join'd with 'em; nor see one seat in my own garden, or one room in my own house, without a Phantome of you, sitting or walking before me" (2:388). This last comment was part of a "Cheddar" letter that Pope, Gay, Bolingbroke, and Mrs. Howard (Gay assured Swift) jointly composed, consisting of a map of the Cotswold village of Byberry with which Pope had fallen in love, and several lost plans of gardens that Pope and Swift had seen together.

By the summer of 1727 Swift thought his suspicions were justified. She was no shepherdess, he thought, when she was in London; and judging by a "Character" of her he wrote in June but never published in his lifetime, he may not have believed in the image wherever she was, even at Marble Hill.[94] In this essentially negative "Character," he summed up his doubts about her with this sentence: "If she had never seen a Court, it is not impossible that she might have been a friend." A few years later in some verses on his own death, Swift crudely wrote:

> From *Dublin* soon to *London* spread,
> 'Tis told at Court, the Dean is dead.
> Kind Lady *Suffolk* in the Spleen,
> Runs laughing up to tell the Queen.[95]

Swift's attitude toward Mrs. Howard is important because it establishes a context for his poem about Marble Hill, *A Pastoral Dialogue between Richmond-Lodge and Marble-Hill*,[96] composed in June 1727, the same month in which he wrote her "Character." In this poem he indulges the view that the best way to gain the ear of Princess Caroline at Richmond Lodge was through Mrs. Howard at Marble Hill. He has the two houses, which have been abandoned by their respective mistresses for St. James's, Kensington, and Hampton Court, meet to commiserate with each other and "talk of News," for as Swift wrote, "by old Proverbs it appears,/That Walls have Tongues, and Hedges, Ears." Most important, the poem reveals Swift's opinion of the house and his friends', especially Pope's, connection with it. It is a sort of obituary on both houses, particularly Marble Hill, whose mistress is now "imprisoned" at Court.[97]

Swift prefixed the following note to his poem sometime after 1731, specifically naming Pope the "contriver" of the landscape:

> 'Marble Hill *is a House built by Mrs.* Howard, *then of the Bed-chamber, now Countess of* Suffolk, *and Groom of the Stole to the Queen. It is on the* Middlesex *Side, near* Twickenham, *where Mr.* Pope *lives, and about two Miles from* Richmond Lodge. *Mr.* Pope *was the Contriver of the Gardens, Lord* Herbert *the Architect, and the Dean of St.* Patrick's *chief Butler, and Keeper of the* Ice House. *Upon King* George's *Death, these two Houses met, and had the following Dialogue.'*

Swift is the speaker as the poem opens, acknowledging that he is writing the poem without the approval of Pope and Gay, who presumably objected to his featuring Mrs. Howard and her country seat in this mild political satire:

> In Spight of *Pope*, in Spight of *Gay*,
> And all that He or They can say;
> Sing on I must, and sing I will
> Of *Richmond*-Lodge and *Marble*-Hill.

(1–4)

The following selected passages in the dialogue speak for themselves:

RICHMOND-LODGE.
My Royal Master promis'd me
To raise me to a high Degree:
But now he's grown a King, God wot
I fear I shall be soon forgot.

. . . .

Marble-H. My House was built but for a Show,
My Lady's empty Pockets know:
And now she will not have a Shilling
To raise the Stairs, or build the Cieling.

. . . .

    No more the Dean, that grave Divine,
Shall keep the Key of my (no) Wine;
My Ice-house rob as heretofore,
And steal my Artichokes no more;
Poor *Patty Blount* no more be seen[98]
Bedraggled in my Walks so green:
Plump *Johnny Gay* will now elope;
And here no more will dangle *Pope*.

. . . .

    Some *South Sea* Broker from the City,
Will purchase me, the more's the Pity,
Lay all my fine Plantations waste,
To fit them to his vulgar Taste;
Chang'd for the worse in ev'ry Part,
My Master *Pope* will break his Heart.

. . . .

Richmond-L.
I then will turn a Courtier too,
And serve the Times as others do.
Plain Loyalty not built on Hope,
I leave to your Contriver, *Pope*:
None loves his King and Country better,
Yet none was ever less their Debtor.
Marble-H. Then, let him come and take a Nap,
In *Summer*, on my verdant Lap:
Prefer our *Villaes* where the *Thames* is,
To *Kensington* or hot St. *James's*;
Nor shall I dull in Silence sit;
For, 'tis to me he owes his Wit;
My Groves, my Ecchoes, and my Birds,

Plate 61. Marble Hill. Pencil drawing by John Buckler, 1831.

> Have taught him his poetick Words.
> We Gardens, and you Wildernesses,
> Assist all Poets in Distresses,
> Him twice a Week I here expect,
> To rattle *Moody*[99] for Neglect.
>
> (15–18, 23–26, 43–50, 67–72. 79–96)

In addition to her immersion at Court, Mrs. Howard also had other troubles at the time with her irresponsible son, her itinerant husband, who was renewing his claims on her, and her finances, apparently with the result that in 1727 all building at Marble Hill seems to have stopped.[100] By 1731, though, all these troubles had cleared up, and she was also beginning to have more time to herself. "I shall now often visit Marble-Hill," she wrote to Gay, "my time is become very much my own; and I shall see it without the dread of being oblig'd to sell it."[101]

Except for a prolonged problem of access across Mrs. Howard's land claimed by adjacent neighbors, in which Pope mediated because it concerned his landlord, Thomas Vernon,[102] he scarcely mentions any landscaping at Marble Hill after 1725. This suggests that the major part of the layout was complete by then. Almost twenty years later, Mrs. Vernon's death in 1742 removed the last obstacle to Mrs. Howard's long dream—twenty years old by that time—of owning extensive acreage all around her house, thus ensuring her privacy and providing her house with the parkland setting fitting for a country seat. In 1743, the year before Pope's death, she and her second husband, George Berkeley, purchased from Mrs. Vernon's daughters a total of twenty-one acres in Plumbush Shot and Marble Hill Shot, and in following years a few other lands were added to the estate.[103]

Mrs. Howard, who did not begin to live at Marble Hill until her retirement from Court in November 1734, outlived all the people connected with the purchase, building, and landscaping of Marble Hill, and continued to live there until her death in 1767. She actually lived into another era of landscape gardening and claimed Horace Walpole as a close friend.[104] His *History of the Modern Taste in Gardening* (1771) could well have been heavily indebted to what she had to tell him about those halcyon days when for a brief period, from 1724 to 1726, Marble Hill caught the fancy and genius of Pope and other leaders of the new style of English landscaping.

7

Lord Peterborough's "little Amoret"

at Bevis Mount

"I confess the stately Sacharissa at Stow, but am content with my little Amoret" (3:310). Thus Charles Mordaunt, the third Earl of Peterborough, commented to Pope in August 1732 after having seen Stowe for the first time. The "little Amoret," very likely an allusion to the pictorial and rustic scene of bathing nymphs in James Thomson's *Summer*, was Bevis Mount in Southampton, and Peterborough was using this allusion to contrast his recently acquired sanctuary to the more majestic Stowe, in which, as he said, "Immensity, and Van Brugh appear in the whole, and in every part."[1] His reflection upon Stowe is not fair, but his comment is understandable if we see him at this time as the lord of a new demesne, delighted with the house and the variety of his grounds, infatuated with his newly acquired status as a gentleman-farmer-sage, and smug about how little money he (not the nation), as compared especially to the Marlboroughs at Blenheim or Robert Walpole at Houghton Hall, had spent on his estate. Geographically, he was far removed from the "world"; philosophically, even more so. He did not fail (in the short time he had there) to iterate the themes of simplicity and virtuous living in retirement and to adopt the pose of the *beatus vir* in his letters to friends. Pope, too, as we shall see, fell easily into that attitude, and encouraged it, when he visited Bevis Mount.

"The last of the knights errant"

The Earl of Peterborough probably did not acquire land at Bevis Mount until 1730,[2] by which time the new gardening was well advanced. Until then, he lived principally at his London house on Bolton Street in Piccadilly, where at least since 1719 Pope had been a frequent guest.[3] When they met, no later than 1718,[4] Peterborough's colorful and fascinating career as soldier and diplomat was over. He had earned his fame in 1705 as a general by bravely and successfully leading a siege on Barcelona with almost no military training. In the years following he darted about Europe in ambassadorial roles at such a pace that Swift was once compelled to write to Gay, "When my Lord Peterborow in the Queen's time went abroad upon his Ambassyes, the Ministry told me, that he was such a vagrant, they were forced to write at him by guess, because they knew not where to write *to* him" (3:416).[5] Both during and after his career, it was primarily his quixotism, bravado, gallantry, and chivalry that generated and sustained his reputation and, even,

Plate 62. Charles Mordaunt,
third Earl of Peterborough. Oil
painting by M. Dahl.

notoriety. Macaulay called him "the last of the knights errant . . . if not the greatest yet
assuredly the most extraordinary character of that age."

When Pope was only in his teens, he had heard from William Walsh about the rare
combination of wit and military prowess in Peterborough (1:21–22).[6] Shortly after first
meeting him, Pope referred to him in explaining that even a courageous warrior like
Hector understandably may flee from an Achilles: "no less a Hero than my Lord
Peterborow, when a person complimented him for never being afraid, made this answer;
'Sir, shew me a danger that I think an imminent and real one, and I promise you I'll be as
much afraid as any of you" (1:493). But Peterborough's most appealing quality, to Pope at
least, was his impetuosity and his happy readiness to try new ideas and do new things.
Pope, we recall, called him and Bathurst "the two most impetuous men I know"; and
there were other resemblances between these two that help explain why Pope was so
attracted to Peterborough. On one occasion, in a letter written sometime between 1725
and 1727 to Mrs. Howard, Peterborough tried to account for that "sympathy and
tendernesse" that had arisen between himself and Pope:

> I have been consulting myself about my latter friend, and find that
> sympathy and tendernesse arise naturally amongst those whose Circum-
> stances have some resemblance. I am satisfyed Mr Pope and my self are to be

177

ranked amongst the unhappy men; . . . the same comforts he wantes for his Body, I want for my Mind. We unfortunately know enough not to be pleased with common things. Our souls are made up of the restlesse uncontented atoms, which make him saunter from breakfast to breakfast, from Lady to Lady, which make me turn from Tree to Tree, from book to book, perhaps desirous of more than we deserve, but to be sure of more than we shall obtaine.

Mutuall complaints of humane things, our common disappointments & disgusts, create a reciprocall compassion, add some equall share of esteem, and these are most of the ingredients which make up the Composition of Love and Friendship.[7]

Pope saw the Earl, as well as Bathurst, as a type of patriarch. In a letter dated 24 August 1732—the first extant letter between the two since 1723—Pope told him: "The great Turk, you know, if often a Gardiner, or of a meaner trade: and are there not (my Lord) some circumstances in which you would resemble the great Turk? The two Paradises are not ill connected, of Gardens and Gallantry" (3:307). The surviving correspondence between the two unfortunately is scant,[8] so the record of their intimate friendship is slight compared with Pope's and Bathurst's. Still, we know that as early as 1719, on his visits to London from his recently acquired Twickenham home, Pope began to stay on occasion—mostly he stayed at Charles Jervas's on Cleveland Street—with Peterborough at his home in Parson's Green, Fulham. Landscaping may have been a common interest and topic of conversation on these visits, and together they must have visited Riskins and Cirencester more than once; and, of course, Peterborough must have been a frequent guest at Pope's villa during those important years when the poet's garden was taking shape.

Parson's Green

One important difference between Bathurst and Peterborough in these early years was that while Bathurst owned two large estates, Peterborough had only his small garden in Parson's Green. Parson's Green was a start on retirement for Peterborough, though Swift in 1723 was skeptical when he wrote to Pope, who was staying there: "I have no very strong Faith in you pretenders to retirement" (2:199). Peterborough summed up his own view on that in one of his many letters to Mrs. Howard in the early 1720s, mentioning his favorite pastime: "I was gone to Branford about garden affaires, the most important perhaps, that may fall to my Share in the remains of life."[9] Even about a decade earlier, he seems to have been serious about his landscaping. After one occasion in May 1712, when perhaps as a member of the Brothers Club Peterborough had entertained Tory wits and politicians at Parson's Green, Swift recorded in his *Journal* that a feast under a canopy was held in Peterborough's arbor; he commented, "I never saw anything so fine and romantick."[10] Passing through Putney in his travels around Britain, John Macky thought Peterborough's gardens worthy of mention in an area that was distinguished for its lovely seats and gardens: "At *Putney*, which is a very large village, are

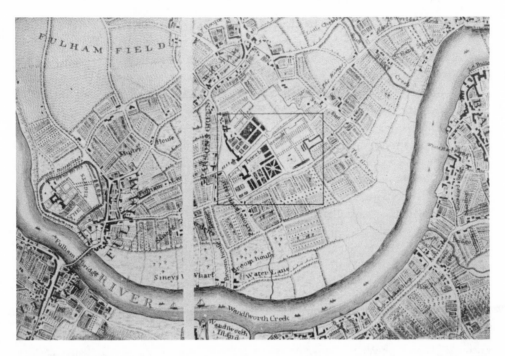

Plate 63. Detail of Lord Peterborough's gardens at Parson's Green, from J. Rocque, *An Exact Survey of the City's of London, Westminster, . . . and the Country Near Ten Miles Round* (London, 1746).

several charming Seats, with their large Gardens, Fish-ponds, and Groves; and indeed the whole Parish is one continued Garden. . . . in my way to London saw Parson's Green, an old Seat of Lord Peterborough with fine gardens."[11]

It seems likely, in fact, that Parson's Green was a botanical garden of some interest. The area of Putney and Fulham along the Thames just outside London had by the 1720s become well known for gardens containing exotics. Henry Compton, the Bishop of London, had in his garden at the Bishop's Palace in Fulham the best collection of American, especially Virginian, plants in England. He had sent a few of his clerics, such as James Blair, the founder and president of the College of William and Mary in Williamsburg, Virginia, to the colonial South as much to gather plants for him as to preach the Gospel. As J. D. Hunt writes, divines like Compton may have been motivated after the Restoration to set their clerics to studying horticulture as an "antidote to both religious enthusiasm and emblematic readings of nature."[12] Peterborough must have known Compton's garden well; perhaps he also knew Christopher Gray's garden in Fulham, where, as the naturalist Mark Catesby wrote in his *Hortus Britanno-Americanus* (London, 1737), there was "a greater variety of American forest-trees and shrubs" than almost anywhere else in England. We do know that Peterborough had achieved great things with the Virginian tulip tree.[13]

A sketchy plan of Parson's Green in John Rocque's *An Exact Survey of the City's of London, Westminster . . . and the Country Near Ten Miles Round* (1746)[14] shows Peterborough's house and gardens (plate 63). They are the largest gardens on the sheet, rectangular in shape and consisting of about ten acres, or roughly twice the size of Pope's. The gardens did not have an axial design; there is some suggestion of slanting walks running along the thousand-foot-long garden and of irregularly placed groves presumably penetrated by winding paths with secret arbors. Whether by a "wilderness" at Parson's Green Richard Bradley meant a naturalized area planted promiscuously with exotics and "secret" in character, or the old-fashioned set grove rigidly enclosed and regularly planted, is not clear; but he does use the word in connection with the exotic tulip tree as if to suggest that it was an appropriate setting. One of the results of the new scientific interest in plants in the late seventeenth century was that gardens had to be designed to accommodate experimentation. It would not do to experiment with plants within the confines of an idle and frivolous garden. John Evelyn had a lot to say about that. In any case, it makes sense to see Peterborough planning a wilderness in this spirit and anticipating his bold and imaginative designs at Bevis Mount.

There is but one reference to the garden by Pope, in a letter probably dated August 1723, that vaguely alludes to some garden features. Another of Peterborough's trips to the Continent is imminent, so Pope jokingly sentimentalizes his friend's self-banishment and his own forlorn condition without him, much like a wife who pines away during her husband's exile. Pretending epicenism with a touch of burlesque, Pope projects himself as Peterborough's wife, for whom their gardens have no meaning in her husband's absence: "What alas to me are your Houses that you leave me, your Gardens, your Groves, your Ponds, & the full Command of all but your Carps & Grandsons?

> Tityrus hinc aberat, ipsæ te Tityre pinus
> Ipsi te fontes, ipsa & hæc ar[busta vocabant].[15]
>
> (2:189–90)

Peterborough's pride in his gardens is evident in his own brief reference to them when writing, gallantly, to Lady Mohun, who lived in Iver Green, Buckinghamshire, not far from Bathurst's Riskins Park, and whose house and gardens Peterborough had just seen: "I was pleased your house was so pretty, but did not consider it would putt the garden att Parson's Green in the same condition with the master [;] we are now both jealous, in despaire, & without hopes of pleasing, but Madame, some little remembrance in your charming place of the Cypress Grove, & the Tulip Tree, I was going on I had something more to wish and desire."[16] This is a tantalizing allusion to his cypress grove; did Pope in his own garden years later perhaps find the idea of planting cypresses up to the obelisk in memory of his mother from Peterborough's grove? A grove of cypresses, at least, must have been a somber and meditative garden area at Parson's Green.

Mrs. Howard's "unfortunate gardiner"

Peterborough's letters at the time pertaining to Marble Hill, most of them written in 1723, show his enthusiasm not only for the gardening project but also for Mrs. Howard herself;[17] these can only be called love letters on his part and evasive replies on hers. He also addressed a love song to her that was printed in the *British Journal* on 28 December 1723;[18] and between her and Lady Mohun, the wife of Peterborough's nephew, he was thought of as "our gallant Gardiner."[19] Thus gallantry as much as gardening made Peterborough excited over Marble Hill.

But the gallant gardener soon became the unfortunate gardener. He became jealous over the roles Lords Pembroke, Ilay, and Bathurst were playing at Marble Hill. When Pope and Bathurst were busy with the landscaping, Peterborough wrote to Mrs. Howard somewhat peevishly, submitting a kind of letter of resignation.[20] He complained over "the disappointments I am to meet with, where I did not expect them," and he confessed that he disliked rivals who were alive more than those who were dead. "Must I yield to Lord Herbert, and Lord Ily," he protested: "if I had built the castle of Blenheim, and filled the Land with Domes and Towers, I had deserved my fate for I hear I am to be Layed aside as an extravagant person fitt to build nothing but palaces." Nonetheless, he wished the house and the garden well, "under all these mortifications": "may every Tree prosper planted by whatever hand, may you ever be pleased & happy, what ever happens to your unfortunate Gardiner, & architect degraded, & Turned of." Still, there was comfort in being able to say, after sending Mrs. Howard a nosegay, that he was "the only gardiner who may have that privilege."[21]

He was also chronically envious of Blenheim and Walpole's Houghton Hall, which he sneeringly referred to as Marlborough's "castle" and one of the "prodigies of Norfolk." His reference to his "little Amoret," apart from its picturesque allusiveness, is a smug rationalization of not having been rewarded as Marlborough was for his military successes. When he was happily settled at Bevis Mount, he could not forbear inviting Mrs. Howard to his "Amoret" with another sneer at Blenheim, stressing his own economy and unambitiousness: "My Blenheim would not afford lodgings for two maids of honour and their equipage, and yet I cannot forbear wishing that you might somehow or other see my purchase of fourteen pounds a year. Though you had seen the prodigies of Norfolk the day before, I should depend upon your partiality to Bevismount, the noble title of my palace, which has put the public to no expense."[22]

Implicit in these kinds of comments were also social, artistic, and even ethical distinctions, to which Pope and his friends were committed, between the villa and the large country house. Morris Brownell has explained how for them the villa became a retreat of "Roman self-sufficiency" identifiable with the patriot opposition to Walpole. Peterborough attempted to evoke the sense of Bevis Mount as a "poetical villa," as Pope did successfully with his own villa. This attempt, which we have witnessed in some form or other in all the villas discussed in these pages, was a function of the strategy to disseminate the moral and artistic superiority of the villa over the larger country house. It is a theme that John Summerson has identified as a central issue in the history of the eighteenth-century country house.[23] It was a theme, in fact, which Pope had played with briefly in 1718 regarding Buckingham House, the Duke of Buckingham's enormous house near London. That house was so large that it, too, may easily have been termed a palace, but Pope cited Pliny in praising its practical and sensible uses. Pliny had been rediscovered by the Burlington circle as a fine authority on classical architecture and was freshly presented to the public in 1728 in Robert Castell's *The Villas of the Ancients* (1728).

"I have been reading the description of Pliny's house with an eye to yours," wrote Pope; he believed that Pliny "would have been glad to have chang'd both his houses for your Grace's one; which is a country-house in the summer, and a town-house in the winter" (1:508) What pleased Pope especially about Buckingham House was that while it was a palace in scale, it was a villa in temper and style. Peterborough would have approved of his remark to Buckingham that the value of such a house is that it is "the properest habitation for a wise man, who sees all the world change every season without ever changing himself." Buckingham House also presented the theme of antiquity in many ways, not least in its gardens, where greenhouses and a kitchen garden were (according to a "Letter" that Buckingham himself wrote and Pope published in his edition of His Grace's *Works*) "full of the best sorts of fruit" and where "a little wilderness" was populated by blackbirds and nightingales.

"Retirement" at the Mount

The earliest known mention of Peterborough's residence at Bevis Mount is by Pope in a letter to John Knight on 23 August 1731: "My next Journey is to Southampton to my Lord Peterborow, where also I have a Catholick Friend who will take care of my soul & shall dine with a Jesuit, thrice a week (3:218). Peterborough's undated letter to Mrs. Howard, sneering at Blenheim and Houghton, and teasing her about *his* independence at Bevis Mount, could have been earlier than that; he saw his estate as "a wild romantic cottage" from which he was indifferent to courts and castles unless Mrs. Howard was in them. The "purchase of fourteen pounds a year" refers to his rental of the house and land for that sum, but we do not know when he began leasing or when he purchased the land. If he had been at Bevis Mount much earlier than 1731, undoubtedly Pope would have visited before then and said so somewhere in his correspondence. So a reasonable guess is that he moved there no earlier than 1730.

As for Pope's first visit, he did not go from Stowe to Bevis Mount as he said he would; James Dormer took him to Rousham instead. Letters to David Mallet and Aaron Hill in early September 1731 mention Stowe, but not Bevis Mount; and since Hill had just written a poem, *Advice to Poets*, flattering Peterborough, Pope would surely have mentioned Bevis Mount in his letter if he had just been there. It is likely, however, that he paid his friend a visit later in the fall, before winter had set in—one cannot imagine Pope delaying a trip like that too long with all that landscaping waiting to be done. An allusion to the main gate at Bevis Mount (see plate 71 on p. 204) in *To Burlington* (line 30) suggests that Pope had seen the ornamented gate before the poem was published in December 1731. By August 1732, at any rate, he was referring to the landscape in his letters as if he knew it.

We do know precisely what piece of land Peterborough inhabited when Pope planned on visiting him in 1731. There exists a map dated 1658 of what was in the Middle Ages owned by the Priory of St. Denys,[24] showing various pieces of land separately owned in the seventeenth century and totaling about twenty-eight acres (plate 64).[25] One of those pieces of land, owned by a Mr. Harsint, was known as Sir Bevoys Hill; it

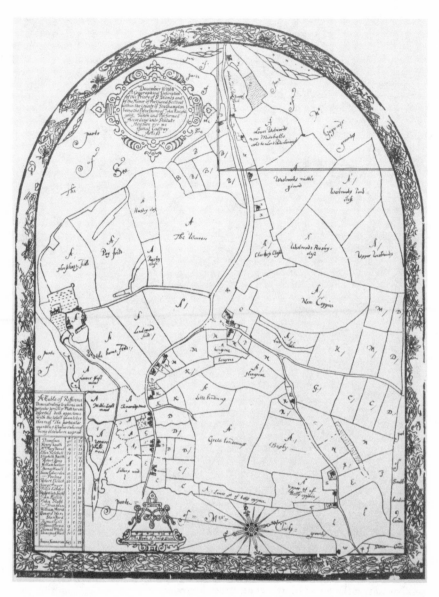

Plate 64. "A Geographical Description of the Priory of St. Diones [Denys] and of the Manor of Portswood . . . within the County of Southampton." Measured by Jonat. Godfrey, 10 December 1658. Within the lined-in area at the top were Peterborough's lands. "Sold to Lord Peterborough" has been written in twice at a later date in the eighteenth century.

took its name from the legend that the Saxon hero, Sir Bevois of Hamton, was entombed there at the top of a hill overlooking the river Itchen. Peterborough took from it the name for his estate. A plan of the Bevis Mount estate redrawn from a larger map of Southampton published in 1843 shows that the portions of the St. Denys property known in 1658 as Ser Bevoys Hill and Mitchell's Close almost exactly corresponded with

183

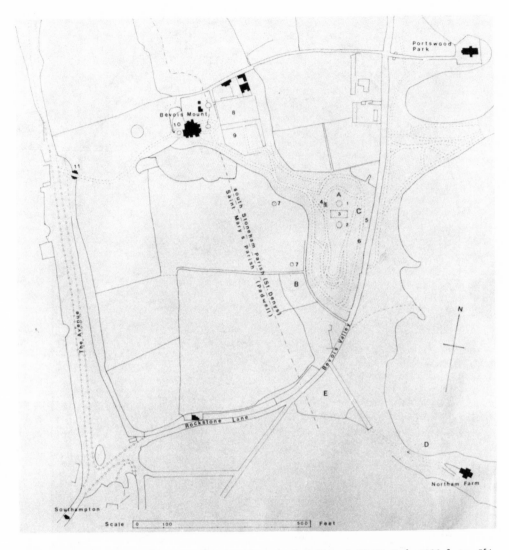

Plate 65. Detail of Bevis Mount from a map of Southampton by I. T. Lewis (1843). Scale: 1300 feet to 5⁵⁄₁₆ inches. References: A. Bevis Mount; B and C. positions used to identify views and angles in the garden; 1 and 2. small mounts at the top of Bevis Mount; 3. bowling green; 4. steps up to the bowling green area; 5. approximate position of the tomb of Sir Bevois; 6. Pope's Walk; 7. fountains; 8. kitchen garden; 9. orchard; 10. house (with later wings); 11. entrance gate. Redrawn by Ian Teh.

the acreage shown in 1843 as South Stoneham Parish (plate 65).[26] The site of Peterborough's "romantic cottage" within South Stoneham Parish is shown, along with the approximately nine acres of splendid gardens winding eastward and culminating in the mount itself. It was this St. Denys land, then, east of the parish boundary separating South Stoneham from St. Mary's parish that Peterborough in 1730 either leased or purchased.[27] In 1735 he became the owner of the land west of the parish boundary, about forty-three acres, which in the Middle Ages was known as the Padwell estate and was bestowed by charter of Edward III upon Queen's College, Oxford, in 1343. The Mr. Gaywood indicated on the 1658 map was a tenant on the Padwell lands because Peterborough acquired the land from Queen's College by exchanging these forty-three acres, worth about thirty-five pounds per year, for some land in Buckingham valued at about fifty-seven pounds per year.[28] He may have held the Padwell land as tenant at the same time as, or soon after, he acquired the St. Denys acreage. He finally purchased it in 1735, the year of his death, in order to ensure that his widow would be secure at Bevis Mount and that the lovely gardens would not be encroached upon to the south and west by another owner. Thus in 1735 Peterborough owned about seventy acres around his house, though only nine contained the gardens Pope admired; had he lived longer he might have landscaped some of the new acreage in a manner similar to Lord Cobham's management of Home Park at Stowe.

Given the devout Catholicism of Lady Peterborough, it is tempting to speculate whether it was she who knew of and chose the site of their rural retreat. Both pieces of land, as it turned out, had associations with religious houses dating back to the Middle Ages. Padwell was owned in the twelfth century by Gervase le Riche, who in 1196 founded the Hospital of St. Julian or God's House and annexed Padwell to it.[29] The Bevis Mount gardens comprised part of the lands belonging to the Black Canons of St. Augustine, for whom St. Denys Priory was founded.[30] It is possible that in some way or another Lady Peterborough through her religious connections was told about the religious houses and these lands with their beautiful prospects, and urged her husband to have a look.

What is fairly well documented is Lady Peterborough's cloistered life at Bevis Mount in the style of a prioress. Peterborough cultivated this image of her as part of his pose of turning his back on the "world." He wrote to Pope on one occasion with a double allusion to the lady's religious devotion and its rural setting at Bevis Mount: "Whenever you apply as a good Papist to your female Mediatrix, you are sure of success; but there is not a full assurance of your entire submission to Mother-church, and that abates a little of your authority. However if you will accept of country letters, she will correspond from the haycock and I will write to you upon the side of my wheelbarrow" (3:281). This passage points up an interesting marriage of the themes of rural "retire-ment" and Elysium. Pope and Peterborough liked to reconstruct this personal reading of the "Mount" into variations on the mountain-valley journey of Everyman—as in this passage from Peterborough to Pope: "I have Lead my Self out of Temptation, and brought my Self into the ways of Pennance, which the Lady approves of, it has a good Catholick Sound. I have left the Mount to gett into the bottom, making Tryall of the Bath watters" (3:468). Prayers on the mountaintop never entirely sufficed; not infrequently, the spa at Bath had to play its part in Peterborough's salvation.

From time to time Pope used Bevis Mount not only as a place where he might comfortably lick his wounds, but also as a retreat where he could actually have them healed. Even if he was not up to, as Peterborough put it, "an entire submission to Mother-church," his Catholicity responded to this image of the Lady as the presiding spiritual Genius of the Place. Lady Peterborough, his "Catholick Friend" at Bevis

Mount, would "take care of my soul & shall dine with a Jesuit, thrice a week, worth all the Priests in Essex." He connected the beauty of Bevis Mount as a healing force with the healing power of Lady Peterborough's prayers, as in a letter to Mrs. Knight in 1734: "I have been but in a poor state of health ever since I set out from home; and can scarce say I have found rest till (where you would least expect it) under my Lord Peterborow. This place is beautiful beyond imagination, and as easy as it is beautiful. I wish you and Mrs. Elliot saw it. Here is a very good Catholic lady in the house, and she and I might pray together for you" (3:426).

Pope was not a keen, church-going Catholic, but this talk of praying with the Lady of Peterborough is more than just a playing with words. Bevis Mount revived in Pope's mind the outdated emblem of *hortus conclusus*. As J. D. Hunt has written, eighteenth-century landowners and poets found uncongenial the self-deprivation inherent in the "spiritual vigors of proper rural solitude and meditation"; and seventeenth-century poets like Abraham Cowley and Andrew Marvell had been somewhat uneasy with the emblem, although the Renaissance garden had for long accepted the emblem in some form or other as a vital element of layout and feeling.[31] On solitary walks by moonlight, hikes amid abbey and castle ruins, or poetic "excursions" to sacred gardens ranging from the Christian Paraclete in *Eloisa to Abelard*[32] to Calypso's pagan bower in the *Odyssey*, Pope certainly felt emotional "highs"; but one always feels that his fervor at such moments derived chiefly from an aesthetic rather than meditative urge. The romantic beauty of the scene moved him more than any meditative strain he may have told Martha Blount was inspired by the scene. He liked to feel uplifted in such scenes and he deployed his wit to make others appreciate just how much. At Bevis Mount it was different, though. From the start, Bevis Mount for Pope was religiously, philosophically, and physically benefi-cent. It was a genuine retreat, a *hortus conclusus*, where at the same time as the gardening provided a vital part of his enjoyment and relaxation, he responded profoundly to the reign of Spirit personified by the Lady, the dramatic beauty of the setting, its remoteness from high society, and the eccentricities of its owner, as if they were all part of a comprehensive allegory. The Bevis Mount landscape was therefore unique in Pope's life.

Two Pope letters in 1732 acknowledge Peterborough's pride in Bevis Mount and his landscaping interests. Replying to his friend's preference for his "little Amoret" over the 'stately Sacharissa" at Stowe and perhaps playing a little on his prejudices regarding other estates, Pope commented in September on Queen Caroline's Hermitage at Richmond, where the busts of Robert Boyle, John Locke, Sir Isaac Newton, William Wollaston, and Dr. Samuel Clarke had been placed and were being praised in innumera-ble poetical celebrations:[33] "I fear it will a little raise your envy to find all the Muses imployed in celebrating a Royal work, which your own partiality will think inferior to Bevis-Mount. But if you have any inclination to be even with them, you need but put three or four Wits into any hole in your Garden, and they will out-rhyme all Eaton and Westminster. I think Swift, Gay, and I, could undertake it, if you don't think our Heads too expensive" (3:311–12). Although Kent erected the Hermitage for Queen Caroline in 1732, Pope thought it was ridiculous. The poetry contest in the *Gentleman's Magazine* to which he alluded produced hundreds of verses celebrating the Hermitage, most of them complimentary, but his own poetic Muse would not stoop to such service.[34] He thought it showed a lack of good sense, for example, to put a bust of Dr. Clarke, who was suspected of Arianism, in such a Hermitage;[35] furthermore, there were political feelings that Pope shared with his friends in the Opposition—and with Peterborough—that made them little disposed to applaud this instance of Queen Caroline's garden art.[36]

Pope also understood the fulfillment Peterborough was enjoying as a gentleman-gardener-sage-farmer at Bevis Mount.[37] By 1732 he was joking about his friend's gardening life in a manner resembling his exchanges over the years with Bathurst. In a letter to Peterborough in August,[38] he touches on a number of themes connected with landscaping in "retirement" that, though spoken here in sport, had intrigued him for more than a decade. Since it contains Pope's most explicit estimate of Peterborough in his new setting, most of the passage may be cited. Peterborough had just returned from a ramble:

> I presume you may before this time be returned from the contemplation of many Beauties, animal and vegetable, in Gardens; and possibly some rational, in Ladies; to the better enjoyment of your own at Bevis-Mount. I hope, and believe, all you have seen will only contribute to it.... I think you happy, my Lord, in being at least half the year almost as much your own master as I am mine the whole year: and with all the disadvantagious incumbrances of quality, parts, and honour, as meer a gardiner, loyterer, and labourer, as he who never had Titles, or from whom they are taken. I have an eye in the last of these glorious appellations to the style of a Lord degraded or attainted; methinks they give him a better title than they deprive him of, in calling him Labourer: *Agricultura*, says Tully, *proxima Sapientiæ*, which is more than can be said by most modern Nobility of Grace or Right Honourable, which are often *proxima Stultitiæ*. (3:306–07)

Pope pays Peterborough a great compliment: one would guess from the latter's lifestyle in retirement that he was a mere "gardiner, loyterer, and labourer." In defense of his calling Peterborough a laborer, Pope quotes Tully, who urged that through agriculture and farming man can best acquire knowledge of the universe. He had suggested the same connection in a note to the *Odyssey* 18: "The truth is, the greatest persons follow'd such employments [plowing, mowing, harvesting] without any diminution of their dignities; nay, a skill in such works as Agriculture was a glory even to a King: *Homer* here places it upon a level with military science, and the knowledge of the cultivation of the ground is equall'd to glory in war."[39] Whether or not Peterborough actually did any "ditching" (as Swift put it) in his garden is beside the point; Pope's letter acknowledges an expansion of his friend's life through his new vocation as a gardener and "labourer." The *Odyssey* note, incidentally, seems especially apt when applied to Peterborough, though it was written several years before he acquired Bevis Mount: his life now qualifies him as a descendant of Odysseus since it combines a knowledge of military science and agriculture. Pope drew the same analogy in *The First Satire of the Second Book of Horace*, which he wrote five months after his letter and which contains his single allusion in verse to Peterborough's landscaping:

> And He, whose Lightning pierc'd th' *Iberian* Lines,
> Now, forms my Quincunx, and now ranks my Vines,
> Or tames the Genius of the stubborn Plain,
> Almost as quickly, as he conquer'd *Spain*.
>
> (129–32)

As for being called a "loyterer," Peterborough was flattered to have that "most noble title, Loiterer," applied to him. If he were a heathen, he would dedicate a temple to laziness; "No man sure could blame my choice of such a Deity," he told Pope, "who considers, that when I have been fool enough to take pains, I always met with some wise man able to undo my labours" (3:310). That passage contains the keynote to his self-image at Bevis Mount.

Pope's earliest known letter from Bevis Mount was written to John Caryll on 24 September 1733 (3:387).[40] By then the landscape design was well advanced. Back home after a three-week visit, he wrote to Lord Oxford enthusiastically that he had just spent three weeks "as agreably and as healthfully as I ever did in my Life." Since his return, however, town habits had made him sick again and made him wonder whether he ought to adopt the Bevis Mount style of retirement at Twickenham (3:389). Quietness and uplift were among the attractions of the place—especially since it was to him a new landscape without any melancholy associations. He had told Caryll his desire to "get off from Lord Bathurst" as soon as he could, and in a letter to Martha Blount, which probably ought to be dated mid-October, he was upset by the melancholy mood of Cirencester and could say, "I really can find no enjoyment in the place; the same sort of uneasiness as I find at Twitnam, whenever I pass near my Mother's room" (3:385). Gay's death and Swift's absence, but especially his mother's death in June, had fixed a mood upon Cirencester and other familiar places that was difficult to dissipate and from which he found he could escape somewhat on the hilltop at Bevis Mount. Ladyholt, that other "retreat," also offered him badly needed "contentment" in the aftermath of his mother's death, but at that time he preferred the Catholic lady on the mount even to Caryll's Catholic retreat.

Remembering his comfort at Bevis Mount the year before, Pope returned there for some six to seven weeks in 1734. In none of his rambles during the preceding fifteen summers did he ever stay that long at any friend's estate. He arrived there in July, being careful to avoid giving the impression to John Caryll that he was neglecting Ladyholt; he immediately wrote to Dr. Arbuthnot:

> I left Lord Bathurst a week ago. . . . My present Landlord gave me an account of your Condition, which he is really concerned at, as he is really a man of humanity, & (like all Men of true Courage) beneficent: He has often wishd you in This air, which is excellent, & our way of life quite Easy, & at liberty. I write this from the most beautiful Top of a Hill I ever saw. . . . (3:424)

Pope himself in the spring had been suffering from one of his recurring illnesses, but he found rest and comfort immediately "under my Lord Peterborow"; "I am in more Retirement than I have been many years," he announced to Hugh Bethel (3:426). In any case, there was just no time for sickness there, with Peterborough planning all sorts of excursions—one right away to see the Duchess of Montagu "within ten miles of us, at Bewley, which, I'm told, is a fine situation on the sea, and I shall see it to-morrow" (3:426). Health, a sense of ease, and good air and food gave him the energy to write a good deal and to participate in adventures that, for him, were unique.[41]

A valuable part of Pope's visits to Bevis Mount was his ability to write poetry there effectively. Even after Peterborough's death in 1735, on visits to Lady Peterborough he composed parts of his greatest satires. The 1734 visit was especially distinguished in this regard because it was then that he "put together" and completed the *Epistle to Dr. Arbuthnot*. Arbuthnot, as we have noted, was especially on Pope's mind during this visit. Soon after he arrived at Bevis Mount there was a letter for him in which the doctor reported his painful illness and advised Pope to continue to attack vice but less personally. Arbuthnot's ideas about general rather than specific satire, with which Pope disagreed, set the poet thinking of how he could honor in verse his friend of twenty years and at the same time demonstrate his own theories of effective satire. The result was the *Epistle*, on which he probably spent some considerable time while at Bevis Mount—he wrote three hundred lines of it there. His letter to the doctor in late August refers to the advice in his poem: "I took very kindly your Advice, concerning avoiding Ill-will from writing Satyr; & it has worked so much upon me (considering the *Time & State* you gave it in) that I determine to address to you one of my Epistles, written by piece-meal many years, & which I have now made haste to put together; wherein the Question is stated, what were, & are, my Motives of writing, the Objections to them, & my answers" (3:428).

In order to do this writing at Bevis Mount, Pope would have had to bring with him an armful of working manuscripts of the poem made up of several fragments composed over the years.[42] This was undoubtedly what he did, since in 1734 he was busy preparing his poems for the second collected volume of his *Works* to be published in April of the next year, and he would have had to bring much other material with him as well. *To Dr. Arbuthnot* was published separately the following January, a month before Arbuthnot's death. Although they are an example of Pope's recurring poetic theme about the positive values of old Roman simplicity, the following lines from *To Dr. Arbuthnot* nonetheless have a cast to them inviting the conjecture that they received an impulse from his experiences and feelings at Bevis Mount during these weeks:

> Oh let me live my own! and die so too!
> ('To live and die is all I have to do:')
> Maintain a Poet's Dignity and Ease,
> And see what friends, and read what books I please.
> Above a Patron, tho' I condescend
> Sometimes to call a Minister my Friend:
> I was not born for Courts or great Affairs,

I pay my Debts, believe, and say my Pray'rs,
Can sleep without a Poem in my head,
Nor know, if *Dennis* be alive or dead.
　　Why am I ask'd, what next shall see the light?
Heav'ns! was I born for nothing but to write?
Has Life no Joys for me? or (to be grave)
Have I no Friend to serve, no Soul to save?

(261–74)

Of all Pope's documented visits to friends, the one to Bevis Mount in 1734 must be the most interesting. Peterborough tended to bring out the adventurous spirit in him. They went on many excursions together, some of them physically demanding. As late as 25 August, with a fortnight remaining in Pope's visit, several "Excursions into Hamshire" were still being planned (3:428). Several years later in a letter to Swift, Pope referred especially to an abortive expedition that took place on his 1734 visit. "I went some years agoe with Lord Peterborow," he wrote, "about 10 leagues at Sea, purely to try if I could sail without Seasickness, and with no other view than to make yourself & Lord Bolingbroke a Visit before I dy'd. But the Experiment, tho almost all the way near the Coast, had almost ended all my Views at once" (4:179–80). As Thomas Tyers described the episode in his critical *Historical Rhapsody on Mr. Pope* (1782), Pope "put to sea, from Southampton, with Lord Peterborough, by way of experiment, but was disordered by the sickness incident to that element, like Virgil in the Bay of Naples, and glad to retire again."[43] Remarkable enough as evidence of how ready Pope was to join Peterborough in an adventure, the episode anticipates the poet's more remarkable inclination, in the light of his health, to take to the sea in 1735 as the dying Peterborough's companion and nurse in a voyage to Lisbon.[44]

Pope's experimental sail with Peterborough in 1734 for ten leagues along the coast should not be confused with what was very likely the outstanding event of his 1734 visit: his and Peterborough's sail to see the ruins of Netley Abbey on Southampton Water.[45] Fortunately, Pope sent a detailed description of this expedition to, not surprisingly, Martha Blount.[46] While supplying evidence in 1734 of Pope's ideas about the romantic and picturesque in landscape,[47] the description is also an appropriate extension of his response to the landscape of Bevis Mount. Two aspects of this letter need to be understood separately. The first is the manner in which Pope described the excursion; the second is the experience itself.

He acknowledges a special loyalty to Martha Blount in writing this description for her—just as he had when he wrote to her about Sherborne, or about the lovers killed by lightning at Stanton Harcourt, or about the Bath-Bristol landscape he walked through in 1739 (see chapter 8). His narration is embroidered by his imagination and his taste for the "poetic" (or emotive) character of a landscape. Setting out "boldly" with Peterborough, his "Bold Leader" on what he called an "Adventure and Discovery," Pope sees himself and his friend as characters in a type of Gothic romance well stocked with rocky and woody cliffs, old Gothic ruins, abandoned barns and gardens, moonlight, remote seashores, and lonely boats quietly gliding past each other in the fading daylight—just the emotive stuff that frequently colored his response to landscape. And there is no doubt that the setting at Netley Abbey was widely known in southern England as a place of "venerable ruins" where, as the Southampton *Guide* (1774) announced, "by a judicious management of trees, which have spontaneously sprung up among the mouldering walls," the owner "has greatly improved the beauty and solemnity of the scene, and by that means, rendered it as well worth visiting as any object of that kind in Great Britain." The whole scene, added the *Guide*, "inspires the most pleasing melancholy."[48] But a Gothic romance needs more than just such setting; it needs also a story to match, and Pope has one for Martha:

> to conclude with a Story, which is necessary to a Romance, (for hitherto you have had only a Description) it is confidently affirmed here, by 2 or 3 who are still living & remember the thing, that a Carpenter having bought a side of this church of Sr B.L. dream'd that his brains were beaten out by pulling down the Great window, & would have gone from his bargain; till being laughd out of his fears, he fell to work, & was crushd on the spot. The fact is undoubted of the Man's death, & the Dream is taken for granted here.

Pope was fond of this kind of local legend or tale; it was part of the evocative *topos* he was portraying. He learned of another tale, too, on this visit to Bevis Mount, concerning a witch in the parish called Mother Batts who was befriended by Peterborough but scorned by eveyone else. He told Lord Oxford he had "an incomparable Story" to tell him about the witch which "would fill 2 sheets of paper" (3:430).[49] The romantic beauty and remoteness of Bevis Mount, together with the eccentricity of its owner, encouraged this Gothic vein in the poet.

Once he was on the excursion, Pope quickly forgot about the possibility of being seasick and got into the spirit of adventure on the high seas. Peterborough manned a "Yatcht . . . under a Flag of the English Colours, & we sail'd prosperously from the Port of Southampton, mann'd only by himself & me with three Mariners. . . ." It sounds as if they were already on the open seas, not merely in the Solent, when they "saluted" a French boat from which they stored up with six bottles of brandy, Frontiniac, and claret before heading for the Isle of Wight, where they purposed "to refresh our selves & anchor by the way, at a Castle [what else?], on evry side inviron'd by the Sea." (The word "inviron'd," incidentally, suggests Pope's picture-consciousness.) The tide was against them, though, so they headed for a promontory that somehow Pope knew contained a "large Prize of Shells of all sorts." He was always on the lookout for shells and minerals of diverse shapes, sizes, and colors with which to adorn his famous grotto, and perhaps Mrs. Howard's too. Again, the tide prevented him from collecting some shells, so they sought out some more accessible coastline near which sat a castle upon a steep hill. Immediately Pope's pictorial sense was "struck with the beauty of it," especially the "aspect of the Towers." They had to explore.

Nowhere else in all of Pope's writings do we get self-portraits in a wilderness such as now follow. Peterborough decided they should explore separately, so Pope was left to

Plate 66. "Netley Abbey and Castle" in *Beauties of England and Wales* (1808), engraved by S. Rawle from a drawing by J. Britton.

his own devices, far from the civilized glories of Twickenham, trying not to get "lost in the Thickets." "I apprehended Snakes & Toads might be among the ruins," he says, and soon he was stopped by an impassable bog that made him turn back. He was looking for a suitable place to dine when suddenly he saw a picture through, or framed by, "a glade of Trees" of an old deserted barn "where was nothing but Emptiness & open doors, but very cool & shady: Round it were very high oaks, planted in a regular Grove."[50] Looking down from that elevation, he reveled in the stagelike scenery of the sea "opening in a hundred broken [by the trees] views." This was a perfect outdoor "theatre" in which to dine; besides, it had good open air and "a fine Turf," thought the landscaper. When he was at last found by Peterborough, however, the latter would not hear of dining there and marched him off to see his own discovery—the ruins of Netley Abbey (plates 66 and 67)[51] where they dined with fallen pillars for a table and seats.

The abbey turned out to be a sort of Gothic dream-come-true for Pope, but the pictorial beauty of the ruins amid the ivy, weeds, and wild flowers struck him most. Pope first saw them framed "thro' the Woods" and then was enchanted by the multiplicity of prospects and optical allusions through arched windows and in between pillars and partition walls, upward of the steeple that "lookd terribly," and beneath the "vast" height of the altar. His description of the position of the ruins in relation to nature in the scene recalls his suggestions for landscaping the ruins of old Sherborne Castle. He admired how with classical-like simplicity the "great Trees of Elder &c," the ivy and

Plate 67. "Netley Abbey," oil painting by William Marlow (1740–1813). Exhibited at the Royal Academy in 1771.

weeds, and most picturesquely melancholy of all, the "Remains of an old Garden & Bowlingreen, & something circularly sloping like an Amphitheatre" naturally "finish" the scene with a touch of elegance through variety. There is even another classical theme, the *simplex munditiis* of Horace, in his appreciation of their dinner being augmented by a "Sallad of Alisander, a very pretty-tasted herb which grew in plenty there."[52] To be eating so well, with wine and freshly picked greens, neatly in the midst of ruins and wilderness, far from home, delighted him. This was a wilder version of the idea of the geniuses of nature and art cohabiting in a landscape garden. To be able to carry on civilized living in the lap of nature (shaped or wild) was to him particularly satisfying. It is what he stressed in a letter he wrote one day from the top of Peterborough's mount, "the most beautiful Top of a Hill I ever saw"; he could sit there in a "little house that overlooks the Sea, Southampton, & the Isle of Wight" and "study, write, & have what Leisure I please" (3:424).[53]

After their return from this excursion, Pope stayed at Bevis Mount about three weeks more. When he left, he looked on Bevis Mount, unknowingly, for the last time as the earthly paradise of its robust master. Such adventures as have been described, and the camaraderie that went with them, were not to be enacted again there or anywhere else. Pope may have planned on another visit in September 1735—he seemed to enjoy early autumn at Bevis Mount—but by midsummer of that year Peterborough's health had worsened, requiring an operation in Bristol and a despairing journey to Lisbon in search of a healing climate. He died on 25 October 1735, shortly after arriving there.

Pope witnessed some of the spectacle of Peterborough's last days at Bevis Mount, and characteristically it was full of heroism and pathos. Peterborough wrote to Lady Suffolk that the example of the Emperor Julian showed him how a soldier, "how a philosopher, how a friend of Lady Suffolk's ought to die. I want to make an appointment with you, Mr. Pope, and a few friends more to meet upon the summit of my Bevis Hill, & thence, after a speech & a tender farewell, I shall take my leap towards the clouds (as Julian expresses it) to mix amongst the stars."[54] The old general called Pope there for what both men knew would be a final meeting, and he urged him to bring with him their mutual friend Bathurst—who, as far as we know, had never visited Bevis Mount. Pope immediately wrote to Bathurst in August telling him he was about to rush to Peterborough's side. It seems remarkable that even in this exigency Pope thought it was necessary to humor Bathurst into returning Peterborough's visit the previous summer:

> My Lord Peterborow has desired me to see him once more at Southampton, before he parts, in all probability for ever, for France [Peterborough later decided in favor of Lisbon] at the end of this month. I cannot refuse it, tho I've but just got up from a slight Fever. He writes me three lines, the last of which is. "If you can persuade Lord Bathurst to repay me my Visit, it will be the only trouble I may give him. pray do if you can." In the opinion that Riding is Physick & Strength at once to your Lordship, whereas to me it is Sickness & Pain, I hope this is not quite an Unreasonable Desire, that you would meet me there, after the 24. till the 30. which will be all the time I can stay: and to see the Last of an old Hero, the last Sparks of Such a Noble Flame, it will be a thing to dwell on our Memory & to talk of in our old age."[55] (3:483–84)

As it turned out, Bathurst did not repay the visit and Pope visited alone in late August, relieving the melancholy character of his stay with talk about gardens—in a weak voice, though spirited, Peterborough "talked of nothing but the great amendment of his condition, & of finishing the Buildings & Gardens for his best friend," Lady Peterborough (3:487). During this farewell visit Pope promised his friend he would supervise the completion of their joint landscaping ideas at Bevis Mount. Thus it was that while not above a month later Peterborough said farewell forever to his "little Amoret," Pope would visit twice the following year, staying for lengthy periods as Lady Peterborough's guest, and once in 1737, presiding alone over the completion of the landscape.

During a two-week visit in June 1736 Pope was able to review the needs of the landscape, study the layout with a view to introducing new visual effects, and reassure Lady Peterborough that he would take things in hand in a manner that would have pleased her husband. The largest consideration, as we shall see, was how to landscape the adjacent Padwell estate, so that the land would be visually integrated with the areas around the mount to the east. He was not sure what could be done to advance these projects in September, the month he had designated for his second journey, but he was definitely in the spirit of landscaping at this time. As he told Ralph Allen, a new personality in his landscaping world, he might as well landscape at Bevis Mount as at home: "I will . . . travel, in a week or two, to Southampton, if I find I can be of any Use there: If not, I'll go on Gardening here; Tis an innocent Employment, & the same that

God appointed for his First Man" (4:31). In another letter in September to William Fortescue, he anticipated spending upward of five weeks at Bevis Mount, and he mentioned some of the attractions that the place had always held for him, including much writing, gardening, and a "rational" form of melancholy, by which he meant a feeling of romantic quietude and remoteness. The following passage may be taken as a summary and description of Pope's fondness for Bevis Mount and his appetite for the romantic:

> I am as you guess'd, returned from one Journey [Cirencester], & now I must add I am going on another: But to the quietest place I can go to, where I never yet pass'd a fortnight, but by a fatality, I think, I fall to writing verses. I wrote there my last Epistle; & began an Imitation of the finest in Horace this spring; which I propose to finish there this autumn. I mean Lord Peterborow's at Southampton, where I am to put the last hand too to the Garden he begun, & lived not to finish. It is a place that always made me Comtemplative, & now Melancholy; but tis a Melancholy of that sort which becomes a Rational Creature, & an Immortal Soul. I propose to go next week & stay till the middle or toward the End of October. (4:33–34)

The "last" epistle he mentions may be either *To Dr. Arbuthnot* or *To a Lady*; the *Imitation of Horace* he began at Bevis Mount in June and hoped to finish on his next visit could be either the *First Epistle of the Second Book of Horace* ("To Augustus") or the *Second Epistle of the Second Book of Horace*.

Clearly Bevis Mount continued to put him in the Horatian as well as romantic spirit: the beauty of the place generated the romantic while the comfort and peace he found, of both mind and body, induced in him the philosophical detachment and objectivity wherewith to advance moral and religious virtue and disparage vicious and corrupt hearts. As so often before, illness delayed his visit, but, again as before, he felt healed and "at ease" when he arrived. "This place is very pleasing to me," he told Ralph Allen; "Here I live very much in my own way; Nor is the Ease & Enjoyment of it lessened, but advanced, by the Employment of planting & improving many Parts of it" (4:36).

The little gardening benefited his health, but he stayed for only two weeks, going from there to Stowe with Lady Suffolk later in November. Amidst busy work in his own garden, he was thinking of plans for Bevis Mount in the months to come and acquiring some Bath stone from Allen for garden ornaments that he was designing.[56] We do not know what the designs were for, but some monument or pedestal in memory of Peterborough may have been planned.

Pope's last known visit to Bevis Mount was in August 1737, but nothing is known of it; he only mentions that he "rambled" to Southampton and Portsmouth, intending to embark on a boat to the Isle of Wight but being disappointed by the weather. It is not unlikely that from July 1738 to April 1739 Bolingbroke, who had returned to England to oversee the sale of Dawley Farm, was staying with Pope, so that during that time the poet may have stayed closer to home except for the occasional visit to Bathurst and, of course, London. Moreover, he was exhausted by his journeys and he complained that his health would not allow him his annual visit to Southampton unless at the end of it he could stay a full month at Prior Park. During a long visit with the Allens in November 1739 he planned an excursion to Bevis Mount, but we do not know if he took it. He had his last view of the place in July 1740 (see 4:252). And there, as far as we know, ended Pope's connections with Bevis Mount. We can only wonder if he ever completed his improvements in the landscape and brought it to that stage of design that he and Lord Peterborough had discussed and projected before the latter's death.

The fame of the garden remained and even grew in the years following. The Southampton *Guide* for years regularly included a section on Bevis Mount, drawing many visitors to see the garden. One of the first tourists to come, while Pope was still living, was his friend Aaron Hill, who in 1738 saw the landscape just after Pope's final touches; he described his visit, though what he wrote says very little about the layout. His account instead stresses the spiritual value of the gardens that held such an attraction for Pope— a "serener satisfaction":

> I stole the delight of conversing, great part of a day, with some vegetable children of yours, in Lady *Peterborough's* gardens, at *Mount Bevis*. I was so pleased, with many things I saw there, that I could have worshipped, in her groves, like a Druid:—I forgot myself, for many hours, into an escape from the proportion of pain, which imbitters our most tender reflections, when they relate to our offspring of a less grateful and prunable kind, into an enjoyment of that serener satisfaction, which you are intitled to receive, above most men; and more capable, perhaps, of receiving, *under* the increase of your flourishing green families.[57] (4:94)

The landscape

Although during the five years Peterborough lived at Bevis Mount he continually invited Pope's friends there, there is no record that any of their mutual gardening friends ever saw the landscape. The only evidence we have to go on, therefore, regarding the layout of the gardens is to be found in some random references to the garden features in Pope's correspondence, an abstract of Bevis Mount included in the 1742 edition of Daniel Defoe's *Tour thro' the Whole Island of Great Britain*, contemporary guidebooks to Southampton, and some early nineteenth-century maps, all of which enable us to reconstruct the garden and which account for the ecstatic reports (not descriptions) that Pope sent back to his friends near London.

A good place to begin is with Defoe's *Tour*. The abstract of Bevis Mount in the expanded 1742 *Tour* was written by someone who had seen the gardens between 1735 (the year of Peterborough's death) and 1742; and the observer most likely saw the gardens after Pope had completed his improvements there in 1736–37. The description is important because it is the most detailed we have of the gardens, as well as because it was written within Pope's lifetime. The first part of the description portrays the setting of the area around the mount itself on the edge of a ridge high above the river Itchen, along with some legendary history attached to the spot:

> About a mile from this town [Southampton] on the banks of the river Itching, is a waste large pile of earth, which rises in the form of a cone, from a large wide foundation of great extent and circumference, which they call Bevis Mount. It is supposed to be an ancient fortification, thrown up by the Saxons, under the command of Bevis, to oppose the passage of the Danes over the river, who lay encamped on the other side. The river is not very large, but the tide running up into it a good way beyond the town, forms a kind of bay just under this great Mount, which being contiguous to an estate belonging to the Earl of Peterborough, his Lordship purchased it and converted it into a kind of wilderness.[58]

Much as the Digbys of Sherborne acquired some emblematic history with national associations when they took possession of Sherborne Castle, Lord Peterborough inherited a landscape at Bevis Mount imbued with legendary connections to the great Saxon military hero called Sir Bevois of Hamton. Sir Bevois was here wrongly identified with Southampton, being the hero of a popular verse romance of the early fourteenth century whose story was retold by Michael Drayton in *Poly-Olbion* (1612–22). In 1724 Defoe himself had been sceptical about the various legends concerning the by then rechristened Bevis of Southampton, but he testified to strong local belief in their veracity: "Whatever the Fable of *Bevis* of *Southampton*, and the Gyants in the Woods thereabouts may be deriv'd from, I found the People mighty willing to have those Things pass for true."[59] In Drayton's version, as in local legends, Sir Bevois was a Christian, crusading military hero (sometimes giant) who performed many tasks on behalf of distressed maidens, his Saxon brethren, and his country. He therefore endowed Bevis Mount with just the right associations to suit the military, chivalrous, and gallant Peterborough. The ghosts of these medieval legends inhabited the landscape as palpably as did Sir Walter Raleigh's at Sherborne.

Legend or history, Pope would have valued the "character" the scene derived from its associations with medieval times and an early English hero. This "character" was a mild example of the emblematical in landscape whereby a period of English history, heroism, and Christianity could be recalled. It was a mild example because it was, as Thomas Whately put it, "reconcileable with beauty"—that is, the sources of the allusive power of the scene could not draw attention to themselves because they were, except possibly for the tomb of Sir Bevois, discussed below, nowhere to be seen.[60] Unless it is conspicuously documented with abbeys, castles, relevant topographical features, and the like, a legend cannot be seen; but it can be felt, and its mood and atmosphere can be enhanced by the landscaping. At Bevis Mount Pope found, and perhaps helped establish, a landscape that leant itself to "allegorical" and "metaphoric" (Whately's terms) meditation. Or to put it another way, the landscape placed him in certain psychological and philosophical moods. The former showed themselves in an uncharacteristic exhibi-

197

tion of bravado, as at Netley Abbey. He expressed the latter in the Horatian poems he wrote at Bevis Mount and in his enthusiasm at Netley Abbey for the romantic landscape and ruins.

Another virtue of the Bevis Mount landscape was the mount itself. It sat atop a high bank and was a prominent feature in the garden, seen both from the house and gardens to the west and from across the river to the east. It was the natural centerpiece of the whole of the landscape. Up its slopes and all around its base was a wild area full of trees and brambles. As the *Tour* writer described it, Peterborough turned the mount and the area around it into a "wilderness":

> as it [the mount] is full of Trees and Brambles, he has cut through them divers circular Walks and Labyrinths, so very intricate, that it is hardly possible to avoid being lost in them. His Lordship used frequently to divert himself by dropping his Friends in the midst of this Wilderness, and stealing away, letting them wander up and down, till they found their Way out of it.[61]

Before describing the mount further, we ought to consult the available plans of the Bevis Mount landscape for an overall picture of its shape, the arrangement of its features, the variety of elevations, its position in relation to the bank overlooking the river, and its dimensions. Plate 65 is the earliest plan (1843) of the landscape that I have been able to find, but it shows the entire garden layout much as it existed when the writer in Defoe's *Tour* saw it. Fortunately, a few years later the layout was beautifully illustrated with great detail in the colorful new twenty-five-inch ordnance survey map series on Southampton published in 1866 and surveyed in the late 1840s (plate 68). Except for one almost perfectly circular path that it shows at the northern end of the mount area, the survey map reveals that the earlier plan is accurate in its outlines of the garden, its sketch of the circular walks around and up to the mount, and its representation of the garden area and paths connecting the mount to the house; but in fascinating detail the later map shows features that are not included in the earlier one but that I have sketched into it.[62] Identified on plate 65, these features include steps at the summit of the mount leading from a path onto the plateau at the top (4); fountains (7); and the elevations of the garden, including the slope eastward down from the mount to a path (6) running alongside the bank (5). Perhaps its major value is that it provides an idea of the size of the garden. It shows that the length of the wilderness area, from north to south, was about eighteen hundred feet and that the house was just under half a mile from the mount, though the long strip of land between the two was only about three hundred feet wide and therefore did not include a great amount of acreage.[63]

Circular paths surround the mount, the top of which is shown in plate 65 as ringed by the inner loop of pathways and marked as A. According to the 1866 map, the eastern slope of the mount fell thirty-five feet before meeting the outer loop or pathway (6), from which the views out over the river Itchen were uninterrupted by trees because the land continued to slope abruptly until it reached the river below. These views must have pleasantly surprised a walker who was just emerging from the darker winding pathways

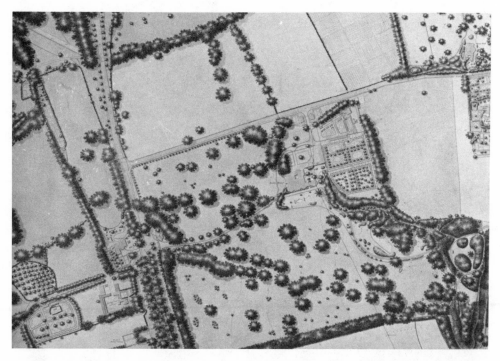

Plate 68. Detail of the Bevis Mount landscape taken from the twenty-five-inch ordnance survey map (1866).

going around, up, and down the northern, southern, and western slopes. It is on this eastern pathway that the fabled tomb of Sir Bevois, as legend had it, was supposed to sit. Undoubtedly there was some tomb or monument there, if not Sir Bevois's, because in a drawing of about 1830 by T. G. Hart the tomb is shown with the lovely views of the river below, where, as the writer in the *Tour* noted, at high tide it has widened into a bay.[64] Hart must have been standing approximately at position C when he drew it. The title of Hart's drawing indicates that in the early nineteenth century the pathway along the higher bank was known locally as "Pope's Walk"[65]; it would not be surprising if this lovely section of pathway, with distant views, had been Pope's favorite scene in the landscape. Another drawing of "Pope's Walk" at about the same time, by F. Young (plate 69), may be of the same spot, with its perspective instead toward the house.

In the Southampton *Guide* for 1768 there is a description of Bellevue House, which belonged to Dr. Nathaniel St. André, the skillful but notorious anatomist and surgeon who was Peterborough's personal physician and operated on him in 1735. Bellevue House stood about one-half mile south of Bevis Mount, close to the bank above the river, and enjoyed an advantage over Peterborough's house in that from it one could see the river. But it was a view similar to the one from the mount, and its description highlights the beauty that Pope found so inspiring: sublimity, an expansive body of water, pictorial motion, contrast of lights and shades, and generally the campagna appearance presented

Plate 69. "Pope's Walk, Bevis Hill." Drawn by F. Young, ca. 1820s. Photographed from a faded sepia postcard.

by the scene were elements of the prospect that perfectly suited the aesthetics of the new gardening:

> From the Terras, but especially from the Windows, the Eye takes in a very grand Prospect; the River being cut off by its winding Course, makes Southampton Water appear like a spacious Bason; the moving of many Boats, the Contract made by the improved and uncultivated Parts, the keeping down, as we say in Painting, that is the intervening Shades, and those of the distant Hills thrown on the nearer and more glaring Objects, exhibit a Landscape truly picturesque, and sufficient to exercise the Genius of a Claude, a Bloswert, or Waterloo.[66]

The features and ornaments with which Peterborough endowed the top of the mount are, with the available evidence, impossible to reconstruct because of the uncertain location of two additional smaller mounts rising from the summit and variously described by our *Tour* writer as "two Spires" and by Pope in Spence's *Anecdotes* as "Lord Peterborow's two hills by Southampton."[67] With the summit measuring roughly three hundred feet by six hundred feet, there is room for doubt as to where they were placed. Thanks to the *Tour*, however, we know how, if not where, they were placed in relation to what else Peterborough brought onto his "mountain" top. The description lists in considerable detail what else was up there:

> The Mount terminates above, as is feign'd of *Parnassus*, in a kind of Fork; and between the two Spires is a Bowling-green [3], or Parterre, adorn'd with fine *Italian* Marble Statues, brought by his Lordship from abroad. It lies open on the Side facing the River, and when the Tide is in, gives a most agreeable Prospect. On one Side of this Parterre, declining gradually from the Top of one of the Spires to the Green, is planted a little Vineyard, exposed to the South; and on the other Side on the very Summit of the Spire, stands a very fine Summer-house, very elegantly built and contrived, with a good Cellar under it, where his Lordship kept his Wines, having no Cellerage at his House, which is near a quarter of a Mile from the Mount, from which his Lordship called it *Bevis-Mount*. . . . The Beauty of the Improvements which his Lordship has made in this Mount, are hardly to be conceived. He adorn'd it with Statues, Grottoes and Alcoves; and diversify'd it up and down with something new and surprising at every Turn, peculiar to his own fine Taste and Genius in Gardening, wherein no Noblemen excell'd and few equall'd him, in *Europe*.[68]

It is not clear from this description whether the steps (4) onto the summit of the mount (shown as A) brought one right up to the bowling green, in between the two mounts. If such were the case, it would have been a symmetrical arrangement and would have confined the garden to the northern end of the summit, the rest of the summit remaining as a lofty wilderness cut through with twisting paths. On the other hand, the 1866 ordnance survey map shows a wide swath running east-west cut out of the woods south of the northern circular area; this might have been the bowling green, and in that event the southern of the two mounts would have stood about in the middle of the summit area. Considering that the total length of the summit area was about six hundred feet, it seems unlikely that two mounts, each perhaps at least one hundred feet in diameter at the base, and one bowling green about one hundred feet wide were squeezed into the northern circular area. For that reason I have located the two mounts (1 and 2) and bowling green (3) as shown in plate 65. With this positioning, the garden features at the summit were asymmetrically arranged, probably with small paths in between them all. The bowling green was "open on the side facing the river" and at high tide commanded an "agreeable prospect" of the river basin below, so there were no trees at its eastern end. Plate 65 confirms this arrangement, as it shows thick trees on the eastern side of the northern circular area that would have entirely obscured the prospect of the river at that point. We know Pope valued the moving scene of boats floating by his own villa; here he had a more romantic or dramatic view of the river traffic along the Itchen.

201

The allusion to Parnassus is apt. Sacred to the Muses, Parnassus also had two peaks, one sacred to Apollo, the other to Dionysus. It is inviting to see Pope regarding Bevis Mount as his own Parnassus. Notwithstanding the religious allusions in his correspondence to the sacred Lady of the house, the Jesuit priest, and the spiritual regeneration at Bevis Mount, his few references to the mount itself sound a classical, not Christian, note. And Peterborough's provisions for the garden up there were designed to create a setting for Apollonian and Dionysian rather than Christian pursuits. For his bowling green, he brought over from Italy numerous marble statues, conceivably of Roman deities, poets, and emperors; the 1768 *Guide* states that the mount area was ornamented throughout with statues. On the southern slope of the northern mount he cultivated his own vineyard, while in a cellar beneath the summerhouse at the summit of the southern mount he kept a ready stock of wines. The "elegantly built and contrived" summerhouse itself, in which Pope did much of his writing, was probably classically styled—perhaps even Palladian. This was the environment in which Pope put together the *Epistle to Dr. Arbuthnot* and finished his *Sober Advice from Horace*. It was Apollonian with a strong current of the Epicurean and Dionysian, as he suggested to Lord Oxford: "You cannot think how happy we are here; I wish, my Lord, you Saw it: If you did, you would be very well pleas'd, very well fed, and very Merry, if I am not very much mistaken: We have the best Sea fish & River fish in the world, much tranquillity, some Reading, no Politiques, admirable Melons, and excellent Bowling-green & Ninepin alley" (3:430). The 1768 *Guide* states that the cellar was not used exclusively for wines but was combined as an icehouse to keep such culinary provisions as the melons (grown in the kitchen garden) and fish.[69] This icehouse was a case of necessity being the mother of invention because at such a distance from the main house the summerhouse would have been an awkward place to dine if food had to be carried back and forth. Peterborough may have got the idea from Mrs. Howard, who had an icehouse. With all of this comfort, ease, and romantic inspiration, the mountain "glory" at the top of Peterborough's mount consisted more of the nourishment and gratification of the poet's imagination and body than the spiritual regeneration he was more apt to find down at the main house with the Lady and her priest. It was the "Sweets of pure Parnassian Air" that Pope breathed up there.[70]

Although the summit of the mount was the climax of the garden, the *Tour* and *Guide* both recognized imaginative landscaping along its slopes as well. Those winding paths up and down the mount are described by the 1742 *Tour* with a vocabulary that somewhat dates it: "diversified," "intricate," "new and surprising," "fine taste," and "genius in gardening." Compared with the 1768 *Guide*'s more effusive description of the "winding gravel Walks which are extremely romantic and agreeable,"[71] and a later *Guide*'s (1787) mention of "the solemn gloomy wilderness behind the house, towards the river, [which] contains fine serpentine walks,"[72] the *Tour* is representing more of a composition in landscape. Apparently, that was Peterborough's intention: there was an abundance of statuary and grottoes, and little alcoves, designed to unfold little surprises and vignettes in verdure and stone.

The Itchen below offered prospects of water here and there—the 1787 *Guide* observed that "the late Lord Peterborough made it an established rule to admit no stranger into his gardens, except when the tide was up, that the prospect might be complete"[73]—but there appears to have been no water or sound of water along these slopes. To the west of the immediate area of the mount, however, but within the St. Denys half of the estate, there were, according to the 1866 ordnance survey map, two fountains. They do not appear in the 1843 plan, but that is not significant because almost no ornamental features are shown on it. The difficulty in accounting for the presence of these fountains is part of the larger problem of explaining the evolution of the landscape between the main house and the mount that appears so clearly in the map. Peterborough intended to landscape that area, the *Tour* tells us without authority: "He intended to rebuild the house, and convert all the grounds lying between it and the Mount into gardens, had he lived a little longer." We know that he purchased the Padwell estate in 1735, undoubtedly because he wanted to provide his wife with some landed security and ensure that the Bevis Mount gardens would not be encroached upon by any future residents in the Padwell area; also he might have aimed to join this new land with the existing gardens according to a new and comprehensive landscape design. In any case, between the house and mount the main path ran by some little groves themselves cut with smaller paths and dotted with seats. With groves, kitchen garden, orchards, and house in such close proximity, this area possessed a concentrated variety for which Pope might have been responsible.

Whatever landscaping Pope did after Peterborough's death, it took him only one year to complete it. One question is whether the improvements he promised Peterborough were more substantial than what he achieved. The 1866 ordnance survey map shows how the Padwell area was eventually landscaped. The planting of trees in the area suggests an avenue or ride extending from the Gate Lodge to a point in the mount area, along one of the winding paths, where there appears to be a hint of a monument or building placed as a terminal focus to the ride. These trees and others in the area are shown as quite mature, so that although the 1843 plan does not show any trees there at all, it is certain they were there long before then. Perhaps in one fell swoop, therefore, the Padwell and mount areas were joined together into one landscape garden. Not much seems to have been done with the perimeter to the Padwell area except for the planting of thick woods. Pope could have conceived this design and supervised it in one year. The trees could have been his "vegetable children" that Aaron Hill saw in 1738. As for the two fountains just west of the mount, the southern one is situated precisely in the middle of the long ride so as to be clearly visible from the monument or building in the mount area at the end of the ride. Pope could have designed this and the other fountain, and had them built with the Bath stone he was awaiting in November 1736. Perhaps he hit on the idea of developing the classical associations of the mount with the two fountains alluding to Aganippe and Hippocrene at the foot of Mount Helicon, sacred to the Muses and believed to inspire those who drank there.

The ground level rose gradually westward, from roughly where the southern fountain stood at forty feet to over ninety feet near the Gate Lodge.[74] From the valley in which the fountain stood the ground rose abruptly eastward up the mount. It was along this shallow valley that T. G. Hart sketched another view of the southern tip of Bevis Mount (plate 70) looking south to the widened river basin and Blackberry Mount.

Peterborough's entrance gates (plate 71) were angled toward the southeast so that

Plate 70. Bevis Mount: drawing by T. G. Hart of a view south to the widened river basin and Blackberry Mount. At the left it shows the south tip of the wilderness area. Mid-nineteenth-century.

East View of the Present Entrance to Bevis Mount, near Southton. August 18th 1824

Plate 71. Entrance to Bevis Mount. Pencil drawing by John Buckler, 1824.

from what was then a footpath and is now called the Avenue one could look through them and straight down the ride. They could have been noteworthy because of military emblems that might have adorned them. Twice Pope may be alluding to them in his poetry. In *To Burlington* there is a passage about "Imitating Fools" who try to outdo Lord Burlington's architectural taste; one of them is a fool who "Turn[s] Arcs of triumph to a Garden-gate" (line 30). This jibe would not really be surprising since in the same poem Pope also takes aim at Bathurst. Burlington's gate at Burlington house was justly famous, thought Pope, for it epitomized the Palladian style; but if Peterborough had ornamented his gate with such a gimmick, that was another matter. The other possible allusion to the gate occurs in the *Epistle to Bolingbroke* (1737):

> Our Gen'rals now, retir'd to their Estates,
> Hang their old Trophies o'er the Garden gates.
>
> (7–8)

On a piece of ornamental masonry at the top of the gate was written "Ostendo non Ostento [I display, but boast not]."

Peterborough was not being falsely modest when he assured Mrs. Howard that his "Blenheim" would not afford lodgings "for two maids of honour and their equipage"; he called his "palace" a "wild romantic cottage." That his house was small, perhaps even smaller than Pope's, is suggested from a drawing presumed to be of the house, dating from no later than the 1840s, when it was purchased by William Betts, who added on two wings, both as large as the original house, and a conservatory (plate 72). The drawing suggests that the house resembled Pope's villa and Marble Hill, with a small classical portico and venetian windows decorating the south front, but if Horace Walpole thought Pope's effort at the Anglo-classic style of architecture was "small and bad,"[75] there is no telling what he would have thought of Peterborough's. While the *Tour* remarks that Peterborough intended to rebuild the house, it nonetheless seemed pleased enough to call it neat, elegant, and well proportioned.

Landscaping ideas that we know Pope conceived or appreciated at Twickenham and elsewhere existed in abundance at Bevis Mount: variety; serpentine paths leading to secret arbors off main pathways; elevation; river prospects; the use of statuary, water, and buildings to provide visual foci and suggest attitudes toward scenes; expressive elements of landscape; and the use of alleys and vistas to draw together distant parts of a landscape. Peterborough always realized, and doubtless Pope kept telling him, that the situation at Bevis Mount was uniquely beautiful. They both understood that any of the new landscaping ideas used there would have very special results. An apt allusion to Peterborough's "tilling" of these beautiful grounds up to his last days was later added by his nephew in an inscription to a seat in the garden (see plate 73).[76]

Plate 72. Bevis Mount house, showing some of the grounds on the south front and the path winding off to the east in the direction of the mount. Photograph of a newspaper illustration (*Southern Evening Echo*).

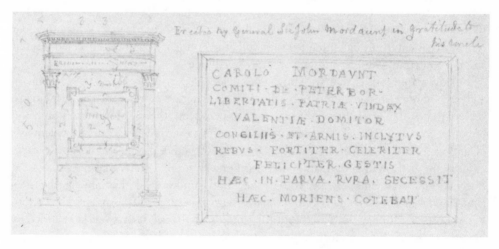

Plate 73. Seat with inscription placed in the garden at Bevis Mount by Lord Peterborough's nephew. Pencil drawing by John Buckler, 1824.

8

The Closing Scenes at Bath

Mr. Allen's Prior Park

The last landscape garden Pope helped design was Prior Park, the home of Ralph Allen, about two miles up Widcombe Hill south of Bath. Of all the landscapes discussed in this book in which Pope involved himself, it was the first that belonged to one whose rank never rose above that of a commoner, and whose brilliant career in the Post Office up to the time Pope first met him in the mid-1730s had been considerably patronized by the Whig administration of the Opposition's archenemy, Robert Walpole.[1] On the face of it, Ralph Allen would have appeared to Pope as another of these newly rich Whig capitalists in search of respectability as part of the landed gentry. "Piecemeal they win this Acre first, then that,/Glean on, and gather up the whole Estate" (lines 91–92), he had complained in his adaptation of John Donne's *Second Satire*. Events that transpired before Pope met Allen, however, alerted him to the positive character of this prominent and successful citizen of Bath, and suggested that he might be a worthy new friend to fill the vacuum, at least partially, that Bolingbroke's departure and Peterborough's death in 1735 inevitably left in his life. There were also practical reasons why a friendship with Allen was worthwhile.

"Virtue's example in degenerate days"

Back in the spring of 1730, when Lord Burlington was in the process of laying out new areas with new buildings and other decorative stone structures in his Chiswick gardens, Allen had met him and suggested the merits of Bath stone for such uses. The story of Allen's successes quarrying and selling Bath stone, beginning in 1724, need not be retold here,[2] but as the leader of the Palladian movement and as the widely acknowledged "Man of Taste" in architectural works of several kinds, public and private, Burlington was just the man to promote the reputation of Bath stone, and Allen knew that. When in 1731 Pope invoked Burlington to "Erect new wonders,"

> Bid Harbors open, public Ways extend,
> Bid Temples, worthier of the God, ascend,[3]

presumably he did not then think of Allen as providing the required stone from his beloved quarries, but he probably had already heard of Allen from Burlington if not also from other sources. Apparently Burlington decided to try out this new stone with some urns, the designs for which Allen was awaiting on 20 May 1730, when he wrote congratulating Allen for his service to his country and thanking him for the "Publique Introduction of a Stone that wil on easie terms answer the best purposes of building."[4] Allen's contributions to such large-scale building projects that Burlington was patronizing were both celebrated and prophesied four years later in Mary Chandler's poem *A Description of Bath* (1734):[5]

> from the Mountain's rocky Sides [the quarries] he drew[6]
> A thousand shining Palaces to view:
> Temples, and Hospitals in ev'ry land,
> From Age to Age, his Monuments shall stand.

It would have sounded an appropriate moral note in *To Burlington* if Pope had been able to ally Allen's name as the stone merchant with Burlington's as the arbiter of taste. In any case, if Allen used the stone for the urns, Pope would have seen them long before August 1736, when he and Allen in the early stages of their friendship visited the gardens together (4:36).[7]

After his extended rambles during the summer of 1734 Pope journeyed to Bath with Bolingbroke in September, staying there for close to one month and seeing much of Martha Blount, Lady Suffolk, and Burlington, who had arrived earlier. There was a stir in Bath at the time owing to the visit of Princess Amelia, whose hand was kissed by Martha, among others, and whose presence was to be celebrated, according to Pope, by the laureate Colley Cibber in unmemorable verses (see 3:435). There were other perhaps more memorable verses dedicated to the Princess on that occasion, including the ones by Mary Chandler, the hunchbacked resident poetess. Her poem contained a concluding passage on Allen and his projected plans for a mansion and some beautiful gardens below it on the slopes of Widcombe Hill. This passage was quite informative about Allen, and given the poem's popularity may be said to have brought him to the attention of a large section of the public outside Bath who had not known much, if anything, about him.

If he read the poem, Pope would have been interested in two types of information about Allen that Mary Chandler celebrates: his moral qualities and the style of house and gardens that he had in mind. Allen's biographers have explained his moral virtues such as selflessness, charity, and humility, which would have surprised and appealed to Pope, who saw himself as a defender of these and other social values magnified in his poetry of the 1730s. As for Miss Chandler's prophesies concerning Prior Park, they parallel and counter the fictional sketch that Pope had drawn of Timon three years earlier, a parallelism that Benjamin Boyce has suggested Miss Chandler deliberately drew.[8] So here was not only a good man, but also one who hoped to evolve a landscape and house in line with the principles of taste that Pope had publicly advocated.

But how could Mary Chandler be as accurate as she was in describing a landscape garden that had not yet begun to take shape? To begin with, she knew the site of the mansion overlooking a steep slope and vale on a "fair Eminence" and could easily conclude that the gardens would be laid out on the slopes beneath it. She also knew that viewed from the house "the craggy hills irregular and rude" where "nature sports romantic" would justify only an irregular plan in which

> The Hill, the Dale, the River, Groves, and Fields,
> Vary the Landscape which thy Prospect yields;
> Whose Vales of Fruit-trees give our Eyes Delight,
> Yet scorn alone to gratify the Sight.[9]

Moreover, the lines about "vales of Fruit-trees" were somewhat conventional, indebted to the country house tradition of poetry, where ripe orchards reflected the lord's or master's abundance and generosity. Miss Chandler also recognized that the existing woods "by Art improv'd" were ideally suited to being cut by winding walks leading to openings, "shady" seats, and "open Vista's," and that numerous springs on Allen's land, if channeled skillfully into fountains, cascades, streams, and basins, could contribute to the irregular beauty of the scene.

One feature described, however, is specific enough to suggest that it was already in place. She says that the quieter scene at the bottom of the hill was dominated by an "ample Bason" that was "the Center of the Place." Later maps of Prior Park show that this was indeed the case and that Allen, years after Pope's death and after the basin had been naturalized into a lake, had a Palladian bridge built next to it to enhance its central importance in that area of the landscape.

The occasion of Allen's first letter to Pope[10] was his offer to pay for a new complete edition of the poet's letters.[11] In 1734 Allen may have known even less of the truth about Pope's character than Pope knew about him, but in the early summer of 1735 his ignorance and misunderstanding—largely the result of the asperity of Pope's satires and the literary skirmishes in which he frequently took part, especially the Chandos controversy—were being dispelled by the appearance of various editions of the poet's letters, including the pirated edition by Edmund Curll. The letters showed Pope's disposition as kind and sincere, attentive and serviceable to friends and acquaintances, and witty. As William Warburton noted in his edition of Pope's *Works*, "Mr. Allen's friendship with the Author was contracted on the sight of his Letters, which gave the former the highest opinion of the other's general benevolence and goodness of heart."

Most important for us here was Allen's discovery that Pope was often talking and thinking about gardens and landscape; if *To Burlington* did not totally convince him, the letters certainly showed that here was the genius and expert of the new landscaping. As a landscape gardener, Pope could not have asked for a better *curriculum vitae* than that which Edmund Curll provided with his pirated edition. One advantage of a friendship with Pope would be his landscaping advice, and perhaps architectural advice, too; and Allen was just then ready for such advice.

Allen did not long delay a visit to the famous poet. On a visit to London for business concerning St. Bartholomew's Hospital, at the end of March or beginning of April 1736, he came to see his new friend's famous Twickenham garden, grotto, and house. Pope also took him to see Burlington's gardens at Chiswick (see 4:36), where Allen's eyes were opened still more to what could be done in a limited space through the skillful placement of stonework in a variety of garden settings. Neither Chiswick nor Pope's garden was as "romantic" as the Widcombe hillside on which Allen would lay out his gardens, but Pope showed him what could be achieved in small and independent areas with water and grove work to vary his landscape. Chiswick, with its cascade and canal, might have given him some ideas on how to work with water specifically, which he had in abundance at Prior Park; and there were also the numerous temples and statuary, possibly built with his own Bath stone, that illustrated the classical treatment of landscape.

Allen returned home from this trip confident that he would be receiving useful advice from Pope. An awkward incident occurred after he left,, however, which anticipates misunderstandings in the future and hints at Pope's lack of ease with him. Allen left behind his friend and traveling companion, James Leake, the Bath bookseller,[12] who tried to see Pope's garden two or three hours later and was inadvertently turned away by the servants in the poet's momentary absence. Pope quickly wrote off to Allen thanking him for his visit and the "Extreme Zeal and Friendship you manifested to me," and apologizing for Leake's treatment because while generally the servants never show the house in his absence, he said, "the Garden I never hinder them to show, but when I have Company with me. Had I had the least Imagination of Mr Leake's meeting you, I had taken more Care, & had mentiond him." In this first known letter to Allen, Pope also wished his new friend the enjoyment of pursuing all the plans they had just discussed, "first your Schemes, & then the Execution, & then the Completion, of them; for those are three distinct pleasures: I know that in every one of these you make the Enjoyment they give your Friends a main part . . . " (4:9–10).

Pope immediately took a part in the Prior Park project by arranging for the portrait painter Johan Van Diest, already in the employ of Allen, to copy some paintings in order to adorn the walls of the future mansion.[13] The paintings to be copied had to be chosen to illustrate the moral and aesthetic values of the master of the house, a view that Pope shared with Allen: "A Man not only shews his Taste but his Virtue, in the Choice of such Ornaments: And whatever Example most strikes us, we may reasonably imagine may have an influence upon others, so that the History itself (if wellchosen) upon a Richmans Walls, is very often a better lesson than any he could teach by his Conversation" (4:13).[14] Here Pope might just as well have been speaking of the use of iconography and emblem in landscape whereby the beauties of natural scenery can be arranged to delineate a moral landscape reflecting its owner's moral worth.[15] As we shall see, a statue of Moses striking water out of a rock above a high cascade was a step in this direction at Prior Park, even if a statue of General Wade fronting the house was not.

"Slide him into a rhime"

Pope recognized Allen's moral force as a valuable help to him in his efforts to establish a public persona that would lend credence and greater authority to his satirical and ethical voice in the poems of the thirties. The edition of the letters reflects that recognition. As a background to their joint landscaping at Prior Park, however, their friendship needs to be qualified.

Pope's feelings for Allen were in some ways analogous to his feelings about John Kyrle, the Man of Ross in *To Bathurst*. Pope did not know Kyrle; neither in a sense did he know Allen, perhaps at least not in the intimate and personal manner he knew Digby, Bolingbroke, Bathurst, Peterborough, and even Burlington. One point that bears on their relationship is that Allen did not rejoice in a family the way Digby and Bathurst did, for example. Benjamin Boyce, Allen's biographer, writes impersonally about the Prior Park "group," which included Allen, his wife, niece, and a circle of admirers. There was not much sense in this "group" of a family institution of age or strength. Peterborough and Bolingbroke at their estates did not satisfy Pope's instinct to be with or know a good and substantial family either, but they at least had wives in whom the poet took an affectionate interest. Mrs. Allen, on the other hand, seems always to have remained remote, and the niece, Gertrude Tucker, briefly became an antagonist in Pope's personal affairs.

Another factor in Allen's and Pope's relationship was that Allen was "low-born" and his riches were new wealth. Pope made a virtue of Allen's low birth—that is, he made symbolic use of it. Allen stood for more, did more, and believed more in the way of moral and Christian goodness, he would say, than most people of higher rank. "I wish the World," he confessed to Allen in 1737, "would let me give myself more to such people in it as I like, & discharge me of half the Honours which persons of higher Rank bestow on me, & for which one generally pays a little too much of what they cannot bestow, Time & Life" (4:74).[16] A direct compliment in verse he paid to Allen in Dialogue 1 of the *Epilogue to the Satires* (1738) reinforced this attitude:

> Let humble ALLEN,[17] with an aukward Shame,
> Do good by stealth, and blush to find it Fame.
> *Virtue* may chuse the high or low Degree,
> 'Tis just alike to Virtue, and to me.
>
> (135–38)

While he praised Allen frequently in his letters, however, this is the single instance of such specific praise in his verse, and one, furthermore, that he suspected would be misunderstood by the general public. Henry Fielding, who praised Allen extensively in print,[18] may have suspected that Pope thought Allen was too "low-born" to celebrate in verse. He rebuked Pope for being a poet "who may condescend to hitch him [Allen] in a Distich, or to slide him into a Rhime with an Air of Carelessness and Neglect, without giving any Offence to the Reader."[19] There was no condescension intended in the phrase "low-born," subsequently changed to "humble" in deference to possible misinterpretations, but it is true that Pope preferred to idealize in verse worthy men of higher rank, perhaps thinking that they would lend more power to his ethical themes.[20]

Pope usually reserved the role of the civilized and enlightened landowner for aristocratic owners of large estates. In 1734, for example, he conferred a version of that role upon Hugh Bethel, who was a relation of the first Earl of Cadogan, his mother's cousin. Bethel had been a friend of the poet's for over twenty years. He was a man of simple and wholesome pleasures whom Pope knew as one who walked "in the common way," neither "in a ditch or on a terras," as he had put it in the first of his surviving letters to Bethel in July 1723. "I know your humanity," he had written, "and allow me to say, I love and value you for it: 'Tis a much better ground of love and value, than all the qualities I see the world so fond of" (2:178–79). With his love of quietness and humanity, and his old-fashioned housekeeping at Rise, his freehold estate up in Yorkshire, Bethel was seen by Pope in terms similar to the poet's appreciation of Allen, and yet the poet chose him as the model for one of his most important ethical satires—a distinction Pope never gave Allen. That Pope never had as much to do with Rise, Bethel's estate, as he had with Allen's was because Rise was so far away;[21] in any case, this did not stop him from adopting Bethel and Rise for his poem, a paraphrase of *The Second Satire of the Second Book of Horace*,[22] and composing what he called in the poem "Bethel's Sermon" (line 9)—a restatement, in his friend's frank and down-to-earth manner, of positive attitudes toward land management belonging to Horace's Ofellus.[23]

Bethel, then, was an old friend, and old friends, like old-fashioned virtues, were very important to Pope. One feels from his correspondence that most of his friends never got to know Allen very well, if at all. Swift, of course, never met him, but Pope (as far as we know) did not even write to Swift about him. There is little evidence, either, that Bolingbroke was much interested in Allen, and generally Allen is left out of the constant well-wishing that takes up so much space in Pope's letters to his friends. Neither does Pope mention Martha Blount in his letters to Allen until 1741. A measure of Bethel's intimacy is the number of times the poet mentions her to him. She shared Pope's appreciation of Bethel's simple life; "I begin to think of you and your Sisters," she wrote to Bethel in 1731, "a warm fire-side, two or three friends in a room, a party at quadrille, and no door open at one's neck" (3:233).[24]

Martha Blount's troubles with the Allens, in fact, suggest the uncertain nature of Pope's friendship with them and elucidate the less personal quality of his contributions to their landscaping. He apparently never felt compelled to describe the landscaping at Prior Park to her in a letter, although in November 1739, a few days after he had arrived in Bath for his first visit with the Allens, he did send her two lengthy descriptions of the hilly landscape between Bath and Bristol (4:201–2, 204–5). Those descriptions, extraordinarily detailed, enthusiastic (even breathless) accounts of the colorful, high, rocky, and distant views atop the Clifton downs near Bristol (see plates 74 and 75) sprang from a world quite separate from Allen's. Allen was not part of this experience, which Pope said was "like a Dream," in the way Lord Peterborough had been part of the Netley Abbey adventure—and this was not simply a matter of Peterborough's presence in the latter and Allen's absence in the former. Pope's letters to Allen, Martha Blount, or anyone else seldom evoke much sense of Allen's identification with the spirit of his landscape. We know Allen consulted Pope about the gardens, but there is a lingering feeling that he was less interested in consulting the "Genius of the Place" at Prior Park. In order to describe enthusiastically a garden scene to Martha Blount, Pope had to feel that the place could offer her a sanctuary and mode of symbolic well-being, whether it was a wilderness like Netley Abbey or a well-tempered garden like Sherborne. To put it another way, there had to be a feeling of Windsor Forest about the landscape, a sense of place that recalled that

Plate 74. "The Northwest Prospect of the City of Bristol," 1734.

original landscape of affection and meaning in their lives, and evoked a setting where Pope could imagine her presence or "Idæa," as he put it. Allen's landscape seems to have been wanting in this regard.

Prior Park did possess, nonetheless, the beauty of variety that Pope articulated in *Windsor Forest* and that he continually celebrated and wanted to experience—indeed, that is very likely the chief reason why he told himself he wanted to put his landscaping talents to use there. After he had finished laying out the second stage of his own garden and had seen his most recent gardening world evaporate with the embarkation of Lord Peterborough for Portugal, his landscaping work had come to almost a complete halt. He had not been in this position for as long as he could remember, nor would he have enjoyed the prospect of being an outdated and inactive garden designer when Kent, Robert, eighth Lord Petre, Spence, Philip Southcote, and a number of others were coming into their own. So when Prior Park rose up in his western horizons, he was naturally eager to play a part in designing its gardens. If his correspondence is a valid indication, however, he never could muster that union of spirit and art at Prior Park that characterized his work in the other gardens considered in this book and that he considered an essential requirement for sensitive and enlightened gardening. One cannot imagine him going out into Prior Park's garden expecting to meet Martha's "Idæa" as at Stowe, or envying himself "the delight of it, because [not] partaken" by her. As for the lady of Prior Park, it was not with her as it had been with the "Lady of La Source," or his "female Mediatrix" at Bevis Mount, or the shepherdess Howard at Marble Hill, or Mary Caesar at Bennington Hall, or the Catholic lady at Ladyholt, and so on. Mrs. Allen could not appear to him as a sympathetic figure in the landscape. The most enthusiasm he could generate for her in the garden was via her faddish hobby of adding grottoes. Since she must have her grotto, too, and since he was improving his own grotto in the early 1740s, he did display an interest in hers.

For this complex of reasons, Pope was slow to bring Martha within the pale of the Allen family. And when he did so things did not work out at all well. In 1741 he began to include her good wishes in his greetings to the Allens, and in the winter of 1742–43 he

Plate 75. "The Avon at Clifton." Watercolor by Thomas Stothard, 1813.

was beginning to think hard of getting her away from her difficult family situation at home and of settling her for a time in Bath. This happened to coincide with the Allens' move from their Bathampton Manor House to Prior Park, but whether it is more than a coincidence that Pope had his eyes set on the vacated Bathampton house, Mrs. Allen's childhood home, as a residence for Martha with a more or less permanent lease is open to conjecture (see 4:430). Regardless, Allen's biographers agree that Pope's urging of this plan offended Mrs. Allen in the summer of 1743.[25] A quarrel ensued that, uniquely in Pope's landscaping career, almost alienated him permanently from a landscape garden that he had helped create. It is ironic that Martha very likely was the root cause. The rift could have resulted from a misconstruction that Allen's niece perhaps willfully placed on the fact that every morning, during the time Martha and Pope were both staying at Prior Park and had rooms next to each other, "between 6 & 7 o'clock, Mrs. Blount usd to come into his Chamber, when she heard them talk earnestly together for a long time, & that when they came down to breakfast, Mrs. B: usd alys to ask him how he had rested that night."[26] Erskine-Hill has pointed out that Martha Blount was probably simply administering nursing services to the invalid Pope, which he would have preferred her to do instead of one of Allen's servants. Nevertheless, if Gertrude Tucker told Mrs. Allen, as she said she did, that Martha Blount was acting as Pope's mistress inside her house, we can understand their subsequent coldness toward her.[27]

Pope was accustomed to taking his good friends' hospitality somewhat for granted, and they, Allen included, made allowances for him. But it is difficult to imagine this kind of quarrel in the summer of 1743, occurring with any of his other friends—the Bathursts, Burlingtons, Bethels, Bolingbrokes, Peterborough, and so on. It must have been with some chagrin that he wrote to Bethel in August: "I am glad first, of your being the better for your Journey, & then, that Mrs Blount will seé you, who has not been the better at all for hers, neither am I for mine. Would to God we were all together, somewhere, for most of our life, to come: Since if there be any Comfort in Life, it is to find honest people together, assisting one another to bear it" (4:467). After he left Prior Park in late July 1743 he never saw it again; he was dead less than one year later. Still, his future editor-commentator, the Reverend William Warburton, whom he had introduced to Allen at Prior Park in November 1741, smoothed out the ruffled feathers on all parties, and by next March the Allens were again visiting Pope at Twickenham.

Planting and "setling Plans"

To turn the calendar back a few years, it would appear that by the summer of 1737 Pope had not yet seen the Prior Park landscape and perhaps only imagined what it was like from Mary Chandler's poem.[28] He had planned to "pass a few weeks there, (you may guess the reason)" in the planting season during the autumn of 1736 (4:37), but nothing came of the plan. In September 1737 he finally got to Prior Park, where he hoped, he told Allen in August, to be of "Service to you in your Wood"; but because he was still bringing "Buildings forward, setling Plans, &c." at Cirencester, he could stay only for two or three days (4:84). His imaginative energies seemed to be everywhere except at Prior Park. If it was not Cirencester, it was his own garden or Buckland (Fortescue's seat) that caught his interest.[29] In a September letter to Fortescue he says nothing of Prior Park, where he had just been, but he is full of Buckland and admonishes Fortescue "to concert this Michaelmas some improvements of your wood, . . . factura nepotibus umbras. But cut out some walks for yourself, while you yet have legs, and make some plain and smooth under your trees to admit a chaise or chariot when you have none. I find myself already almost in the condition, tho' not the circumstances, of an aged judge, and am forced to be carried in that manner over lord Bathurst's plantations" (4:85). Among the attractions of Buckland, incidentally, that Pope prized were its age and its old connection with the Fortescues—their "Paternal Seat," as he puts it, from a past age of good manners, hospitality, and taste (4:355). His fondness for those old Elizabethan and Jacobean houses was always coming to the surface when he wrote letters to their owners. The Palladian palace that Allen was building at the time somehow pales in that emotional and historical context, notwithstanding Allen's benevolence and good architectural judgment.

We do not hear any more about Allen's landscape until April 1739,[30] when Pope wishes him and Fortescue the pleasure of each other's company "rather by a Fireside, than on your delectable Mountains in this Weather" (4:173). There was a chance he could manage a visit to Bath in the summer, but there still was a lot of activity at the time in his own garden. The preceding November he had put in his order with Allen for six stone urns that he had designed, presumably for his own garden, and now in May he had the services of Allen's mason, Biggs, to set up these urns and others that were a gift from the Prince of Wales, and to repair his portico "where the Rain overflowed the Stucco" (see 4:144, 181). In the middle of this, Bolingbroke, for whom at Pope's request Allen had dispatched bottles of Bath water in the autumn, had finally just sold Dawley Farm and departed immediately for France, leaving the poet rather dejected.

By August Pope had given up the idea of a visit to the Allens until the end of the year, feeling out of sorts and spending his time instead arranging for Allen to send a "Pillar" to Sir Thomas Lyttelton at Hagley and designing three garden buildings there; he was also supervising the laying of a pavement by Biggs in his own garden, one of the "Vanities" that he declared was soon to be "at an end" but that he would excuse "to the Connoisseurs by setting over my door, in conclusion of them, *Parvum Parva decent*" (4:190–91). Allen, he remarked, was to blame for his and his friends' vanities, with his abundant supplies of stone. He could not have suspected that after his long visit with the Allens at Widcombe from November to February he would return home infected by a desire for one last vanity that he lived with for the rest of his life: the refurbishing of his grotto with rocks, stones, minerals, and the like from Cornwall and elsewhere.[31]

The November trip to Bath was partly due to poor health; possibly Viscount Cornbury's positive reports about Allen and Prior Park also roused him. In any case, he finally arrived at the Allen household for an enjoyable three-month visit. It would be only a year and a half before the Allens moved into Prior Park, but there was still time to consult the landscape with renewed care and guide its design. Pope was glad of the rest, too. The diet of his pleasures consisted of reading, writing, planting, and relaxed conversation with his host—all at his own leisure. "If you can write me a Line," he said to Bethel, "it will find me at Ralph Allen's Esq's at Widcomb, where I shall live, read, & plant away my time, leaving the Madness of the Little Town [Bath] beneath me" (4:206). One would expect him to have been working on landscape designs from the start of his visit, but January came and Allen would not let him go; as he told Fortescue, he still hoped to "serve him [Allen] a little in laying out his Garden &c." (4:217).

Apparently the gardens were then almost finished, or so we may surmise from a letter Pope wrote to Allen in May 1740, three months after returning home, in which he speaks of the completion of the gardens—a sanguine comment, certainly, but one that hints at the large amount of planting, cutting of paths through woods, clearing of prospects, management of water, and so on that must have gone on during the winter. "It is my firm resolution," he announced, "to inhabit the Room at the end of your Gallery one Fortnight at least in September, & as much longer as I can, to see your Gardens finish'd (ready for Mrs Allen's Grotto and Cascade the following year) I must inquire, next after hers & your health, after that of the Elms we planted on each Side of the Lawn? & of the little Wood-work to join one wood to the other below, which I hope you planted this Spring" (4:239). One supposes from this passage that until Pope's visit in the winter of 1739–40 not much significant planting had been done on the predominantly treeless slopes of the hill. It was then that they planted elms on either side of the central lawn, north of the house; the "little Wood-work" Pope mentions, joining upper and lower woods, which they decided had to be planted in the spring, could be the thin lines of

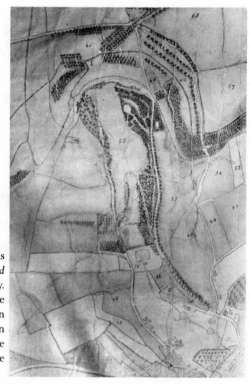

Plate 76. Detail of Prior Park house and gardens from the *Survey of the Manors of Hampton, Claverton, and Widcombe*. Author unknown, late eighteenth century. This shows how the gardens were naturalized in the second half of the century: the outlines of the lawn have been softened, the kitchen garden has been replaced by an irregularly planted grove, and three ponds (with a Palladian bridge) have replaced the single central basin.

trees (shown on plate 76) along the western side of the central lawn connecting larger areas of woods to its north and south. It could well have been his idea since he asks about it in particular. At least it would have been characteristic: in addition to increasing the visual continuity of the garden as it proceeded downhill, it provided a line of woods through which a path could be cut leading from the top southern end of the gardens down to the lower northern area with its centrally placed basin (see plate 77).

According to Richard Jones, they also planted, in true Bathurst fashion, an astounding number of trees—55,146 pines all over and around the estate, some of them along with elms and other types, just above (south of) the house, where they appear to have lined roadways and paths radiating from the so-called Upper Lodge (shown on plate 76 and identified on plate 78). These tree-lined pathways are shown particularly well on Thomas Thorpe's 1742 survey (plate 79), and two of them are pictured later in the large *Survey* of Allen's estates (plate 76) as being lined up with a statue of General George Wade (father of Allen's first wife), who eventually attained the rank of field marshal. In a letter he wrote on 10 May 1763, Samuel Derrick, master of ceremonies at Bath, described the statue and the landscaping around it with the variety of propects that were opened up along the perimeter of the estate:

> Before the house is a handsome lawn with a statue of General Wade, upon a pedestal, in a Roman habit, grasping a truncheon. The ground about is charmingly disposed and improved; the gardens well watered and laid out in

217

Plate 77. "Prior Park, the Seat of Ralph Allen Esq. near Bath." Engraved by Anthony Walker, 1752. This shows in detail the long wilderness on the right, with winding paths; the kitchen gardens to the left; and the central basin, at the bottom of the sloping lawn. Also shown is Allen's invention of a machine for transporting quarried stone.

taste, and Mr. Allen has planted a vast number of firs in the neighbourhood, which thrive well. The ride bordering round the grounds is miles in extent in which the views of the city, river, and adjacent country, are every minute so varied, that to me it wears the appearance of fairy-ground.[32]

For the base of the statue Van Diest designed four panels, which hang today inside the house; they depict Wade's projects in Scotland.[33] But one cannot help feeling that the dramatic position the statue enjoyed just south of the house, set off as it was by lines of trees, justified something with more associative relevance to the area in which it stood.

With these trees recently planted, Pope's eagerness to hear about their progress is understandable. He had asked Omer, Allen's mason who was then at Twickenham, "about a hundred questions concerning the Garden, Trees, the House, & Finishing, &c." (4:247). He was also eager to have the Allens see his grotto, particularly Mrs. Allen, because as he hinted in his earlier letter of 15 May (4:239), the gardens of Prior Park needed to be in readiness to receive a grotto and cascade that, in keeping with the growing ladies' fad, seemed to be in her charge. Whether by carefully mentioning Mrs. Allen in subsequent letters Pope was simply being diplomatic about a woman who seemed less fond of him than was her husband, or whether he was being respectful of her taste for grottoes, he included her in his excitement about his grotto. Having decided that he could not get back to Bath until the end of September, he wrote in August to "rejoice extraordinarily that Mrs Allen has begun to imitate the Great Works of Nature, rather than those Bawbles most Ladies affect." "I hope," he added, "you have not

Plate 78. Auction map of Prior Park Estate, early nineteenth century. Certain features are identified, such as the "Bath House," the serpentine, "Pope's Grotto," "Bason and Fountain," Upper Lodge, and the Priory.

impoverishd Your Rock to beautify mine" (4:254). Mrs. Allen, then, had at least started her gardening experiment with the underground "Works of Nature," and Pope wanted to go and join in. Jokingly, two months later, he offered to come in his own "little Chair, which would be highly useful to me when with you, in securing my very crazy person from Cold in the works in your Garden, Rock, &c." (4:280).

The landscape: "this delightful spot"

The Allens moved into Prior Park at last in the late spring of 1741, by which time the outlines, at least, of the gardens below the house must have been complete. There were details, too, that on the basis of Thorpe's 1742 *Survey* and a 1752 engraving of Prior Park might be judged to have been complete by then and probably were facilitated by Pope on his visit. To begin with, the shape and disposition of the central lawn, on either side of which Pope said he helped plant elms, must have looked much as it does in the engraving of the gardens by Anthony Walker. This engraving, which shows in more detail than any other extant print or map the enviable position of the house and several important features of the gardens as they were when Pope knew them, pictures the lawn with a straight edge along the eastern side and a serpentine edge on the western. The reason for one being straight and the other serpentine is that while the latter matched the

219

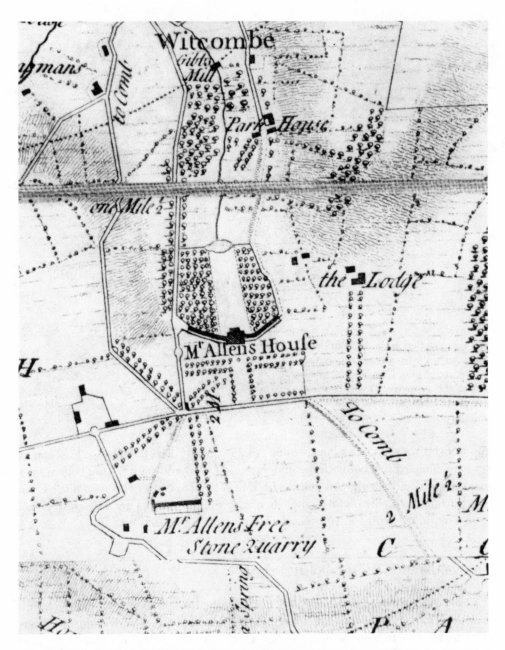

Plate 79. Detail of Prior Park ("Mr. Allen's House") from Thomas Thorpe's *Actual Survey of the City of Bath* (Bath, 1742). The planting is roughly and misleadingly shown.

wilderness character of the woods planted on the western side, then about twenty feet high, with winding walks through them and twisting rivulets emanating from springs and falling down a cascade, the former more prosaically separated the lawn from the kitchen gardens. Thorpe's *Survey*, though earlier, is surely not correct in picturing groves on the eastern side of the lawn of equal extent to those on the western side. This hill had

220

few trees on it when Pope and Allen started planting, so if there were groves to the east they must have planted them; and yet, one cannot believe that in that event they would have cut them down again by 1752 to clear the area for the kitchen garden.

Another interesting detail shown by the 1752 engraving is that on the kitchen-garden side the separation from the lawn was in the form of a hedge while on the wilderness side, already abundantly natural in character, the separation appears to have been a solid wall. It is impossible to say when they were placed there, but the engraving also shows four urns on pedestals placed along the hedge at equal intervals (with one by the entrance to the kitchen garden) from upper to lower terrace. The effect resembles that of the Exedra at Chiswick, which Allen saw on two separate occasions. The governing scheme of this area, with kitchen garden along one side and wilderness along the other, resembled on a larger scale the layout of Pope's own garden.

The lawn itself comprised an open terrace directly facing the north front of the house and shaped by the curving arcades, followed by the flat, smooth-shaven, sloping lawn extending and narrowing down to a second terrace, on the center of which was placed the basin. As has been stated, the basin, which was fed by springs up on the hills, occupied visually a central position in the gardens as seen from the house. To enhance the basin's visual importance in this spot and to create the illusion of greater length (though the garden was long as it was), the lawn narrowed considerably until, when it reached the bottom, it was the same width as the basin—recalling Pope's observation on perspective: "You may distance things by . . . narrowing the plantation more and more toward the end, in the same manner as they do in painting."[34] The basin was also landscaped as a theater, monument, or building might be, but not with verdure. It was flanked by raised walls that curved around it; off to the east side there could have been steps leading to a lookout point with another urn and pedestal, from which to the east one would look out upon fields and livestock.[35] Later, in 1769, the Palladian bridge was built over two newly floated lakes where the basin had been (see plate 80).

Prominence was also given to the kitchen (fruit and vegetable) garden. Mary Chandler's poem, we recall, had prophesied that Allen's gardens would be the complete opposite of Timon's, especially in that his fruit trees would not simply "gratify the Sight." The proximity of the kitchen garden to the pleasure gardens recalls Riskins, where the "Promiscuous Kitchen Quarters" were actually part of the pleasure gardens; and as at Riskins, Allen's kitchen garden contained decorative (as well as functional) paths, some winding and some straight, which made it enjoyable to the casual observer.[36] Walker's engraving shows one of the paths leading out onto the lawn and another to the elevated structure next to the basin. By way of decoration there was a fountain in the kitchen garden just in front of the "offices" of the east wing of the house, identified in Daniel Smith's auction map as a "Bason and Fountain" (plate 78); and Walker also shows a graceful-looking building, surrounded by trees, next to this fountain and by the lawn entrance to the kitchen garden, which Smith called a "Bath House." It housed a cold bath but looked rather like an orangery. Boyce speaks of a greenhouse, and chicken yards and guinea fowl, near the house,[37] but it is not clear where these would have been; the building shown by Walker may have doubled as a greenhouse. The greenhouse apparently was for, among other things, growing pineapples, which on Pope's recommenda-

221

Plate 80. Eighteenth-century view of Prior Park mansion with the Palladian bridge (built in 1769) and lake in the foreground. The naturalization of the sloping lawn has by this time been carried to the point where sheep are allowed to graze upon it.

tion and advice, and with his gardener John Searle's and Burlington's Mr. Scot's expert guidance, Allen successfully cultivated.

Scot was about to leave Burlington's employ and "Set up for himself in the Art of Gardening, in which he has great Experience," Pope told Allen in late summer 1741. He had a scheme for making pineapples cheaper and was to visit Allen shortly. "I know you'l make him welcome," Pope remarked, "& he may be of some Use to instruct & enlarge the Idæas of Isaac" (4:360)—Isaac Dodsley, Allen's gardener, was the bookseller Robert Dodsley's brother. Since as Burlington's gardener Scot would have acquired considerable and varied experience, especially by working with Kent at Chiswick in the 1730s, Pope probably is referring to general experience here, not just to knowledge of the cultivation of pineapples.[38] An interesting and, I think, ironic footnote to the exchanging and gifts of gardeners that Pope frequently arranged for his friends and himself is that after his death, John Searle, who had been with him for over twenty years, was hired by Allen to join Isaac as one of his head gardeners at Prior Park. Since Prior Park was the only garden, besides his own, for which in his last few years Pope did any planning, Searle certainly would have heard a good deal about it and even offered his opinions; he therefore was not going to an unfamiliar garden. It is not unlikely, it seems to me, that Robert Dodsley, who through his brother possibly kept in close touch with the goings-on at Prior Park, as a bookseller initiated the idea of Searle's producing a plan and account of the deceased poet's famous garden, which he published in 1745. To the confluence of these circumstances at Prior Park, therefore, we may owe the only surviving graphic evidence of what Pope's garden looked like. In any case, it was quite a plum for Allen to get Pope's gardener.

If we go back to Allen's gardens as they existed in 1741, the area that looks as if it received most of Pope's attention, though you could not guess it by Thorpe's treatment of it in his *Survey* (to which the poet had subscribed), was the wood on the west side of the lawn, stretching all the way down to the basin. As shown by Walker, it was a tantalizingly irregular and dark area cut through with a network of mazelike paths. A writer in the May 1754 number of the *Universal Magazine* who described the landscape was especially impressesd by these groves:

> The gardens are laid out with a profusion of fancy, yet with great œconomy, as to the expence. For, Mr. Allen being contented with the situation, instead of forcing nature to bend to art, he has pursued only what the natural situation has pointed out to him; and, by that means rendered it one of the cheapest, and, at the same time, one of the most beautiful seats in England. He has levelled no hills, but enjoys the beauty of the prospects they afford; he has cut down no woods, but struck through them fine walks, and has, by that means, a delightful grove always filled with birds, which afford the rural ear a music transcending all others.[39]

The large *Survey* of Allen's estates and Smith's auction map both give an idea of how interesting this wood was. In addition to the twisting paths, there was a large secluded opening or "room" into which one of these paths led. After Pope's manner at Twickenham and elsewhere, there probably were more, smaller, secret areas not shown that were decorated with seats and other stone ornaments. In his early nineteenth-century published memoirs and papers on the literary associations of Bath, the Reverend Francis Kilvert spoke of "the Walks, which serpentine through this delightful Spot, [and] are decorated with Vases, and other Ornaments in Stone."[40]

The most interesting feature in the area, however, was the arrangement of waterworks. Perhaps it was Samuel Richardson, a friend of Allen's, who, when adding to Defoe's *Tour* for a new edition in 1748, called Allen the "Genius of the Place" and decided that this wood was original and spectacular enough to be described separately. Leading from the lawn, says the *Tour*,

> winding Walks made through a little Coppice opening to the Westward of those Slopes; but all these are adorned with Vases, and other Ornaments, in Stone-work; and the Affluence of Water is so great, that it is received in three different places, after many little agreeable Falls, at the Head of one of which is a Statue of Moses down to the Knees, in an Attitude expressive of the Admiration he must have been in after striking the Rock, and seeing the

Water gush out of it. The winding Walks were made with great Labour; and, tho' no broader than for two or three to walk abreast, yet in some places they appear with little cliffs on one Side, and with small Precipices on the other.[41]

This statue of Moses, which as Boyce comments continued in the Christian theme of some of the paintings in the house by Van Diest,[42] stood at the top of a high falls, perhaps as much as twenty feet high,[43] producing a rush of water that must have sounded throughout the wood and across the lawn, and been heard even up at the house. Such water effects immeasurably pleased Pope, who remembered the romantic cascade at Sherborne and was very fond of the cascades and "jetts" in Venus's Vale at Rousham. More than that, though, this scene of grove, spring, falls, and rustic stonework seems very likely to have derived from Pope's frequently demonstrated commitment in gardening to the classical *locus amoenus*. Professor Mack wrote in *The Garden and the City* about how Pope's innovations in English gardening were influenced by his recall of the classical figure of the rocky cave.[44] Pope's own grotto, which he was refurbishing at about the same time as this watery "cave" at Prior Park was being created, owed its thematic underpinnings to the renderings of such a scene by the classical poets, especially Homer, Virgil, and Martial. As Professor Mack points out, Pope's *Guardian* essay alone amply illustrates that, as does his translation of Calypso's bower in book 5 of the *Odyssey*. If there is any part of the Prior Park gardens that "belongs" to Pope in that it was central to his fundamental "poetic" approach to gardening as allusive and classical, it was this spot. The Moses figure represents no problem in this context because it was merely a Christian allusion added on in deference, doubtless, to Allen's Christian benevolence and bountiful generosity to others. Milton would have approved, one feels, of that version of Christian humanism, and Pope himself had "read" both a Christian and classical meaning at Sherborne and elsewhere.

As for the falling water that the 1748 *Tour* mentioned, it comprised the head of a large serpentine stream that appears on both the large *Survey* and Smith's map. Across the serpentine was a "Sham-Bridge" possibly designed by Pope,[45] which probably appeared as one of the illustrations of buildings on Allen's estates in the large *Survey*; Pope never mentioned it in his correspondence and, surprisingly, neither did the 1748 *Tour*. Its style resembled the little rustic bridge at Sherborne.

Along these rivulets of paths at the edge of the wood was located a grotto identified in Smith's map as "Pope's Grotto." Could this have been the rustic grotto that in 1740 Pope had said Mrs. Allen was creating? There are still in this spot some tumbled stone walls that suggest the rustic character of a grotto. There is a small octagonal stone-wall structure with a pointed thatch roof, shown as one of the buildings (L) in the large *Survey*, that might have been this grotto, though it is identified as the "Thatch'd House."[46] With its pointed roof of thatch it resembles somewhat Merlin's Cave at Richmond. Finally, along the western wall of these groves there were two exits to the tramway that ran alongside Prior Park, one of which, according to Walker, was at the beginning of a straight path to the basin.

As an example of a so-called second stage (1730s) of the new landscaping, Prior Park was impressive. Pope was unable to get down to see the Allens in their new mansion and occupy a room overlooking the gardens until the end of autumn "in the planting Season." "I hope you enjoy Yours," he wrote to Allen in July; "When I can encrease my own happiness by seeing yours there, I cannot be certain, but think about the beginning of Septr. . . . if our old project of a Short Stay upon Clifton down, & a Voyage to Wales were practicable, I would aim at it then" (4:350). This was not an idle comment because eventually, in August 1743, less than a year before his death, he "went over the channel to Wales" (4:467)—his first and only known visit there—without Allen. Meanwhile, he proposed meeting the Allens at Cirencester and then embarking on a ramble together "to Cornbury, Rowsham, Lord Litchfields, D. of Shrewsbury's, all of which are worth seeing, and (above all) Stowe" (4:347). The Allens did come, but not until October, and we do not know whether they saw these places. They took Pope back with them to Prior Park. In July he was assisting Allen in the choice of four busts, including ones of Milton and Sir Walter Raleigh (another echo of Sherborne), probably for the house, though not inconceivably for the garden (4:351); and in August he was planning the October visit: "If a little Planting be necessary in my Garden, it shall be hasten'd at the beginning of October, so as to reach you time enough [to assist] you in Yours" (4:358).

This visit was momentous less because of the gardening they did than because in November, at Allen's urging, Pope invited Warburton to come to Prior Park. To work together for a month or more on Pope's idea of a "General Edition" of his poems, to be edited by Warburton, who could thereafter assume he would be Pope's "official" commentator-editor, in this "Inviolable Asylum" of a house, would be in the interest of posterity.[47] An ambitious man, Warburton came immediately and from then on rose in Allen's esteem, spending more and more time at Prior Park until in 1746 he eventually married Allen's niece, Gertrude Tucker.[48] Pope's biographer, then, as well as his gardener, eventually became a fixture at Prior Park (see plate 81).

Pope was at Prior Park again with Warburton, who preceded him there, in October, having received a visit from the Allens at Twickenham in August. He had two weeks with Warburton, discussing among other things the new *Dunciad* he was preparing with an increased body of humor and satiric footnotes. After Warburton left, Pope stayed on until the end of November. During this time he applied himself to building a "Pine-house" for the pineapples, located close to the house in the kitchen garden because Allen was apprehensive that "the Chimney of the Pine-house might smoke so as to be offensive to the new building" (4:429). Pope tried to reasssure his friend: "John [Searle] assures me it will not; there need be no fires all the day, & the quantity, when once the house is tight, & the Glaziers work good, so small, that it evaporates within a few yards of the place." He was eager to have the experiment succeed because of Mrs. Allen's fondness for the fruit and "because it is the only piece of Service I have been able to do you, or to help you in" (4:429). By this comment we may judge that the gardens by then were fairly complete as far as Pope was concerned. He was relieved to hear the next week that the smoke was not a problem; "I should be sorry to blacken you any way," he added (4:431). Pope performed one final service for Allen in April 1743 when he passed on advice from Burlington on how to care for the new fawns in the small deer park above the house (4:452).

There is some irony to that last remark in light of the quarrel in the summer of 1743

Plate 81. Pope, Ralph Allen, and William Warburton at Prior Park. Painting by the Reverend Francis Kilvert.

involving Martha Blount. As has been mentioned, Pope did think of moving to Mrs. Allen's old home, Hampton Manor, or to Widcombe; but he had occasion to write to Jonathan Richardson, the painter, after the quarrel and put to rest a rumor that he was about to move to Bath. Although he just did not like the city of Bath, his firmness and the perceptibly sour note in the following passage from the letter to Richardson were possibly induced by the aftertaste to that quarrel:

> But for your News of my quitting Twitnam for Bath, inquire into my Years, if they are past the bounds of Dotage? ask my Eyes, if they can See, & my nostrils if they can smell? To prefer Rocks & Dirt, to flowry Meads & silver Thames, & Brimstone & Fogs to Roses & Sunshine? When I arrive at these Sensations, I may settle at Bath; of which I never yet dreamt, further, than to live just out of the Sulphurous Pit & at the Edge of the Fogs, at Mr Allen's for a month or so. I like the place so little, that Health itself should not draw me thither, tho Friendship has, twice or thrice.[49] (4:484–85)

Sadly, after he left Prior Park unhappily in the summer of 1743, Pope never saw it again. Today it is a school and its landscape, though neglected and forlorn, has survived without any encroachment by housing estates or any other forms of development.

Epilogue

The intensely personal character of Pope's landscape gardening is, I hope, now evident. Spence caught the right note in a conversation with Pope in 1743, the year before the poet died. "I pity you, Sir," he said to Pope, "because you have now completed everything belonging to your garden"—and most everything belonging to others of his favorite landscapes, he might have added. "Why," Pope replied, "I really shall be at a loss for the diversion I used to take in laying out and finishing things. I have now nothing to do...."[1]

As the art of biography acknowledges, the inward and spiritual life of a person is largely affected by his outward, day-to-day life. This was certainly true of Pope's landscaping. His youth, reading, and friends, as well as places, situations, timing, politics, and social vantage point, all determined it, the most practical of the arts he practiced.

He was a famous landscaper from the early 1720s to the end of his life because, like most geniuses, he had a highly assimilative intellect. That is why although his pictorial landscaping principles—summarized in *To Burlington* and recorded by Spence—remained unchanged during the quarter-century of his gardening fame, his notions of landscape possibilities, from Ladyholt and Chiswick to Prior Park, were continually expanding. He moved with the times, and in the increasingly high value he placed on expressive and irregular landscape effects, he helped direct English landscaping toward the midcentury Picturesque era. He was by no means an outdated landscaper when he died, as Prior Park showed. His garden, twenty-five years after he acquired the use of its five acres, was one of the best-known private gardens in England, and friends and acquaintances still asked him for landscaping advice, which, his health permitting, he gladly gave. He was less apt to ask his gardener John Searle to "Shut, shut the door" against interested landscapers than against mad poets and scribblers.

Pope's reputation as a gardener was won as a landscaper, not as a horticulturist, although his correspondence reveals that he was a knowledgeable vegetable and fruit grower. There were other more knowledgeable men, like Philip Miller, foreman in the Chelsea Botanical Garden and author of *The Gardener's and Florist's Dictionary* (1724), to whom he and his contemporaries could turn for expert horticultural advice.[2] Pope's reputation was largely founded on his own garden and his landscaping for other public figures featured in this book who could be counted upon to spread the word about his genius for design. Much of this fame in his lifetime was circulated that way, by word of mouth, though Switzer mentioned him briefly in some of his writings and Pope himself declared his authority as artist-landscaper in *To Burlington*.

Most of all, however, it was Pope's own garden that perpetuated his gardening reputation; it drew visitors and tourists right up until the time it was destroyed by Baroness Howe in 1807. Unbelievably, however, apart from Kent's stylized engraving of the Shell Temple and a recently discovered painting by Jonathan Richardson (frontispiece), there are no known contemporary illustrations of the garden. Morris Brownell has recently dramatized this fact. He has illustrated just how much in vogue the villa was as a subject for paintings throughout the eighteenth century; his exhibition in the summer of 1980 at Marble Hill of views of Pope's residence revealed the extensive proportions of its iconography, which was perpetuated by the famous, like Jonathan Richardson and J. M. W. Turner, as well as by the not-so-famous.[3] But this exhibition, entitled "Views of Pope's Villa, Grotto and Garden: a Microcosm of English Landscape," may have been mistitled because it demonstrated how little visual evidence there is of the garden itself. The exhibition's one exciting addition to the almost nonexistent iconography of Pope's garden is the painting by Richardson, for long thought to be lost but now part of the Paul Mellon Collection at the Yale Center for British Art, showing Pope in his garden with the obelisk memorializing his mother in the faint background. Even that, however, does not reveal much about the garden layout. Many visitors came but few, apparently, stopped long enough to sketch. One exception, though not contemporary, was John Buckler, who came to the garden in 1826 and did several sketches of the grotto interior and entrance on the garden side and the setting for the obelisk Pope set up in memory of his mother.[4]

The absence of graphic evidence of what Pope's garden looked like must have been one reason why his role in the establishment of the English landscape garden was underrated after he died. In the last half of the century, his reputation diminished as the so-called Picturesque movement—which featured "Capability" Brown, Humphry Repton, William Gilpin, and Richard Payne Knight—superseded his ideas, and as Horace Walpole, Thomas Whately, and, surprisingly, even Spence (and his friend Robert Dodsley) tended to play down his early influence in favor of Kent's, Willliam Shenstone's,[5] Philip Southcote's, and Lord Petre's (a Catholic naturalist and the mutual friend of Pope and John Caryll). Spence, indeed, may well have thought of himself in the 1750s as a practicer of landscape techniques that had long since outstripped Pope's ideas and made them appear old hat. Indeed, it may be the prevalent judgment among garden historians today that by midcentury, just six years after Pope died, his gardening ideas (and garden) had become outdated. Without its presiding poetic genius to quicken and energize its interplay of images and effects, so the reasoning may go, and with another owner present instead who blurred the personal and almost mythical associations of its glades and recesses, the garden tended to become a mere tourist attraction, a museum piece. One writer recently commenting upon Mrs. Patrick Delany's gardening tastes felt that "in her admiration for Pope's garden at Twickenham, she was plainly old-fashioned" but that in her capacity also to admire "the work of 'the ingenious Mr. Brown'

[Capability Brown] at Longleat in 1760 or landscaping based on the designs of Humphry Repton" she redeemed herself.[6] But what is surprising is that Spence, Walpole, and Whately were all inclined to give Kent the biggest role even in those early years, partly because (one suspects) Kent had turned professional landscape gardener in the late 1730s and therefore had convincing credentials to add to his genius.

Still, for all that, one of Kent's principal credentials they did not forget was his friendship with Pope when the poet was in the vanguard of the movement. Though Spence, Walpole, and Whately do not speak much of Pope's actual landscaping at several estates throughout the country, from which they would have learned a good deal more about his ideas than they knew, they recognize that his innovations in English landscaping could in one sense never become old-fashioned; he brought the "poetic" to garden design, the mentality of the artist who sees finely and with heightened nuance. A quick survey of Spence's observations and anecdotes on Pope's gardening reveals this. He makes only one or two great claims for Pope the gardener, but at the same time he articulates in bits and pieces the new world of artistic gardening that Pope introduced. The 1742 visitor to the Twickenham garden recognized as much in his halting way, and stated the prevalent attitude, when he concluded his description by announcing that the gardens could not have been designed by anyone but Pope—not by Kent, Petre, or Spence himself. "They are fancyed in a manner so truely Poetical," wrote the visitor.[7]

Pope's contribution was inherent in English landscaping for the rest of the century and afterward. It was even manifest in some imaginative landscapes that few garden commentators saw but that, if they had, might well have affected their late-century assessments of his styles and techniques. If nothing else, these landscapes would have illustrated to them his ability to work upon larger canvases than his own garden provided. In fact, the matter of scale is relevant, as I have tried to suggest, in assessments of this kind. In his own garden Pope landscaped only five acres because he did not want any more. He had some trouble, as we have seen him sometimes declaring half-seriously, in simply getting around the expansive landscapes of his friends. Committed to his small demesne, he obviously accepted constraints upon his efforts to create the illusion of space and distance. It was precisely through a contrast of the irregular with the regular, of the straight with the curving line, of the open and flat with the winding and hidden, that this illusion and multiplicity of effects were achieved. Without that contrast which garden historians have been inclined to call "transitional," Pope could not have created such variety, and yet it is just that element of contrast or balance which appears outdated in the face of what followed later in the century.[8]

One other feature of Pope's gardening taste that bears mentioning here again is his obvious nostalgia in preferring landscapes and houses that had remained in a single family's possession for generations. Clearly one of the facts that drew him to Sir William Codrington's seat at Dodington Hall in Gloucestershire was that it was a beautiful Elizabethan house set unobtrusively in a gentle vale where the family had long lived. The house itself, as well as the sloping lawns and rolling hills and woods around it, spoke to him of a past age of simple and honest tastes and values. It was the same with Sherborne, Rise, Cirencester, Stanton Harcourt, Ladyholt, and a number of others. Good house-

229

keeping and sensible economy seemed to him synonymous with those places, where a garden was a thing of use as well as delight. Usefulness was, of course, also an ancient quality he found in classical gardens. If a modern garden could display that kind of good sense at the same time as it looked forward to new imaginative pictorial techniques, it seemed to him it was on the right track.

It is clear from Pope's sustained love of gardening and taste for open landscape that landscaping allowed him the scope for a pleasing mode of self-consciousness, a poetic and emotive self-expression that he did not indulge as much in his poetry after the first edition of his *Works* (1717), except for his Homer translations. Whatever the reasons for this shift of temper and subject in his poetry,[9] Pope never outgrew the poetic sensibility for landscape that began to be especially nourished when his family moved to Binfield, the evocative landscape of his youth, where at the age of twelve his schooling began in the pictorial uses of landscape. His letters to Martha Blount describing the terrain like the downs he saw in 1739 between Bath and Bristol or the gothic-like hilly wilderness around Netley Abbey in 1734 show that this sensibility became progressively more intense and was sharpened by his painter's perspective. In this vein he remained during his lifetime a (largely) unacknowledged influence not only upon landscaping but also upon attitudes toward open landscapes.[10] The force behind these impulses in him is glimpsed in a passage from a recently discovered letter he wrote around 1737: "The Country is a Study at this time," he told Ralph Allen, "& I think the Noblest in ye World: It is ye Study of God & Nature, in the most beautiful of his Manifestations."[11]

Since Pope's poetry was headed in other directions in the 1720s, it was vital, emotionally and aesthetically, that landscaping afforded him an artistic focus for this pictorial and romantic sensibility. It was also essential that Martha Blount was the ideal listener and correspondent in whom he could confide when he was infected by contemplative, melancholic, and rapturous moods in natural scenery. Her "Romantic Taste," as he put it, made him write to her as he did to no one else. He did not keep her within the garden with the flowers and idle pleasures for which his contemporaries thought women were suited. He put her in the landscape, where with him she ranged (in his imagination) sympathetically and understandingly.

Appendix A

Morris Brownell's contention that in his description of Horatio's gardens in the *Essay on Pope's Odyssey* Spence was really describing Pope's garden[1] is unconvincing, even though it is tempting to depend upon it for further ideas of what Pope's garden looked like. It is appropriate here to suggest why.

After Spence wrote part 1 of his complimentary and judicious *Essay on Pope's Odyssey* (1726), Pope made a point of getting to know him, so that by the time Spence got around to writing part 2, and publishing it in 1727, Pope had probably welcomed him at Twickenham and, as we know, made some suggestions for part 2. On the basis of one or more visits to Twickenham, Spence acquired a knowledge of Pope's garden, which Brownell has cited as evidence that in his description of the gardens of Horatio in part 2, he was really describing Pope's gardens as a compliment to the poet. One might comment initially that if Spence had wished publicly to compliment his new friend's garden, he would not have obscured the praise in this fashion. There is also the troubling fact that never once in all his writings, many of them about gardening and gardens, did Spence mention that he had described Pope's garden in his *Essay*—and neither did Pope.

Beyond that there are substantive reasons for not allowing the interpretation. To begin with, if it is agreed that Spence is describing Twickenham, we are nonetheless disappointed to find that the description is so general, and many of the features are so common, that we do not learn much from it about the appearance of the garden. We would, however, be reassured from it that the garden, as a transitional garden, was not "unapologetically regular" as was later argued by people who never saw it—and by modern garden historians. Still, we can draw that conclusion on the bases of other descriptions and Searle's *Plan*.

Moreover, if Spence had wanted to compliment Pope as a gardener, he would have described the garden as it was, and would not have modified it as we must conclude he has done if we believe he is describing Pope's garden. The garden was special, as I have shown, because of the particular location of its features, and Spence perhaps would have insulted Pope, not complimented him, if he had altered the design in his account of Horatio's gardens. Here is a list of discrepancies between Spence's account and what we know of Pope's garden: (1) Spence describes a Great Walk down to the river, but there was no such feature on the grass plot on the riverside. (2) Philypsus and Antiphaus, the speakers, sit down by a fountain in full view of the river, but Pope had no such fountain on the riverside. He did have a "Spring of the Clearest Water" (2:296), as he told Blount, but that was not in full view of the river and, in any case, it was in the grotto. (3) There were no gates leading into the Great Walk—the mount was at the eastern end of the walk. (4) Spence's description of "that single Grot yonder, and the hanging Precipice over it," suggests that the grotto was another feature, far removed from the house, and situated next to a romantic-looking precipice. There was nothing remotely like such a precipice in Pope's landscape; the slopes, groves, and walks in the garden, all laid out on gently sloping land, if sloping at all, could hardly be what Spence had in mind with his "hanging Precipice." (5) While Spence stipulates that there was scarcely any feature in Horatio's gardens that did not take advantage of prospects, there were several—as I have shown—that did not in Pope's garden. Indeed, prospects were only available from the house, the mount, the theater, and perhaps the slope at the western end of the garden. The Newcastle visitor mentioned only the mount as affording prospects. (6) Conceal-ment of bounds was no longer so unique in Pope's garden in 1727 that Spence would have had to be thinking of that garden when mentioning it as a distinctive feature of Horatio's. (7) Spence does not at all mention kitchen gardens, and yet they were an important feature in Pope's plan. In short, there is certainly room for doubt that the evidence "overwhelmingly supports the identification of Pope's Twickenham with the gardens of Horatio."[2]

Appendix B

Although Pope does not appear to have landscaped much at Marble Hill after 1725, one detail about the landscaping commanded his attention in 1725 and, remarkably, continued unresolved for about twenty years.[1] The matter illustrates again his readiness to come to the assistance of his friends in their times of need, and it shows how thoroughly involved he was with Mrs. Howard's landscape. The drama, which went on unresolved for over fifteen years, concerned Mrs. Howard and those acting on her behalf (including Pope), on the one hand, and Mr. and Mrs. Thomas Vernon, Pope's landlords, on the other. Vernon had sold Marble Hill Shot to Lord Ilay, acting for Mrs. Howard, back in 1724, but he continued to occupy lands on either side of Mrs. Howard's new gardens— lands owned by the trustees of something called Death's Charity. Vernon's occupancy would have posed no problem for Mrs. Howard except for a lingering nuisance in the form of a public right of way cutting across her land between her gardens and the river. Apparently she did not mind a public access east-west next to the river, well away from the house, so Pope was authorized to arrange an alternative terrace-way along the Thames bank. He needed the cooperation of local tenants to achieve this, but they did not mind as long as they had the alternative access along the river (2:249). However, in order to lay out the two-thousand-foot terrace-way, Mrs. Howard ideally needed to purchase the charity land, then occupied by the Vernons, on either side of her own. Thomas Vernon refused to relinquish the tenancy, even for a good price, and after he died in 1726 his wife, apparently faithful to his wishes, also refused to cooperate (see 2:446, 3:34–35). Even Robert Walpole was exasperated by the Vernons' conduct; Pope wrote Fortescue on 23 September 1725 "that Mr. Walpole swore by G—d Mrs. Howard should have the ground she wanted from V—n" (2:323).

The part of the terrace-way that could be built, by virtue of being on Mrs. Howard's land, was nearing completion early in 1726;[2] in August Lord Ilay wrote to Mrs. Howard: "I thought it best to leave Your friend Vernon to himself 2 or three days to see if upon recollection he would be A little more Christian I mean humane. instead of that he Yesterday sent me to know Your answer, so that I think I am at the end of my string with him. . . . You are really in love with Your grounds, he knows, & therefore is so cruel [.] God forgive him for I never will" (5:5). The Vernons did, however, agree to sublet the land to Mrs. Howard. After her husband's death that year, Mrs. Vernon decided to exploit the awkward position in which her husband had placed Mrs. Howard by requesting some additional money in return for allowing Mrs. Howard's continued lease of the two acres. She sent this request to Pope, who clearly was embarrassed by it, as he reveals in his letter to Mrs. Howard in October 1727: "It amounts to about 23 pound more than I believe you have any cause to pay. This is the matter so Important. But sure tis a Family-fault; & the Widow, like a good woman is very sollicitous to perform the *Will of the Dead*, which was, to Impose upon you every way" (2:446).[3]

Since the annual rent had been thirty shillings, this was an exorbitant demand by the widow, whether made in the memory of her husband or not. According to a letter Pope wrote to Mrs. Howard in May 1729, she did not pay any additional money and the situation worsened (3:34–35). The widow then tried to terminate Mrs. Howard's sublet and evict her from the land. Some confusion followed, resulting from Mrs. Howard's belief that Pope had agreed to her paying the widow more money (see 3:34–35); she rebuked him and he defended himself.[4]

It is clear that it was out of the question for Mrs. Howard to return the land to Mrs. Vernon. It had already been assimilated into the Marble Hill landscape, as Pope intimates with some more information about the gardens: "The Fact is, that these 2 acres, in the Lease, which I remember to have read some years since, are said to lye *between Capt. Grays ground & the West Side* (toward the Alehouse) So that it may be anywhere among those grounds behind the Horsechestnuts, for any thing said in the Writings" (*Corr.* 3:35). As Lord Ilay put it, Mrs. Vernon knew that Mrs. Howard was "in love with her grounds," and she was not going to give in, even though her efforts to get more money were unsuccessful.

Things coasted along for about ten years until William Plomer in September 1738 demanded his right of way along the river, which of course Mrs. Howard could not grant without owning the two acres or the lease to them. He was stalled, largely by Pope, and in August 1739 accused Pope of bad faith and threatened legal action (5:19). Mrs. Vernon, however, died in just over two years, after which Mrs. Howard acquired the lease to all the lands involved along the river wherewith to complete the terrace-way. Undoubtedly, this was one landscaping transaction Pope would have happily passed up.

Appendix C

There are several sketches by Pope preserved among the Homer manuscripts, in the British Library, some of which have been referred to elsewhere in this book. Including the ones under our attention here (see plates 82, 83, 84), they were done on the backs of letters, on which Pope also translated passages of Homer—which, as students of Pope know, was the way he translated a good percentage of Homer. All of these sketches are of architectural or gardening subjects and appear to be related to Pope's villa for the following reasons: (1) Pope's identification of the two entrances of the building in plate 82 as facing a street and a garden respectively and with a window on the "2d floor, to reflect Gardens"; (2) in the house in plate 83, the presence, on the garden side, of an arch on the ground floor, a portico on the first floor, and a balustrade on the second; (3) the similarity of floor plans between plates 82 and 83; (4) the squarish garden plat shown in plate 82; and (5) the trellis facing the river for a "Prospect," which might have been an early version (1719–20) of a design for his grotto entrance.[1]

The sketches are reproduced here, by kind permission of the British Library, as examples of Pope's sketches of this kind, and with the hope that students of Pope and architecture may be able to shed some light on them.[2]

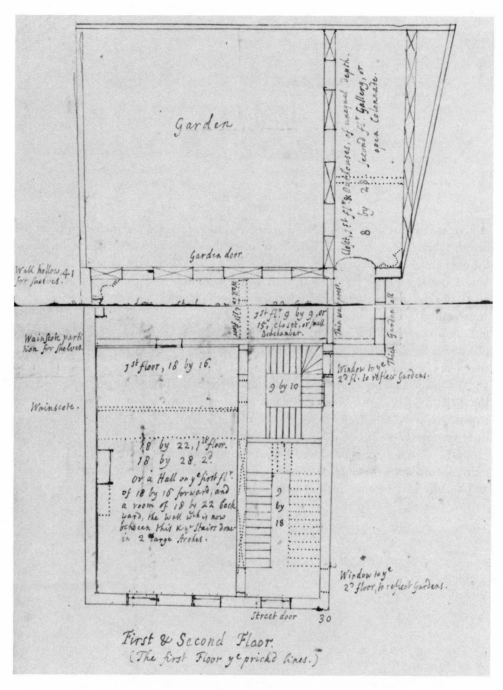

Plate 82. Pope's sketch of the floor plans for a house facing a street on one side and a garden on the other. The drawing is on the reverse side of a letter written to Pope on 29 February 1724, on which he also translated the *Odyssey* 7, lines 357–83. He drew the plan on two separate pieces of paper because he had torn the letter in half to obtain two sheets for his translation. He shows an awareness here of the relationship of the house to the gardens by noting that one of these windows did "reflect Gardens."

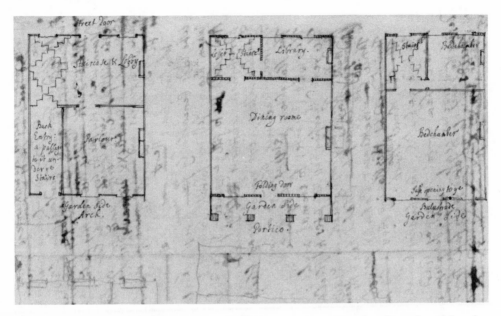

Plate 83. Pope's sketch of the floor plans for a house facing a street on one side and a garden on the other, ca. 1717–18. Drawn on the reverse side of a letter to him dated 16 October 1717, on which he also translated the *Iliad* 16, lines 839ff.

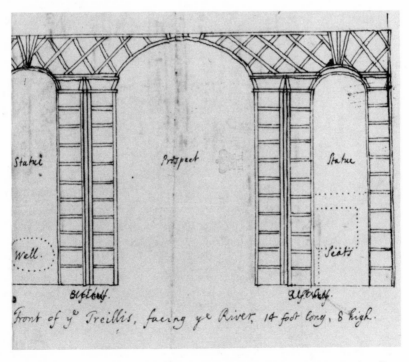

Plate 84. Pope's sketch for the "Front of yᵉ Treillis, facing yᵉ River, 14 foot long, 8 high." This could have been an early (unused) design for the entrance to his grotto. He drew it on a letter on which he also translated the *Iliad* 21, lines 529–52.

237

Notes

Abbreviations

Add. MS   British Library, Additional Manuscripts

Corr.   *The Correspondence of Alexander Pope*. Edited by George Sherburn. 5 vols. Oxford, 1956.

PRO   Public Record Office (London)

Swift, *Corr.*   *The Correspondence of Jonathan Swift*. Edited by Harold Williams. 5 vols. Oxford, 1963.

TE   *The Twickenham Edition of the Poems of Alexander Pope*. General editor, John Butt. Vols. 1–6, the original poems; vols. 7–10, the Homer translations. London and New Haven, 1938–61, 1967.

Introduction

1. In fact, Pope was much more interested in the architecture of his new home. He asked the architect Colin Campbell to design it and perhaps even tinkered with some plans himself if we presume that some of his sketches in the Homer MSS (Add. MS 4804, 30v) were intended for the London house.

2. Maynard Mack, *The Garden and the City* (Toronto, 1969), pp. 9–11, considers some of the reasons for the move.

3. This is part of a recently discovered description of Pope's garden; see Malcolm Andrews, "A New Description of Pope's Garden," *Journal of Garden History*, 1 (1) (January–March 1981):35–36.

4. Volume and page references in the text refer to *Corr*.

5. Some of these were: Appscourt Manor (Surrey), Amesbury (Wiltshire), Bevis Mount (Hampshire), Blenheim, Buckland-Filleigh (Devon), Chiswick House (Middlesex), Cirencester Park (Gloucestershire), Dawley Farm (Middlesex), Down Hall (Essex), Easthampstead Park (Berkshire), Gosfield (Essex), Hagley Park (Worcestershire), Ladyholt (Sussex), Letcombe (Berkshire), Leighs (Essex), Mapledurham (Berkshire), Marble Hill (Middlesex), Prior Park (Somersetshire), Riskins (Buckinghamshire), Rousham (Oxfordshire), Sherborne (Dorset), Stan-

ton Harcourt (Oxfordshire), Stowe (Buckinghamshire), Tottenham Park (Wiltshire), Wimpole (Cambridgeshire).

6. Joseph Spence, *Observations, Anecdotes, and Characters of Books and Men*, ed. James M. Osborne, 2 vols. (Oxford, 1966), 1, 609. Hereafter cited as Spence. Osborne organized Spence's anecdotes into two sections devoted to gardening: one recorded Pope's comments on the subject (602–20), and the other, the more "advanced" ideas of Spence himself, Southcote, and others in the 1750s (1059–1147). References to this work cite volume and anecdote numbers unless pages are specified. See also Morris Brownell, *Alexander Pope and the Arts of Georgian England* (Oxford, 1978), p. 108. Hereafter cited as Brownell.

7. On Pope's father's skillful landscaping at Whitehill, see Brownell, pp. 120–21; Lucius Fitzgerald, "Pope at Binfield," *Home Counties Magazine* 2 (1900):57; and George Sherburn, *The Early Career of Alexander Pope* (Oxford, At the Clarendon Press, 1934), pp. 277–78.

8. The poems are part of a volume of manuscripts titled "Epistolary Conversations in Verse and Prose Between a Lady, under the Name of Amica, And her Friends" on the first page of which is scribbled, "Hʸ Hoare To His Daughter Anne, anno. 1825." Amica, who becomes a Mrs. W—t, remains unidentified, but she must have become a member of the Hoare family of Stourhead as some of the poems of the late eighteenth and early nineteenth centuries in the volume were written to and for members of the Hoare family. I cite from the volume with the kind permission of Mr. Norman Kitz.

9. Pope's "romantic" susceptibility to landscape is thoroughly examined by Brownell, pp. 71–101.

10. Brownell, pp. 186–232, considers these gardens, though not in as much detail.

1. A Master Key to Popery in Gardens

1. For an excellent and convenient anthology of the most important writing about gardening in the eighteenth century, the reader can do no better than turn to *The Genius of the Place*, ed. John Dixon Hunt and Peter Willis (London, 1976).

2. Heavy use is made of Spence's *Anecdotes* in this study. He was himself a devoted and talented gardener. His landscaping has recently been the subject of a series of essays by R. W. King, "Joseph Spence of Byfleet," *Garden History*, 6 (3); 7 (3); 8 (2); 8 (3). See also Peter Martin, "Joseph Spence's Garden in Byfleet: Some New Descriptions," *Journal of Garden History* (April–June 1983), pp. 121–29.

3. See John Dixon Hunt, *The Figure in the Landscape* (Baltimore, 1976). One of Hunt's theses in this book deals with the effects of the eighteenth-century art of gardening upon the human mind—especially upon poets. Chapter 2 discusses how gardening helped Pope achieve a style of human involvement with the natural world generally, and how his garden and grotto evoked poetic associations that in turn contributed to his self-image and its subtle deployment in the ethical and satiric poems of the 1730s.

4. Mack, *Garden and the City*, especially ch. 1.

5. Spence 1, 559. Brownell, pp. 102–17, considers at length Pope's concept of garden design chiefly in terms of the poet's taste or eye for the "picturesque."

6. Spence 1, 612.

7. Spence 1, 603, uses this phrase around 1751.

8. "The History of Modern Taste in Gardening," in *Horace Walpole: Gardenist*, ed. Isabel Chase (Princeton, 1943), p. 25. Hereafter cited as Chase.

9. Spence 1, 612.

10. Spence 1, 604, records Pope as saying that "all the beauties of gardening might be comprehended in one word, "variety.""

11. For an account of Pope's experience as a painter, see Brownell, pt. 1. Norman Ault effectively described this tendency of Pope's as a poet in *New Light on Pope* (London, 1949), ch. 5.

12. Spence 1, 606.

13. Spence 1, 607.

14. Pope's use of this word and its early eighteenth-century meaning has been subjected to a wide range of interpretations. Recently Brownell, pp. 85–101, has seen in Pope's sense of the word not only allusions to landscape and garden effects that look like pictures, "*ut pictura horticultura*" as Horace phrased it, but also the emotive or psychological dimension of landscape in the moonlight, for example, or around antique ruins of castles, abbeys, and the like. As far as Pope is concerned, I prefer to separate these two aspects of his response to landscapes and gardens. As I explain later in this chapter, his poetic sensibility to emotionally evocative landscape relates more intelligibly to his antiquarianism and "romanticism"—to his imaginative powers—than to his precise aesthetic criteria for preferring one kind of landscape over another. There is no evidence that Pope used the word "picturesque" to mean anything more than a scene that presents pictorial effects. Another analysis of the word from a psychological standpoint is by Wylie Sypher, "Psychological Picturesque: Association and Reverie," *Rococo to Cubism in Art and Literature* (New York, 1960), pt. 2, ch. 3. One of the clearest assessments of picturesque gardening is by Edward Malins, *English Landscaping and Literature, 1660-1840*, ch. 7.

See also Kenneth Woodbridge's recent comments on the excessively liberal use of the word "picturesque," in "Irregular, Rococo or Picturesque," *Apollo* 108 (November 1978):356; and "The Nomenclature of Style in Garden History," a lecture given at the Victoria and Albert Museum in June 1979, on the occasion of the exhibition entitled, "The Garden," and published in *British and American Gardens in the Eighteenth Century: A Collection of Essays*, ed. Peter Martin, a special issue on garden history of *Eighteenth-Century Life*, 8 (2) (1984); reissued by the Colonial Williamsburg Foundation (Williamsburg, Va., 1984). Woodbridge feels that Pope's garden with its grotto may have evoked a "visionary scene" but that it cannot be seen as a paradigm of the picturesque garden since there is no extant picture of it to illustrate the point. In his lecture he argued that if "picturesque means anything as a style, it is the direct appeal by purely visual means," but that historically this style (for example, William Kent's designs) has embraced both the "natural" (that is, "irregular") and "rational" (that is, geometrical and "classical"). It is misleading, he writes, to associate the former exclusively with the picturesque. Pope's garden, while it contained elements of the "irregular," also displayed (according to Searle's plan) the geometric and other "rational" factors implied by association.

15. Spence 1, 605.

16. Spence 1, pp. 252–55.

17. See *The Guardian*, no. 173, Tuesday, 29 September (1st ed.; London, 1714), 2:336–40. My citations from this essay are taken from this edition.

18. Mack has presented the literary background to Pope's gardening in *Garden and the City*, pp. 21–25, 37–40, 51–57; he also discusses the image of the garden in the literature of retirement, upon which Pope drew for both his gardening and poetry (pp. 82–107). John Dixon Hunt has more recently argued the Italianate, classical and modern, coloration of Pope's Twickenham garden and grotto in his essay, "Pope's Twickenham Revisited," *British and American Gardens in the Eighteenth Century*.

19. Riskins may well have been the first landscape garden Pope got to know well. For circumstantial evidence that he may have known Riskins by 1713, see ch. 3.

20. Temple's essay was published in *Five Miscellaneous Essays by Sir William Temple*, ed. Samuel Holt Monk (Ann Arbor, 1963), pp. 1–36. Temple prefaced this remark with the phrase "for aught I know," implying that he was writing too early in the history of the new gardening to be sure about the "rules" of the "best" garden design. Pope does not reflect Temple's tentativeness here. Horace Walpole in his "History of the Modern Taste in Gardening" also examined the importance of Homer's description; see Chase, pp. 4–6.

21. He also cites Virgil's description in the *Aeneid* of the old Corycian's garden.

22. In *The Seventh Epistle of the First Book of Horace* (1738), lines 77–78, Pope referred to his childhood demesne: "A little House, with Trees a-row/And like its Master, very low."

23. Although both Addison and Temple praise Chinese gardening, Pope mentions it only once (as far as I know), in a letter to Robert Digby in 1725 (*Corr.* 2:314–15). On the Chinese element in the new gardening, see Rudolf Wittkower, *Palladio and English Palladianism* (London, 1974), pp. 184–90. See Brownell, pp. 122–23, on Pope's probable feelings about Chinese "Sharawadgi."

24. See G. R. Hibbard, "The Country House Poem of the Seventeenth Century," *Journal of the Warburg and Courtauld Institutes*, 19 (1956):159–74. See also Mack, *Garden and the City*, pp. 91–94; reprinted in *Essential Articles for the Study of Alexander Pope*, ed. Maynard Mack (Hamden, Conn., 1968).

25. Spence 1, 1115. Mack, *Garden and the City*, pp. 85–86, briefly touches on Temple's gardening influence upon Pope.

26. Brownell, pp. 40–50, 78–85, discusses Pope's appreciation of and response to pictorial landscape in Homer. See also David Clark, "Landscape Painting Effects in Pope's Homer," *Journal of Aesthetics and Art Criticism* 22 (1963):25–28; reprinted in Mack, *Essential Articles for the Study of Alexander Pope*.

27. *The Second Satire of the Second Book of Horace* (1734), line 135.

28. Spence 1, 616.

29. TE 9:242n.

30. See Malins, *English Landscaping and Literature*, pp. 21–23; Brownell, p. 105; and Elizabeth Manwaring, *Italian Landscape in Eighteenth-Century England* (New York, 1925), pp. 124–25.

31. The incidence of color words in the Alcinous passage is one in every four lines, the highest of any verses he ever wrote. He had been taking painting lessons with Charles Jervas, the portrait painter, that year, but perhaps equally influential was Addison's *Spectator* no. 412, which urged the importance of color in descriptive verse. Pope may have set out to demonstrate to Addison that he was more responsive to color than almost anyone else. *Spectator*, ed. Donald F. Bond (Oxford, 1965).

32. *Spectator* 3:549–52.

33. "The Moralists," *Characteristicks of Men, Morals, and Manners* (London, 1711), 2 (pt. 3):231.

34. For an account of the fame of Pope's garden, see Brownell, pp. 124–37. Brownell elaborates on the possibility that Spence spread the fame of Pope's garden through his use of it as a model for the portrait of Horatio's garden in his *Essay on Pope's Odyssey* (London, 1727), but see my reservations about this identification in Appendix A.

35. In the discussion that follows I am not suggesting, of course, that certain descriptive art-historical terms should never be used, but that a reliance upon them for explaining Pope's concepts of garden design is bound to prove confusing and imprecise.

36. Malins in *English Landscaping and Literature*, ch. 1, summarized the French and Dutch influence. See also Christopher Thacker, *The History of Gardens* (Berkeley and Los Angeles, 1979), chs. 9–11.

37. Thomas Whately in his *Observations on Modern Gardening* (London, 1770), p. 151, was the first to write at length about associationism in gardening, which he said "should seem to have been suggested by the scene . . . not sought for, not laboured." Hunt, *Figure in the Landscape*, ch. 2, has recently written on this subject and drawn the distinction between the emblematic and expressionistic in early eighteenth-century gardens.

38. "William Kent: Heresy in Stowe's Elysium" in *Furor Hortensis: Essays on the History of the English Landscape Garden in Memory of H. F. Clark*, ed. Peter Willis (Edinburgh, 1974), p. 55.

39. See Richard E. Quaintance, "Walpole's Whig Interpretation of Landscaping History," *Studies in Eighteenth-Century Culture*, vol. 9, ed. Roseann Runte (Madison, 1979), pp. 285–300.

40. TE 7:3, 7, 18.

41. Hunt, *Figure in the Landscape*, p. 85. See Hunt's interpretation of how *Eloisa to Abelard* illustrates Pope's notion that "what stirs the mind at any moment influences what the eye sees in the world around it" (pp. 71–73).

42. *Liberty* 5:698.

43. Brownell, pp. 195–207, speculates extensively on Pope's possible influence upon the conception of the Elysian Fields of Stowe, though nowhere does the poet hint he had anything to do with them. Still, as both George Clarke and Brownell have suggested, Pope probably contributed some ideas toward the iconographic conception of the Elysian Fields. The principal authority on Stowe's gardens is Clarke. See especially his essay "The Gardens of Stowe," *Apollo* 92 (June 1973):558–65; and "Grecian Taste and Gothic Virtue," *Apollo* 92 (June 1973):566–71. See also Brownell, pp. 195–207; Christopher Hussey, *English Gardens and Landscapes 1700–1750* (London, 1967), pp. 89–113; Laurence Whistler, *The Imagination of Vanbrugh and His Fellow Artists* (London, 1954); and Sylvia Crowe Ransom, *Garden Design* (London, 1958), pp. 55–64.

44. As quoted by Whistler, *Imagination of Vanbrugh*, pp. 182–83.

45. From the letterbook of the Marchioness de Grey, 5 July 1748, Bedfordshire County Record Office; as quoted by G. Clarke, "William Kent," p. 49.

46. Speaking to Spence in 1739 about his boyhood in the forest, Pope reminisced: "I followed everywhere as my fancy led me, and was like a boy gathering flowers in the woods and

fields just as they fall in his way. I still look upon these five or six years as the happiest part of my life" (Spence 1, 24). See also Pope's letter to the Blount sisters, *Corr.* 1:428–29.

47. Pope's letters to Martha Blount are discussed by Brownell, pp. 86–95 passim.

48. Reports of the Historical Manuscripts Commission, *Carlisle*, 6:143–44, 23 December 1734; Spence 1, 1122.

49. On this question see Kenneth Woodbridge, "William Kent as Landscape-Gardener: A Re-Appraisal," *Apollo* 100, no. 150 (n.s.) (August 1974):133–34; G. Clarke, "William Kent," pp. 49–55; and Clarke, "The Gardens of Stowe," pp. 562–63.

50. West, *Stowe, The Gardens of the Right Honourable Richard Lord Viscount Cobham. Address'd to Mr. Pope* (London, 1732), line 6. West was apparently induced to address the poem to Pope because the latter praised Stowe in *To Burlington*. Connecting the poem with Pope's name would certainly not harm its reception either. On West's poem, see the illuminating discussion by Brownell, pp. 196, 200.

51. One of the best summaries of these themes is by Brownell, pp. 201-4. See also Clarke, "Moral Gardening: The History of Stowe—X," *Stoic* 24 (July 1970):118–19; and "William Kent," p. 50.

52. On the value of ruins to a landscape garden, see Hussey, *English Gardens and Landscapes*, p. 145. Brownell has examined Pope's taste for open and hilly landscape, pp. 85–98; see also his treatment of Pope's description of Sherborne, pp. 113–17.

53. Horace Walpole, "History of Modern Taste in Gardening," p. 29, on the basis of visual observation, asserted that Pope exerted his influence upon Kent's designs for the "opening and retiring of Venus's Vale"—or rather that Kent took his management of the grove work there from Pope's garden itself. Kenneth Woodbridge has written the definitive history of Rousham's early eighteenth-century gardens in "William Kent's Gardening: The Rousham Letters," *Apollo* 100 (October 1974):282–91. See also Malins, *English Landscaping and Literature*, pp. 30–31; Brownell, pp. 178–81; and Christopher Hussey, "A Georgian Arcady—I, William Kent's Gardens at Rousham, Oxfordshire," *Country Life* 99 (14 June 1946):1084–85.

54. Brownell, p. 182, enumerates the features Rousham and Sherborne are supposed to have in common, but I fail to see as much resemblance, except that both gardens feature a slope; even there, though, Sherborne's is much steeper and has a more dramatic and gloomy feeling about it.

2. Chiswick and Twickenham: The Beginnings along the Thames

1. Mack, *Garden and the City*, p. 17 and n.

2. For accounts of Twickenham and the surrounding Thames area in the first half of the eighteenth century, see John Cornforth, "When the Thames was England's Brenta," *Country Life Annual* (1963), pp. 73–75; Christopher Hussey, "Twickenham—I," *Country Life* 96 (8 September 1944):420; Nicholas Lawrence, ed., *Six Views of Twickenham in the Eighteenth-Century* (Richmond, n.d.); Madame Van Muyden, trans. and ed., *A Foreign View of England in the Reigns of George I and George II: The Letters of Monsieur César de Saussure to his Family* (London, 1902), pp. 143–44; Hugh Phillips, *The Thames About 1750* (London, 1902), pp. 176–95; Henrietta Pye, *Short Account of the Principal Seats and Gardens in and about Richmond and Kew* (London, 1760); John

Walker, "The Thames through Eighteenth-Century Eyes: Augustine Heckell and his Imitators," *Country Life* 146 (3 July 1969):24–27.

3. Defoe, *A Tour thro' the Whole Island of Great Britain* (London, 1724), 1:168. Defoe's *Tour* was published in stages, with volume 2 appearing in 1725 and volume 3 in 1727. A three-volume edition appeared in 1738, added to perhaps by Samuel Richardson; a third edition, which appeared in 1742, is cited later for descriptions of Chiswick and Bevis Mount.

4. *A Journey through England in Familiar Letters from a Gentleman Here to His Friend Abroad* (1722), 1:37. Hereafter cited as Macky. By way of a preface, Macky observed how surprising it was that while "there have been many printed Voyages to Italy, so many Tours of France . . . there should never yet have any Thing of this Kind been undertaken here; since Great-Britain affords a much larger Mixture of Curiosities in the Seats, Parks, and Gardens" (1:ii). However, see John Dixon Hunt and Peter Willis, *The Genius of the Place* (London, 1975), p. 44, n. 23.

5. His description of Petersham Lodge, an unexpectedly early appreciation of a garden "wildly dispos'd," appears in his letter book describing his travels in England in 1712–13 (Civic Record Office, Southampton, D/M/1/3). It was first published by A. J. Sambrook, "Pope's Neighbours: An Early Landscape Garden at Richmond," *Journal of the Warburg and Courtauld Institutes* 30 (1967):444–46.

6. See Manwaring, *Italian Landscape in Eighteenth-Century England*, pp. 121–66. Mack, *Garden and the City*, plate 7 and p. 282, also reproduced and noted the Joli painting.

7. Macky 1:37. Mack, *Garden and the City*, pp. 13–21, discusses this reputation of Twickenham as an Anglo-classic paradise and explains it in terms of the currency in eighteenth-century England of Virgil's second *Georgic*.

8. Rudolf Wittkower, *Palladio and English Palladianism*, ch. 12.

9. For accounts of Burlington's role in the Palladian revival, see Wittkower, *Palladio and English Palladianism*, ch. 8. See also John Summerson, *Architecture in Britain, 1530–1830* (London, 1954), ch. 20; and Brownell, ch. 11.

10. For an excellent study of the Italian Renaissance garden, see Georgina Masson, *Italian Gardens* (London, 1961), chs. 4–5.

11. Sherburn decided on this date and it is accepted here (*Corr.* 1:338–39).

12. For a review of this first stage of these alterations, see Brownell, pp. 151–53; James Lees-Milne, *Earls of Creation* (London, 1962), pp. 140–48; Jacques Carré, "Lord Burlington's Garden at Chiswick," *Garden History* 1 (3) (Summer 1973):23–30; H. F. Clark, "Lord Burlington's Bijou, or Sharawaggi at Chiswick," *Architectural Review* 95 (May 1944):125–29; and Woodbridge, "William Kent as Landscape-Gardener," pp. 130–31. For a discussion of the significance of the Chiswick gardens in Burlington's artistic world, see Hunt, *Figure in the Landscape*, pp. 93–98. Jacques Carré has recently published and discussed the eight Jacques Rigaud views of the Chiswick gardens commissioned by Lord Burlington, in *Journal of Garden History* 2 (2) (April–June 1982).

13. *John Gay: Poetry and Prose*, ed. Vinton A. Dearing with the assistance of Charles E. Beckwith (Oxford, 1974), 2:203 (lines 1–5). Dearing notes that the date usually assigned to Gay's journey, and therefore to the poem, is a year too early; as Pope's correspondence shows (*Corr.* 1:347, 349), Gay took a journey to Devonshire in July 1716 (Gay, *Poetry and Prose* 2:581).

14. On Kent's career, see Margaret Jourdain, *The Work of William Kent* (London, 1948).

15. Woodbridge, "William Kent as Landscape-Gardener," pp. 126–29. Woodbridge provides a good deal of evidence of Kent's knowledge of specific Italian gardens, and he suggests how they must have impressed themselves on his imagination.

16. Woodbridge, "William Kent as Landscape Gardener," pp. 127–28.

17. Spence 1, 619. Brownell, pp. 152–53, considers especially Pope's and Lord Petre's roles, according to Spence 1, 1123, in laying out a flower garden perhaps next to the Bagnio or Casino at Chiswick.

18. See Ronald Paulson, "The Pictorial Circuit and Related Structures in Eighteenth-Century England," in *The Varied Pattern*, ed. Peter Hughes and David Williams (Toronto, 1971), pp. 165–70.

19. Chase, pp. 28–29. For an account of Pope's and Kent's relationship, see William K. Wimsatt, *The Portraits of Alexander Pope* (New Haven, 1965) pp. 107–36.

20. The seminal study of the origins of Pope's pictorialism in his Homer is Jean Hagstrum, *The Sister Arts: The Tradition of Literary Pictorialism and English Poetry from Dryden to Gray* (Chicago, 1958), pp. 210–22, 229–33. See also David Clark, "The Landscape Painting Effects in Pope's Homer," *Journal of Aesthetics and Art Criticism* 22 (1963):25–28, reprinted in *Essential Articles for the Study of Alexander Pope*, ed. Maynard Mack (Hamden, Conn., 1968); and Brownell, pp. 40–50.

21. TE 7:9.

22. Jervas had a fine collection of Italian masters in his London home, Bridgewater House in Cleveland Court, where Pope was a frequent guest.

23. Carré, "Lord Burlington's Garden at Chiswick," p. 27.

24. Colin Campbell mentions the Bagnio as the first of Burlington's classical buildings at Chiswick; see his *Vitruvius Britannicus* (London, 1725), 3:8.

25. Graham and Collier to Burlington, Chatsworth MSS 154.1.

26. Macky, 1:61.

27. Defoe's *Tour* (1742), 3:287–90, describes Chiswick; the description is also cited in Hunt and Willis, *Genius of the Place*, pp. 170–71.

28. Carré, "Lord Burlington's Garden at Chiswick," pp. 23–24, proposes that Bridgeman, who very likely worked at Chiswick, did so as the executant of Burlington's designs for the layout of Chiswick. He points out that when Kent modified the landscape in the 1730s he did not eliminate the hedges and straight allées as he did those that Bridgeman designed elsewhere, as at Stowe; this might have been in deference to the fact that they were his patron's ideas, not Bridgeman's. Carré also cites Macky's contention, in 1724, that "the whole contrivance of 'em [the Chiswick gardens] is the Effect of his Lordship's own genius, and singular fine Taste" (Macky 1:86).

29. See Spence 1, 610, 611.

30. Chase, p. 28.

31. Defoe, *Tour* (1742) 3:101, 289–90.

32. Wittkower, *Palladio and English Palladianism*, pp. 120–21, gives evidence of manuscripts and drawings at Chatsworth in stating that the house was begun no later than 1725 and was probably standing in 1727, with interior work left to be done. Burlington, he said, was entirely responsible for building it. The Grand Allée at Chiswick, incidentally, was not centered on the main axis of either the old or the new house, though the wide grass walk leading eventually to the

Exedra was aligned with the Palladian addition. In this way Burlington avoided the dominating or autocratic central perspective that existed in a house-landscape relationship designed, let us say, by Sir John Vanbrugh, where the house lorded it over the landscape in an affirmation of human power or pride.

33. A young protégé of Burlington, Castell dedicated this work to him. The work is based on the Younger Pliny's letters concerning his two villas at Tusculum and Laurentum. It was very influential when it appeared; not only did it demonstrate the advanced state of classical authority in architecture and landscaping by 1728 and suggest that the ancient Roman villa gardens closely imitated nature (see Masson, *Italian Gardens*, p. 125), but in the "Preface" it also classified Roman villas, and by application contemporary English villas, into three main types: (1) the *villa urbana* or country residence quickly accessible from the city and, as in the case of Chiswick House, in need of being "supplied with most of the Necessaries of Life from a neighbouring Market-Town" except for some home-grown vegetables and fruit; (2) the *villa rustica* into whose landscape design, as at Riskins, Dawley Farm, and possibly Marble Hill, "a proper Distribution of all Things in and about the Villa" was observed, "particularly with relation to the Farm-House, which in this Sort of Buildings, according to the more ancient Roman Manner, was always join'd to the Master's House, or but very little remov'd from it"; and (3) the entirely self-sufficient villa, which might even export produce. See Hunt, *Figure in the Landscape*, pp. 98–100.

34. Lees-Milne, *Earls of Creation*, pp. 144–45.

35. TE 3 (2):180–81. The manuscript of Pope's piece at Chatsworth is in the handwriting of Lady Burlington who seems to have acted as his amanuensis on occasion in the early 1730s.

36. Defoe's *Tour* (1742) 3:290 described the new cascade as follows: "At the End of the River, next the [Chertsey] Road, is a fine Cascade lately erected [1738], which by an Engine to raise the Water, his Lordship proposed to have a constant Fall into the River; but the Engine failing, it is but seldom the Cascade can play, and then but for a short time."

37. See Woodbridge, "William Kent as Landscape-Gardener," pp. 130–31. Kent also designed an Exedra with which he intended to replace a grove of trees facing the garden front of the new house. It was perhaps too natural for Burlington, who rejected it and chose a more formal version, with hedges; Kent later used his sketch for the Temple of British Worthies at Stowe. See Hunt, *Figure in the Landscape*, pp. 96–97.

38. Spence 1, 1060, 1064.

39. See Wimsatt, *Portraits*, p. 111.

40. Wimsatt, *Portraits*, pp. 111–14. See especially Kent's letter to Burlington, 28 November 1738 (Corr. 4:150).

41. If the trees were planted at roughly the same time the Casino was built, then twenty or twenty-one years later would be 1737–38—a likely date for the petition.

42. *Corr*. 4:323–24. David Nokes, "Pope's Epigrams on William Kent: A New Manuscript," *Yearbook of English Studies* 5 (1975):109–14, has found a manuscript in the British Library that on one folio has two epigrams very probably written by Pope in September 1738 at the expense of Kent's architectural and landscaping schemes. One of them reads: "When Kent was employ'd for the speaker to plan/He struck out Walk Hedgerow & Border/His Honour who thought the Devil in the Man/Cried out to his Trees pray to Order." Burlington would be the "speaker."

43. Kent mentioned in 1738 having designed "New Works" in Pope's garden; see H. A. Tipping, ed. "Four Unpublished Letters of William Kent," *Architectural Review* 63 (1928):180, 182. According to Brownell, p. 174n, these may have been urns Kent designed for the garden (see *Corr.* 4:413).

44. Howard Erskine-Hill has given a good account of the Caryll family, and Pope's relationship to it, in *The Social Milieu of Alexander Pope: Lives, Example and the Poetic Response* (New Haven, 1975). Hereafter cited as Erskine-Hill.

45. Erskine-Hill, p. 58.

46. See Hibbard, "The Country House Poem of the Seventeenth Century," pp. 159–74.

47. See Erskine-Hill, pp. 69–71, 87–92, for an explanation of Pope's neglect of Caryll. Pope's letters mention only one certain visit after an intended visit in 1717 (*Corr.* 1:442), and that was in 1733 on his way to Bevis Mount, induced chiefly by his mother's death (*Corr.* 3:387).

48. See, for example, *Corr.* 1:157, 161, 168, 219, and 289.

49. See Erskine-Hill, ch. 2.

50. Add. Mss 28227–28235.

51. See Add. MSS 28229, f. 413; 28230, ff. 284–89, 334–422, passim; 28231, ff. 180–268, passim; 28232, ff. 121–312, passim; and 28235, ff. 412–13.

52. From letters exchanged between the second Duke of Richmond, of Goodwood House near Chichester, and Sir Matthew Fetherstonhaugh, of nearby Uppark, concerning the purchase of Ladyholt in 1760 (Uppark Archives, West Sussex Record office), one gets the impression that the major beauty of the landscape, apart from its high position, was its trees. Richmond assured Fetherstonhaugh at one point in the negotiations that "the beauty of Lady-holt consisted in the Timber which he [Caryll, the grandson of Pope's friend] had not the least intention to destroy." Clearly, Caryll had done a good deal of planting earlier in the century.

53. The emblematic nature of Pope's retirement at Twickenham is analyzed in Mack, *Garden and the City*, chs. 1–3; and Brownell, ch. 5.

54. This description appeared in the January 1748 issue of the *Newcastle General Magazine, or Monthly Intelligencer* 1:25–28; it has been published recently in Mack, *Garden and the City*, Appendix A (see p. 238).

55. See "The Muse of Satire," *Yale Review* 41 (1951):80–92; reprinted in Mack, *Essential Articles for the Study of Alexander Pope*. See also Mack, *Garden and the City*, pp. 232–36.

56. On the dimensions and size of Pope's garden, see A. J. Sambrook, "The Shape and Size of Pope's Garden," *Eighteenth-Century Studies* 5 (3) (Spring 1972):450–55. In addition to studies by Brownell, Mack, and Sambrook already cited, the following studies on Pope's garden may also be consulted: Sambrook, "Pope and the Visual Arts," in *Writers and Their Background: Alexander Pope*, ed. Peter Dixon (London, 1972), pp. 143–71; J. Burke, *English Art 1714–1800*, Oxford History of English Art, vol. 9 (Oxford, 1976); Hunt, *Figure in the Landscape*, pp. 75–85; Hussey, *English Gardens and Landscapes*, ch. 5; George Sherburn, *Early Career* (Oxford, 1934), ch. 10; and R. Paulson, "The Pictorial Circuit," pp. 165–70.

57. *The Letters of John Gay*, ed. C. F. Burgess (Oxford, 1966), p. 43.

58. Mack, *Garden and the City*, p. 16n, notes that in a memoir of himself Gibbs refers to his additions to "Alexander Pope's villa." See also Brownell, p. 279; Bryan Little, *The Life and Work of*

James Gibbs (London, 1955), p. 85; and Howard M. Colvin, *A Biographical Dictionary of British Architects, 1660–1840* (London, 1954), p. 235.

59. On Pope's interest in architecture, see Brownell, pt. 3.

60. For a sensitive interpretation of Pope's Anglo-classic building as reflecting his notions of proportion and harmony, and the unity of the cosmos, see Mack, *Garden and the City*, pp. 32–36.

61. Add. MS 4809, f. 86v and 84v respectively. Sambrook published the sketches in "Pope and the Visual Arts." There are several other sketches by Pope of gardening and architectural ideas in the Homer MSS; see Appendix C.

62. Mack, *Garden and the City*, pp. 238–39.

63. See Mack, *Garden and the City*, p. 238. See also Brownell, pp. 372–80, and Brownell, *Alexander Pope's Villa: Views of Pope's Villa, Grotto and Garden: A Microcosm of English Landscape*, catalogue of the exhibition at Marble hill, Summer 1980 (Greater London Council, 1980).

64. Spence 1, 613, 620.

65. See Mack, *Garden and the City*, Appendix B. Mack sensitively and perceptively discusses the iconography of Pope's riverside monument, pp. 37–40.

66. *Mr. Pope's Literary Correspondence* (London, 1735), 2:79 (last series in pagination). Cited by Sherburn, *Corr.* 2:263n, and in Mack, *Garden and the City*, p. 308.

67. In spite of Searle's presence, Bathurst said that his man Burton would come with the trees "to see them transplanted with care" (*Corr.* 2:263).

68. See Searle, *A Plan of Mr. Pope's Garden* (London, 1745), plate 19 (B). The features of the garden are numbered and lettered on this *Plan*: hereafter they are cited in the text. In the discussion that follows regarding the size of Pope's trees, the reader may wish to refer to Mack's comments in his notes on illustrations of Pope's house, *Garden and the City*, pp. 283–84. See also Brownell's remarks on the trees in *Alexander Pope's Villa*, passim.

69. Chase, p. 24. The chiaroscuro effect achieved through the planting was a unifying element. On the aesthetic principle of unification, see Carole Fabricant, "Binding and Dressing Nature's Loose Tresses: The Ideology of Augustan Landscape Design," *Studies in Eighteenth-Century Culture*, ed. Roseann Runte, 8 (1979):112–16.

70. This fact was discovered by Sambrook, "Shape and Size of Pope's Garden," who noticed inconsistencies in some of the angles shown by Searle. Until his discovery it was always thought that the house and garden were lined up at right angles to each other.

71. Pope was struck by the beauty of a flood in the first year of his residence: "I found our House exactly like Noah's Ark in every thing.... The Prospect is prodigiously fine: It is just like an Arm of the Sea, and the Flood over my Grassplot, embraced between the two Walls, whose tops are only seen, looks like an open Bay to the Terras. The opposite meadow where you so often walked, is coverd with Sails" (to Teresa Blount, *Corr.* 2:59).

72. Andrews, "A New Description of Pope's Garden," p. 35. The manuscript is in the British Library, Add. MS 22,926 (pp. 92–94).

73. Spence 1, 602, was unsure when the mount was made, but he was certain that Kent designed it "in the natural taste, but in the execution all the rise was as stiff and bad as the point of view at the top of it was good and well chosen." He also noted that the plan of the mount by

Kent was at Oatlands, Lord Lincoln's seat; it is now lost. It is unlikely that Kent designed the mount in the early 1720s; there is no record of his landscaping for Pope or anyone else (except possibly Burlington) that early. On the other hand, we know he was doing something in Pope's garden in 1738, at which time he might have been altering the mount. For other citations on the mount, including Elizabeth Carter's brief comment on the views from the top of it (cited from G. Hampshire, "Johnson, Elizabeth Carter, and Pope's Garden," *Notes & Queries*, n.s., 19 [June 1972]:221), see Brownell, p. 130.

74. Edward Blount on several occasions received some of Pope's most complete descriptions of his gardening and embellishments of the grotto. In the above letter, for example, we have one of the earliest instances (1721) of Pope's romantic taste for a medley of landscape effects combined with a sense of a house's age and traditions. He is writing about Rentcomb, not far from Cirencester, the seat of Blount's brother-in-law, Sir John Guise, where he is staying: "I look'd upon the Mansion, Walls, and Terraces; the Plantations, and Slopes, which Nature has made to command a variety of Vallies and rising Woods; with a Veneration mixt with a Pleasure" (*Corr.* 2:86).

75. Oxford was laying it out in the spring of 1726.

76. The scholarship on Pope's grotto has been extensive. In addition to Mack's chapter in *Garden and the City*, pp. 41–76, there is a bibliography of such studies in his book, p. 41n. More recently, see Brownell, pp. 254–71, for an analysis of the grotto as an example of Pope's garden architecture; Hunt, *Figure in the Landscape*, pp. 81–85, on the grotto as part of the garden; and Hunt, "Twickenham Revisited," in *British and American Gardens in the Eighteenth Century*.

77. On the whole question of how the grotto served as both a mirror and a lamp of Pope's imagination, see Mack, *Garden and the City*, ch. 2. Brownell, p. 257, considers how these lines on the grotto amount to a description of the garden, too.

78. For the complete text of the original poem, see TE 6:225–26.

79. Mack, "Introduction to Homer," TE 7:ccxxiv, observes that Kent's sketch of Calypso's grotto for the headpiece of *Odyssey* 5 resembles the interior of Pope's grotto as shown by Searle in his "Perspective View," published in his *Plan*.

80. *Verses on a Grotto by the River Thames at Twickenham, composed of Marbles, Spars, and Minerals* (1741), lines 3–6, TE 6:382. This poem was published, along with five others on the grotto and garden, in Searle's *Plan*. For some background on the composition of these verses, see Morris Brownell, "Walter Harte, Nicholas Hardinge, and Pope's 'Verses on the Grotto,'"*Notes & Queries*, n.s., 24 (May–June 1977):245–47.

81. Writing to Aaron Hill in April 1731, Pope claimed that when he arrived for a visit Hill would "see a Place seeming more fit for me than it is; looking Poetical" (*Corr.* 3:188).

82. A brief background to the camera obscura is given by Marjorie Nicolson and G. S. Rousseau, *'This Long Disease, My Life': Alexander Pope and the Sciences* (Princeton, 1968), pp. 282–85; see also Brownell, p. 258; and, on other visual effects in the grotto, Mack, *Garden and the City*, pp. 44–47.

83. Hunt, *Figure in the Landscape*, pp. 81–85, discusses the variety of the grotto's "essentially private iconography" and the psychological "excitement" that Pope elicited from it. Hunt

sees in the variety of the grotto an eloquent summation of the psychological provisions of the entire garden.

84. Andrews, "A New Description of Pope's Garden," p. 33, briefly discusses the 1742 description of the Shell Temple; see also Brownell, pp. 251–54.

85. Spence 1, 619.

86. The Newcastle writer does not mention the theater either, making it likely that it had disappeared before Pope's death; neither does the 1742 visitor mention it.

87. Commentators have thought that Pope pulled these workmen away from Carlton House in Richmond, but I agree with Peter Willis, *Charles Bridgeman and the English Landscape Garden*, Studies in Architecture, vol. 17 (London, 1977), ch. 3, that he probably took them from Marble Hill, which was closer by and where Bridgeman was currently employed. On Pope's relationship with Bridgeman, see also Brownell's useful summary, pp. 163–70.

88. Masson, *Italian Gardens*, p. 88. Another beautiful surviving example of a green theater is the one at Villa Rizzardi in Veneto; it is one of the largest and finest of its kind in Italy. Probably the earliest example of a garden theater in Italy was the one Donato Bramante designed for Villa Belvedere at the Vatican in the early sixteenth century (Masson, pp. 124–25). It was more in the style of an amphitheater modeled after the ancient Roman theater. On the theater in the English landscape garden, see Hunt and Willis, *Genius of the Place*, pp. 36–37. See also S. Lang, "The Genesis of the English Landscape Garden," in *The Picturesque Garden and Its Influence outside the British Isles*, ed. N. Pevsner, Dumbarton Oaks Colloquium on the History of Landscape Architecture (Washington, D.C., 1974), pp. 22–29.

89. The "Last Will and Testament of Alexander Pope, Esq." (printed in Mack, *Garden and the City*, Appendix D) mentions numerous pieces of statuary that were in Pope's garden, including some garden urns that were bequeathed to Martha Blount. Pope used a mason called Biggs, recommended by Ralph Allen, to carve the statuary (*Corr.* 4:181, 353, 360). From time to time Pope was consulted by friends on the choice and location of statuary for their gardens.

90. Willis, *Charles Bridgeman*, ch. 3, also chose this spot as the most likely site of the theater; his second choice, between the Shell Temple and the mount, seems unlikely because that area was already cramped for space.

91. TE 3 (2):183. Willis, *Charles Bridgeman*, ch. 3, discusses Pope's relationship with Bridgeman, as does Brownell, pp. 167–69, who argues that Pope may have been frustrated chiefly by the spectacle of Bridgeman, the deferential professional, being unwilling to be praised in a poem that attacks the tastes of his "Great" clients.

92. Walpole actually called these trees the quincunx, not the groves, and Pope in his *Epistle to Fortescue*, line 130, wrote that Lord Peterborough "Now, forms my Quincunx, and now ranks my Vines." But if the garden had a quincunx, evenly spaced rows of trees making up a succession of squares with a fifth tree in the middle, why did not Searle show it in his *Plan*? Spence, in fact, himself queried whether Pope in his letter to Jervas mentioning the "solitary Groves" meant "his two quincunx groves?" (1, 602). It seems unlikely that Searle, who knew the garden on a day-to-day basis, would have forgotten the quincunxes. The solution to this puzzle lies in the current usage of the word "quincunx" as defined by A. J. Dézallier d'Argenville in his

Theory and Practice of Gardening (1709), trans. John James (London, 1712); the newer meaning of the word applies to what Pope had in his garden. See my note elaborating this, "Quincunx or Groves in Pope's Garden?", *Notes & Queries*, n.s., 24 (3) (June 1977):243–45.

93. See below, ch. 6; and Edward Malins and the Knight of Glin, *The Lost Demesnes: Irish Landscape Gardening 1660–1845* (London, 1976), ch. 2.

94. See R. W. King's four-part account of Spence's gardening, "Joseph Spence of Byfleet."

95. See Brownell, pp. 124–35. For my argument against this suggestion, see Appendix A.

96. Spence 1, 610.

97. Cf. the description of Calypso's bower in lines 80–94. Pope said of the scene, "It is impossible for a Painter to draw a more admirable rural Landskip" (TE 9:176, line 80n).

98. Chase, p. 29.

99. See W. K. Wimsatt and John Riely, "A Supplement to *The Portraits of Alexander Pope*," *Evidence in Literary Scholarship: Essays in Memory of James Marshall Osborn*, ed. René Wellek and Alvaro Ribeiro (Oxford, 1979), pp. 123–64; and Mack, *Garden and the City*, p. 29.

100. As has already been noted, in a letter to Burlington on 12 September 1738, Kent refers to "new works" in Pope's garden that "I design'd there"; see H. A. Tipping, "Unpublished Letters," pp. 180–83. What these new improvements were is not known; they could have been alterations to the mount, which Spence said Kent designed. See Spence 1, 603, 1060, 1062.

101. See Spence 1, 279; *Corr.* 4:153, 365.

3. The Great Patriarch: Lord Bathurst and His Parks

1. *Lives of the English Poets by Samuel Johnson*, ed. G. B. Hill (Oxford, 1905), 2:36.

2. *Boswell's Life of Johnson*, ed. G. B. Hill, rev. and enlarged by L. F. Powell (Oxford, 1934), 3:347.

3. For details of Bathurst's family background and early years, see Lees-Milne, *Earls of Creation*, ch. 1.

4. Sir Benjamin had purchased the Oakley property in Gloucestershire, just west of the town of Cirencester, in 1695 from Frances Poole, Countess of Newburgh, so that from the age of eleven Allen Bathurst lived in the old Jacobean house, known as Oakley Grove. It finally became his at the age of twenty. For centuries these woods had been a portion of unregistered (unowned) woodland in that area, later belonging to the Abbey at St. Mary. See Welbourne St. Clair Baddeley, *A History of Cirencester* (Cirencester, 1924), p. 264. Simultaneously, upon his father's death, he inherited Riskins, which his father had acquired through marriage to Frances Apsley, granddaughter of Sir Peter Apsley, who had originally purchased the estate for the Apsley family. See George Lipscomb, *The History and Antiquities of the County of Buckingham* (London, 1847), p. 517.

5. In 1683 Queen Anne had bestowed upon Bathurst the post of treasurer of her household, while Bathurst's mother, Frances, had been on very friendly terms with Princesses Mary and Anne. When she became Queen, Anne remained close to the couple, and on 28 August 1709 she stayed overnight with them at Oakley Grove on her way to Bath (St. Clair Baddeley, *A History of Cirencester*, pp. 265–66).

6. He was named as a commissioner of the Treasury in 1714 (see Swift, *Corr.* 2:78–79).

7. Prior, who was a member of the earlier but not the later club, nicknamed Bathurst "Batty." The beginning of Prior's friendship with Pope is difficult to date, however; it is likely that it developed later than the others, making it doubtful that Prior introduced Pope to Bathurst. I am indebted to Professor H. Bunker Wright for advice on Prior's earliest contacts with Pope.

8. Goldsmith, *The Life of Thomas Parnell, D.D.* (London, 1770), pp. 35–37.

9. See Charles Kerby-Miller, ed. *Memoirs of the Extraordinary Life, Works, and Discoveries of Martin Scriblerus* (New Haven, 1950), pp. 36–48.

10. *Mr Popes Welcome from Greece a copy of Verses wrote by Mr Gay upon Mr Popes having finisht his Translation of Homers Ilias,"* lines 87–88 (Gay, *Poetry and Prose* 1:257).

11. See Pope to Digby, 20 July 1720, May 1722, and 12 August (ca. 1725) (*Corr.* 2:50, 115–16, 314–15).

12. See also Digby to Pope, 2 July 1725 (*Corr.* 2:305).

13. Pope also playfully described Digby's cousin, Viscountess Scudamore, as a rustic (*Corr.* 1:473). Her gardens, for which Bathurst considered some improvements in the 1720s, was at Holm Lacy in Herefordshire. Preserved among the manuscripts at Badminton House, Gloucestershire, is an elegy written upon Lady Scudamore's untimely death from smallpox in 1729. It celebrates her rustic life at Holm Lacy and, in the process, mentions some details of her gardens.

14. See his letters to Caryll (June 1718) and Burlington (2 February 1719) (*Corr.* 1:475; 2:2–3).

15. *Epistles* 1.15.45–46 (*Corr.* 1:488–89). Translated: "only men like you are wise and live well—whose invested wealth is displayed in garish villas" (*Horace: Satires, Epistles and Ars Poetica*, trans. H. Rushton Fairclough, Loeb Classical Library [London, 1926], p. 347).

16. Thomson dedicated "Spring" to her as a young woman, and to her also Shenstone dedicated *Rural Elegance*. Shenstone's intimacy with her did not begin until after her move to Riskins, which appears in his poem as the "rural calm retreat" where nature was by "Seymour's winning influence charmed." See Helen Sard Hughes, "Shenstone and the Countess of Hertford," *PMLA* 46 (1931):1113–27.

17. Reprinted from the Alnwick Castle manuscripts, *Percy Family Letters and Papers*, vol. 28 (1743), in Helen Sard Hughes, *The Gentle Hertford: Her Life and Letters* (New York, 1940).

18. *Correspondence between Frances, Countess of Hertford (afterwards Duchess of Somerset) and Henrietta Louisa, Countess of Pomfret, between the years 1738 and 1741*, ed. William Bingley, 2nd ed. (London, 1806), 3 vols. Hereafter cited as *Hertford-Pomfret Corr.*

19. William Brogden has recently written that Switzer very likely drew the "Epitomy" for *The Practical Kitchen Gardener* (1727), in which he also described Riskins, but that it was left out of that publication for some unknown reason, perhaps financial. He bases this suggestion on some phrasing in the Appendix to his 1742 edition of *Ichnographia Rustica*. See Brogden, "The Ferme Ornée and Changing Attitudes to Agricultural Improvement," in *British and American Gardens in the Eighteenth Century*.

20. It included, among other additions, the "Epitomy" of Riskins and an appendix (possibly written before 1730 since it refers to the layout of Dawley, begun in 1726, as "now a doing") entitled "A Further Account of Rural and Extensive Gardening." On further details

regarding the dating of the appendix, see Brownell, p. 223n. This appendix reflects the influence of the landscaping done in the *ferme ornée* style by Bathurst, Bolingbroke, and (less clearly) Cobham at Riskins, Dawley, and Stowe respectively in the years just preceding. Switzer called these three men "improvers."

The only lengthy study on Switzer is by William Brogden, "Stephen Switzer and Garden Design in Britain in the Early Eighteenth Century" (Ph.D. thesis, University of Edinburgh, 1973). See also Brogden's essay, "Stephen Switzer: 'La Gran Manier,'" in *Furor Hortensis*, pp. 21–30.

21. Switzer may first have met Bathurst when he sold him seeds for the "Promiscuous Quarters" of his estate (*Ichnographia Rustica*, 1742, vol. 3, Appendix). According to Brogden, Switzer began his independent career in 1710 at Grimsthorpe, Lincolnshire, the country seat of Robert Bertie, Marquess of Lindsey; a form of the Grimsthorpe design was used by Switzer in the 1718 edition of *Ichnographia Rustica* as the Manor of Paston, of which Switzer included a plate, with an attached commentary. See Brogden, "Switzer: 'La Gran Manier,'" pp. 25–28. Brownell, pp. 229–32, discusses Riskins and Switzer's probable role there.

22. Even before Addison's essay, Riskins could have existed essentially as it did when Switzer praised Bathurst in 1718. In any case, Sir William Blathwayt's Dyrham Park, Gloucestershire, which Switzer describes at length in *Ichnographia Rustica* (1718) as a "beautiful rural Garden," clearly was a matured garden and not his work.

23. *Ichnographia* (1718 and 1742), vol. 3.

24. Brogden, "Switzer: 'La Gran Manier,'", p. 28. Switzer said of Louis XIV's motives in directing Le Nôtre's designs at Versailles and elsewhere: "He might allure and dazle the Eyes of *Europe*, and thereby easier carry on Scheme of Universal Monarchy he had all along been aiming at, [but this] is not my Business, neither do I pretend to determine" (*Ichnographia* [1718] 1:40). James Turner has challenged Brogden's contention regarding Switzer's garden politics, arguing it is a "fallacy" to assume that Switzer's politics can be separated from his gardening; see his essay "Stephen Switzer and the Political Fallacy in Landscape Gardening," *Eighteenth-Century Studies* 11 (1978):489–96.

25. "A Proemial Essay," *Ichnographia* (1742) 1:11–12.

26. Pope's editor, William Warburton, noted that "this office, in the original plan of the poem, was given to another; who not having the SENSE to see a compliment was intended him, convinced the poet it did not belong to him" (TE 3 (2):144, line 74n).

27. *Ichnographia* (1718) 3:43. See William Stukeley's drawings of Grimsthorpe in Brogden, "Switzer: 'La Gran Manier,'" plates 4a–5b.

28. Pope mentions Apscourt, Surrey, once in his correspondence (*Corr.* 4:451); according to Searle's *Plan*, p. 8, Pope acquired "several Humming Birds and their Nests, from Antony Brown, Esq; of Abbscourt" as ornaments for his grotto. Pope also refers to the fields of "delightful *Abs-court*, if its Fields afford/Their Fruits to you" (*The Second Epistle of the Second Book of Horace*, lines 230–33).

29. *Ichnographia* (1742), Appendix, 3:8–9.

30. On Castell's work, see Hunt, *Figure in the Landscape*, pp. 70–76. On Switzer, see Brownell, pp. 223–24. H. F. Clark, "Eighteenth Century Elysiums," *Journal of the Warburg and Courtauld Institutes* 6 (1943):165, pointed to Castell's *Villas* to illustrate that by 1728 there was an

awareness of what irregularity in a garden could mean, and he added that the book influenced the transition to the landscape garden and helped make it palatable to his age.

31. *Hertford-Pomfret Corr.* 1:272. In a letter to her son in 1743, she referred to the place over the dining room fireplace "where Mr. Pope used to hang" (Hughes, *Gentle Hertford*, p. 247).

32. *The Lamentation of GLUMDALCLITCH, for the Loss of GRILDRIG: A Pastoral*, lines 57–59 (TE 6:273).

33. Although located in the parish of Iver, Riskins was closer to (and just north of) Colnbrooke. See W. H. Ward and K. S. Block, *A History of the Manor and Parish of Iver* (London, 1933).

34. According to Lady Hertford, the owner previous to Sir Peter Apsley, the Bathursts' grandfather, was a Mr. Britton, but she says she cannot discover who built the house. Ward and Block, *Iver*, state that a Dame Ursula in her will mentioned in detail the furnishings of the house back in 1649. William Salter purchased Riskins in 1656, and when he died in 1664 he left the "capital messuage commonly called Richkinge alias Richkine in the parish of Iver" mortgaged to one Mistress Lucy Webbe. In 1678 Sir Peter Apsley acquired the estate.

35. *Hertford-Pomfret Corr.* 1:198.

36. She overestimated its length, later putting it at 555 yards, but even this seems too long if we judge according to Switzer's scale; his "Epitomy" or plan suggests that the length was about one thousand feet.

37. *Hertford-Pomfret Corr.* 1:245–48.

38. Daines Barrington, "The Progress of Gardening," *Archaeologia* 7 (1785):36–39.

39. Hughes, *Gentle Hertford*, p. 154.

40. In a letter to her son, 10 June 1743, Lady Hertford spoke of being attacked by the resident duck, which lived on an island in the canal, as she was removing weeds from "the Gravel Walk betwixt the Basin and the Serpentine Water" (Hughes, *Gentle Hertford*, p. 264).

41. This canal still exists today. John Rocque's *Topographical Map of Middlesex* (London, 1754) shows how in the next ten years the sequence of rivulets, canals, and serpentine brooks at Riskins, then called Percy Lodge, were naturalized: they were widened somewhat and connected into one continuous waterway that flowed into the main canal (see plate 34). See also Rocque's "Specimen" in *Proposals for publication by Subscription . . . An Actual Survey of the Counties of Oxford, Buckinghamshire, and Berkshire*, on four sheets on a scale of one inch to the mile; it contains a section of the Iver area with Riskins shown as Percy Lodge. Cf. also the twenty-five-inch ordnance survey map of 1875, which shows the water system, virtually unchanged, more clearly.

42. 1 August 1742 (Hughes, *Gentle Hertford*, p. 158).

43. Digby to Pope, 2 July 1725 (*Corr.* 2:305). This letter is a reply to a joint letter from Gay and Pope at Riskins to Digby. Apparently this letter, which has been lost, described the gardens at Riskins (see Sherburn's note).

44. Digby joked that the salmon Bathurst "expected Old Thames should bring into the Kitchen, I should have expected from him who calls himself a Fisherman"; he urged Pope to bring Bathurst to Holm Lacy, where the nearby Wye would make him a real fisherman "with some huge Salmon of dimensions worthy to be recorded by his own pencil on the Kitchen-wall, & where it may remain a Trophy of his Skill in Fishery" (*Corr.* 2:305). The canal was also stocked with carp and tench.

45. In 1743 Lady Hertford wrote to her son that she had discovered in the wood yard an old boat or canoe of the finest cedar that "some of the garden-men and the carter say . . . has lain in the same place to their knowledge for fifteen years" (Hughes, *Gentle Hertford*, pp. 298–99). She remarked that Lord Bathurst, who must have used it as one of his vessels on the water, could not have known it was made of such fine cedar, or else he would not have allowed it to go to waste.

46. *Hertford-Pomfret Corr.* 2:259–61.

47. Hughes, *Gentle Hertford*, pp. 154–55.

48. Hughes, *Gentle Hertford*, p. 260.

49. She seemed to know that the site of the greenhouse was the former site of St. Leonard's Chapel (*Hertford-Pomfret Corr.* 1:271), which is shown in several later maps as north of and directly in line with the main canal.

50. To Lady Pomfret, 21 May 1740 (*Hertford-Pomfret Corr.* 1:273).

51. *Hertford-Pomfret Corr.* 1:248.

52. *Hertford-Pomfret Corr.* 1:306–8. Perhaps Lady Luxborough's example at Barrell's stimulated her. Influenced by her brother Bolingbroke's "farming" at Dawley Farm, Lady Luxborough set about landscaping her estate in the late 1730s. In the early 1740s she kept in close touch with Lady Hertford, as well as with Shenstone and his *ferme ornée* at the Leasowes. "In the house I have turned a dairy into a library," she told Lady Hertford; "I have also made a little summer-house that is stuccoed and adorned with the busts of my Brother Bolingbroke, Pope, Dryden, Milton, Shakespeare, Newton, and Locke. I keep about three score pounds a year in my hands that I may see a few cows, sheep, etc. near me. . . . But why do I tire you with such insignificant descriptions? I believe it is self-interest, hoping to hear [of] your own improvement at your bergerie" (Hughes, *Gentle Hertford*, p. 153). Lady Luxborough, incidentally, urged her friend to have some drawings or prints made of several of the views at Riskins by Thomas Smith of Derby, who had done some of Lord Lyttelton's seat, Hagley Park, and who had approached Shenstone to do the same at the Leasowes. Shenstone told Lady Luxborough about Smith in 1748, but there is no record that Smith made any prints of either Riskins of the Leasowes (Hughes, *Gentle Hertford*, pp. 165, 445 n. 92).

53. John W. Croker, ed., *Letters to and from Henrietta, Countess of Suffolk . . . 1712–1767* (London, 1824), July 1734, 2:80. Hereafter cited as Croker.

54. See *Corr.* 2:464, 524, 532; 3:157, 295–96. In a letter to Gay on 10 July 1732, Swift mentions Riskins as one of the places he will be staying if he comes to England that year: "My scheme was to pass a month at Amesbury, & then go to Twitenham & live a winter between that & Dawly, & sometimes at Riskins, without going to London" (*Corr.* 3:297). On 12 August he wrote Gay again: "I want to be Minister of Amesbury, Dawly, Twitenham, Riskins and Prebendary of Westminster, else I will not stir a step" (*Corr.* 3:303–4).

55. In a letter of early spring 1725, for example, Pope combined the image of the Patriarch with a joke over being overwhelmed by Bathurst's Turklike tyranny (*Corr.* 2:292).

56. In a letter to Swift on 30 June 1730 Bathurst saw himself as an absolute "Monarch" at Cirencester, but satirically imputed the role of "great" man and tyrant to Robert Walpole, using the same joke of transplantation as he had above with Pope in a critical vein: "here I am absolute

Monarch of a circle of above a mile round, at least 100 acres of Ground, w^{ch} (to speak in the Stile of one of the Country-men) is very populous in Cattle fish & fowl. To enjoy this power, wch I relish extreamly, & regulate this Dominion, wch I prefere to any other, has taken up my time from morning to night. There are Yahoos in the Neighbourhood, but having read in History that the southern part of Britain was long defended agst the Picts by a wall, I have fortified my territories all round; that wise People the Chinese yu know did the same thing, to defend y^{m}selves agst the Tarters. . . . now that I am in the midst of my own Dominions, I think of nothing but preserving them, & grow fearfull lest a certain great man [Walpole] shou'd take a fancy to them & transport them into Norfolk to place them as an Iland in one of his new-made fish-ponds or if y^{u} take this for too proud a thought I will only suppose it to be hung out under a great Bow-window" (Swift, *Corr.* 3:400–401). For its sheer immensity, in both house and garden but especially the former, Walpole's Houghton Hall was a recurring feature of the Opposition argot.

57. See his comments on this with respect to a recently discovered letter from Pope to John Caryll, Jr., dated 1 May 1712, in "'My Ordinary Occasions': A Letter from Pope," *The Scriblerian* 9 (1) (Fall 1976):1–7.

58. Pope continued to apply the image of the beast to his friend. He told Atterbury that whereas Bathurst was likely to turn into a "Happy Beast" grazing upon his countless acres, Pope was in danger of the more ethereal alternative of being "turn'd to converse, not with the beasts of the field, but with the birds of the grove" (*Corr.* 2:109). It is interesting that in September 1721 Pope had used the same image of birds lodging in trees to describe the lodging he and Lady Mary Wortley Montagu were likely to find on a visit to Cirencester, whereas those (like Bathurst), "with a more Earthly or gross temperature, with the Beasts of the field," may lodge on the ground (2:82–83).

59. Swift, *Corr.* 4:409.

60. Pope once told Robert Digby, "One of his Lordship's Maxims is, that a total Abstinence from Intemperance or Business, is no more *Philosophy*, than a total Consoption of the Senses is *Repose*" (*Corr.* 2:315). Bathurst frequently showed concern that Pope was wearing out his body by "letting his soul ride it too hard," and he was ready to help him with a program of exercise at Cirencester: "I positively insist upon your coming down to me that I may put you into a new regimen." He believed especially in riding throughout his extensive acres (see Swift, *Corr.* 3:455; 4:232). Bolingbroke once recalled that the "Lord of Cirencester prescribes exercise to prevent indigestion" (to Sir William Wyndham, 20 February 1736, among the Bolingbroke papers at Petworth House, West Sussex).

61. *To Burlington*, lines 130–31, TE 3 (2):150.

62. Both Bridgeman and Kent worked at Houghton, though only Bridgeman is known to have designed any landscape. He laid out the parkland and "Mr. Eyre, an imitator" is said by Horace Walpole to have laid out the gardens consisting of about forty acres (Chase, p. 25). It is the seven-hundred-acre parkland that seems to have drawn attention and specific admiration, not the approximately forty-acre garden fenced off from the parkland by a "ha-ha." Sir Thomas Robinson, who may have seen the plan of Houghton published by Isaac Ware (*Plans, Elevations, and Sections; Chimney-Pieces, and Ceilings of Houghton in Norfolk* [London, 1735] showing in detail the

design of the parkland and vaguely indicating the garden, visited Houghton in late November or early December 1731. His approving account of what he saw says comparatively little about the gardens and much about the parkland:

> The enclosure for the Park contains seven hundred acres, very finely planted, and the ground laid out to the greatest advantage. The gardens are about forty acres, which are only fenced from the Park by a *fosse*, and I think very prettily disposed. Sir Robert and Bridgeman showed me the large design for the plantations in the country, which is the present undertaking; they are to be plumps and avenues to go quite round the Park pale, and to make straight and oblique lines of a mile or two in length, as the situation of the country admits of. (Reports of the Historical Manuscripts Commission, *Carlisle* 6:85)

It is likely that Bridgeman told Pope about Eyre's designs within the pleasure gardens and thus provided Pope with some detail for his Timon portrait. Houghton may have had "ha-ha's," not walls, but the gardens had "very little full-grown timber" ("Trees cut to Statues") and "not a drop of water for ornament" (Reports of the Historical Manuscripts Commission, *Carlisle* 6:85). On Houghton Hall as a model for Timon's villa, see K. Mahaffey, "Timon's Villa: Walpole's Houghton," *Texas Studies in Literature and Language* 9 (1967):193–222; and Mack, *Garden and the City*, Appendix F. Brownell, Appendix C, has urged that Blenheim is an even more likely model than Houghton.

63. 30 June 1730, Swift, *Corr.* 3:400–401. Literally speaking, Bathurst was not well placed to talk about solid foundations: the house at Cirencester had poor foundations in masonry, though its lineage was solid enough, going back to 1600.

64. Bathurst demolished Sir Robert Atkyns's house and later used the stone for some buildings in Oakley Wood.

65. Rudder's plans do not indicate the boundaries of the parks of which Cirencester park is an amalgamation, but Hussey notes that in addition to Sapperton to the west, Home Park to the east, and Oakley Park in between, there was also a Lodge Park. The amalgamation was not complete when Bathurst died (Hussey, *English Gardens and Landscapes*, p. 82). See also St. Clair Baddeley, *History of Cirencester*, pp. 263–67.

66. Hussey, *English Gardens and Landscapes*, p. 80, cites the Duke of Beaufort's estate at Badminton, Gloucestershire, as an example of this type.

67. Bathurst did not derive an income from his afforestation. Given his expenses on the landscaping at Cirencester, his finances grew progressively more awkward until he eventually sold Riskins in 1739. He also borrowed £2,000 from Pope in 1738 (*Corr.* 4:149n).

68. 6 December, Swift, *Corr.* 5:79. Bathurst admonished Swift to farm in his garden for economic reasons (see his letter of 19 April 1731, Swift, *Corr.* 3:454).

69. TE 3 (2):133.

70. See 8 in plate 37. See Hussey, *English Gardens and Landscapes*, p. 82.

71. Later commentators have identified him as Benjamin Styles of Moor Park (see TE 3 [2]:144n).

72. TE 3 (2):146n.

73. TE 3 (2):180–82.

74. Brownell, pp. 188–95, 272–75, has written on Cirencester's gardens and garden buildings.

75. Lewis held several government posts under Lord Oxford and was an intimate of Tory wits; Bathurst regarded him as his "prose-man" because of his seriousness compared with the effervescence of the wits. He had a fondness for drinking water (see Spence 1, 213 and note). Pope said about Lewis on 13 September: "He will be tractable in time as birds are tam'd by being whirl'd about; and doubtless come not to despise the meanest shrubs or coppice-wood, (tho' naturally he seems more inclin'd to admire God in his greater works, the tall timber . . .)" (*Corr.* 2:13).

76. Gay, *Poetry and Prose* 2:601, line 87n. On these deficiencies of water and wood, see also *Corr.* 3:312.

77. TE 6:195.

78. *History of Gloucestershire*, p. 129. All features in Cirencester Park cited by numbers refer to plates 37 and 38.

79. *History of Gloucestershire*, p. 130.

80. He was wrong. As Lees-Milne pointed out, Bathurst died only fourteen years before the 2.25-mile Sapperton Tunnel was dug under his property. George III opened the tunnel in 1789, and on 22 April 1790 four barges of coal came to Cirencester by water.

81. The "baubling works" Bathurst mentions were far to the west end of Oakley Wood, near to the "Sylvan seat" that became known as Alfred's Hall (G).

82. Croker 2:81.

83. Hussey, *English Gardens and Landscapes*, p. 81. For a useful discussion of Alfred's Hall as garden architecture, see Brownell, pp. 272–75. See also Barbara Jones, *Follies and Grottoes* (London, 1953), pp. 20–22.

84. Swift, *Corr.* 4:199–200.

85. Preserved in Pope's Homer MSS, Add. MS. 4809 f. 97. James Sambrook first published this sketch plan in "Shape and Size of Pope's Garden," fig. 5b.

86. Mrs. Pendarves, later the wife of the Reverend Patrick Delany, wrote her description of Cirencester in a letter to Swift on 24 October 1733 (Swift, *Corr.* 4:199–200).

87. George Sherburn (*Corr.* 4:25n) noted that *Rusticus expectat* alludes to the joke in Horace, *Second Epistle of the First Book*, line 42.

88. The Earl of Orrery wrote to Swift on 7 July 1741: "Lord *Bathurst* is at *Cirencester*, erecting pillars and statues to queen Anne" (Swift, *Corr.* 5:206).

89. Pope was very busy in the mid-1730s designing garden architecture for friends. In 1734 he designed some for Lord Bruce at Tottenham; it wants, he told Burlington, "only a few Temples & ornaments of Building, which I am contriving, in defect of better architects (who are a Rare & uncommon Generation, not born in every Family)" (*Corr.* 3:417). Later additions to the Cirencester landscape included several in a wide clearing or glade just north of Oakley Wood: a Square House, a Round House (9), and an Ivy Lodge.

90. *History of Gloucestershire*, p. 130.

91. British Museum Loan MSS, Bathurst Papers, 57/75, fs. 65–67.

4. Sherborne Castle: A "Situation of so uncommon a kind"

1. This chapter is a revision of an article entitled "Intimations of the New Gardening: Alexander Pope's Reaction to the 'Uncommon' Landscape at Sherborne" that appeared in *Garden History* 4 (Spring 1976):57–87. For several revised (and important) details and corrections I am indebted to Kenneth Woodbridge, "Critique," *Garden History* 4 (Autumn 1976):5–8.

2. Pope's correspondence does not indicate any other visit during the year; neither does it reveal whether he did stop at Wilton House.

3. As Sherburn noted, editors have dated Pope's visit and the letters concerning it in 1722. He places the visit in 1724 (*Corr.* 2:236, 241n), a date that I accept for this discussion.

4. Morris Brownell, pp. 113–17, 316, recently added some insights to Sherborne's importance. Pope's description of the gardens was published in Hunt and Willis, *Genius of the Place*, pp. 208–11. Apart from this, see the scattered references and accounts in Malins, *English Landscaping and Literature*, pp. 41, 155; Mack, *Garden and the City*, pp. 22, 42; and Hunt, *Figure in the Landscape*, pp. 86–87.

5. See Clark, "Eighteenth-Century Elysiums," p. 167.

6. Hereafter the new castle is referred to simply as Sherborne Castle, while the old castle is designated as the ruins.

7. London, 1832. The other four were the grand, beautiful, picturesque, and rural. See Malins, *English Landscaping and Literature*, p. 155.

8. The Norman castle was ultimately destroyed by Cromwell and Fairfax in 1645.

9. *Survey of Dorsetshire* (1732), pp. 124–25. Coker wrote this passage before ca. 1635, when he died.

10. At Coleshill, the family seat in Warwickshire, in 1698–99, Lord Digby took a personal interest in planting trees, ordering them from London and planting them during the "fine season" (British Library, Egerton MSS 1540, f. 132). It would be reasonable to assume that Lord Digby also did a good deal of planting at Sherborne, and perhaps other landscaping. John Hutchins, the Dorset historian, said that Digby built Pinford Bridge across the Yeo on the Sherborne estate (*The History and Antiquities of the County of Dorset*, 3rd ed. [London, 1873], 4:287).

11. Pope wrote to the Earl of Strafford in 1725 that he would "as soon travel to contemplate your Lordships [amateur gardening] works, as the Queen of Sheba did to contemplate those of Solomon" (*Corr.* 2:309). Strafford was a member of Pope's and Swift's close circle of friends in the 1720s.

12. Sherburn notes that this letter could date from 1715, but he prefers 1717 since that is the year that appears (in another hand) on the letter.

13. Erskine-Hill, p. 156. Jervas's will is preserved among the Digby MSS in the Birmingham Reference Library (Digby "B" 173). Erskine-Hill mentions a letter from Robert Digby to Pope on 12 March 1717 in which Digby shows an interest in Leoni's *Palladio*.

14. Erskine-Hill, pp. 132–56.

15. Pope admired the magnificent monument to the memory of the Earl of Bristol in Sherborne Abbey (*Corr.* 2:239).

16. See Pope's letter to Robert's younger brother Edward, the only surviving son to Lord Digby, two days after Robert's death (*Corr.* 2:375–76).

17. TE 6:313–14, lines 1–10; see also notes in TE 6:315–16. Pope mentioned Robert and William Digby in verse again in *An Essay on Man*, Epistle 4, lines 104–6 (TE 3 [1]:138); and in his *Epilogue to the Satires*, Dialogue 2, lines 240–41 (TE 4:326). See Erskine-Hill, pp. 160–63, for a brief account of Pope's relationship to the Digby family.

18. Dorothy Stroud, *Capability Brown*, with an Introduction by Christopher Hussey, 2nd ed., rev. (London, 1975), p. 239. Cornelius Dickinson, one of Brown's working gardeners or foremen mentioned in his one surviving account book, was connected with the work at Sherborne (p. 206).

19. The reclamation of the lake in conjunction with the Somerset River Authority has been completed. In addition to enlarging the lake tenfold into reservoir capacity, this project will help restore the "Capability" Brown character of the lake and pleasure grounds.

20. Originally, I proposed the idea that Pope drew this plan on his 1724 visit, but on the basis of corrections and observations by Kenneth Woodbridge ("Critique," p. 5), I now no longer think so. Woodbridge feels it is highly improbable that Pope could have drawn such a plan on the spur of the moment. Pointing out that the plan is drawn on the same kind of paper as a 1769 plan also in the Sherborne archives, and that "the main divisions of the ground" coincide with those of the 1733 map, he maintains that sometime around 1769 the plan was copied from the 1733 map, with the details added later.

21. "Upon the Gardens of Epicurus; or, Of Gardening in the Year 1685," in *Five Miscellaneous Essays*, p. 27.

22. I am indebted to Woodbridge for pointing out that the canal was French in style and for clearing up some confusion over the location of the *berceau*.

23. See my note, "'Regular' or 'Irregular': Pope's Description of the Groves at Sherborne Castle," *Notes & Queries*, n.s., 22(11) (November 1975):490–91.

24. See Woodbridge's discussion of some early garden plans of Rousham in the Bodleian in "William Kent's Gardening: The Rousham Letters," *Apollo*, n.s., 100 (October 1974):282–91, which helps to date the theater there.

25. As has been explained, however, this map does not show trees where it is certain there were some: the horse chestnut groves, the northwest area, and the row of limes along the garden wall on the east front of the castle.

26. "Eighteenth-Century Elysiums," p. 167.

27. *The History and Antiquities of the County of Dorset*, 4:290.

28. *Observations on Modern Gardening* (London 1771, 3rd ed., pp. 150–51). I was reminded of this passage by J. D. Hunt in "Emblems and Expressionism," *Eighteenth-Century Studies* 4 (3) (1971):295, where he explains the distinction between the emblematic and expressionistic character of a garden in the early eighteenth century.

29. See B. S. Allen, *Tides in English Taste* (Cambridge, Mass., 1937), 2:130–31.

30. Brownell, p. 114, has made a similar point about the stagelike framing that Pope has in mind here, emphasizing the variety through contrast and handling of perspectives, which suggested "the management of stage scenery."

31. See Brownell, pp. 115–17, for an interpretation of Pope's suggestions in terms of what Brownell calls the "essence" of the poet's conception of the landscape-garden.

32. Mack, *Garden and the City*, p. 28.

33. Mack, *Garden and the City*, pp. 28–30.

34. See also *Corr.* 2:47; and Robert Digby's letters to Pope (*Corr.* 2:58, 191).

35. In a passage not quoted, when he refers to noblemen who have raised their villas by plundering other nations in war, or at the expense of the public, Pope is alluding to the Duke of Marlborough and Robert Walpole respectively. In *An Essay on Man*, Epistle 4, lines 295–300 (TE 3 [1]:156), Pope repeats the point possibly with Lord Digby in mind again as a positive contrast to the Marlboroughs and Walpoles.

36. See also R. Digby's letters to Pope (*Corr.* 1:474; 2:47, 51).

37. This was the monument in memory of the third Earl of Bristol. The little church is evidence of Lord Digby's interest in architecture; Erskine-Hill, p. 156n, notes that Lord Digby subscribed to vols. 2 and 3 of Colin Campbell's *Vitruvius Britannicus*.

38. Woodbridge has discovered a drawing by Kent for a seat at Sherborne in the Gothic style, so Kent may, in fact, have done some work at Sherborne; see "Critique," p. 8.

5. Bolingbroke: The Tory Farmer at Dawley Farm

1. The list of biographies of Bolingbroke is lengthy, but the standard modern biography is by H. T. Dickinson, *Bolingbroke* (Oxford, 1970). For an analysis of Bolingbroke's political ideas see Isaac Kramnick, *Bolingbroke and his Circle: The Politics of Nostalgia in the Age of Walpole* (Cambridge, Mass., 1968). Some recent biographies are by Sheila Biddle, *Bolingbroke and Harley* (London, 1975); Jeffrey Hart, *Viscount Bolingbroke: Tory Humanist* (London, 1965); and S. W. Jackman, *Man of Mercury* (London, 1965).

2. Spence 1, 653.

3. Spence 1, 274.

4. *The Works in Verse and Prose of William Shenstone, Esq.* (London, 1765), 2:245.

5. Bolingbroke saw the first volume of Pope's *Iliad* before publication (Spence 1, p. 63n) and he appears to have been painted by the poet in a position of praying, probably around 1713 (Spence 1, 108). See also Spence 1, p. 616.

6. *Verses* on a *Grotto* by the River *Thames* at *Twickenham*, composed of Marbles, Spars, and Minerals, line 10 (TE 6:383). See also Pope's letter to Bolingbroke on 3 September 1740 (*Corr.* 4:261–62).

7. Letter dated 25 November 1735 in the Bolingbroke correspondence in the archives of Petworth House, Sussex.

8. Swift, *Corr.* 2:461. Although Bolingbroke did not marry the Marquise de Villette until 1720, he had been her lover since 1717. La Source is discussed by Kenneth Woodbridge in "Bolingbroke's Château of La Source," *Garden History* 4 (3) (Autumn 1976), pp. 50–64; he includes some interesting plates of the landscape and gardens. My discussion of La Source is much indebted to Woodbridge's essay.

9. Swift, *Corr.* 2:398.

10. Woodbridge, "Bolingbroke's Château of La Source," p. 58.

11. *Histoire de l'Angleterre* (La Haye, 1749), 13:83–84; Woodbridge, "Bolingbroke's Château of La Source," p. 58.

12. Swift, *Corr.* 2:399–400. The plans published by Woodbridge in figure 1 of his article, "Bolingbroke's Château of La Source," show La Source as it probably was when Bolingbroke moved there (Plan 2) and as it was in 1739 after large-scale alterations, which had begun in 1735; we do not have graphic evidence of what Bolingbroke himself did in the gardens, apart from his iconography.

13. Translated:

> On account of faith preserved incorruptly toward the Queen, and the parties,
>> On account of effort strenuously exhibited, at least, in procuring a general
>>> peace,
>> Forced to turn the soil by the madness of an insane faction,
>> Here he is unjustly exiled to the calm source of sacred water,
>>> May he live pleasantly,
>>> H. De B. An. & c.

14. Swift, *Corr.* 2:399.

15. *Georgics* 2, line 149.

16. *Epistle* 1, lines 18, 103.

17. Woodbridge considers that Pope's mood or attitude might have inspired his verses on the nymph of the grotto, sent to Edward Blount on 2 June 1725 (*Corr.* 2:297). See TE 6:248 and n.

18. The Latin lines come from Horace, *Carmina* 3.4. The first four lines of the ode translated are:

> [Listen!] Or is it kind hallucination
> Deceiving me? I seem to glimpse her music,
>> I roam through hallowed groves
> Where pleasant winds and waters wander too.
>>> (5–8)

The next two lines from Horace follow on Pope's own preceding English lines and implore Bolingbroke and his wife to continue their celestial music with

> Accompaniment or else
> Apollo's lyre, or sing, clear-voiced alone.
>> (3–4)

He concludes the poem with line 25 of Horace's poem, "Because I love your fountains and your dances" (*The Odes of Horace*, tr. James Michie [New York, 1963], pp. 128–29). As Norman Ault noted, "lyre" in Pope's last line of his verses was an intended pun on "Loire" since the two words at the time were most likely homophones (TE 6:309n).

19. Mack, *Garden and the City*, p. 62. Pope used his grotto twice, at least, to present this theme, in *The First Satire of the Second Book of Horace*, lines 121–32 (1733); and in *Verses on a Grotto* (1740–43).

20. See Sherburn's note to these lines by Seneca (*Corr.* 2:252). See also Bolingbroke to Swift, 27 June–6 July 1734 (Swift, *Corr.* 4:413).

21. See Kramnick, *Bolingbroke and his Circle*, ch. 6, for an excellent analysis of Bolingbroke's ideas on history.

22. On Pope's relative perceptions of Bolingbroke and Lord Oxford, see my essay, "Rhetoric of Praise and Rhetoric of Blame in Pope's 'Epistle to Harley,'" *South Atlantic Bulletin* 37 (2) (1972):3–9.

23. Poetry had always interested him, however, although perhaps in a dilletantish way. He knew Dryden and contributed commendatory verses to Dryden's translation of Virgil (1697); he was the first person to whom Dryden showed *Alexander's Feast* (see *The Critical and Miscellaneous Prose Works of John Dryden*, ed. Edmond Malone [London, 1800], 1 (1):285).

24. Voltaire was also Lady Bolingbroke's friend; she once sent Swift a copy of the *Henriade* (Swift, *Corr.* 3:279).

25. Spence 1, 277.

26. Mack, "Introduction," TE 7:ccxxxiii–ccxxxiv. Mack uses the phrase Bolingbroke-Odysseus, which I take up below.

27. *The First Satire of the Second Book of Horace*, line 128. *Dawley Farm*, possibly written by Pope, describes Bolingbroke as "Free of Heart, and eloquent of Tongue" (line 49).

28. *Letters*, ed. Lord Mahon (London, 1845), 1:376. Swift made a similar judgment in a letter to Stella in November 1711 (*Journal to Stella*, ed. Harold Williams [Oxford, 1948], 2:401).

29. "Introduction," TE 7:lii–lvi.

30. See books 15, 17, 21, 22, and 24. Pope told Broome, his collaborator, on 8 October 1724 that he had "at last ended the fourteenth book" (*Corr.* 2:265). Odysseus arrives at Ithaca in book 13.

31. Letter to Caryll, 14 August 1713 (*Corr.* 1:185).

32. See *Odyssey* 24:388–400. Another landscape feature in Ithaca whose pictorial and iconographic beauty Pope stressed is the fountain in book 17 (232–45). It had the multiple function of serving the city ("an useful work!"), alluding to the nation's history with its busts of ancient kings, and evoking a sacred setting—a "mossie altar" or grove "sequester'd to the nymphs." The scene has an associative setting, recalling emotions and meaning in the style of Bolingbroke's fountainhead of the Loiret at La Source.

33. See also 24:326–28.

34. *One Thousand Seven Hundred and Forty: A Poem*, line 98 (TE 4:337). See a recent discussion of Pope's political allusions in his Homer, in John M. Aden, *Pope's Once and Future Kings: Satire and Politics in the Early Career* (Knoxville, 1978).

35. The conversations concerned the settling of his affairs vis-à-vis the government and the privileges that he claimed under his pardon.

36. Middlesex Record Office (hereafter cited as MRO), Muniment of Title for Manors of Harlington and Dawley (446/ED 205).

37. 5 August 1711, *Journal to Stella*, vol. 1.

38. The following information on the Bennett family and Dawley is taken from *The Victoria History of the County of Middlesex*, ed. Susan Reynolds (London, 1962), 3:261–67. Lord Ossulstone's younger brother, Henry, was created Lord Arlington, taking his name from Harlington Parish, in which Dawley stood. John Evelyn had laid out Euston Park for him.

39. See MRO, Acc. 446/ED 236.

40. Harlington Enclosure Award map, PRO MPH 236.

41. Brownell, pp. 225–29, stresses Pope's "classical identification" of Dawley Farm with its owner and asks, but does not consider, the question whether Pope's admiration for farmlike gardening affected the gardens of Dawley. See also Willis, *Charles Bridgeman*, pp. 132–33.

42. Sherburn dated the letter August 1726, immediately after Swift's return to Dublin.

43. Gay supped with Bolingbroke and his wife at Cranford on 16 September (*Corr.* 2:400). Bolingbroke was either there or at his house in Pall Mall during this period, and Swift at one point found his movements confusing enough to enquire of Gay where he might write to him (see *Corr.* 2:408, 410).

44. Pope was in Lord Bolingbroke's carriage; as he crossed a bridge near Whitton, the bridge broke, overturning the carriage in the water. He was saved from drowning by the footman and cut only his right hand on the broken window as he was pulled out. See George Sherburn, "An Accident in 1726," *Harvard Library Bulletin*, 2 (1) (1948):121–23.

45. Swift, *Corr.* 3:199–200.

46. Colvin, *British Architects*, p. 233. Bolingbroke was one of several Tory leaders who engaged Gibbs. In 1728 Gibbs published his widely used *Book of Architecture*.

47. *Gentleman's Magazine* 72 (1802):725.

48. TE 6:452. John Butt, Pope's editor, did not accept Ault's attribution of this poem to Pope; see TE 6:453–55. Brownell, however, tells me he is about to publish an essay claiming coauthorship by Pope and Swift.

49. *Letters of Lady Luxborough* (London, 1775), pp. 22–23. In spite of the architectural work at Dawley during this time, there is no evidence suggesting that Bolingbroke himself was responsible for any designs; rather, Gibbs probably had an entirely free hand. As Pope told Spence in 1739: "Lord Bolingbroke is not deep either in pictures, statues, or architecture" (Spence 1, 280).

50. Bolingbroke Family Papers, Add. MS. 34196. See also letters for 3 June 1728, 28 May 1729, 5 June 1730. His last letter from Dawley in this collection is dated 7 May 1734; the next, in July 1735, is from Chantelou in France.

51. "Reflexions upon Exile" (1717), in *The Works of Alexander Pope*, ed. W. Elwin and W. J. Courthope (London, 1871–89), 8:478–79. Pope told Spence in 1735 that while Bolingbroke was in exile "he wrote 'A Consolation to a Man in Exile' so much in Seneca's style that was he living now among us one should conclude that he had written every word of it" (Spence 1, 271). As has been suggested, Bolingbroke's mood in retirement, first at La Source and then at Dawley, was influenced by Seneca.

Laelius, whose name in Pope's mind became a pseudonym for Bolingbroke (see TE 3 (1):11n), was an apt reference here; Elwin and Courthope, *Works* 8:479, observed that Laelius "was celebrated for his statesmanship, his philosophical pursuits, and his friendship" and was "described by Horace as delighting, on his retirement from public affairs, in the society of the poet Lucilius. Thus the name was fitted to the functions of Bolingbroke, and the relation in which he stood to Pope."

52. See Malins, *Lost Demesnes*, ch. 2, especially pp. 31–36; and below, ch. 5.

53. Swift, *Corr.* 3:213 (6 June and 11 June). Who the person from Suffolk helping him to make Dawley "richer" might have been is not known to me. By "poor farm" Bolingbroke conceivably meant poor in agriculture.

54. Swift, *Corr.* 3:264.

55. Swift, *Corr.* 3:267.

56. "I never knew him live so great and expensively," Swift wrote to Pope on 16 July 1728, "as he hath done since his return from Exile; such mortals have resources that others are not able to comprehend" (*Corr.* 2:505). He was still more concerned by April 1729, writing to Bolingbroke and Pope: "My Lord, I have no other notion of Oeconomy than that it is the parent of Liberty and ease, and I am not the only friend you have who hath chid you in his heart for the neglect of it, tho' not with his mouth, as I have done" (*Corr.* 3:28).

57. Swift, *Corr.* 3:350 (30 August). A few months later (21 March 1730) Swift intimated the financial troubles that the longevity of Bolingbroke's father was causing the son and the likelihood that the Dawley pleasures might soon come to an end if the old Lord did not die: "and how does my Lord St. John? which last question is very material to me, because I love Burgundy, and riding between Twickenham and Dawley" (*Corr.* 3:99).

58. Lady Luxborough, who eventually acquired her own *ferme ornée* at Barrell's, gave her version of these paintings to William Shenstone on 28 April 1748: "When my brother Bolingbroke built Dawley, which he chose to call a Farm, he had his hall painted in stone-colours, with all the implements of husbandry placed in the manner one sees or might see arms and trophies in some General's hall; and it had an effect that pleased every body. I believe Pope mentions it in one of his letters to Swift" (*Letters of Lady Luxborough*, p. 23). We may speculate whether she was thinking of an analogy to Lord Peterborough's military emblems at Bevis Mount. To a bemused Lord Archer in 1749, she also wrote concerning Dawley: "My brother's calling it a Farm was only meant that it really was one; for he then kept £700 per annum in hand: but that the house was much too fine and large to be called a Farm. But on the other side, its environs were not ornamented, nor its prospects good" (p. 24). (One may wonder how Dawley got to this state from that pictured by Kip.) Lady Luxborough was justly proud of her own *ferme ornée*: she once told Shenstone, who was helping her with the design of Barrell's, that a mutual friend "will be heartily welcome to the beans and bacon my Farm produces, and to the cheese of my own dairy" (p. 39).

59. Note the resemblance of *Dawley Farm*, lines 33–34, to Pope's lines in the *Epistle to Dr. Arbuthnot* (1735): "Not Fortune's Worshipper, nor Fashion's Fool,/Not Lucre's Madman, nor Ambition's Tool" (lines 334–35). With the reference to the character as a "Plebeian" (Marlborough was knighted) and a hint of senility, the entire satiric passage (lines 33–38) could well be satirizing the Duke of Marlborough and Blenheim, which Pope, incidentally, was fond of doing; see, for example, *A Character* (TE 6:358–59), especially the lines, "Go then indulge thy age in Wealth and ease/Stretch'd on the spoils of plunder'd palaces . . ./*The trophy'd Arches, story'd Halls invade,/And haunt his slumbers in the pompous Shade*" (lines 11–12, 17–18).

60. Swift, *Corr.* 3:383.

61. See above, note 58. In a conversation with Bolingbroke, overheard and one part of which was recorded by Spence, Pope refers to certain visual effects—possibly at Dawley—which included apparently mediocre prospects and natural views (Spence 1, 614).

62. Add. MS. 34196, f. 19. His wife had been in Paris for some time attempting to recover from an illness.

63. TE 6:454.

64. It was entitled, *To the Author of a Poem intituled Dawley Farm*, printed in *Fog's Journal* (10 July 1731).

65. The whole subject of Bolingbroke's influence on Pope is exceedingly complex and largely a matter of conjecture; the reader should consult Mack, "Introduction to *An Essay on Man*," TE 3 (1):xxix–xxxi. See also Mack, Appendix A, "The *Essay on Man* and Bolingbroke's Fragments," p. 169.

66. Spence 1, 310. See also Spence, Appendix B to item 310, pp. 632–33. Mack, TE 3 (1):xxx, notes that the collection on "the happiness of contentment" was a specific influence on Epistle 4 of *An Essay on Man*, but as James Osborn observed, this prose collection may have been aimed at the initial general plan for a much larger moral work of which the ethical epistles, including the *Epistle to Burlington*, were to be a part (Spence 1, p. 139). This is borne out by Spence's mention of the "gardening poem," the *Epistle to Burlington*, to which apparently parts of Bolingbroke's prose collection related. See F. W. Bateson's discussion of the relationship of several of Spence's anecdotes to the four ethical epistles and *An Essay on Man* (TE 3 [2]:xx–xxii). On the identity of "the gardening poem," see also Spence, Appendix A to item 310, 1, p. 631. See also Robert W. Rogers, *The Major Satires of Alexander Pope*, Illinois Studies in Language and Literature (Urbana, 1955), 60:32–44.

67. On the likelihood that Pope was instead attacking Robert Walpole's Houghton Hall and the Duchess of Marlborough's Blenheim Palace, see Kathleen Mahaffey, "Timon's Villa: Walpole's Houghton," *Texas Studies in Literature and Language* 9 (1967):193–22; Mack, *Garden and the City*, Appendix F; Brownell, pp. 381–83.

68. Subtitled *A True and Perfect Key to Pope's Epistle to the Earl of Burlington*" (TE 3 [2]:176–88).

69. *Master Key*, p. 187. That Pulteney, one of the leaders of the Opposition, lacked a country seat was unique. Bateson notes that Pulteney's parsimony compelled him not to proceed with Burlington's design for a "House with an Arcade," which was published in Kent's *Designs of Inigo Jones* (London, 1727). See also Pope to Swift, 17–19 May 1739 (*Corr.* 4:179). Pulteney leased John Caryll's Ladyholt in 1718.

70. "To *Alexander Pope*, Esq.," *St. James Evening Post*, 1–3 March 1733; quoted in TE 6:455.

71. See Bolingbroke and Pope to Swift, March 1732 (*Corr.* 3:274–76).

72. In 1733–34 he also wrote the essays later published as *A Dissertation on Parties*. See Kramnick, *Bolingbroke and His Circle*, p. 275, n. 62, for an account of its publication.

73. See John Butt, TE 4:xxxvi–vii; also John M. Aden, *Something like Horace: Studies in the Art and Allusion of Pope's Horatian Satires* (Nashville, 1969); Thomas Maresca, *Pope's Horatian Poems* (Columbus, 1966); Reuben Brower, *Alexander Pope: The Poetry of Allusion* (Oxford, 1959), especially ch. 9; G. K. Hunter, "The 'Romanticism' of Pope's Horace," *Essays in Criticism* 10 (1960):390–404; and R. E. Hughes, "*Imitations of Horace* and the Ethical Focus," *Modern Language Notes* 71 (1956):569–74.

74. See Dixon, *Pope's Satires*, pp. 99–107.

75. Such passages appear in *To Bethel* (1733–34), lines 137–38, 141–47; *Versification of*

Donne's Second Satire, lines 109–14; the Man of Ross sketch (written possibly before May 1730) and the sketch of Old Cotta and his son in *To Bathurst*; and *The Second Epistle of the Second Book of Horace*, passim.

As Mack, *Garden and the City*, p. 168, explains, regarding the use of the landscape-farm or homestead as part of his self-portrait in the poems of the 1730s, Pope stressed his bourgeois diet at Twickenham in stating a favorite Opposition theme concerning the true meaning of liberty. Examples are: "Give me again my hollow Tree!/A Crust of Bread, and Liberty!" (*The Sixth Satire of the Second Book of Horace*, lines 222–23); "Give me, I cry'd, (enough for me)/My Bread, and Independency" (*The Seventh Epistle of the First Book of Horace*, lines 69–70); or especially Bethel's "Sermon" on temperate living and Pope's agreement in *The Second Satire of the Second Book of Horace*, lines 1–110 and 129–50. See also *The Sixth Satire of the Second Book of Horace*, lines 137, 165–70.

76. Some of the letters were published in William Coxe, *Memoirs of the Life and Administration of Sir Robert Walpole* (London, 1800), 3. In the Petworth archives they are arranged by date only, not by folio numbers.

77. Ironically, his father lived for seven more years. In this collection of Petworth letters, one written on 18 January 1737 mentions that he would not sell Dawley "if my Lord St. John should happen to drop, which is no improbable contingency."

78. Add. MS. 34196, f. 10.

79. Aristippus was Bolingbroke's favorite philosopher; see *Corr.* 3:29 and the *Epistle to Bolingbroke*, line 31.

80. Cf. Pope's *Epistle to Bolingbroke*, line 51.

81. See Pope to Bathurst, 23 November 1738 (*Corr.* 4:148). Among other avaricious demands, Vanneck wanted "the gardens and timber for nothing."

82. To Swift, 17–19 May 1739. In this letter Pope describes Bolingbroke's writing.

6. Pope, Mrs. Howard, and Friends at Marble Hill

1. Add. MS. 22626, f. 29 (5 July 1723?).

2. Gay, *Letters*, p. 44.

3. As Sherburn noted, on the back of this letter Pope translated a part of the *Odyssey* 5, which his letter to Broome on 14 July indicates was done before that date. Peterborough in his letter also mentions Lord Bolingbroke's presence in London, which dates his letter after 23 June, the date of Bolingbroke's arrival in England.

4. It was not until March 1724 that Lord Ilay, one of the trustees of the Prince of Wales's settlement on Mrs. Howard, began to acquire the land piecemeal for her (Syon MSS. Book K. 2.1.1, Letter H, ff. 233–35). Two other trustees appointed by the Prince were the Duke of Argyll and Robert Britiffe, a lawyer from Norfolk. For a brief history of Mrs. Howard's place at Court, her acquisition of the land, the building of the house, and its ownership after Mrs. Howard in 1767, see Marie P. G. Draper, *Marble Hill House and Its Owners* (London, 1970). I am heavily indebted to Marie Draper's research with original manuscripts at Blickling Hall and

elsewhere for many details and references. She does not provide much detail about the layout of the gardens, though she explains how the land was acquired (ch. 2).

5. Mrs. Howard had a fortune of £6,000, but it was in the form of trusts. Otherwise, she and her husband had very little cash, a condition that was aggravated by her husband's drinking and gambling habits (see Add. MS. 22627, ff. 40–46).

6. Horace Walpole esteemed her highly; see *Reminiscences, Written by Mr. Horace Walpole for . . . Miss Mary and Miss Agnes Berry*, ed. Paget Toynbee (London, 1924), pp. 65–66. Lord Hervey, who might have been disposed to think of her as an "enemy," also commended her for her "good sense, good breeding, and good nature" (*Lord Hervey's Memoirs*, rev. ed., ed. Romney Sedgwick [London, 1963], pp. 11–13.

7. For further details of Mrs. Howard's early married life, see Draper, *Marble Hill*, pp. 7–11.

8. See Pope's letter to Teresa and Martha Blount (*Corr.* 1:427).

9. TE 6:182.

10. This is assuming that Sherburn is correct in identifying the "Mrs. H." whom Pope mentions in his letters to Judith Cowper in 1722 as Miss Mary Howe, another maid of honor. See *Corr.* 2:136n. Gay did write to Mrs. Howard from France on 8 September, 1719 (Gay, *Letters*, pp. 135–37). One piece of evidence connecting Pope and Mrs. Howard in 1721 is the appearance of her name as a subscriber to Giovani Battista Buononcini's *Cantata*, published that year. This composer made a friend of Pope while he stayed in Twickenham during the summer of 1721; her name as well as those of others of Pope's good friends in the subscription list suggests that he solicited subscriptions for the composer.

11. Gay, *Poetry and Prose*, 1:256, line 62.

12. "On Modern Gardening," Chase, p. 80. On Pope and Richmond Lodge, see Brownell, pp. 156–57.

13. Sherburn notes Warburton's comment (Pope's *Works* [1751]) that this was a favorite remark of Sir Thomas Hanmer's (*Corr.* 2:14n).

14. "Charles Bridgeman: The Royal Gardens," in *Furor Hortensis*, pp. 41–47; see also Willis, *Charles Bridgeman*, ch. 3. See also Judith Colton, "Merlin's Cave and Queen Caroline: Garden Art as Political Propaganda," *Eighteenth-Century Studies* 10 (1) (Fall 1976):1–20; and Christopher Hussey, "Richmond Green, Surrey—I. Oak House and Old Palace Place," *Country Life* 95 (5 May 1944):722–25.

15. According to David Green, *Gardener to Queen Anne: Henry Wise and the Formal Garden* (London, 1956), p. 156, Wise seems to have been impervious, perhaps deliberately, to the landscaping movement. Neither Bridgeman's execution of some original thoughts at Chiswick nor later his designs at Eastbury, Rousham, Stowe, and so on, nor Caroline's patronage of Bridgeman—even after she became Queen in 1727—moved Wise to naturalize his landscape ideas. Wise had never had much use for topiary work, however.

16. She had long been credited with the making of the serpentine in Kensington Gardens and Hyde Park in 1731; and shortly after the King's death in 1727 she directed Bridgeman to plant and develop some one hundred fifty acres of Hyde Park, which George I had appropriated

for Kensington Gardens, after "the fashion of the Elector of Hanover's gardens at Herrenhausen" (Green, *Gardener to Queen Anne*, pp. 77–78).

17. César de Saussure observed on 14 June 1726 that Queen Caroline took "great interest in the gardens" and "greatly embellished them" (*A Foreign View of England*, p. 143). For an account of Queen Caroline's early gardening interest, see Willis, *Charles Bridgeman*, ch. 4.

18. Colton, "Merlin's Cave and Queen Caroline," pp. 4–20.

19. See Willis, *Charles Bridgeman*, chs. 1–3, for a thorough account of Bridgeman's early professional landscaping.

20. See Robert Halsband, *The Life of Lady Mary Wortley Montagu* (Oxford, 1966), pp. 97–98.

21. *The Complete Letters of Lady Mary Wortley Montagu*, ed. Robert Halsband (Oxford, 1965), 2:30.

22. *Down-Hall*, line 30 (*Literary Works of Matthew Prior*, ed. H. Bunker Wright and Monroe K. Spears [Oxford, 1959], 2:552). On Pope's relationship with Bridgeman at Down Hall and with other members of Harley's circle of Tory virtuosi, see Willis, *Charles Bridgeman*, p. 26. See also Brownell, pp. 165–66.

23. See Willis, *Charles Bridgeman*, pp. 79–80.

24. Reports of the Historical Manuscripts Commission, *Bath* 3:498 (16 March 1721). For a discussion of Down Hall, see Willis, *Charles Bridgeman*, pp.73–76.

25. See "A Poet's Gardener," *Listener* 62 (24 December 1964):1007–9.

26. Reports of the Historical Manuscripts Commission, *Bath* 3:488–89.

27. Without their help, Lady Mary, with a competitive edge, spent considerable sums of money on her garden from 1724 to 1727. See Halsband, *Life of Lady Mary*, p. 124, and the Wharncliffe Muniments 108, on deposit in the Sheffield Central Library.

28. Halsband, *Letters of Lady Mary*, 2:30.

29. See Colton, "Merlin's Cave and Queen Caroline," p. 3 and n. 8.

30. *A Journey through England* 1:65–66.

31. Chase, p. 30.

32. Rocque's plan even shows a type of *ferme ornée*. At the entrance to the gardens, just opposite "Richmond Green" (identified on the plan), a tree-lined avenue started off to the southeast and continued along the southern perimeter of the royal garden adjacent to open fields until it arrived at the southeast corner next to the river; then it extended westward along the river, affording lovely views of the river all the way, until it met and ended at a smaller entrance into the middle section of the gardens—a "wilderness" of woods cut through with winding paths and hiding secret arbors and seats. This circular avenue resembled the pathway around the perimeter of Home Park at Stowe, which Bridgeman designed beginning in 1726, and it performed the similar function of affording views of the house and the gardens within, as well as of the fields outside. See Willis, "Charles Bridgeman: The Royal Gardens," pp. 42–43.

33. To Lord Peterborough, September 1732 (*Corr.* 3:311–12); *Epistle to Burlington*, lines 77–78 (TE 3 [2]:144 and n); and *The Poems of Jonathan Swift*, ed. Harold Williams (Oxford, 1963), pp. 662–64. See also Willis, "Charles Bridgeman: The Royal Gardens," pp. 44–45. On Queen Caroline's use of garden art in Merlin's Cave for political purposes, see Colton, "Merlin's Cave and Queen Caroline." One of the outlandish features of Merlin's Cave was the appointment of "thresher" poet Stephen Duck as the cave's resident hermit. As the century progressed, this fashion of hiring hermits for specially built hermitages reached what to us seems outrageously

comic proportions. Although Pope was his own style of hermit in his grotto, his presence in the grotto was more than a picturesque pose of meditation and retreat for him. It was instead a vital element in a process of private reflection about which he wrote in his ethical and satirical poems of the 1730s. Had he suspected that he was inadvertently promoting the meaningless display of archetypal hermitages in gardens later in the century, he would have been scandalized and felt serious reservations about the iconographic fame his grotto was earning. See Hunt's discussion of hermitages in *Figure in the Landscape*, ch. 1.

34. Gay, *Poetry and Prose*, 1:258, line 112n. Norman Ault, *New Light on Pope* (London, 1949); pp. 172–82, argued that Pope's friendship with Argyll was very close. See Pope's letter to Martha Blount, December 1716 (*Corr*. 1:379).

35. Add. MS. 22627, f. 94 (29 April); as quoted in Draper, *Marble Hill*, p. 12.

36. Hervey, *Memoirs*, pp. 277–78.

37. Whitton Park is shown on Rocque's 1746 *Exact Survey of the City's of London, Westminster*. . . . It is about one mile from Marble Hill. See Draper, *Marble Hill*, n. 52, for reference to Whitton in the Syon MSS. See also Henrietta Pye, *A Short Account of the Principal Seats and Gardens, In and About Richmond and Kew* (London, 1760), pp. 41–42. Spence's description of the trees at Whitton in the 1750s may be found in the Spence papers at the Beinecke Rare Book and Manuscript Library at Yale.

38. To Pope (*Corr*. 2:183).

39. On Lord Herbert's architectural activities, see Lees-Milne, *Earls of Creation*, ch. 2.

40. Add. MS. 22625, f. 107, cited in Draper, *Marble Hill*, p. 15. Pope undoubtedly encountered the eccentric Lord Herbert and his dog Fop, not to be confused with Mrs. Howard's dog by the same name, frequently at Marble Hill. As C. F. Burgess noted, Pope's poem *Bounce to Fop*, with which Swift probably helped on his visit in either 1726 or 1727, was more likely satirically directed against Herbert than Mrs. Howard (Gay, *Letters*, p. 96n). Peterborough would have appreciated the satire.

41. See figure in Draper, *Marble Hill*, p. 13. On the following page Draper explains the methods and arrangements of the purchase. Plate 56 is a reconstruction of the Marble Hill landscape based on the outlines provided by a plan in a deed of 23 August 1901; Draper, p. 13, published a plan of the outlines. Brownell, pp. 157–61, considers evidence of Pope's work at Marble Hill.

42. Hereafter the numbers cited of features on the landscape are from plate 56.

43. An account dated October 1725 by Roger Morris, Mrs. Howard's architect for work completed from June 1724 to July 1725, included the item, "Railing in ye Meadow" (Hobart MSS in Norfolk Record Office, 8862, 21 F4). See *Corr*. 2:181, 281, 292, 435.

44. See Horace Walpole, *Collected Works*, ed. R. Berry (London, 1798). I have cited this verse from a manuscript at Rousham House, with the permission of Thomas Cottrell-Dormer.

45. Pye, *Principal Seats and Gardens in . . . Kew*, p. 19.

46. Reproduced from "Marble Hill, Middlesex," *Country Life* 39 (25 March 1916):399. No authority was given for this small plan, but in several respects it is accurate and appears to be based on a reliable source.

47. While the Heckell and Mason engraving shows the ground to the west of the groves, it does not show it as far to the east, so the alley could have run along the eastern boundary.

48. Swift, *Poems* 2:407–11.

49. Wilton MSS, Archives of the Earl of Pembroke, Wilton House.

50. Add. MS. 22628, f. 57.

51. See Malins, *Lost Demesnes*, pp. 41–43.

52. The icehouse is mentioned in the gardener's contract for responsibilities and costs sometime soon after Mrs. Howard's second marriage in 1735 (Norfolk Record Office, Hobart MS. 8863, 21 F4). Lord Peterborough, who kept a close watch on Marble Hill, might have taken the idea for his own icehouse atop Bevis Mount hill from Mrs. Howard's.

53. Norfolk Record Office, Hobart MS. 8862, 21 F4.

54. Add. MS. 4809, f. 161v.

55. In a letter to Broome on 29 June 1725, Pope states that while waiting for *Odyssey* 16 to go to press, he has finished "two books of verse," perhaps *Odyssey* 15 and 17 (2:302 n. 3).

56. Hunt, *Figure in the Landscape*, p. iv.

57. A facetious allusion to the mounts at Riskins, of which Pope disapproved.

58. The couplet is Pope's adaptation of Gay's couplet in 1714 inviting Robert, Earl of Oxford, to attend a Martin Scriblerus Club gathering (see Gay, *Poetry and Prose* 1:127).

59. Bathurst was at Marble Hill again in September (*Corr.* 2:317).

60. Add. MS. 22626, f. 9. The year of the letter is not given, but I have placed it in 1725 on the basis of Pope's visit to Stowe in July of that year and his designing for Mrs. Howard during the year. Martha Blount goes on to compliment the gardens at Marble Hill (see below), so the letter could not date from 1724, when there was little to see there in the way of landscaping. As for 1726, by then Pope's contribution to the landscape appears to have diminished; he was also busy with the pleasure of entertaining Swift on his first visit to England for years.

61. Add. MS. 22628, f. 13.

62. Norfolk Record Office, Hobart MS. 8862, 21 F4. Cited in Draper, *Marble Hill*, p. 15.

63. See Peter Willis, "Creator of the English Garden: Charles Bridgeman's Tools and Techniques," *Country Life* 153 (17 May 1973):1401–4. Willis explains how the tools mentioned in Bridgeman's inventory of 1738 link him to the new natural style of gardening.

64. Norfolk Record Office, Hobart MS. 8862, 21 F4. Cited in Draper, *Marble Hill*, p. 36.

65. Draper, *Marble Hill*, p. 38. The document is an estimate for repairs by Henry Edmead (Norfolk Record Office, Hobart MS. 8862, 21 F4). The buildings were demolished in 1908, but an article entitled "Of Garden Making," by F. Inigo Thomas in *Country Life* 7 (24 February 1900):235–37, shows one of them. This essay includes a plan of Marble Hill's gardens as they existed on the river side, neglected, in 1900 . It is not known from what period this remnant of the garden dates.

Brownell, pp. 161–62, cites Marble Hill's mount as an old-fashioned feature it had in common with Sherborne and Pope's garden. He notes Batty Langley's stricture, in *New Principles of Gardening* (1728), p. vii, that Mrs. Howard's "*Slopes* . . . being view'd at the River *Thames*" were rendered in a "low mean Manner" by being terraced or "broken." But Langley is here speaking not of mounts, but rather of terraced sloping ground. Two paragraphs earlier he spoke of the "poor and trifling" effect of terracing mounts, but there is no suggestion by Langley or anyone else that Mrs. Howard's, Digby's, or Pope's mounts were terraced instead of having uninterrupted slopes. It was apparently Mrs. Howard's terraces, not her mount or other features of the garden, that Langeley found "stiff and regular."

66. *Letters Written by the Late Right Honourable Lady Luxborough to William Shenstone, Esq.* (London, 1775), p. 23.

67. Add. MS. 22626, fs. 11–11v.

68. Add. MS. 22626, f. 56. Judging by a letter Lady Hervey wrote to Mrs. Howard on 24 July 1729, either on her own or someone else's initiative Mrs. Howard was widening the circle of friends who contributed in some way to her gardens. She had asked Lord Hervey, Pope's Sporus in the *Epistle to Dr. Arbuthnot*, for some plants from his estate. "Marble-Hill will receive," Lady Hervey remarked in her letter, "some considerable addition to its present beauty" (Add. MS. 22628, f. 22).

69. 2 August 1730 (Gay, *Letters*, p. 96).

70. Add. MS. 22626, f. 58.

71. Malins, *Lost Demesnes*, p. 46. Malins, ch. 2, analyzes in detail Swift's, Mrs. Delany's, and other friends' landscaping, especially in the 1720s.

72. Swift, *Poems* 1:278; see also letter to Archbishop King, 28 September 1721 (Swift, *Corr.* 2:406).

73. Swift, *Corr.* 3:60 (27 May 1725); see also Sheridan to Swift, 23 June and 13 August 1735 (Swift, *Corr.* 4:355, 376).

74. Swift, *Corr.* 3:76. Sir Walter Scott told of an amusing incident in the gardens at Quilca in which Sheridan was supposed to have had the better of Swift. According to Scott's tale, to surprise Sheridan with some improvements in the gardens during his absence, Swift speedily had a long canal cut; formed an arbor, which he called "Stella's Bower," at the end of it by transplanting some trees; and built a dry stone wall around some land about the canal with stones from the ground. Though Swift gave directions that these improvements should be kept secret, Sheridan learned of them before he returned home, so that when he and Swift walked by the area, Sheridan confounded Swift by pretending not to see anything (Thomas Sheridan, *Memoirs of Jonathan Swift, D.D.*, ed. Sir Walter Scott, Edinburgh, 1814, pp. 313–14).

75. Swift, *Corr.* 3:302. Swift spent long periods there from June 1728 to February 1729, June 1729 to October 1729, and June 1730 to September 1730. In between the visits to Market-Hill Swift intimated to Knightley Chetwode the importance of gardening to him: "I shall think [it] very unwise in such a world as this, to leave planting of trees and making walks, to come into it" (Swift, *Corr.* 3:317).

76. There is a description of the house and gardens, as they appeared in 1744, in *The Autobiography and Correspondence of Mary Granville, Mrs. Delany*, ed. Lady Llanover (London, 1861), 2:308, 314; see also F. Elrington Ball, *The History of the County Dublin* (Dublin, 1917), pt. 6, pp. 129–33; and Malins, *Lost Demesnes*, pp. 36–40.

77. J. Cooper Walker, *The Rise and Progress of Gardening in Ireland* (Dublin, 1791), p. 63.

78. On the authorship of this poem, see Swift, *Poems*, 3:1107–8. I cite the poem from a manuscript at Rousham House, with the permission of Thomas Cottrell-Dormer.

79. *Correspondence of Sir Thomas Hanmer* ed. Sir Henry Bunbury (London, 1838), pp. 216–17.

80. Pope mentioned Hanmer disparagingly in *Corr.* 1:216 ("A Fig too for H———r/Who prates like his Grandmere") and 234. Later, Hanmer's edition of Shakespeare induced Pope to include him in *The Dunciad*, book 4, lines 105–10 (TE 5:351), as Montalto.

81. Swift, *Corr.* 3:397; see also 3:446.

82. Swift, *Corr.* 3:286.

83. Swift, *Corr.* 4:170.

84. Swift, *Corr.* 4:199, 339.

85. For Swift's opinion of this name for the estate, see his letter to Mary Pendarves, 29 January 1736 (Swift, *Corr.* 4:455).

86. Swift, *Corr.* 4:252, 415. It is also interesting that while during these years Mary Pendarves was spending much time in Fulham and extolling its beauties to Swift, Peterborough was doing his best to get Swift to come visit him at Bevis Mount: "I should have been glad of any thing of Swift's, pray when you write to him next, tell him I expect him with impatience, in a place as odd, and as much out of the way, as himself" (to Pope, October 1732, *Corr.* 3:317; see also 3:28).

87. Swift, *Corr.* 4:199.

88. Her drawings may be seen in the British Library and the National Museum, Dublin.

89. Bathurst saw her in London in May of that year as well, as she told Swift later: "We then talked of your vineyard: he seemed pleased with every subject that related to you" (Swift, *Corr.* 4:159).

90. *Lost Demesnes*, pp. 33–34.

91. The wall gave Swift a sense of industry about his garden and he cited it several times in the next five years as his single extravagance in that line. See Swift, *Corr.* 3:14, 59, 373, 383.

92. Swift, *Corr.* 3:196.

93. See *Corr.* 2:436, 332; and Martha Blount to Mrs. Howard, Add. MS. 22626, f. 9.

94. Swift, *The Prose Works*, ed. Herbert Davis et al. (Oxford, 1939), 5:214.

95. Swift, *Poems* 2:559, lines 177–80.

96. Swift, *Poems* 2:407–11.

97. In April 1732, Peterborough asked Pope, "why is our Shepherdess in voluntary slavery?" (*Corr.* 3:281). Though married, Mrs. Howard was still mistress of the robes.

98. On 29 February 1728, Swift wrote to Martha Blount from Dublin: "How will you pass this Summer for want of a Squire to Ham-common and Walpole's lodge [in Richmond Park]; for, as to Richmond lodge and Marble-hill they are abandond as much as Sr. Spencer Compton. . . . Your greatest happiness is that you are out of the chiding of Mrs. Howard and the Dean" (Swift, *Corr.* 3:268–69).

99. The gardener at Marble Hill apparently, of whom I have found no other mention.

100. According to receipts and bills cited by Draper, *Marble Hill*, p. 38.

101. Add. MS. 22626, ff. 53–54. Cf. Gay to Swift, 20 March 1728 (Swift, *Corr.* 3:272).

102. Regarding Pope's mediation in litigation about Marble Hill, see Appendix B.

103. See Draper, *Marble Hill*, pp. 42–46, for a summary of further purchases.

104. Walpole moved to Strawberry Hill, his Gothic villa in Twickenham, in 1744. A passage in a letter he wrote to her from France on 20 September 1765 reflects their common interest in gardening: "Their [the French] Country Houses wou'd appear to me no more rural than those in Paris. Their gardens are like Desserts, with no more verdure or Shade. What trees they have, are shipped up, and cut strait at top; it is quite the massacre of the Innocents" (Add. MS. 22626, f. 83).

7. Lord Peterborough's "little Amoret" at Bevis Mount

1. See Brownell, p. 217n.

2. What might be the earliest reference to his residence at Bevis Mount is an oblique one in a letter Peterborough wrote to Mrs. Howard in October 1730 (?): "and give me leave to add that the Elysian fields in this world are our own" (Croker 1:390). See F. J. C. Hearnshaw, "Bevis Mount," *Papers and Proceedings of the Hampshire Field Club and Archaeological Society* 5 (pt. 1) (1905):114–15.

3. Cf. *Corr.* 2:1. According to H. B. Wheatley, *London Past and Present* (London, 1891), 1:218, Peterborough lived on Bolton Street from 1710 to 1724. Wheatley also states that Peterborough lived in Peterborough House (Grosvenor House after 1735) in Millbank, Westminster, built possibly by the first Earl; the house had "a fine garden behind it," he noted (1:545).

4. Cf. *Corr.* 1:493.

5. See Spence 1, pp. 112–16. Swift, *Poems, To the Earl of P-b-w,* 2:398, lines 4–9, also wrote these verses about Peterborough's perpetual rush throughout Europe:

> In Journeys he out-rides the Post,
> Sits up till Midnight with his Host,
> Talks Politicks, and gives the Toast.
>
> Knows ev'ry Prince in *Europe's* Face,
> Flies like a Squib from Place to Place,
> And travels not, but runs a Race.

For a life of Peterborough, see William Stebbing, *Peterborough* (London, 1890).

6. After the Hanoverian succession, when Peterborough began to be cut off from the Court and politics, the notion of his possessing too much wit for his own good in those "corrupt" times became rather commonplace. Pope voices it in a letter to Swift in 1723: "I tremble for my Lord Peterborow (whom I now lodge with) he has too much wit, as well as Courage to make a solid General, & if he escapes being banish'd by others, I fear he will banish himself" (*Corr.* 2:184–85).

7. Add. MS. 22625, ff. 112–13. See my note, "Pope, Lord Peterborough, and Mrs. Howard: Fresh Glimpses from an Unpublished Letter," *Scriblerian* 9 (1) (Fall 1976):55–56.

8. Much of it, along with three volumes of manuscript memoirs, may have been burned after Peterborough's death in 1735 by his wife, the former Anastasia Robinson. No letters written between 1723 and 1732 have been discovered.

9. Add. MS. 22625, f. 116.

10. *Journal to Stella*, 31 May 1712.

11. *A Journey through England* 1:210. See also Miles Hadfield, *Gardening in Britain* (London, 1960), p. 225. Lady Mohun admired the "beauty" of Parson's Green in a letter to Mrs. Howard (Add. MS. 22625, f. 125).

12. Hunt, *Figure in the Landscape*, pp. 25–36.

13. Richard Bradley, in *New Improvements of Planting and Gardening* (7th ed.; London, 1739, p. 102), wrote: "I find that Plants of Virginia and even those of the North Parts of Carolina, will

bear over Frosts, if they are managed with judgment. The Tulip-Tree, which flourishes so well in the Earl of Peterborough's Wilderness at Parson's-Green, is a Virginia plant."

14. Sheet no. 10.

15. The Latin passage is from Virgil, *Eclogues*, 1.38–39. Translated:

Tityrus was not there. The very springs and pine-trees
Called out, these very orchards were crying for you, my friend.

(*The Eclogues and Georgics of Virgil in the Original Latin with a Verse Translation*, ed. and tr. C. Day Lewis [Garden City, N.Y., 1964], p. 9).

16. Add. MS. 22625, f. 33. There is no date to this letter, though the early 1720s seem likely, when he and Pope were especially busy in their gardens.

17. Croker 1:130–74. Croker mistakenly assigns all the letters to 1723. The last one in the series (1:172) written from Bevis Mount is plainly misdated since Peterborough did not begin to live at Bevis Mount until 1730. There are several Croker did not print in which Peterborough does refer to gardens and his and Mrs. Howard's friendship with Pope. I refer to these later on. Draper, *Marble Hill*, pp. 14–15, cites a few of these letters.

18. See Croker 1:xlvi.

19. Add. MS. 22625, f. 123–25.

20. Add. MS. 22625, f. 107.

21. To Lady Mohun, Add. MS.22625, f. 33.

22. Croker 1:173.

23. For revealing discussions of distinctions between the villa and the larger country house, see Brownell, pp. 214–16, and John Summerson, "The Classical Country House in 18th-Century England," *Journal of the Royal Society of Arts* 107 (July 1959):552.

24. See F. J. C. Hearnshaw, "Bevis Mount," *Papers and Proceedings of the Hampshire Field Club and Archaeological Society* 3 (2):155–69.

25. Hearnshaw, "Bevis Mount," pp. 109–14.

26. I. T. Lewis, *Southampton* (Southampton, 1843).

27. On the 1658 map of the St. Denys Priory estate, someone has marked the "Ser Bevoys" and "Mitchell Close" areas as "sold to Lord Peterborough."

28. A special act of Parliament was required for this exchange (Act of 8 George II, 1735), entitled "An Act for exchanging of lands between the Right Honourable Charles, Earl of Peterborow and Monmouth and the Provost and Scholars of the Queen's College, in the University of Oxford." The land was described as follows: "All that Grange or parcel of Ground called Padwell with all Closes Meadows Pastures Feedings and other commodities to the same Grange . . . and being within the liberties of the Town of Southampton that is to say on the north and west parts of the highway leading from the aforesaid Town towards Winchester" (Hearnshaw, "Bevis Mount," pp. 111–112, 115).

29. *Victoria County History: A History of Hampshire and the Isle of Wight*, ed. William Page (Westminster, 1903) 2:160–64.

30. See J. S. Davies, *A History of Southampton*, partly from the MS of Dr. Speed in the Southampton archives (1883), pp. 434–37. See also the Rev. Theodore C. Wilks, *A General History of Hampshire, or the County of Southampton* (London, n.d.), vol. 22, part 22, pp. 274–75.

54. Add. MS. 22625, f. 46. See Spence 1, 260–61; *Corr.* 3:487–88, 489–90, 508–9. Pope described Peterborough's suffering to Martha Blount: "He has with him, day after day, not only all his Relations, but every creature of the Town of Southampton that pleases. He lies on his Couch & receives them: tho he says little. When his Pains come, he desires them to walk out, but invites them to stay & dine or sup" (*Corr.* 3:488). Edith Sitwell, *The English Eccentrics* (London, 1950), described how the Earl invited his friends (Pope included) to be present when he died. He had arranged to die on a couch in the grounds of Bevis Mount, but though he made a powerful farewell speech, death did not come even at his command. He managed, in fact, another trip to London before his departure for Lisbon; Spence (1, 262) saw him there. The "very uncommon chirurgical operation" was performed by the notorious Dr. Nathaniel St. André, who was suspected of poisoning George Berkeley in 1725; he later married Berkeley's wife and took her down to Southampton.

55. See also *Corr.* 3:485.

56. See his letter to Allen, *Corr.* 4:40–41.

57. Apparently Hill enjoyed a fairly close friendship with Peterborough. He wrote the poem *Advice to the Poets*, which includes a passage on Peterborough to which Pope referred in a letter to Hill on 4 April 1731 (*Corr.* 3:188).

58. Defoe, *Tour* (1742), 1:140. For the most part, the sections on Bevis Mount in all the Southampton *Guides* from 1768 onward were taken from this abstract.

59. Defoe, *Tour* (1724), 1 (Letter 2):81.

60. Whately, *Observations on Modern Gardening*, pp. 150–51..

61. Defoe, *Tour* (1742), p. 204.

62. Unless otherwise indicated, numbered and lettered garden features refer to plate 65.

63. In 1844 the Bevis Mount estate was sold to William Betts, a contractor from Dover, who immediately began to divide it into lots for building purposes. The 1866 ordnance survey map (OSM) shows how rapidly development was carried out once it began. Housing completely surrounds the estate; it also has severed the house from the mount and wilderness area—a critical point in the disappearance of the gardens. Gravel pits and brick fields first encroached upon the wilderness, and eventually the entire mount was covered by houses.

64. The supposed tomb is thought to have remained in this position until the mid-nineteenth century, when it was removed in the course of development of the site. Brownell, plate 45, published this sketch. T. G. Hart was a local Southampton artist who lived in the area from 1825.

65. See Elwin and Courthope, *Works* 10:187.

66. Pp. 47–48. As in the case of the *Guide*'s description of Bevis Mount, which is taken from the 1742 edition of Defoe's *Tour*, this description seems to have been written by someone with a knowledge of painting.

67. Spence 1, 608. This particular view of the two hills is mentioned in nineteenth-century guide books: see *Stranger's Guide to Southampton*, 21st ed. (Southampton, 1890), p. 86.

68. Defoe, *Tour* (1742), 1:204–5.

69. *Guide* (1768), pp. 48–49. The *Guide* for 1787, pp. 56–57, states that "the ice-house, which is very fine, has good vaults under it which serve for cellars."

70. Peterborough, we recall, once made the tongue-in-cheek comment to Pope that he was paradoxically leading himself "out of Temptation" and into "ways of Pennance" by leaving the mount "to gett into the bottom" (*Corr.* 3:468).

71. *Guide* (1768), p. 49.

72. *Guide* (1787), p. 57.

73. *Guide* (1787), p. 57.

74. The twenty-five-inch OSM (1866) indicates elevations. It might also have occurred to Peterborough and Pope to use the Padwell area in the manner that Lord Cobham used Home Park at Stowe—that is, encircle the area with a walk along which advantageously placed temples and seats could command views back toward the mount and the house and at the same time provide views and perspectives of positions around the perimeter from the house and mount. Since the land rises across Padwell to the west, the views also would have included the river.

75. Cf. letter to Horace Mann (20 June 1760), *The Correspondence of Horace Walpole*, ed. W. S. Lewis, Warren Hunting Smith, and George L. Lamm (New Haven, 1960), 21:417.

76. Sir John Mordaunt, Peterborough's nephew who lived at Bevis Mount after Lady Peterborough died in 1755, erected a tablet in memory of his uncle somewhere in the garden; it was subsequently removed to the main house, where it remained until the house was taken down at the beginning of this century. The tablet was inscribed in Latin and, translated, read:

> To Charles Mordaunt,
> Count of Peterborough
> Defender of the freedom of the Fatherland
> Conqueror of Valencia
> Famous for his Counsels and his Arms,
> When Matters had been Conducted Bravely
> Swiftly, and Fortunately,
> He retired into These Small Estates,
> Dying, he kept Tilling These.

8. The Closing Scenes at Bath: Mr. Allen's Prior Park

1. The authoritative biography of Ralph Allen is by Benjamin Boyce, *The Benevolent Man: A Life of Ralph Allen of Bath* (Cambridge, Mass., 1967). Hereafter cited as Boyce. The reader is referred to this interesting study for details of Pope's friendship with Allen, in chs. 5–7. Another and more recent study of Allen's relationship to Pope is included in Howard Erskine-Hill's *The Social Milieu of Alexander Pope*, ch. 7; this chapter emphasizes the moral qualities of Allen's character that held symbolic importance as a background to Pope's verse portrayal of his own social values. My own chapter here is naturally heavily indebted to both these studies, particularly the former: my intention has been to gather together certain details of the Pope-Allen friendship as they relate to the Prior Park landscape and to other individuals who have figured prominently in this book. Brownell, pp. 207–13, has also considered in some detail Pope's influence in the Prior Park gardens.

2. See Boyce, chs. 3–4; and Erskine-Hill, pp. 218–24.

3. *Epistle to Burlington*, lines 192, 197–98.

4. Letter from the Burlington MS. 162.2, at Chatsworth, cited by Boyce, p. 42.

5. The second, enlarged edition was printed in London 1734, for J. Gray and James Leake, the Bath bookseller and good friend of Allen's. The first edition was also published in 1734.

6. Allen invented a "machine" to ascend and descend the road or wagonway in order to carry stone from his quarries at the top of Widcombe Hill down to the town. It is shown in the engraving by Anthony Walker in 1752 (plate 77). R. E. M. Peach, *The Life and Times of Ralph Allen* (London, 1895), pp. 78–81, cited a document of 1731 stating that Allen constructed a wagonway on his land.

7. Allen's interest in architecture is discussed by Erskine-Hill, pp. 217–18; his friend General George Wade, himself a resident of Bath, possibly advised Allen on architectural matters. Wade had a house built in Bath, ca. 1720, after Inigo Jones's house in Lincoln's Inn Fields, and Burlington designed a house for him in London in 1715. Wade was also a good friend of Lord Cobham's.

8. See Boyce, ch. 5.

9. Cited in Boyce, pp. 57–58.

10. Boyce, p. 66, suggests that Allen first wrote to Pope sometime between June 1735 and late March 1736.

11. Warburton stated that Allen made this offer, in Pope, *Works*, 9:313n.

12. Mary Chandler's *Description of Bath* (Bath, 1734) was printed for him; he owned the bookshop just across the way from Allen's townhouse in Bath. Allen found him useful as a source of books (see Boyce, p. 64). Defoe's *Tour* (1742), 2:258, noted that Leake's bookshop was "one of the finest Booksellers Shops in Europe"—an opinion colored by Richardson's being Leake's brother-in-law.

13. See Boyce, pp. 67–68, 104–5. Allen decided on "the Discovery of Joseph to his Brethren" and Scipio's "Resignation of the Captive" (*Corr.* 4:13), while Pope decided on Poussin's *Death of Germanicus*. Burlington had a good copy of the Scipio, so Pope was arranging for Van Diest to see that one. See also *Corr.* 4:20. Pope's arrangements for Van Diest's work at Prior Park are considered in Brownell, pp. 333–34.

14. See a recent article on Shaftesbury's influence upon the identification of the morally good with the aesthetically attractive by John Andrew Bernstein, "Shaftesbury's Identification of the Good with the Beautiful," *Eighteenth-Century Studies* 10 (3) (Spring 1977):304–25.

15. See a recent review essay by Ronald Paulson, "Thoughts on Landscape Theory," *Eighteenth-Century Studies* 10 (2) (Winter 1977):245–61, which summarizes scholarship in recent years on garden history and, among other things, puts the emblematic and iconographic landscape gardening in the eighteenth century into helpful perspective.

16. See also his letter to Allen on 6 July [1738]: "So much higher is my Respect for Virtue than for Title, that You might suffer as much from the Importunity & Assiduity of an honest Heart, as your Betters (in this world) do, from that of an Interested one" (*Corr.* 4:108).

17. On Pope's changing "low-born" to "humble," see *Corr.* 4:144–45.

18. See Boyce, ch. 7 passim.

19. *The History of Tom Jones*, book 8, ch. 1.

20. Allen is included, without mention, in Pope's poem *One Thousand Seven Hundred and Forty*, lines 89–98, as one of several honest men who have lost faith and hope (TE 4:337). The reason for Pope's neglect of Allen in his poetry could have been Allen's connection with Robert Walpole and the embarrassment Allen might have felt at being praised in poetry that relentlessly attacked the government. Erskine-Hill, pp. 235–40, analyzes the political implications of Pope's experience with Allen.

21. See Pope to Bethel, 19 November 1738 (*Corr.* 4:146–47).

22. TE 4:54–69. In July 1731, after having just composed one of the epistles in *An Essay on Man*, Pope wrote as follows to Bethel: "I have just finished an Epistle in Verse, upon the Nature & Extent of Good nature & Social affection; & am going upon another whose subject is, The True Happiness of Man, in which I shall prove the Best Men the happiest, & consequently you should pull off your hat to me, for painting You as the happiest man in the Universe" (*Corr.* 3:209).

23. See Dixon, *Pope's Satires*, pp. 77–78.

24. In the same letter, Pope alludes to Bethel's friendship with Burlington and the former's appetite for hunting.

25. As Boyce, pp. 139–40, explains, the Allens were looking for the right person to lease the house as their neighbor, it being only four miles from Prior Park. Apparently they were not interested in Martha Blount as a neighbor. During his visit to Prior Park in December 1742, the lease on Pope's villa came up for sale, and he declined the opportunity to buy it. At the time, however, after seeing the Bathampton Manor House with its soft rural surroundings, he considered moving into it; and the Allens, who were desirous of intellectual and artistic stimulation, seemed to have been attracted to the prospect of Pope as their neighbor. Nothing came of this and the next summer Pope was trying to convince Allen to let him and George Arbuthnot (son of Dr. John) use it during their visit with the Allens while Martha stayed at the main house. Wishing to avoid the precedent this would set, Allen insisted that they all stay in the main house. According to Boyce, p. 148, Mrs. Allen might well have felt some jealousy over these designs on her old family residence.

26. She told this to William Mason many years later; it is quoted from Duncan C. Tovey, *Gray and His Friends* (Cambridge, 1890), p. 281; see also Boyce, pp. 146–47, and Erskine-Hill, pp. 234–35.

27. See her letter to Pope from Prior Park soon after Pope had left, 28 July or 4 August (*Corr.* 4:462).

28. Although the landscaping at Prior Park during these earliest years of Pope's connection with it is not documented, the building of the main house is. In 1737 the basement story of the house was being built, and already erected were the so-called offices at the western end of what became a dramatically long, curving line of buildings on a terrace about two-thirds of the way up the long slope of Widcombe Hill. See Boyce, pp. 42–44. Henry Wood's drawings of the house are in the Bath Reference Library (plates 6 and 7 in Boyce).

29. Buckland-Filleigh, near Great Torrington, Devon. Pope had encouraged Fortescue to landscape Buckland-Filleigh the previous year, noting that unlike himself Fortescue had a daughter who would enjoy it after him (*Corr.* 4:34). As early as 1731, Pope had given Fortescue practical building and gardening advice. He advised him how to prune "old trees or copsewood

for Hedges" so as to produce an "excellent effect in widening the Walk & giving air in the closest woodworks" (*Corr.* 3:225). And as late as 1741 Pope hoped that Fortescue was still "improving your Paternal Seat, and planning agreable Groves, under whose Shadow *in otia tuta recedas*, whenever you are weary of the *Dignitas sine Otio*" (*Corr.* 4:355). In spite of Pope's long-term interest in Fortescue's Devon seat, I have found no plans or descriptions that could give an idea of its layout or suggest the nature of Pope's probable influence upon it.

30. Pope intended but failed to visit Allen in the winter 1738 (see *Corr.* 4:134, 157).

31. For the details of Pope's last efforts at making grottoes, see his "Mr. Pope, in Bath, Improves the Design of His Grotto," *Restoration and Eighteenth-Century Literature*, ed. Carroll Camden (Chicago, 1963), pp. 143–53. Brownell, pp. 258–70, analyzes the last stages of the grotto in light of Pope's interest in geology. See especially Pope's description of the grotto in a letter to William Borlase, an expert on Cornish geology, on 8 June 1740 (*Corr.* 4:245–46). Pope had the services of another of Allen's masons, a man named Omer, who was over at Twickenham as soon as May or June to execute the placement of "materials from the Mines and from the Quarries" (*Corr.* 4:230, 239, 245–46).

32. Quoted in W. Gregory, *Ralph Allen and Prior Park* (Bath, 1886), p. 27. General Wade received a special copy of Pope's 1737 *Letters* (*Corr.* 4:68, 74).

33. See Boyce, pp. 113–14. At this time Van Diest was also designing some statues for the Prior Park library (*Corr.* 4:247).

34. Spence 1, 610. Boyce, p. 113, informs us that the gardens at the top, immediately below the house, were just under half a mile wide; from that point to the basin was also about half a mile.

35. Plate 76 shows that the path through the kitchen garden led to the lookout point, where there was an opening in the wall for access. Built against the basin was a weir from which the stream flowed north until, as Thorpe's 1742 *Survey* shows, it reached a mill owned by one Gibbs.

36. Plate 76 shows that the kitchen garden was eventually (in the late 1760s) removed to the west of the house next to the entrance lodge. The old kitchen garden was then planted as groves; the map indicates young trees in the area. This *Survey* map also reveals other changes that naturalized the gardens. The eastern side of the central lawn was made to curve somewhat and, above all, the central basin was replaced by two lakes end-on-end with a Palladian bridge, designed after the example of the famous Palladian Bridge at Wilton House, crossing one of them (see plate 80). A "Dairy Building" was built in the 1750s facing one of the lakes. Thomas Potter, the second son of the Archbishop of Canterbury, close friend of William Pitt's, and secretary to Frederick, Prince of Wales, until 1751, visited Prior Park in 1756; in a letter to Pitt he noted this process of naturalization: "The scenes at Prior Park change every hour. . . . The present joy at the birth of an heir [Ralph Allen Warburton, who died in 1775] does not respite the labours of a gardener. Half the summer will show the bridge; the dairy opens to the lake; vast woods have taken possession of the naked hills and the lawns slope uninterrupted to the valleys" (*The Correspondence of William Pitt, Earl of Chatham*, ed. J. H. Pringle and W. S. Taylor [London, 1838–40] 1:154).

37. Boyce, p. 114.

38. In August 1738 Pope asked Burlington the favor of Scot's assistance to build a stove for pineapples in his garden (*Corr.* 4:118). See also Pope to Allen 24 March 1743 (4:449), concerning the need to delay Isaac Dodsley's appointment to do some work in Pope's garden.

39. Anonymous, "*A Description of the Seat of* Ralph Allen, *Esq; near the City of Bath*," *Universal Magazine of Knowledge and Pleasure* (London, 14 May 1754):193. This passage is little more than an adaptation of the description of Prior Park in Defoe's *Tour* (1742) 2:265, and suggests the reputation the gardens were acquiring.

40. "On the Connection of Pope with the West of England in General, and Bath in Particular," published in the Rev. Francis Kilvert's *Remains in Verse and Prose* (Bath and London, 1866).

41. *Tour* (1748), 2:301–2. See Boyce, p. 129.

42. Boyce, pp. 114–15. Boyce observes that many thought it was a flattering "companion piece" to the statue of General Wade on the other side of the house; it was, however, much more meaningful than the general's banal statue. Boyce also supposes that Allen may have asked Pope for an inscription for the statue. See also Brownell, pp. 209–10, on some possible attributions for the waterworks.

43. The Rev. Richard Pococke, *The Travels through England*, ed. James Joel Cartwright (London, 1889) 2:153.

44. Mack, *Garden and the City*, pp. 51–57. See also Hunt, "Twickenham Revisited," in *British and American Gardens in the Eighteenth Century*.

45. Richard Graves in *The Triflers* (London, 1805), p. 65, said that the serpentine "is ornamented by a fictitious bridge, designed by Mr. Pope, to conceal it's termination." This suggests that the bridge was placed at the north end of the serpentine. Boyce, pp. 292–93, interprets the drawing of the bridge as "neither pure Palladian nor pure rustic."

46. Boyce, pp. 114–15, mentions that in 1931 there was a stone grotto in this area with a grave of a dog, conceivably the dog Bounce, which Pope gave to Allen in 1739 as "a Guard to your house & Companion to you in your Walks" (*Corr.* 4:181); but he proposes that Mrs. Allen's grotto could have been a building with an open portico, Gothic arches, and a flat crenellated roofline that is identified in a 1785 print as "The Grotto" and shown in the large *Survey* as the "Gothic Temple in the Woods" (see plate 10.e in Boyce). Mrs. Allen did not appear to make much progress with her grotto; on 12 March 1742 Pope wrote to Allen as follows: "I hope whenever Mrs Allen begins her works of that sort, they will be sooner brought to perfection [than his own], & I will attend them as diligently as my own, in the Autumn, before it is too cold" (*Corr.* 4:444).

47. See Pope's letter of invitation (*Corr.* 4:370–71).

48. Warburton's connections with the Allens and Prior Park are discussed by Boyce, pp. 121–98 passim.

49. Years earlier (1723) on a visit to the Blounts' residence at Torbay, Pope expressed his dislike of assemblies at Bath with a contrasting image of a pictorial prospect over the sea; he wrote to Edward Blount, saying he would rather drink tea in the Blount summerhouse on a "Promontory that overhangs the Sea" than go "to an Assembly" at Bath as he had been planning (*Corr.* 2:176).

Epilogue

1. Spence 1, 620.

2. See, for example, Pope's letter to Miller on behalf of Lord Cornbury, in 1734, asking for help in supplying Cornbury with several varieties of fruit (*Corr.* 3:451–52).

3. See the catalogue by Brownell, *Alexander Pope's Villa . . . A Microcosm of English Landscape* (London, 1980).

4. Add. MS. 36371, ff. 26, 29–32.

5. Evidence of Shenstone's own neglect of Pope's and Bathurst's role may be found in his "Ode" to Riskins, written in honor of the Countess of Hertford, Bathurst's successor there. He mentions Pope and other wits in passing, but gives entire credit for the landscaping there to the Countess' picturesque touch.

6. D. Chambers, review of Ruth Hayden, *Mrs. Delany: Her Life and Flowers* (London, 1980), in *Journal of Garden History* 1 (4) (October–December 1981):418.

7. Andrews, "New Description of Pope's Garden," p. 36. For some additional background to Spence's regard for Pope as a gardener after the poet's death, see Peter Martin, "Joseph Spence's Garden in Byfleet: Some New Descriptions," *Journal of Garden History* 8 (1) (January–March 1983).

8. In his "Conclusion," Brownell, pp. 364–65, has spoken of Pope's "picturesque sensibility to accommodate conflicting aesthetic values" and remain open to "a synthesis of the critical and creative principles." Thus Pope, says Brownell, was able to illustrate through gardening and other "sister" arts the principles of "true" or "humanistic" as opposed to pedantic or dogmatic taste.

9. See Mack, *Garden and the City*, chs. 3–6, for a study of this shift in Pope's poetry; and Dixon, *Pope's Satires*, chs. 5–9.

10. Hunt has written the history of this influence in *Figure in the Landscape*; see especially ch. 2.

11. See Joan Metcalfe and Aubrey Williams, "A Letter From Pope," *Scriblerian* 13 (2) (Spring 1981):74.

Appendix A

1. See Brownell, pp. 124–35.

2. Brownell, p. 135.

Appendix B

1. An account of the legal squabbles involved may be found in Draper, *Marble Hill*, pp. 41–43.

2. A letter from Gay to Mrs. Howard dated 17 March 1726 confirms this; it is preserved among the Blickling Hall MSS.

3. I am treating this as a separate instance of Mrs. Howard's problems with Mrs. Vernon

because of Sherburn's dating of the letter on the grounds that Pope's allusion to her "uneasy, tormenting situation" refers to her efforts to obtain a legal separation from her husband. However, Pope's reference to "Mrs. V's paper" may be cited as evidence for dating the letter in the spring of 1729, when Pope referred again to a "Paper" in a letter to Berkeley (*Corr.* 2:259).

4. It is likely that the incident about which Pope writes in this May 1729 letter is, in fact, identical with an incident regarding a "Paper" to which he referred in a letter to George Berkeley (*Corr.* 2:259), whom Mrs. Howard married in 1735, and with an incident he mentioned in a letter to Mrs. Howard (*Corr.* 2:446). The May 1729 letter is the only one of the three Pope dated.

Appendix C

1. Brownell, pp. 131–32, has speculated that what he called Pope's possible "obsession with prospect" might be suggested by the sketch of the garden trellis, which shows the arched opening letting in a "Prospect."

2. These sketches also suggest Pope's architectural interest in the theories of Palladio and the work of Lord Burlington and his circle. See Peter Dixon and Avril Henry, "Pope and the Architects: A Note on the Epistle to Burlington," *English Studies* 51 (October 1970):1–4; and Charles A. Beaumont, "Pope and the Palladians," *Texas Studies in Literature and Language* 17 (1975):461–79. See plates 19 and 20. More recently, see Brownell, ch. 11.

Bibliography

ADDISON, JOSEPH. *The Spectator*, Nos. 411, 412. Edited by Donald F. Bond. Oxford, 1965.

ADEN, JOHN M. *Something like Horace: Studies in the Art and Allusion of Pope's Horatian Satires.* Nashville, Tennessee, 1969.

ALLEN, BEVERLY SPRAGUE. *Tides in English Taste 1619–1800.* 2 vols. Cambridge, Mass., 1937.

ALTENBERND, A. LYNN. "On Pope's Horticultural Romanticism." *Journal of English and Germanic Philology* 54 (1955):470–77.

ANDREWS, MALCOLM. "A New Description of Pope's Garden." *Journal of Garden History* 1 (1) (January–March 1981):35–36.

ATKYNS, SIR ROBERT. *The Ancient and Present State of Glostershire.* London, 1712.

AULT, NORMAN. *New Light on Pope.* Ch. 5. London, 1949, reprint Hamden, Conn., 1967.

BALL, F. ELRINGTON. *The History of the County of Dublin.* Dublin, 1917.

BARRINGTON, DAINES. "The Progress of Gardening." *Archaeologia* 7 (1785).

BEAUMONT, CHARLES A. "Pope and the Palladians." *Texas Studies in Literature and Language* 17 (1975):461–79.

BIDDLE, SHEILA. *Bolingbroke and Harley.* London, 1975.

BINGLEY, WILLIAM, ED. *Correspondence between Frances, Countess of Hertford (afterwards Duchess of Somerset) and Henrietta Louisa, Countess of Pomfret, between the years 1738 and 1741.* 3 vols. 2nd ed. London, 1806.

BLOCK, K. S., AND W. H. WARD. *A History of the Manor and Parish of Iver.* London, 1933.

BOSWELL, JAMES. *Boswell's Life of Johnson.* Edited by G. B. Hill, revised and enlarged by L. F. Powell. 6 vols. Oxford, 1934.

BOYCE, BENJAMIN. *The Benevolent Man: A Life of Ralph Allen of Bath.* Cambridge, Mass., 1967.

————. "Mr. Pope, in Bath, Improves the Design of His Grotto." In *Restoration and Eighteenth Century Literature*, edited by Carroll Camden. Chicago, 1963.

BROGDEN, WILLIAM. "The Ferme Ornée and Changing Attitudes to Agricultural Improvement." In *British and American Gardens in the Eighteenth Century: A Collection of Essays*, edited by Peter Martin. Special issue of *Eighteenth-Century Life* viii (2) (1983); to be reissued by Colonial Williamsburg Foundation, 1984.

————. "Stephen Switzer and Garden Design in Britain in the Early Eighteenth Century." Ph.D. thesis, Edinburgh University, 1973.

287

————. "Stephen Switzer: 'La Gran Manier.'" In *Furor Hortensis: Essays on the History of the English Landscape Garden in Memory of H. F. Clark*, edited by Peter Willis. Edinburgh, 1974.

BROWER, REUBEN. *Alexander Pope: The Poetry of Allusion*. Oxford, 1959.

BROWNELL, MORRIS. *Alexander Pope and the Arts of Georgian England*. Oxford, 1978.

————. *Alexander Pope's Villa: Views of Pope's Villa, Grotto and Garden: A Microcosm of English Landscape*. Catalogue of exhibition at Marble Hill House, Summer 1980. London, 1980.

————. "The Garden and the Topographical View." *Journal of Garden History* 1 (3) (July–September 1981):271-78.

————. "Walter Harte, Nicholas Hardinge, and Pope's 'Verses on the Grotto.'" *Notes & Queries*, n.s., 24 (May–June 1977):245–47.

CAMPBELL, COLIN. *Vitruvius Britannicus*. London, 1725.

CARRÉ, JACQUES. "Lord Burlington's Garden at Chiswick." *Garden History* 1 (3) (Summer 1973):23–30.

————. "Through French Eyes: Rigaud's Drawings of Chiswick." *Journal of Garden History* 2 (2) (April–June 1982):133–42.

CASTELL, ROBERT. *Villas of the Ancients*. London, 1728.

CHANDLER, MARY. *A Description of Bath*. Bath, 1734.

CLARK, DAVID. "Landscape Painting Effects in Pope's Homer." *Journal of Aesthetics and Art Criticism* 22 (1963):25–28. Reprinted in *Essential Articles for the Study of Alexander Pope*, edited by Maynard Mack. Hamden, Conn., 1968.

CLARK, H. F. "Eighteenth-Century Elysiums: The Role of 'Association' in the Landscape Movement." *Journal of the Warburg and Courtauld Institutes* 6 (1943):165–89.

————. *The English Landscape Garden*. London, 1948. Reprinted, Gloucester, 1980.

————. "Lord Burlington's Bijou, or Sharawaggi at Chiswick." *Architectural Review* 95 (May 1944):125–29.

CLARKE, GEORGE. "The Gardens of Stowe." *Apollo* 97 (136) (June 1973):558–65.

————. "Grecian Taste and Gothic Virtue: Lord Cobham's Gardening Programme and Its Iconography." *Apollo* 97 (136) (June 1973):566–71.

————. "Moral Gardening: The History of Stowe—X." *Stoic* 24 (July 1970).

————. "William Kent: Heresy in Stowe's Elysium." In *Furor Hortensis: Essays on the History of the English Landscape Garden in Memory of H. F. Clark*, edited by Peter Willis. Edinburgh, 1974.

COKER, JOHN. *Survey of Dorsetshire*. London, 1732.

COLTON, JUDITH. "Kent's Hermitage for Queen Caroline at Richmond." *Architectura* 2 (1974):181–91.

————. "Merlin's Cave and Queen Caroline: Garden Art as Political Propaganda." *Eighteenth-Century Studies* 10 (1) (Fall 1976): 1–20.

COLVIN, HOWARD M. *A Biographical Dictionary of British Architects 1660–1840*. London, 1954.

CORNFORTH, JOHN. "When the Thames was England's Brenta." *Country Life Annual* (1963):73–75.

COXE, WILLIAM. *Memoirs of the Life and Administration of Sir Robert Walpole*. 3 vols. London, 1800.

CROKER, JOHN W., ED. *Letters to and from Henrietta, Countess of Suffolk...1712–1767*. 2 vols., London, 1824.

DEFOE, DANIEL. *A Tour thro' the Whole Island of Great Britain*. 3 vols. London; vol. 1, 1724; vol. 2, 1725; vol. 3, 1727.

————. *A Tour thro' the Whole Island of Great Britain*. 2nd ed. 3 vols. London, 1738.

————. *A Tour thro' the Whole Island of Great Britain*. 3rd ed. 4 vols. London, 1742.

DELANY, MARY GRANVILLE. *The Autobiography and Correspondence of Mary Granville, Mrs. Delany*. Edited by Lady Llanover. 2 vols. London, 1861.

DE SAUSSURE, CÉSAR. *A Foreign View of England in the Reigns of George I and George II: The Letters of Monsieur César de Saussure to His Family*. Translated and edited by Madame Van Muyden. London, 1902.

DÉZALLIER D'ARGENVILLE, A. J. *The Theory and Practice of Gardening*. 1709. Translated by John James. London, 1712.

DICKINSON, H. T. *Bolingbroke*. Oxford, 1970.

DIXON, PETER. *The World of Pope's Satires: An Introduction to the 'Epistles' and 'Imitations of Horace.'* Chs. 3 and 4. London, 1968.

————, AND AVRIL HENRY. "Pope and the Architects: A Note on the Epistle to Burlington." *English Studies* 51 (5) (October 1970):1–4.

DOBSON, AUSTIN. *At Prior Park & Other Papers*. London, 1912.

DRAPER, MARIE P. G. *Marble Hill House and Its Owners*. London, 1970.

ERSKINE-HILL, HOWARD. *The Social Milieu of Alexander Pope: Lives, Example and the Poetic Response*. New Haven, 1975.

EVELYN, JOHN. *The Diary*. Edited by E. S. de Beer. 6 vols. Oxford, 1955.

FABRICANT, CAROLE. "Binding and Dressing Nature's Loose Tresses: The Ideology of Augustan Landscape Design." In *Studies in Eighteenth-Century Culture*, vol. 8, edited by Roseann Runte. Madison, Wis., 1979.

FIENNES, CELIA. *The Journeys of Celia Fiennes*. Edited by Christopher Morris. London, 1949.

FITZGERALD, LUCIUS. "Pope at Binfield." *Home Counties Magazine* 2 (1900).

GAY, JOHN. *The Letters of John Gay*. Edited by C. F. Burgess. Oxford, 1966.

————. *Poetry and Prose*. Edited by Vinton A. Dearing. 2 vols. Oxford, 1974.

GILPIN, WILLIAM. *A Dialogue upon the Gardens of the Right Honourable the Lord Viscount Cobham at Stow in Buckinghamshire* (1748). Edited by John Dixon Hunt. Augustan Reprint Society, Publication no. 176. Los Angeles, 1976.

————. *Observations on the Western Parts of England, relative chiefly to picturesque beauty*. London, 1798.

GOLDSMITH, OLIVER. *The Life of Thomas Parnell, D.D.* London, 1770.

GRAVES, RICHARD. "Trifling Anecdotes of the late Ralph Allen, Esq. near Bath," in *The Triflers*. London, 1805.

GREEN, DAVID B. *Gardener to Queen Anne: Henry Wise and the Formal Garden*. London, 1956.

GREGORY, W. *Ralph Allen and Prior Park*. Bath, 1886.

GROSE, FRANCIS. *The Antiquities of England and Wales*. 3 vols. London, 1789.

GUILLAUME, GEORGE. *Architectural Views and Details of Netley Abbey*. Southampton, 1848.

HADFIELD, MILES. *Gardening in Britain*. London, 1960.

HAGSTRUM, JEAN. *The Sister Arts: The Tradition of Literary Pictorialism and English Poetry from Dryden to Gray*. Chicago, 1958.

HALSBAND, ROBERT, ED. *The Complete Letters of Lady Mary Wortley Montagu*. 3 vols. Oxford, 1966.

————. *The Life of Lady Mary Wortley Montagu*. Oxford, 1956.

HAMPSHIRE, G. "Johnson, Elizabeth Carter, and Pope's Garden." *Notes & Queries*, n.s., 19 (June 1972):221.

HANMER, SIR THOMAS. *The Correspondence of Sir Thomas Hamner*. Edited by Sir Henry Bunbury. London, 1838.

————. *The Garden Book*. Edited by E. S. Rohde. London, 1933.

HARRIS, JOHN. *The Artist and the Country House: A History of Country House View Painting in Britain 1540–1870*. London, 1979.

HART, JEFFREY. *Viscount Bolingbroke: Tory Humanist*. London, 1965.

HASSELL, JOHN. *Tour of the Isle of Wight*. London, 1790.

HEARNSHAW, F. J. C. "Bevis Mount," *Papers and Proceedings of the Hampshire Field Club and Archaeological Society* 5 (part 1) (1905):109–25.

HIBBARD, G. R. "The Country House Poem of the Seventeenth Century." *Journal of the Warburg and Courtauld Institutes* 19 (1956):159–74. Reprinted in *Essential Articles for the Study of Alexander Pope*, edited by Maynard Mack. Hamden, Conn., 1968.

HUGHES, HELEN SARD. *The Gentle Hertford: Her Life and Letters*. New York, 1940.

————. "Shenstone and the Countess of Hertford." *PMLA* 46 (4) (1931):1113–27.

HUNT, JOHN DIXON. "Emblems and Expressionism in the Eighteenth-Century Landscape Garden." *Eighteenth-Century Studies* 4 (3) (Spring 1971):294–317.

————. *The Figure in the Landscape: Poetry, Painting, and Gardening during the Eighteenth Century*. Baltimore, 1976.

————. "A Silent and Solitary Hermitage." *Annual Report of the York Georgian Society* (1970): 47–61.

————. "Twickenham Revisited." *British and American Gardens in the Eighteenth Century: A Collection of Essays*, edited by Peter Martin. Special issue of *Eighteenth-Century Life* 8 (2) (1983); to be reissued by Colonial Williamsburg Foundation, 1984.

————, AND PETER WILLIS, EDS. *The Genius of the Place: The English Landscape Garden 1620–1820*. London, 1975.

HUSSEY, CHRISTOPHER. *English Gardens and Landscapes 1700–1750*. London, 1967.

————. "A Georgian Arcady—I. William Kent's Gardens at Rousham, Oxfordshire." *Country Life* 99 (14 June 1946):1084–85.

————. *The Picturesque: Studies in a Point of View*. London, 1927. Reprinted, Hamden, Conn., 1967.

————. "Richmond Green, Surrey—I. Oak House and Old Palace Place." *Country Life* 95 (5 May 1944):722–25.

HUTCHINS, JOHN. *The History and Antiquities of the County of Dorset*. 3rd ed. 4 vols. London, 1873.

IBBETSON, JULIUS C. *A Picturesque Guide to Bath, Bristol.* . . . London, 1793.

IRELAND, SAMUEL. *Picturesque Views on the River Thames.* London, 1792.

JACKMAN, S. W. *Man of Mercury.* London, 1965.

JACQUES, DAVID. "The Art and Sense of the Scriblerus Club in England, 1715–35." *Garden History* 4 (Spring 1976):30–53.

JOHNSON, SAMUEL. *Lives of the English Poets by Samuel Johnson.* Edited by G. B. Hill. Oxford, 1905.

JONES, BARBARA. *Follies and Grottoes.* London, 1953.

JOURDAIN, MARGARET. *The Work of William Kent.* London, 1948.

KERBY-MILLER, CHARLES, ED. *Memoirs of the Extraordinary Life, Works, and Discoveries of Martin Scriblerus.* New Haven, 1950.

KILVERT, REV. FRANCIS. *Remains in Verse and Prose.* Bath and London, 1866.

KING, R. W. "Joseph Spence of Byfleet." *Garden History* 6 (3) (Winter 1978):38–64; 7 (3) (Winter 1979):29–48; 8 (2) (Summer 1980):44–65; and 8 (3) (Winter 1980):77–114.

KRAMNICK, ISAAC. *Bolingbroke and His Circle: The Politics of Nostalgia in the Age of Walpole.* Cambridge, Mass., 1968.

LANG, S. "The Genesis of the English Landscape Garden." In *The Picturesque Garden and Its Influence outside the British Isles*, edited by Nikolaus Pevsner. Dumbarton Oaks Colloquium on the History of Landscape Architecture 2:22–29. Washington, D. C., 1974.

LANGLEY, BATTY. *New Principles of Gardening.* London, 1728.

LAWRENCE, NICHOLAS, ED. *Six Views of Twickenham in the Eighteenth-Century.* Richmond, n.d.

LEES-MILNE, JAMES. *Earls of Creation.* London, 1962.

LIPSCOMB, SIR GEORGE. *The History and Antiquities of the County of Buckingham.* London, 1847.

LITTLE, BRYAN. *The Life and Work of James Gibbs.* London, 1955.

LUXBOROUGH, LADY. *Letters of Lady Luxborough.* London, 1775.

MACK, MAYNARD. *The Garden and the City: Retirement and Politics in the Later Poetry of Pope 1731–43.* Toronto, 1969.

————. "The Muse of Satire." *Yale Review* 41 (1951):80–92. Reprinted in *Essential Articles for the Study of Alexander Pope*, edited by Maynard Mack. Hamden, Conn., 1968.

MACKY, JOHN. *A Journey through England in Familiar Letters from a Gentleman Here to His Friend Abroad.* 3 vols. 1722.

MAHAFFEY, KATHLEEN. "Timon's Villa: Walpole's Houghton." *Texas Studies in Literature and Langauge* 9 (1967):193–222.

MALINS, EDWARD. *English Landscaping and Literature, 1660–1840.* London, 1966.

————, AND THE KNIGHT OF GLIN. *Lost Demesnes: Irish Landscape Gardening 1660–1845.* London, 1976.

MANWARING, ELIZABETH. *Italian Landscape in Eighteenth-Century England: A Study Chiefly of the Influence of Claude Lorrain and Salvator Rosa on English Taste 1700–1800.* Especially ch. 6. New York, 1925.

MARESCA, THOMAS. *Pope's Horatian Poems*. Columbus, Ohio, 1966.

MARTIN, PETER. "The Garden and Pope's Vision of Order in the 'Epistle to Burlington.'" *Durham University Journal* 65 (3) (June 1973):248–69.

———. "Intimations of the New Gardening: Alexander Pope's Reaction to the 'Uncommon' Landscape at Sherborne." *Garden History* 4 (1) (1976):57–87.

———. "Joseph Spence's Garden in Byfleet: Some New Descriptions." *Journal of Garden History* 3 (2) (April–June 1983):121–29.

———. Pope, Lord Peterborough, and Mrs. Howard: Fresh Glimpses from an Unpublished Letter." *Scriblerian* 9 (1) (Fall 1976):55–56.

———."Quincunx or Groves in Pope's Garden?" *Notes & Queries*, n.s., 24 (3) (June 1977):243–45.

———. "'Regular' or 'Irregular': Pope's Description of the Groves at Sherborne Castle." *Notes & Queries* n.s., 22 (11) (November 1975):490–91.

MASSON, GEORGINA. *Italian Gardens*. London, 1961.

NEALE, JOHN P. *Views of the Seats of Noblemen and Gentlemen*. London, 1824.

NICOLSON, MARJORIE HOPE, AND G. S. ROUSSEAU. *'This Long Disease My Life': Alexander Pope and the Sciences*. Princeton, 1968.

NOKES, DAVID. "Pope's Epigrams on William Kent: A New Manuscript." *Yearbook of English Studies* 5 (1975):109–14.

PARKINSON, JOHN. *Paradisus in Sole: A Garden of All Sorts of Flowers . . . Herbs*. London, 1629.

PAULSON, RONALD. *Emblem and Expression: Meaning in English Art of the Eighteenth-Century*. Ch. 2. Cambridge, Mass., 1975.

———. "The Pictorial Circuit and Related Structures in Eighteenth-Century England." In *The Varied Pattern*, edited by Peter Hughes and David Williams. Toronto, 1971.

———. "Thoughts on Landscape Theory." *Eighteenth-Century Studies* 10 (2) (Winter 1977):245–61.

PEACH, R. E. M. *The Life and Times of Ralph Allen of Prior Park, Bath*. London, 1895.

PEVSNER, NIKOLAUS, ED. *The Picturesque Garden and Its Influence outside the British Isles*. Dumbarton Oaks Colloquium on the History of Landscape Architecture, vol. 2. Washington, D. C., 1974.

———, AND S. LANG. "Sir William Temple and Sharawaggi." *Architectural Review* 106 (1949):391–93.

PHILLIPS, HUGH.*The Thames About 1750*. London, 1902.

POCOCKE, REV. RICHARD. *The Travels through England . . . 1750, 1751 and Later Years*. Edited by J. J. Cartwright. London, 1889.

POPE, ALEXANDER. *The Correspondence of Alexander Pope*. Edited by George Sherburn. 5 vols. Oxford, 1956.

———. *Prose Works of Alexander Pope*. Edited by Norman Ault. Oxford, 1936.

———. *The Works of Alexander Pope*. Edited by William Warburton. 9 vols. London, 1751.

———. *The Works of Alexander Pope*. Edited by Whitwell Elwin and W. J. Courthope. 10 vols. London, 1871–89.

————. *The Twickenham Edition of the Poems of Alexander Pope*. General editor, John Butt. Vols. 1–6, the original poems; vols. 7–10, the Homer translations. New Haven, 1938–61, 1967.

PRINGLE, J. H. AND W. S. TAYLOR, EDS. *The Correspondence of William Pitt, Earl of Chatham*. London, 1838–40.

PRIOR, MATTHEW. *The Literary Works of Matthew Prior*. Edited by H. Bunker Wright and Monroe K. Spears. 2 vols. Oxford, 1959.

PUGH, R. B., ED. *The Victoria History of the County of Middlesex*. London, 1962.

PYE, HENRIETTA. *Short Acount of the Principal Seats and Gardens in and about Richmond and Kew*. London, 1760.

QUAINTANCE, RICHARD E. "Walpole's Whig Interpretation of Landscaping History." In *Studies in Eighteenth-Century Culture*, vol. 9, edited by Roseann Runte. Madison, Wis., 1979.

RANSOM, SYLVIA CROWE. *Garden Design*. London, 1958.

ROGERS, ROBERT W. *The Major Satires of Alexander Pope*. Illinois Studies in Language and Literature, vol. 40. Urbana, Illinois, 1955.

ROSS, FREDERICK. *The Ruined Abbeys of Britain*. Ch. 7. London, 1882.

ROUSSEAU, G. S. "A New Pope Letter [describing his excursion to Netley Abbey, Hampshire]." *Philological Quarterly* 45 (2) (April 1966):409–18.

ST. CLAIR BADDELEY, WELBOURNE. *A History of Cirencester*. Cirencester, 1924.

SAMBROOK, JAMES. "The Shape and Size of Pope's Garden." *Eighteenth-Century Studies* 5 (Spring 1972):450–55.

————. "Pope and the Visual Arts." In *Writers and Their Background: Alexander Pope*, edited by Peter Dixon. London, 1972.

————. "Pope's Neighbours: An Early Landscape Garden at Richmond." *Journal of the Warburg and Courtauld Institutes* 30 (1967):444–46.

SCHULZ, MAX. "The Circuit Walk of the Eighteenth-Century Landscape Garden and the Pilgrim's Circuitous Progress." *Eighteenth-Century Studies* 15 (Fall 1981):1–25.

SEARLE, JOHN. *A Plan of Mr. Pope's Garden*. London, 1745. Edited by Morris Brownell. Augustan Reprint Society, Publication no. 211. Los Angeles, 1982.

SHENSTONE, WILLIAM. *The Works in Verse and Prose of William Shenstone, Esq*. 2 vols. London, 1765.

SHERBURN, GEORGE. *The Early Career of Alexander Pope*. Oxford, 1934.

SICCA, CINZIA MARIA. "Lord Burlington at Chiswick: Architecture and Landscape." *Garden History* 10 (1) (Spring 1982):36–69.

SITWELL, EDITH. *The English Eccentrics*. London, 1950.

SPENCE, JOSEPH. *An Essay on Pope's Odyssey*. London, 1727.

————. *Observations, Anecdotes, and Characters of Books and Men*. Edited by James M. Osborn. 2 vols. Oxford, 1966.

STEBBING, WILLIAM. *Peterborough*. London, 1890.

Stranger's Guide to Southampton. 21st ed. Southampton. 1890.

STROUD, DOROTHY. *Capability Brown*. Introduction by Christopher Hussey. 2nd ed, rev. London, 1975.

SUMMERSON, JOHN. *Architecture in Britain, 1530–1830.* 6th rev. ed. Ch. 20. London, 1979.

———. "The Classical Country House in 18th-Century England." *Journal of the Royal Society of Arts* 107 (July 1959).

SWIFT, JONATHAN. *The Correspondence of Jonathan Swift.* Edited by Harold Williams. 5 vols. Oxford, 1963.

———. *The Poems of Jonathan Swift.* Edited by Harold Williams. 2nd ed. 3 vols. Oxford, 1958.

SWITZER, STEPHEN. *Ichnographia Rustica.* London, 1718; 2nd ed., London 1742.

———. *The Nobleman, Gentleman, and Gardener's Recreation.* London, 1715.

———. *The Practical Kitchen Gardener.* London, 1727.

SYPHER, WYLIE. "Psychological Picturesque: Association and Reverie." *Rococo to Cubism in Art and Literature.* New York, 1960.

TEMPLE, SIR WILLIAM. "Upon the Gardens of Epicurus; Or, Of Gardening, in the Year 1685." *Five Miscellaneous Essays,* edited by Samuel Holt Monk. Ann Arbor, 1963.

THACKER, CHRISTOPHER. *The History of Gardens.* Berkeley and Los Angeles, 1979.

THOMSON, JAMES. *The Seasons.* Edited by James Sambrook. Oxford, 1982.

THORPE, THOMAS. *Actual Survey of Bath.* Bath, 1742.

TIPPING, H. A. "Four Unpublished Letters of William Kent." *Architectural Review* 63 (1928):180–83.

TOVEY, DUNCAN C. *Gray and His Friends.* Cambridge, 1890.

TOYNBEE, PAGET, ED. *Reminiscences, Written by Mr. Horace Walpole for . . . Miss Mary and Miss Agnes Berry.* London, 1924.

TURNER, JAMES. "Stephen Switzer and the Political Fallacy in Landscape Gardening History." *Eighteenth-Century Studies* 11 (Summer 1978):489–96.

WALKER, JOHN. "The Thames through Eighteenth-Century Eyes: Augustine Heckell and His Imitators." *Country Life* 146 (3 July 1969):24–27.

WALKER, J. COOPER. *Essay on the Rise and Progress of Gardening in Ireland.* Dublin, 1791.

WALPOLE, HORACE. *The Correspondence of Horace Walpole.* Edited by W. S. Lewis. New Haven, 1937–83.

———. "The History of Modern Taste in Gardening" (1785). In *Horace Walpole: Gardenist,* edited by Isabel Chase. Princeton, 1943.

WARE, ISAAC. *Plans, Elevations, and Sections; Chimney-Pieces, and Ceilings of Houghton in Norfolk.* London, 1735.

WEST, GILBERT. *Stowe: The Gardens of the Right Honourable Richard Lord Viscount Cobham. Address'd to Mr. Pope.* London, 1732.

WHATELY, THOMAS. *Observations on Modern Gardening.* London, 1770.

WHEATLEY, H. B. *London Past and Present.* Vol. 1, p. 218. London, 1891.

WHISTLER, LAURENCE. *The Imagination of Vanbrugh and His Fellow Artists.* London, 1954.

WILKS, THEODORE C. *The History of Hampshire.* 3 vols. London, n.d.

WILLIAMS, AUBREY, AND JOAN METCALFE, EDS. "A Letter From Pope." *Scriblerian* 13 (2) (Spring 1981):74.

WILLIS, PETER. "Charles Bridgeman: The Royal Gardens." In *Furor Hortensis: Essays on the*

History of the English Landscape Garden in Memory of H. F. Clark, edited by Peter Willis. Edinburgh, 1974.

————. *Charles Bridgeman and the English Landscape Garden*. Studies in Architecture, vol. 17. London, 1977.

————. "Creator of the English Garden: Charles Bridgeman's Tools and Techniques." *Country Life* 153 (3960) (17 May 1973):1401–4.

————. "A Poet's Gardener." *Listener* 62 (24 December 1964):1007–9.

WIMSATT, WILLIAM K. *The Portraits of Alexander Pope*. New Haven, 1965.

————, AND JOHN RIELY. "A Supplement to *The Portraits of Alexander Pope*." In *Evidence in Literary Scholarship: Essays in Memory of James Marshall Osborn*, edited by René Wellek and Alvaro Ribeiro. Oxford, 1979.

WITTKOWER, RUDOLF. *Palladio and English Palladianism*. London, 1974.

WOODBRIDGE, KENNETH. "Bolingbroke's château of La Source." *Garden History* 4 (Autumn 1976):50–64.

————. "Irregular, Rococo or Picturesque." *Apollo* 108 (201) (November 1978):356.

————. *Landscape and Antiquity: Aspects of English Culture at Stourhead 1718 to 1838*. Oxford, 1970.

————. "The Nomenclature of Style in Garden History." Lecture delivered at the Victoria and Albert Museum in June 1979. Published in *British and American Gardens in the Eighteenth Century: A Collection of Essays*, edited by Peter Martin. Special issue of *Eighteenth-Century Life* 8 (2);to be reissued by Colonial Williamsburg Foundation, 1984.

————. "William Kent as Landscape-Gardener: A Re-Appraisal." *Apollo* n.s., 100 (150) (August 1974):126–37.

————. "William Kent's Gardening: The Rousham Letters." *Apollo* n.s., 100 (152) (October 1974):282–91.

Index

70; paintings of farm implements at, 134–35; *Plan* by Knyff, P50; Pope describes "farm," 134; reconstruction of landscape, 136–38, P52; sale of, 141–44; Swift advises Pope to garden at, 138; Swift's interest in, 58, 131; verses form *Dawley Farm* on building alterations at, 132–33

Defoe, Daniel: *Tour* (1724), describes Thames region of Twickenham and Richmond, 19–20; *Tour* (1742), describes Chiswick and Bevis Mount gardens, 28–29, 30, 31, 196–203; *Tour* (1748), describes Prior Park gardens, 223–24

De Grey, Marchioness: censures Stowe, 12

Delany, Rev. Patrick: Irish gardens, 167. *See also* Delville

Delville, seat of the Rev. Patrick Delany: Swift and its gardens, 167–70; verses on, 168–69. *See also* Pendarves, Mary

Dering, Daniel, 11

Derrick, Samuel: describes Prior Park gardens, 217–18

Deschamps de Marcilly, Marie-Claire. *See* Lady Bolingbroke

Dézallier d'Argenville, A. J.: *Théorie et la Pratique du Jardinage*, 108. *See also* James, John

Digby, Mary, 85; epitaph for, 101; Pope's guide through Oakley Wood, 101

Digby, Robert: amateur landscape gardener, 98–99; gardening triumvirate with Pope and Bathurst, 99; his family's values, 100–1; epitaph for, 101

Digby, William, 5th Baron, 99, 100

Dodington Hall (Gloucestershire), seat of Sir William Codrington, 98, 229; praised by Pope, 17

Dodsley, Isaac, 222

Dodsley, Robert, 222–23, 228

Dormer, James, 182

Dormer, Robert. *See* Rousham House

Douglas, Mrs. Charles, Duchess of Queensberry: Bridgeman is recommended to her, 166

Down Hall (Essex), seat of 2nd Lord Oxford: bowling green, 50; Bridgeman's work there, 149

Draper, Marie: *Marble Hill and Its Owners*, 155, 159, 162

Drayton, Michael: *Poly-Olbion*, 197

Dryden, John: *To My Dear Friend Mr. Congreve*, 53; translation of Dufresnoy, 26

Dufresnoy, Charles Alphonse: *De Arte Graphica*, 26

Dyrham Park (Gloucestershire), seat of William Blathwayt, 254n.22

Epistle to Bathurst: Man of Ross, 86, 117. *See also* Man of Ross; Pope, Alexander: Works cited

Epistle to Burlington, xxiii, 2, 12; Chandos controversy, 31; deleted reference to Bridgeman, 57–58; hostile response to, 140; veiled criticism of Lord Bathurst, 85–87. *See also* Brydges, James; Pope, Alexander: Works cited; Timon; Villario

Erskine-Hill, Howard: *Social Milieu of Alexander Pope*, 99, 214

Eumaeus: denounces corruption in *Odyssey*, 128

Evans, Dr. Abel, 39

Evelyn, Sir John, 180

Eyre, Mr.: designed gardens at Houghton Hall, 257n.62

Faustinus: Martial on his villa, 65

Fetherstonhaugh, Sir Matthew: conspires with Duke of Richmond to buy Ladyholt Park, 248n.52

Fielding, Henry: censures Pope for poetic treatment of Ralph Allen, 211

Flitcroft, Henry, 148

Fog's Weekly Journal: publishes *Dawley Farm*, 138

Fortescue, William: urged to landscape by Pope, 215. *See also* Buckland-Filleigh

Frederick, Prince of Wales: gifts to Mrs. Howard, 146. *See also* Carlton House

Gardens of Alcinous. *See Guardian* (no. 173), Pope's essay on gardening

Gay, John, 37, 63, 166, 170; at Cirencester Park, 87; finds Marble Hill plans, 145; in Oakley Wood, Cirencester Park, 85; letter to Swift about Pope's gardening, 42; *Mr. Pope's Welcome from Greece*, 24–25, 64, 147, 153

Gentleman's Magazine: poetry competition over the Hermitage at Richmond, 186–87

Gervase le Riche, 185

Gibbs, James (architect): designs temples for Down Hall, 149; Pope's architect, 39, 42; renovated Dawley house, 132

Gilpin, William, 228; idea of picturesque, 8; *Practical Hints on Landscape Gardening*, 97

Goldsmith, Oliver, 64

Gorboduc, 99

300

Shaftesbury, 3rd Earl of. *See* Cooper, Anthony Ashley

Sheffield, John, Duke of Buckingham, 64; Pope's edition of his *Works*, 182. *See also* Buckingham House

Sheffield, Katherine, Duchess of Buckingham: garden schemes at Leighs, 90

Shenstone, William, 228; "Ode" to Riskins, 285; on Lord Bolingbroke and Pope, 119–20; patronized by Lady Hertford, 66

Sherborne Castle (Dorset), seat of the Digby family, 197; and green theaters, 108–9; iconographic value of the Norman ruins, 97–98, 114–16; illustrations of, 102–3, P40, P41, P44, P46, P47; Kent's design of a seat for, P48; map by Ladd, P42; Pope's description of, 96–97, 101–18; relation to Stowe, 15–17; symbolic importance of, to Digbys, 117; theater, 55; view of, from Hutchins's *History*, P45; watercolor of, P43. *See also* Digby, Robert

Sheridan, Thomas: gardening at Quilca, 167–68; verses on Delville, 168–69

Shirley, Lady Elizabeth: Macky mentions her villa, 20

Sir Bevois of Hamton, 183

Sophia, Princess, Electress of Hanover, 146

Southampton *Guide*: on Bevis Mount, 196, 199–200, 202; on Netley Abbey, 191

Southcote, Philip, 213, 228; on Stowe, 14

Spectator: Addison calls for less autocratic gardens, 21. *See also* Addison, Joseph

Spence, Joseph, 119, 125, 221, 229; alludes to Bevis Mount, 200–1; Lord Bolingbroke and Pope planning a "gardening poem," 140; chief recorder of Pope's gardening thoughts, 1; cites Pope: on being finished with landscaping, 227; on cathedrals and temples in trees, 54; on garden ornaments for his garden, 44; on his boyhood in Windsor Forest, 243–44n.46; on "painting" in gardening, 3; on the picturesque at Twickenham, 44; on trees, 6; on variety, 2; on wishing to build a "Roman temple, in trees," 26; claims Kent designed Pope's mount, 249–50n.73; gardening anticipated in *Windsor Forest*, 3; Horatio's gardens and Pope's garden, 58, 231–32; Osborn's edition of *Anecdotes*, 2; Kent's natural taste at Chiswick, 32; Milton and

the new gardening, 6; on Pope's "poetic" gardening, 229; painting of, by George Vertue, P1; records Pope's three gardening "heads," 2; Temple's and Addison's influence, 6

Stanhope, Philip, 4th Earl of Chesterfield: on Bolingbroke's fluency, 125

Stanhope, Sir William: altered Pope's gardens, 61

Stanley, Sir John, 170

Stanton Harcourt (Oxfordshire), seat of Viscount Simon Harcourt, 85, 98; lovers killed by lightning at, 190

Steele, Richard: published Pope's *Messiah* in *Spectator*, xix

Stephenson, Edward: buys Dawley, 144

Stonor Park (Oxfordshire): Pope describes setting of, 12

Stothard, Thomas: watercolor, P75

Stowe (Buckinghamshire), seat of Lord Cobham, xxiii, 176, 195; appearance in 1724, 11–12; "Bridgmannick" theatre, 18; Elysian Fields, 14–17, 28; gardens romanticized in 1730s, 13; Pope describes in 1731, 11; Pope gets ideas there for Marble Hill, 164; Pope's influence, 14–15

Strafford, 3rd Earl of. *See* Wentworth, Thomas

Strawberry Hill (Twickenham, Middlesex): Walpole's verses on, 156

Stroud, Dorothy: on "Capability" Brown, 101

Summerson, Sir John, 181

Swift, Jonathan, 58, 63, 71, 81, 93, 129, 167, 170, 176, 212; *A Pastoral Dialogue*, 160, 161, 165, 172–74; and Dawley Farm gardens, 58, 133–34, 136, 172; and La Source, 120, 121–22, 123; "Character" of Mrs. Howard, 172; contribution to Irish landscaping, 166–70; his Dublin garden, xxiii, 121; on Lord Peterborough's retirement at Parson's Green, 178; relationship with Mrs. Howard and Marble Hill, 58, 166, 170–74; visits English gardens, 166–67; visits Pope, 58; visits Riskins Park, 64; walks at Cirencester Park, 80. *See also* Naboth's Vineyard

Switzer, Stephen, 66–70, 165, 228; *A Farther Account of Rural . . . Gardening*, 70; "Plan of Riskins," 66, P33; attacks vast landscaping schemes, 67–68; censures Bridgeman, 68; dedications of works to Lord Bathurst, 66; *Ichnographia Rustica*, xxi, 2, 4–5, 66, 106; *ferme ornée*, 69; *Nobleman, Gentleman, and*